070.194 CRO

D0265587

International Radio

Journalism

WITHDRAWN

Radio journalists have witnessed much of the history of the twentieth century. From early documentary recordings, to the ground-breaking war reporting of Ed Murrow and Richard Dimbleby, to the sophisticated commentaries of Alistair Cooke and reporters such as Fergal Keane, *International Radio Journalism* explores the way radio has covered the most important stories this century and the way in which it continues to document events in America, Britain, Europe and many other areas of the world.

International Radio Journalism is a theoretical textbook and a practical guide for students of radio journalism, experienced reporters, editors and producers. The book details training and professional standards in writing, presentation, technology, editorial ethics and media law in America, Britain, Australia and other English-speaking countries and examines the differing roles of journalists throughout the world. The author analyses the major public sector broadcast networks such as the BBC, CBC, NPR and ABC and the work of commercial radio and small public radio stations, in the United States, Britain and Australia.

Tim Crook investigates the way in which news reporting has been influenced by governments and media conglomerates and identifies an undercurrent of racial and sexual discrimination throughout the history of radio news. There are unique chapters on comparative media law for broadcast journalists, the implications of multimedia and new technologies, digital applications in radio news, and glossaries which cover the skills of voice presentation, writing radio news and broadcast vocabulary.

Tim Crook is Head of Radio and Lecturer in the Media and Communications Department at Goldsmiths College, University of London, and is an award-winning journalist and live talk-show presenter with LBC.

Communication

and Society

General Editor: James Curran

International

Radio

Journalism

History, theory

and practice

Tim Crook

Routledge

London and New York

UNIVERSITY OF WESTMINSTER
LEARNING RESOURCES CENTRE
ROAD
WICK PARK
HA1 3TP

First published 1998
by Routledge
11 New Fetter Lane, London EC4P 4EE

Simultaneously published in the USA and
Canada by Routledge
29 West 35th Street, New York, NY 10001

© 1998 Tim Crook

Typeset in Perpetua and Bell Gothic by
RefineCatch Limited, Bungay, Suffolk
Printed and bound in Great Britain by
Biddles Ltd, Guildford and King's Lynn

All rights reserved. No part of this book may
be reprinted or reproduced or utilised in any
form or by any electronic, mechanical, or
other means, now known or hereafter
invented, including photocopying and
recording, or in any information storage or
retrieval system, without permission in
writing from the publishers

British Library Cataloguing in Publication Data
A catalogue record for this book is available
from the British Library

Library of Congress Cataloging in Publication Data
Crook, Tim
International radio journalism/Tim Crook.
p.   cm. — (Communication and society)
Includes bibliographical references and index.
1. Radio journalism.
I. Title.   II. Series: Communication and
society (Routledge (Firm))
PN4784.R2C76   1998
070.1′94—dc21   97–16886

ISBN 0–415–09672–3 (hbk)
ISBN 0–415–09673–1 (pbk)

Contents

Part VI

MODERN STYLES OF RADIO REPORTING AND JOURNALISM

Plates

Acknowledgements

This book is dedicated to the following people who have been helpful and incredibly patient with me for the last five years.

Marja Giejgo for untiring and brilliant proof-reading and personal support.

Rebecca Barden for having the patience of a saint and being a supportive editor.

Professor James Curran whose idea it was and for being a nice chap.

John Smith for researching in Australia valuable information and acquiring books that have been helpful.

Trevor John Lecturer in Sound and Radio from the University of Newcastle, Australia for more proof-reading and superb suggestions for improvement.

Jessica Nicholas for more help and Australian intelligence.

Keith Waghorn, **Damien Chalaud**, and **John Beacham** at Goldsmiths College for putting up with me.

Sarah Fuller, **Kevin Steele**, and **Mindy Leigh** at BBC Radio Training, and **Sean McTernan**, BBC Legal Department.

Justin Everard at the BBC and **Nina Bialoguski** at ITN for organising photographs.

Charles Golding at LBC for being a superb Programme Controller. **Trevor Aston**, Deputy Programme Controller and producers **Chris Lowri** and **Steve Campen**.

Derval Fitzsimons at IRN and colleagues at News Direct 97.3 FM.

Bilha and **Gerry Goldberg** at the International Radio Festival of New York for allowing me to be the festival's archivist and have access to thousands of radio news programmes from around the world.

Tim Knight for information and intelligence from Japan.

Charlie Rose, Head of LBC News Information until 1996.

James Schofield, **Caroll Orr**, **Alastair Lawson-Tancred** and **Keir Simmons** for doing so well despite working in my news agency.

Editors: **Mike Best, Peter Thornton, Ron Onions, Phil Taylor, Keith Belcher, David Wilsworth, John Perkins, Nigel Charters** and **Robin Malcolm** – editors who wanted to employ me.

Doctor Fred Hunter for corrections to the text and advice on ethics sources.

Caroline Godwin, Pat Clarke, Sue Clough, Tim and **Joe Wood, Mike Taylor** and other journalist colleagues at the Central Criminal Court and the Royal Courts of Justice.

Jake Ecclestone, Deputy General Secretary of the National Union of Journalists for support in freedom of expression battles.

Extracts from BBC-owned material are reproduced by kind permission of the BBC.

Philip Leask, Chairman, Pavilion Records Limited.

Sara Cornthwaite for copy editing and **Katherine Hodkinson**, desk editor at Routledge.

Last, but not least, my students and trainees over the years.

Due to the unusual nature of this book, extracts, dialogue and reported speech often have several sources. I have endeavoured to provide audio and text sources, both primary and secondary, where appropriate.

Tim Crook

Part I

Introduction
Practice, theory
and history

Chapter 1

From box room
to digital
control room

Radio journalism has been enormous fun, thoroughly exhausting, a decent way of making a living, and a constant education in life. My career began with an interview at the London College of Printing in 1978 when the first editor of UK's Independent Radio News, Dr Fred Hunter, was recruiting trainees for the first vocational radio journalism course in Britain outside the BBC. Up until this time the BBC had been the model for radio journalism practice in Britain. Their reign of cultural domination was at an end. I was an aspiring poet going through a George Orwell *Down and Out in Paris and London* phase and working as a road-sweeper for the Corporation of London. God knows what sort of picture I must have presented. I was applying for the magazine journalism course and, towards the end of an aggressive interview, Dr Hunter piped up 'Would you like to work in radio?' My weak response: 'I suppose so,' was quickly followed up with the question 'Why?'. The answer, 'Because I like the sound of my own voice' is I think an important lesson on how not to answer questions during an interview.

Fred must have been very desperate, because for some reason he offered me a place. There were several months of travelling, writing and a little journalistic freelancing in the Middle East before I turned up in a tiny box-room on the second floor of a tower block at London's Elephant and Castle. My experience of walking naively into the 1978 Israeli invasion of Southern Lebanon did not create a thirst within me for foreign or war reporting. Ignoring United Nations' advice I had travelled to the border only to be greeted with a sustained attack from Palestinian Katyusha rockets. I was convinced there were plenty of other people prepared to observe and write about man's inhumanity to man. Poems seemed to be a more creative and harmless way of fulfilling a role in society. There then followed a gallant attempt to train me in the art of radio journalism by Fred and his colleague Dr John Herbert, an experienced radio news editor from ABC, BBC World Service and IRN. I still do not know why I got on the course.

My first move was to listen to badly scratched vinyl records of news broadcasts by Richard Dimbleby and Ed Murrow. They are hard acts to follow and I do not see myself getting anywhere near their achievements. Over the years as I have delved into archives and blown off the dust lying on books long out of print, I have grown to love the world of radio and the art of its journalistic and creative broadcasters. I believe we are living in an age of Radio Renaissance and this book is an attempt to celebrate its history, present craftsmanship and a great future for a medium that has never lost its importance and value to human society.

In the last few years we have begun to experience the impact of a new techno-logical revolution which has radically changed the efficiency and way that radio journalists can operate. The digital age, 'multimedia' and the implications of communication on the World Wide Web have liberated journalists from the point of view of individual research, have expanded the opportunity of freedom of expression and commercial application of radio news operations. When this book was originally commissioned, it would have been out of date if it had been delivered within two years. I first entered journalism when newsrooms thundered to the clattering of manual typewriters, the cries of copy tasters and the litter of analogue tape. Typewriters disappeared in the middle to late 1980s. In less than three years, entire radio stations have jettisoned the paraphernalia of analogue technology to produce and transmit twenty-four-hour programming from digital work stations. Using reel-to-reel tape machines and analogue mixing consoles, radio journalists would have taken one and a half hours to produce the all-round package of news cuts, wraps and programme pieces. When I introduced digital work stations at my news agency in September 1995 at the Royal Courts of Justice and Central Criminal Court, the same job now took less than fifteen minutes. Research requiring hours of requests to news cutting libraries is achieved in seconds from CD-Roms. This book will endeavour to share the excitement and implications of this technological tornado which is changing the lives of people within the industry as well as the habits of listeners and consumers.

My experience in 1978 throws up a number of important issues. Somebody with my background, doing a labouring job but having a commitment to current affairs, an ability to communicate with the written word and the voice, and a track record of using my initiative to generate news stories was given a break. Once offered, I tried very hard not to throw it back in anybody's face. I may have been an utter pain in the neck to the people who taught me and the patient colleagues who have tolerated me over the years. After twenty years I am relieved to say that some people are prepared to accept that I have contributed something. I am now in the position at Goldsmiths College, University of London, to provide opportunities and to teach and train. I own a news agency which employs radio journalists in national and international news gathering and I am also very active in the radio drama field as a writer, director and producer. I have been and still remain at the coal-face of live presentation and all the developments in digital production and communication.

Over the years I have read a number of excellent books on radio journalism and they are to be applauded and commended, but up until now, I have not come across a book which seeks to provide practical training advice and at the same time give radio journalists the chance to discuss and analyse the history and current practices of their trade, or profession. I also feel that not enough is being done to celebrate the art of radio journalism. It is an honest and fulfilling way of communicating the truth and humanity of our world to other human beings. I want to pay tribute to the courage and example shown by the ghosts of voices from the past and the voices of the present.

Radio is a fast-moving medium of broadcast news for both listeners and journalists. Throughout my career there has been little opportunity to question, to challenge, and to compare in a field where deadlines are literally up to the second. The radio journalist is at the mercy of a telephone call and a clock. Who are we serving? Our peers? The companies for whom we work? Our listeners? Or the communities to whom we broadcast? What are the imperatives which guide us? Are they commercial, social, religious, political, ethical, or professional?

The editor of this series, Professor James Curran and Routledge's Senior Editor Rebecca Barden wanted a book which marries the disciplines of practice and theory. It is an interesting brief given to someone who is teaching and very active in radio at the same time. Throughout the teaching process at Goldsmiths College I have found it very bracing to be challenged and confronted with awkward questions by a multi-cultural and rather unique community of students. In many ways I have gone through a thorough re-evaluation of my journalistic objectives and values.

In this book, there is a great bias towards writing and editorial crafts. I stress the importance of using the voice and achieving competence in a range of specialist areas. Technical knowledge is as important as good judgement in relation to applying the law. But a book of a little more than 100,000 words is never going to be comprehensive and effective on its own. So I have included an extensive bibliography listing a considerable amount of factual spoken word material now available on cassette and compact disk. Live practice is, in my opinion, the only way to learn a professional craft and then you have some credibility when considering an analysis of the hows and the whys. So in the context of training, reading this book should be combined with active journalism.

It is important to understand that this book has not been written by a theoretical lecturer in media and communications. I hope I am not encumbered with

any ideological and doctrinaire baggage. My ideas and opinions about radio journalism and the political and ethical culture which determine my approach to the
craft are based on my own liberal background and a personal respect I have for
individual liberty, democracy and freedom of expression. When academics talk
about the culture of journalism, and seek definitions, there is a danger that they
will make the mistake of deciding that surrounding factors determine its function
and *raison d'être*. I believe that the community of journalism and the existence of
journalists in any society has its own driving force of moral, ethical and political
objectives. I believe that journalists themselves have sought to define these principles independently. Their thoughts and professional spirit are separate from the
control and policy of state governments, business corporations and proprietors.

The appointment of John Birt to the position of Director-General of the BBC
has brought his philosophy of 'Mission To Explain' and the challenge to the 'Bias
Against Understanding' into a new 'Directorate' structure in both BBC radio and
television. He has introduced a culture of specialist correspondents who are
invited to comment on news events and make intelligence assessments. Radio
practitioners are also expected to work in television. This is not a new concept in
America, or Australia. But the bi-media structure of news organisations raises
interesting issues about the relationship between radio and television news, and
the culture of management.

At the same time this change has been attended by political controversy and
accusations that the BBC has buckled to the pressures of real censorship and self-
consorship during eighteen years of uninterrupted Conservative government.

The tensions created by these issues exploded at the UK Radio Academy
Festival in Birmingham in July 1993 when the distinguished foreign correspondent
Mark Tully attacked the reforms John Birt had attempted to introduce. Within
twenty-four hours John Birt responded with a spirited and eloquent apology for
the changes he says are necessary to take the BBC into a new era. He explained
that the BBC had to win the argument to persuade a Conservative government to
renew the Charter and maintain licence fee funding. There have been reports of
catastrophic changes to BBC programming and management culture, and complaints of low morale blowing through this great institution. The industry's trade
magazine, *UK Press Gazette*, once reported that BBC South's Head of Broadcasting
had earned the nickname 'Vlad The Impaler'. This is because his tenure has been
marked by the departure of station managers and senior staff. Aggressive management techniques confronting the culture of radio news journalism have become
a prevailing experience for many in the industry. In the USA the Federal Communications Commission agreed to a process of deregulation which resulted in
the removal of the obligation for all radio stations to maintain newsrooms and
local news services.

While in the grip of recession in the early 1990s, Britain's premier independent speech service, LBC, developed a more aggressive polemical style of 'News Talk' programming. Former *Sunday Times* editor Andrew Neil had a weekday morning editorial and a weekend programme. Presenters such as Australian Mike Carlton and one of BBC television's first woman newscasters Angela Rippon were free to express comment during live programmes. A former *Sun* newspaper columnist Richard Littlejohn repeatedly berated British establishment figures with contempt and irreverence during phone-in programming. These developments followed a disastrous attempt to create two different newstalk radio services on the station's FM and AM frequencies. This was also combined with macromanagement mistakes by the station's holding company. Several years of redundancies, management/union battles and continual crisis management serve as a fascinating case-study on the inextricable link between editorial change and financial imperatives.

The Australian-owned holding company Crown Communications went into receivership and most of the Australian programming management had to leave the station. The Programme Director Charlie Cox had returned the radio station into an operating profit and he showed skill in developing programming initiatives. He remained in Britain and as managing director of DMG, the radio division of the *Daily Mail* and General Trust PLC, he has played a key role in financial investment in UK commercial radio. Mike Carlton returned to Australia taking with him a UK Sony Award and a Gold Medal from the International Radio Festival of New York as well as the ignominy of being the news presenter who insulted many of his listeners by saying, 'Wogs begin at Calais'. His undoubted talent and vigorous style of questioning were never really appreciated by the UK industry and radio critics. He now presents the drivetime sequence on 2BL, the ABC's flagship radio station in Sydney.

Despite an effort by Dame Shirley Porter and her family company Chelverton Investments to secure the franchise for another eight years, the UK Radio Authority decided to award LBC's frequencies to a new consortium called London News Radio headed by LBC's former managing director Peter Thornton. The new company proposed a rolling news format service on FM and a commitment to 'restore journalistic and radio reporting values'. LBC responded with a high profile campaign against closure which involved the collection of thousands of signatures from aggrieved listeners. The axing of LBC and the resulting row generated more publicity for the station than at any time in its twenty-year history. The loyalty shown by listeners for a news and talk station that had been part of London life for twenty years was astonishing. The Radio Authority came under sustained political pressure. The decision to withdraw the licence was taken by an unelected body which sat in secret and gave no reasons for its decision. There was no right of appeal. Thousands of listeners took part in a spontaneous wave of protest and anger and the event has raised important issues about freedom of expression and democratic accountability over the control of broadcasting freedom. The story was to take more dramatic twists and turns. Reuters bought out the winning consortium. There was another relaunch, this time of two separate stations. The FM service was to be dedicated to a rolling news format and self-driven programmes with state of the art technology. D-Cart, an Australian computer news programming package replaced reel-to-reel tape recorders, editing blocks and razor blades. All of the station's continuity sound, from jingles to adverts, were to be transmitted using another computer software package. A UK multi-track computer sound editing system, SADiE, was acquired by the Commercial Productions Department. But despite millions of pounds of investment, Reuters' venture into the competitive field of commercial radio news and talk programming was financially unsuccessful. In July 1996 there was another wave of change as ITN acquired the FM station to run a more concentrated, pacey style of rolling news format, and the Great Western Radio Group, the majority shareholder of the national FM station Classic FM, acquired the AM station to relaunch the brand of LBC which so many listeners wanted to hear again. Both stations moved into the hi-tech ITN news building in central London. Traditional reel-to-reel tape recorders were banned and a senior executive was heard to say that they belonged to the Victoria and Albert Museum.

The FM station has been rebranded as News Direct 97.3FM and the half-hour news sequences resemble the pace and panache of Capital Radio's *The Way It Is* which coincidentally was axed in 1996. The rising of LBC from the ashes with jingles that resonate the sound of the old station has been a success. There was an initial 86 per cent increase in listeners making the station the second most listened to radio service in London and putting it in top position as London's most popular commercial talk station. The station is hoping to sustain this position and subsequent listening surveys demonstrate consolidation of these good ratings. It is a quite extraordinary experience hosting an LBC live programme in 1997 compared to what it was like in 1977. In those days a studio manager controlled the mixing console with a separate Master Control Room monitoring the output of the station. The presenter and guests were in a separate studio recording area. A producer and assistant producer would be responsible for preparing the content of the programme. In the newsroom the assistant producer would be bashing away on an Olympia or Remington style typewriter to run in with copy and cues in triplicate. Associated Press, the Press Association, and United Press International teleprinters would be clattering out reams of paper for the copy taster to evaluate. Adverts would be transmitted on old-fashioned reel-to-reel loop cartridge machines. Programme pieces and pre-recorded interviews would be lined up on large Studer tape recorders.

In 1997 I am sitting in a combined studio/control room the size of a box-bedroom you would find in a semi-detached dwelling on a modern housing estate.

I am responsible for the audio-transmission of the entire station as I read the news, interview guests, and switch in and out of phone-in calls myself. This is known as self-driving or 'self-opping'. My jingles and commercials are run at the touch of hotkeys on a panel controlling a huge digital sound system which automatically loads the material for cueing every fifteen minutes. Programme features or interviews can be selected by number codes on a computer keyboard from D-Cart, or run from the digital Sony mini-disc machine. All the station's news subscriber services and information databases are available on screen at the touch of a keyboard. There is only one producer who is evaluating the calls for the phone-in component of the programme and who sends messages by screenwriter before my very eyes. Music is transmitted from compact discs. Specially sequenced sound montages or effects for quiz programmes are set out on another computer screen which displays computer software programmes such as SAW, SAW Plus, or Samplitude. The graphical interface enables me to move and shift sound in coloured blocks with the click and drag of a mouse button. Furthermore, I can connect to Compuserve or the Microsoft Network to explore World Wide Web pages which offer me near instant pictures, text, sound and video on millions of subjects from millions of sources.

There have been breathtaking developments in other areas of radio news broadcasting. The newest BBC network channel, Radio Five, was axed to make way for an all news and sport channel despite parliamentary and widespread public protest. Radio Five had the fastest growing audience of all the national networks. The editor of the all-news and sport channel *Radio Five Live* was Jenny Abramsky. From April 1994 Radio Five Live has been a success story. Many former LBC producers and journalists have been hired to create a popular blend of immediate news and sports coverage combined with documentary and interesting speech-based programmes during the evening. The transformation of the BBC's fifth radio network claimed a number of casualties. One of these was the weekly 20-minute live children's news magazine programme aimed at 9–12 year-olds. The purpose of *In the News* was to educate and inform a younger audience about national and world issues using music and features in a style appropriate for the target listener. The programme had a take-up of 82 per cent of the country's primary schools and received two thousand letters a week.

At the time of Radio Five Live's launch more cynical insiders bestowed on the station the irreverent title 'Spews'. When BBC Radio experimented with all-news broadcasting during the Gulf War by 'requisitioning' Radio 4's FM frequencies for this purpose, journalists called it 'Scud FM' – a reference to the Russian-made Iraqi missiles which were being fired into Israel and Saudi Arabia.

The UK Radio Authority which regulates the licences of commercial radio stations has responded by awarding a national medium-wave frequency to Talk Radio. This service started inauspiciously with an ill-fated mixture of 'shock-jocks' and banal phone-in sequences. A former LBC senior producer, Jason Bryant, has changed the format with a more gentle and news-informative blend of presenters. Sport is covered heavily at weekends and in the evenings. Listening figures are improving, but the station's financial losses are still reported to be high. Jason Bryant left the station in July 1997.

Both Radio Five Live and Talk Radio are existing on AM frequencies which are criticised in the UK for being blighted by heavy interference during the hours of darkness. To what extent will technical limitations undermine audience appreciation and growth? AM has been a hugely successful spectrum for US and Australian talk stations. Will the promise of Digital Audio Broadcasting in the UK provide the answer? Radio stations established on terrestrial frequencies are finding alternative outlets on Satellite and the World Wide Web which can currently deliver near FM stereo quality on 28.800 modems.

Competition and politics are combining to create a rapidly-changing environment for radio news broadcasting in Britain. These changes raise further fascinating questions about broadcasting power and democracy.

These recent experiences and developments in the United Kingdom are by no means unique to this country. Ideas and styles adopted as new in Britain have been pioneered and well-executed in other countries. Jenny Abramsky has insisted that the BBC's news and sports channel is not going to be a copy of the rolling news format broadcast by WINS in New York where you hear the national and international news every twenty minutes. In a special session at the UK's 1992 Radio Academy Festival in Birmingham the focus of the discussion concentrated on the practices in Britain and the USA. Nobody raised the example of Radio France and France Info, a dedicated national rolling news French network that has been successfully developed on a national FM waveband, and can be found on the Eutelsat satellite service. The French experience of developing and listening to a national news network has been with us for several years and the model has been established only a matter of miles from the cliffs of Dover.

Yet the French experience was not on the agenda during the Radio Academy discussion. It now transpires that BBC Radio Five Live executives travelled to Paris to visit the station. They examined the success of a network providing comprehensive radio news twenty-four hours a day for 365 days of the year. They evaluated how it was possible to provide this service with an annual budget of seven million pounds and only fifty full-time staff. France Info's Editor-in-Chief, Pascal Delannoy, advised the BBC team to keep it simple, and move fast. 'There's only room for one continuous news network in France, and I'm sure the same is true in Britain.' Nicholas Wheeler, who was appointed to relaunch London's News 97.3FM, travelled to France, Philadelphia, New York and Los Angeles to study successful rolling news formats. Whereas BBC Radio Five Live mixes news with sport and magazine programming, News 97.3FM and its successor News

Direct more closely mirror the France Info format with a basic turnaround sequence of thirty minutes. The short news reports, known as 'chroniques' in France, are never more than two and a half minutes.

Radio journalists share common problems and experiences throughout the world. The origins and styles of radio news are also vastly different even within the English-speaking world. This book aims to discover interesting comparisons between UK, USA and Australian radio news operations. Occasionally, I also look at what happens in other countries.

The journalist has a role in any society to report truthfully and to convey information to fellow citizens about events which offend against human decency. There is a moral obligation on the part of journalists to expose abuses of power, injustice, illegality, and wrong-doing. This role will inevitably force the journalist to confront authority and challenge powerful forces within society. In any democracy there is a constant war being fought between the forces of journalism and the forces of censorship and control. Information is power. In a genuine democracy journalists should be allowed a wide discretion to disseminate information as a service to fellow citizens. Radio plays an enormous role in this continuing battle. I have tried to analyse and explain the exercise of this power by the individual radio journalist through the history of the twentieth century.

How is this war being fought? When Richard Dimbleby entered Belsen concentration camp and described what he saw in one of the most evocative broadcasts of the modern age, the BBC did not want to broadcast it. Editors feared that listeners would be unduly distressed, or not able to believe his naked and terrifying depiction of human carnage and depravity. But there was also a more serious background to the issue. The appalling vista of human suffering put on trial not only the extreme Nazis who carried out genocide but also the Allies for their failure to discourage and prevent the slaughter of millions of defenceless people. Richard Dimbleby threatened to resign. His recording was broadcast. The individual radio journalist had asserted his purpose to observe and report the truth. But had he reported the entire truth? There is a risk that people are being left with the impression that he did not provide one reference to the fact that the focus of this genocide was the Jewish population of Eastern Europe. This is because his only reference to Jews has been edited out of versions of his broadcast. But Anne Karpf, the writer of *The War After: Living with the Holocaust*, has asserted in an article for the *Guardian* in June 1996, that 'he scarcely mentioned Jews'. Perhaps he had not spoken the full truth. It is true that he did not emphasise that the target of the Nazis' Final Solution was the Jewish race, but he did observe that thousands of the victims were Jews. It is also a fact that Jewish survivors comprised about half of the people imprisoned at Belsen. I have spoken to survivors myself and analysed other accounts. I do not believe Richard Dimbleby deserves to be condemned for not making the right emphasis. However, I believe the BBC, the War

Cabinet and Foreign Office were fully aware of the operation of genocide against European Jewry and it can be argued that these bodies deserve to be in the dock accused of being indifferent bystanders. First, for failing to believe and respond to the evidence being presented to them. For instance, the Polish government in exile's special envoy, Jan Karski, who had witnessed the horrors of the Warsaw ghetto and the operation of the death camps, had personally briefed four members of the British War Cabinet in November and December 1942. Second, they should also be condemned for censoring the broadcast of accounts of the concentration camps. Third, for not preparing British listeners for the horrors encountered by the young Dimbleby and his fellow allied correspondents.

Ed Murrow created a similarly harrowing broadcast after entering Buchenwald. Why did he omit the fact that most of the bodies and survivors suffering in these camps were Jewish? Since both men are now dead, and no one cared to ask them these questions, we have to speculate about the pressures of self-censorship and the influence of the deeply entrenched cultural anti-Semitism present in Britain and America prior to 1939. The BBC and American networks were wary of providing emphasis on the persecution of Jews because of their sensitivity about stirring up anti-Semitism within their own populations and alienating Germans in overseas broadcasts. The benefit of hindsight and the cultural imperatives of another age justifiably challenge those judgements. More recently, radio journalists have attempted to put into words and engage with the imagination of the listener the equally appalling story of genocide in Rwanda. The BBC correspondent Fergal Keane has been among the more effective communicators on this subject. But the western world appears less concerned about the horrors of this human tragedy. Few journalists covered the trials of Serbian and Croatian soldiers for war crimes arising out of the bloody conflict in the former Yugoslavia. These proceedings at The Hague in Holland were relegated to a few paragraphs in the broadsheet newspapers of English-speaking countries. Not even the BBC allocated a full-time correspondent to ensure full coverage. What determines the exercise of news priorities in radio news? Money, morality or politics?

There is a growing practice in the United Kingdom to give witnesses anonymity in adversarial trials and to hold legal proceedings in secret. Journalists are being prevented from observing the work and decisions of the judiciary. This is a major threat to democracy and liberty. The breaches of the open justice principle are being justified with arguments and platitudes we normally associate with dictators. It is claimed that more criminals will be convicted if their accusers are not identified and put in fear of reprisals. It is claimed that 'sensational reporting' prejudices public respect for justice. These are insidious arguments. They are intellectually shallow and morally suspect. Here we have two examples of where the journalist needs to assert a cultural imperative that is directly linked to the existence and purpose of journalism in a liberal democracy. The journalist has a duty to challenge and expose these events. The journalist is the eyes and ears of the individual citizen. When the journalist is bound and gagged the citizen has no rights. Democracy evaporates.

International Radio Journalism seeks to make sense of the culture of radio journalists, and the moral imperatives which motivate those good people in all parts of the world who practise it well and honourably. I offer a general apology for my failure to acknowledge achievements and radio news broadcasting in areas of the world which I have yet to discover. I express my sincere thanks to the radio writers past and present whose outstanding research has enabled me to begin my task. I hope that what follows interests the professional and inspires, intrigues and goes some way to preparing the student and trainee for the world of international radio journalism.

Chapter 2

Basic skills, listening and contacts

The radio journalist needs to achieve four main areas of competence:

1 Presentation of information through the use of the voice.
2 Ability to write in a radio news style for bulletins, features and programme pieces.
3 Operational ability to use recording, writing and communications equipment and sound production techniques.
4 Editorial judgement in the production of broadcast radio news items.

Quite apart from this quartet of attributes, the radio news reporter needs to possess the instinct and culture of journalism. There are three basic skills needed:

1 Wide and continuing knowledge of news and current affairs.
2 An appreciation of news sense and priority.
3 A tenacious and persistent inquisitorial attitude rooted in the principles of free speech and freedom of expression.

There is much to read and study in the field of radio journalism and this book's philosophy seeks to bring an open-minded and eclectic approach to the subject and to encourage creativity and intellectual analysis in the process of training and work.

Listening

This is perhaps the most enjoyable part of all training. It is vital that habitual listening to the most significant radio news bulletins and programmes forms a central component of the trainee's weekly schedule.

In the UK, BBC Radio 4's *Today* programme should be a regular morning appointment. This should be followed by *The World At One*, *PM* and *The World Tonight*. The key bulletin of the day on Radio 4 is the *6 o'clock News*. Then the listening should take in the more popular news judgement and style of broadcasting on Radio 1 FM with *Newsbeat* at 12.30 p.m. and a new drive-time format in the afternoon. If you are in London, it is recommended that you listen to commercial radio news programmes on Capital Radio, News Direct 97.3FM, LBC, Heart 106.2, Virgin, and nationally, the *Classic Report at Six* on Classic FM. In the regions, trainees should regularly compare the news packaging and content of independent and BBC local radio services.

Independent Radio News supplies news to most of the UK's commercial radio services. Hourly bulletins can be heard on Classic FM throughout the country and a rival radio news network is providing the bulletins for the new national Virgin AM station which has a more viable FM station in London.

BBC Radio 4 broadcasts an excellent range of documentary, feature and investigative news programmes. It is recommended that the trainee studies *File on Four*, *Analysis*, *From Our Own Correspondent* and *You and Yours*. The broadcast times can vary from year to year so it is useful to check the latest schedule in listings magazines such as *Radio Times*. Radio Five Live has built a wider range of audience for news than BBC Radio's flagship Radio 4 whose listeners are mainly drawn from the ABC1 marketing category. The network has demonstrated a lively and popular approach to developing and analysing national and international news stories and fusing this with concentrated coverage of all sports.

The BBC World Service is a goldmine of superb international news programmes. Insomniac trainees can hear these on Radio 4's longwave frequency after close-down. There are two regular programmes which harness the range and power of the BBC's foreign correspondents: *Newsdesk* daily at 0000, 0200, 0700, 1100, 1800, and *Newshour* daily at 0500, 1300 and 2100. These times are Greenwich Mean Time. *Outlook* is described as 'the magazine programme that presents the "human interest stories behind the news"' and has become an international institution in radio. This can be heard Monday to Friday at 1405 and 1905 and there is a repeat on Tuesdays and Saturday at 0105. Other programmes worth catching are *Assignment*, *Network UK*, *People and Politics*, *The World Today* and *World Brief*. Up-to-date times can be found in the magazine *On Air* which is published quarterly. BBC World Service radio programmes are also transmitted in segments on US radio stations and *On Air* gives details of call-signs and frequencies. By April 1997, the BBC World Service had agreed a deal with United States Public Radio International to supply a fifty-minute early morning foreign news programme to 500 US radio stations to follow up the successful provision of a drive-time news programme called *The World* in partnership with PRI and WGBH in Boston.

The trainee in the USA has a rich array of radio news services and programmes to sample and study. National Public Radio has led a revolution in quality and in-depth radio news programming in the last twenty years and with over 300 member stations throughout the States most American radio students should have an opportunity of hearing them. NPR produces three outstanding current affairs programmes: *Morning Edition* for the breakfast audience, *The State of The Nation*, a lunchtime current affairs and phone-in programme, and the drive-time *All Things Considered*. There is also the *Weekend Edition* on Saturdays and Sundays for the weekend breakfast audience. There is a weekly documentary series on national and international affairs called *Horizons*. All major city markets in the USA have a good choice of NewsTalk, All News and varied music format stations. New York has the well-known rolling news format station WINS and there are strong News-Talk stations in other cities such as WRC in Washington. WBAL in Baltimore is an excellent example of a news station in a middle range market. In 1994 WBAL maintained a twenty-four-hour newsroom with nineteen journalists, meteorologists and four mobile news units. In Los Angeles the trainee could sample KFWB, a dynamic and energetic radio news operation making powerful use of 'news helicopters' to give eye witness reports of breaking stories. The leading American networks ABC, CBS, NBC and MBS all put out a varied range of services tailored to streams of format broadcasting. It is a very useful exercise to move around the dial to examine how local stations package the various services. ABC Radio News distributes a weekly wrap-up of national and international news called *World News This Week* which is carried by more than 200 US stations, and the American Forces Radio Network. The Christian Science Monitor set up a net-worked radio news service which had 191 public radio outlets for its news bulletins and features, but rising costs led to closure in June 1997. Syndicated material is sometimes carried by 100 public radio stations. UPI and AP also provide radio news copy and audio on subscription. It has to be said there has been some retreat in the resources applied to radio news gathering. The four main networks are primarily driven by the requirements of television news so most of the reporters and journalists are bi-media. CNN has become a news provider in the radio field but again as an adjunct of primary television news service. This is not the case with NPR.

The Canadian radio scene is also rich with a variety of qualitative radio news services. The Canadian Broadcasting Corporation maintains an impressive array of news bulletins and programme segments. The menu includes the award-winning *Canada At Five*, *The World at Six*, *World Report*, *The World This Weekend*, the political programme called *The House* and the weekly analytical programme on the media *Now the Details* hosted by Mary Lou Finlay. CBC news can be downloaded on the Internet via Real Audio on a brilliant web site: www.radio.cbc.ca. Rogers Broadcasting Ltd maintain one of the leading commercial radio news services in

Canada. Driven editorially from the Toronto flagship station CHFI- FM 98.1, the network produces impressive documentaries and *Sunday, Sunday* a one-hour national news magazine programme distributed across over forty markets coast-to-coast. The programme has co-hosts in Vancouver and Toronto. 1994 saw the relaunch of CHUM Satellite Network National News with a nine and a half minute package of news material originating from studios based at CHUM-Toronto and CFRA-Ottawa. There is no other national radio newscast co-anchored from two cities. Each day, the CHUM newsroom in Toronto polls the newsrooms of affiliate stations, searching for important and interesting stories developing in those markets. The service is also dedicated to looking for *Good News* so that their listeners are hearing about positive developments in medicine, science, business, technology, and human endeavours which are not being reported by other national outlets. Another example of a Canadian radio station originating its own news service is CFPL FM 96 in London, Ontario. CFPL produces regular bulletins, news and magazine programmes covering local, national and international affairs.

Australia, like the USA, is well served by a rich and varied mixture of radio news stations and networks. The political and cultural structure of the country has resulted in a more locally-based industry so that city and town stations feel the need to serve the interests of their own population. The Australian Broadcasting Corporation provides both national network services, which broadcast the same programmes to all the states and territories, and local services in capital cities and regional centres. However locally-tailored and nationally-networked programmes on commercial stations command the higher audience share. As in the USA, Australian state governments control their own education and police services and formulate their own laws. There are four main Australian news networks. Macquarrie News is one of the oldest established. The 2UE Network is based in its H/Q Sydney station. The Australian Radio Network is driven from 2UW in Sydney. The Parliamentary News Network, PNN, distributes a mix of rolling news format, live national sports commentary and federal government proceedings from Canberra. The public sector radio organisation ABC funded by government grant distributes news services to affiliate stations. A good example of this is 2BL 702 in Sydney. The 2BL format utilises a strong news and current affairs base through the day, with talk-based entertainment in the evening, and sport at the weekend. ABC produces two leading news and current affairs programmes to follow the BBC and NPR pattern.

There is a breakfast programme called *AM* on two networks at various times throughout the morning, with the main bulletin at 8 o'clock. *PM* is transmitted at 6 o'clock in the evening. Two of the most famous radio NewsTalk presenters in Australia are Alan Jones at breakfast time and John Laws up until lunchtime on Sydney's 2UE which dominates the market share for talk radio in this part of

Australia. Australia has also seen a rich and fascinating development of community radio services and the listener may find more probing, experimental and pioneering programming on community stations in the large cities. News coverage on these services tends to be more reflective and is often compiled by journalists who have a background in media studies education.

Contacts

Radio journalists need to organise and develop a contacts book from the very start of their careers. There are now some very useful pocket contacts books being published annually in the UK, USA and Australia. The UK *Guardian*'s *The Media Guide* is an excellent compendium of day-time addresses and contacts for newspapers, radio and television, library sources, pressure groups, emergency services, government and trade unions. This type of information needs to be built upon by an individual journalist with the home and night-time telephone numbers of decision makers and contacts in all fields. Even home addresses are worth asking for. Most radio news production involves shifts running through the night and the early hours of the morning. It is when stories break at this time that the good personal contacts book will be like gold dust. When establishing a presence through freelance shifts this personal resource can guarantee future employment. The information technology revolution now offers a range of small electronic gadgets which can hold and update contacts systems on a digital basis. The UK's weekly trade magazine for journalists, *UK Press Gazette*, has published a software programme which is an excellent database for contacts. It contains thousands of pre-existing contacts as well as the capability for adding your own. This software programme called PG Contacts can be easily loaded onto a small laptop and uses minimal disk space.

Chapter 3

Experience, print media, languages and multimedia

The trainee should be sent out on assignments almost immediately. Radio journalism is a practical discipline. There are many people who are good at talking about it and sadly far fewer who are actually good at doing it. The first experience for any radio reporter should involve covering a real news event with a portable recorder and microphone. Industry magazines such as *UK Press Gazette* in the UK publish weekly news diaries, and most journalism schools have access to agency diaries. The trainee needs to cover at least one news event a week. The following brief is fairly typical of what a professional radio reporter is required to provide from one news story:

A Thirty second radio news copy item for bulletins.
B A 15 to 20-second news cut from an interview combined with 10 to 15-second cue for bulletins.
C A 40-second news wrap consisting of voice report with 5 to 10-second news actuality included. This should also be presented with a cue which has a fresh angle and different approach to the news cut cue.
D A 2-minute news programme piece consisting of the reporter's voice and actuality from the news story.

Analysis of Print Media

There was a famous occasion when a former army colonel who had taken over as Managing Director of a British radio service complained to his editors that whenever he walked into the newsroom he found the journalists lounging around reading the morning's newspapers. Radio journalists should have a voracious appetite for all areas of the news media. We would recommend that in the UK, broadsheets such as the *Independent*, the *Guardian*, *The Times* or the *Daily Telegraph* should be studied. It is also important to consider the more popular newspapers. Broadcast journalists should avoid harbouring the snobbish and arrogant attitude that UK papers such as the *Sun*, *Mirror*, and the *Daily Star* are mere 'gutter-press' and pander to the lowest common denominator. These papers are written with enormous skill and professionalism. The language is popular and colloquial and the news judgement is often closely in tune with public opinion. The so-called 'middle-brow' papers such as the *Mail* and the *Daily Express* are also of vital interest to the popular broadcaster.

American broadcast journalists should also be taking the leading broadsheet papers in their cities. The *New York Times* and *Washington Post* are obvious suggestions combined with the larger circulation tabloids. In Australia, the *Sydney Morning Herald* should be combined with *The Australian*, *The Age* in Melbourne and there are similar choices in other Australian states.

News media reading should take in several Sunday papers and a number of weekly publications. The international news magazines *Time* and *Newsweek* are excellent sources of world news and feature stories. The *International Herald Tribune* is a daily publication which could be described as a newsprint 'World Service Programme'.

Regional morning, evening and local weekly newspapers provide good examples of the news judgement and style of coverage in local reporting. The United Kingdom is blessed with some excellent daily papers that are published outside London such as the *Northern Echo* in Darlington, the *Manchester Evening News*, *The Yorkshire Post* and the *Liverpool Daily Post*. The Scottish press is distinguished by the *Glasgow Herald*, *The Scotsman* and *Scotland On Sunday*. Scottish news values are based on many different cultural, political and social priorities. These publications are models of how the perspective on news values changes the further you move away from a country's metropolis. Radio journalists should make a special effort to read the black press in countries such as Britain and the USA. In the UK, *The Voice* is undoubtedly the leading paper for Afro-Caribbeans. The *Pittsburgh Courier* and *Chicago Defender* are leading representatives of the American black press.

Languages

I remember speaking to a European correspondent and asking him with some trepidation how many languages he spoke. The answer was 'One . . . English. I still think there's room for improvement.' The journalist was being rather self-effacing, but in a world made smaller by communications, there is an argument for radio journalists to acquire a range of language skills. It can considerably enhance career prospects and give a journalist the edge when applying for the more exciting assignments. It might be a good idea to learn languages spoken by the world's largest populations or in areas which are the host of significant world events and news stories. Spanish gives the journalist communications skills in the Hispanic areas of the USA, Central and Latin America as well as Europe. German is a significant language throughout Eastern Europe. French has a sphere of influence which takes in large areas of Africa, former French colonies including the Pacific as well as parts of Canada. Fluent speakers of Russian have and will continue to enjoy the reporting of the historic changes in the former Soviet Union. There would be some merit in considering languages such as Arabic, Japanese and Mandarin Chinese and Urdu, since they are spoken in areas which are gaining in political and economic prominence.

Linguistic skills offer many advantages when working as a producer or news bulletin editor. I recall that some of the basic expressions I learned on a Norwegian course were enormously helpful when reporting on the Alexander Keilland oil rig disaster in 1980. As the story was breaking the rescue operation was being coordinated from Stavanger on Norway's west coast. Most of the communications centres were being overwhelmed with telephone calls in English. The courtesy expressed by my attempt at speaking Norwegian resulted in my getting live broadcast interviews with Norwegian coastguards, helicopter pilots and representatives of the oil company which owned the platform. The UK has seen growth and development in modern language degrees and the quality of language teaching. Cassette and video courses are useful starts, but the real progress tends to be made during classes with native speakers. The acquisition of advanced language skills will enable the radio journalist to monitor and assess foreign media with speed and precision and roam around as a field reporter with greater confidence and security.

Multimedia

No modern radio journalist will survive in the twenty-first century without a full grounding and understanding of information technology, the power and research potential of the Internet and World Wide Web, and the applicaton of digital systems to radio news text, production and transmission. Digitally programmed radio stations were a feature of the American and Australian radio scene years before the introduction of the technology into UK radio journalism environments. The BBC has lagged behind its commercial competitors, but is now beginning to catch up. The Corporation as a whole has recently adopted an integrated text and multimedia system. Local radio stations such as GMR (Greater Manchester Radio) and Radio Bristol have taken the step to operate a fully digital operation. Classic FM, London News Radio, LBC and Heart FM made the move much more efficiently and effectively several years before. At the time of publication the latest PC technology could offer stand-alone machines that can supply 200 megahertz central processing units (CPUs), 32 megabytes of random access memory (RAM), 288 and 344 kilobytes per second modem connection to the Internet and two to three gigabytes of random organised memory (ROM).

The residual cost for such a system in the UK is £2,000 at the time of writing with lower actual costs abroad where information technology has a lower economic scale. These systems can be networked for programming, newsroom and integrated transmission operations. The purpose of this book is to fully equip the trainee and professional radio journalist with the necessary intelligence to participate in the revolution sweeping through the industry and connecting the worldwide community of radio journalists into a powerful network of contacts and shared experience. ISDN (Integrated Standard Digital Network) has been used to deliver digital standard outside broadcast connections. ISDN is about to be more comprehensively marketed to domestic computer users as the interface costs are being lowered through greater use. This means that the Internet can deliver digital quality sound. Progressive Networks has developed and successfully distributed the Real Audio player, which, at the time of writing, is offering version four for free download. There is digital stereo quality on 28,800 modems and ISDN line connections. More and more radio stations are establishing real-time broadcast web sites, so it is possible to hear classical music in stereo from Radio New Zealand or CBC in Canada, as it is being broadcast. A Californian software company, Liquid Gold, has created a programme which promises to deliver Dolby Digital Sound quality on 14,400 modems and Microsoft has developed a sound programme called Netshow player version two, which is used to transmit News Direct and LBC in London on the World Wide Web. There are other sound software programmes that can be downloaded within a matter of minutes.

The desk-top publishing packages, Microsoft Office Suite, Lotus Suite, and Word Perfect for Windows all offer the resources for qualitative desk-top publishing which enable the radio journalist to build effective communication resources for letters, leaflets, programming forms and information databases. Dedicated contacts files can be created in these software programmes. Presentation programmes such as Lotus Freelance and Microsoft Powerpoint enable the radio journalist to prepare impressive presentation documents for 'pitches' and memoranda to news directors and programme controllers. They are also essential for the freelance who wants to make an impression to commissioning editors for independent productions and freelance assignments.

Your PC multimedia system must have a decent 16 or 32-bit sound card to link in with a cost-effective and versatile sound editing programme. I am a practised user of a high grade Turtle Beach sound card initialised to Software Audio Workshop 6.0. This has enabled me to use my PC to produce multi-layered news packages with sound effects, music, voice links, and actuality inserts cross-faded and mastered digitally onto Sony Mini-disc or DAT.

The only other necessity for full international connection with World Wide Web news sites and radio stations that transmit on the Web is a subscription to a good Internet service provider. The author uses both Compuserve and Microsoft Network. Compuserve has existing agreements with professional news agencies so that journalists would be able to scan the full UK Professional Press Association Service which is also divided into sub-windows for Law Courts, Financial, Royal, Sport and General news stories. The advantage of an MSN connection is quick access to the outstanding multimedia MSNBC service which is replete with downloadable video and sound news files. Both service providers have elected to support the Explorer 3 web browser which is the software programme which enables the computer to travel across the World Wide Web. MSN has the widest range of 'searcher' programmes which respond to the submission of key words. The latest version of Netscape provides similar access on alternative service providers.

The rapid and accelerating changes in computer technology are so breathtaking that the equipment and services written about here could easily be out of date between completion of the book's manuscript and publication. For example, in an eighteen-month period the best available package in domestic PCs for £2,000 changed from a Pentium 100 processor with 16 megabytes of Ram and a gigabyte hard disk drive, to a system which offers twice these configurations. It is recommended that some consideration is given to acquiring systems that have a long reach of upgrading. Some attention should be given to the motherboard of the PC which is the base that links the various electronic components. The motherboard can be more easily accessed in a tower unit.

The PC does not have to be a tower or base unit with a 15- or 17-inch screen. Portable notebook computers are an alternative provided that proper investment is made in computer architecture which has an independent location for the sound card operation. I have found that the compact nature of many notebook computer structures results in technical compromises. The sound card circuit is sometimes combined with the graphics card which is the electronic circuit responsible for driving the screen. In addition it has been known for the sound card to be joined or placed too closely to the hard disk. This will result in very bad sound interference when mixing and render any production mix-downs unbroadcastable. It is advisable to invest in a portable notebook system which can take add-on components giving the travelling radio journalist the opportunity to produce sophisticated news packages on location, access CD-Roms and the Internet. The Internet also offers an alternative method of transmitting material if there are difficulties with studio ISDN facilities. Many UK national newspapers market entire year collections on CD. This enables radio journalists in the field to carry a year's collection of a respected broadsheet national newspaper such as the *Daily Telegraph* on one CD-Rom and call up relevant copy for a story receiving attention. This is quicker and vastly more efficient than depending on photocopying at the news cuttings or information library. However, a fax modem facility is a crucial resource enabling your newsroom and production office to transmit research material in digital form quickly and efficiently to your portable computer screen. There is now a huge range of on-line newspapers, news agencies and news broadcast organisations available on the Web. I have evaluated the following sites:

The Electronic Telegraph – www.telegraph.co.uk

This site commands the highest respect of working journalists. It was one of the first and remains arguably the best on-line newspaper in the UK and it is updated daily. It is also possible to look at old editions in order to research a series of links to one event. You need to register before exploring the site but this can be bypassed by bookmarking the address using Netscape. Adding the address to the 'favourites' list is the equivalent function using the Microsoft Explorer Web Browser.

The Times and *The Sunday Times* – www.the-times.co.uk

This is a good web site offering daily updates of *The Times* (daily) and weekly editions of the *Sunday Times*. There is also access to information from the *Times Higher Education Supplement*. There is a similar position to the *Daily Telegraph* site where you need to register, but bookmarking bypasses this process.

Scottish Newspapers – the Electronic Herald – www.cims.co.uk/herald/

This is the best Scottish broadsheet site, but you will find more news information from the site for leading Scottish tabloid newspapers the *Daily Record* and the *Sunday Mail* – www.record-mail.co.uk/rm/drsm/front1.html This site is updated daily.

The best international multimedia news agency sites are undoubtedly CNN Interactive and MSNBC. There tends to be a US slant but these sites are quite brilliant in their use of multimedia, design and depth of information resources. CNN hold archival links to current stories for useful background information. The sound files from MSNBC tend to be superior at the time of writing. Addresses: www.cnn.com and www.msnbc.com

The most interesting and available dedicated radio news sites are to be found at www.sms.co.uk/irn providing access to copy script and Real Audio bulletins from Independent Radio News which is the prominent commercial UK radio news provider and CBS news from America on www.cbsnews.com. The Press Association site www.pa.press.net is rather superficial from the point of view of journalistic resources and I recommend the PA service provided through Compuserve at the time of writing. The US international news magazine *Time* maintains a web site at www.time.com which is strong on text but weak on graphics. The American tabloid newspaper *USA Today* runs an excellent online web site at www.usatoday.com with a special file of 'hot sites' published everyday that provide links to news-related subjects. There is a web library of the links for the previous year.

For those needing financial news information there are good sites at the *Wall Street Journal* www.wsj.com (This influential American daily requires a subscription after you have used up your trial period.) The *Financial Times* at www.ft.com and European Business News Interactive at www.ebn.co.uk which has a scrolling screen listing latest information on the state of the European markets and weather news.

Real Audio now runs a sophisticated live radio web site which also lists radio news services available across the world. It is perfectly feasible to hear bulletins provided by the US Pacifica and National Public Radio networks. Australian Music Monolith maintains a links page for Australian radio stations and programmes. Up until October 1996, the University of Queensland co-produced a Community Radio News Service which syndicated news stories with sound news cuts across Australia.

The UK general election of May 1997 became the first multimedia Internet election with the main broadcast services, BBC and ITN, offering substantial World Wide Web sites that contained lateral structures of text, pictures, audio and video information. The web sites were promoted by terrestrial TV and radio channels. This dimension to the election coverage was empowering for the proportion of the audience with computer connections. A listener now had an interactive engagement with the flow and resource of information. In addition to listening to live output on the computer, the listener could also access archive sound files, and background text at the same time. ITN's success with multimedia during the general election provided the impetus for the permanent provision and development of multimedia news. On their web site (www.itn.co.uk) news and archive background files are supplied through text, sound and video stream. LBC and News Direct has also developed and enhanced Internet media communication and it is astonishing that in July 1997 BBC Internet services were being panned by the critics. John Naughton in the *Observer* noticed that Director General John Birt's rhetoric about the digital information revolution was not being served by BBC practice.

Chapter 4

Attitudes and
news

Radio journalism is as much about attitude as it is about basic techniques. You need the right attitude to survive. In this book it is my intention to pass on the benefits of twenty years of experience and offer my observations about what makes a good radio journalist. I shall also make it very clear what it is that makes a bad journalist.

So to begin with let us go back to sources. You need sources to develop stories and the main field of news research in the radio newsroom will be on the telephone to the police, fire brigade, ambulance, coastguard and other public emergency services. In some English-speaking countries paramedics work for the fire service and emergency providers work under a single umbrella organisation. The key to operating well in a radio newsroom is to call and communicate regularly and more critically to call before each bulletin deadline. You need to cultivate these sources so there is a bond of trust and understanding. Speed of communication is important. The knack of dealing with each call and incident is to satisfy the Who What Why Where When and How? questions. When dealing with the identity of individuals you need to remember to obtain first names, addresses, professions, age and sex, marital status and the parental status of adults. You should always check the nature of relationships. If you have forgotten something or there is any lingering doubt about accuracy, you must go back to your source. Furthermore you should always follow the rule 'when in doubt leave it out' and never ever take anything for granted. It is not for journalists to assume or presume.

Curiosity is your watchword. You need to be nosey and analytical. It is the questions that you ask which dig out the best stories. Do not expect to hide in a

1: The modern radio newsroom. At Independent Radio News in London, Keir Simmons writes his scripts, prepares and edits audio cuts to present live on-air using computer technology.

2: The 'Dart' system. Independent Radio News is the largest provider of radio news in the United Kingdom. The service is actually staffed and compiled by Independent Television News. Here all the bulletin voice reports and news cuts have been compressed onto digital floppy disks. This is known as the 'DART' system. It is being used in BBC Regional broadcasting centres such as Plymouth in the south-west of England.

3: The newsroom at London's News Direct 97.3 FM station, Britain's only 'rolling news' format radio station. No reel-to-reel tape recorders are to be seen. The role of journalist, producer and presenter is combined into one.

4: A News Direct journalist at work editing on the 'Dave' computer system. Sound files are represented in 'waveform'.

5: A News Direct radio journalist working on a split screen for news text, agency copy and using a mouse and keyboard to compile and edit cue and sound material into one package.

6: News Direct's intake station. Computer digital systems receive reports and outside broadcast sources by ISDN lines. Radio news communication remains digital from the point of origination all the way through to transmission.

7: News Direct's on-air studios are the size of two small bedrooms. They are identical so that one is on-air and the other is off-air for preparation and production. This is the off-air studio demonstrating a total digital transmission system.

8: News Direct's on-air studio with only one person managing the station's entire output. Complete self-drive news broadcasting is achieved by a purpose-built studio integrated into text and sound editing computer storage systems. The on-air microphone is connected to the headphones giving the presenter mobility within the studio.

9: The control room of London's most popular talk station, LBC, which was Britain's first independent radio station. This photograph was taken when the weekend breakfast programme was being produced, with the producer Steve Campen in the studio. The control room reverts to a self-drive studio for most of the day's programming. LBC use D-Cart for news reports and features, DCS (Digital Commercial System) for adverts and jingles, mini-disc for longer pre-recorded programmes and compact disc for music. The tape recorder is redundant.

10: An LBC studio with sound-proofed windows providing visual contact with each production area. The two computer screens are connected to SADiE – the digital multi-track software editing system which is used to produce more creatively demanding features and programming components such as commercials and drama.

11: Britain's most influential news and current affairs radio programme – *Today* on BBC Radio 4. Production is well infrastructured with producers, reporters, editors and studio managers serving the three regular presenters – James Naughtie, Sue MacGregor and John Humphreys.

crowd, or think it can wait until tomorrow. You need to be hungry for news. When you walk into a radio newsroom you can normally realise within a few seconds who are the high flyers and what separates the very good from the mediocre. The reporter picking his or her nose or gossiping over coffee is not going to run with a story. The radio journalist should never sit back on a shift and the professional radio journalist is never off duty, even when on holiday. I can recall two spectacular stories of very experienced journalists ignoring this rule. The first concerned the defence correspondent who went on vacation to Famagusta when Turkey invaded the northern area of Cyprus in 1974. The journalist concerned made himself unavailable, continued with the delights of eating, drinking and sunbathing and then enthusiastically 'checked in' with his newsroom at London's Heathrow Airport only to discover that his editors had decided on a major career change for him. The other concerned a radio journalist who provoked the despair of his colleagues when taking a gastronomic homage to China during the build-up to the Tiananmen Square massacre in 1989. Again he left no contact numbers or addresses and deliberately refrained from ringing in, even though he was fully aware of the significance of the unfolding story. His name was on the list of redundancies announced six months later. The good radio journalist is always on the lookout for something about to happen. This is true even on a honeymoon.

So what is news? And how is radio news different from newspaper, magazine and television news? This is a complex question. Sometimes it is like observing shifting sands. You can start with anything that is new, interesting and true. But is that enough for it to fit in with the news agenda of your radio station or news network? The answer to this question is very often, 'no'. News organisations very rarely commission scientific surveys of their listeners. Furthermore, many news organisations such as the BBC in Britain are extremely sensitive to political pressure and media criticism. Two hundred letters complaining about the treatment of a news story or the attitude of a news broadcaster can precipitate an enquiry, disciplinary hearing or public rebuke. A severe roasting from a national newspaper reviewer with an axe to grind can also have a negative impact. It does not take much effort for a political organisation or pressure group to orchestrate a distorted public reaction to a news story. The BBC Radio 4 *Today* programme's 'Personality of the Year' award has been somewhat discredited by deliberate attempts from the Conservative and Labour parties to promote their respective leaders as the winning candidates in an open telephone vote.

There are obvious characteristics for a news story. It must be something which interests the listener, and better still many listeners. But how many? Is radio news determined by Jeremy Bentham's Utilitarian philosophy – is radio news dependent on what gives pleasure and interest to the greatest number of people? News needs to be something the listener has not heard before. It could be tomorrow's history today and it needs to represent changes in the status quo.

After twenty years of experience in journalism I have come to the conclusion that there are two important categories of news agenda. The first that tends to operate is the agenda set by the news station and the perception that radio journalists have what is of value to their peers. The second is what the listener needs and finds interesting. The first tends to have priority over the second.

In the first category, radio news journalists value a story that is told quickly and beats the competition in speed of transmission. Scoops are valued as much as in newspaper journalism, but are more quickly forgotten. Generally the radio medium tends to pick up on new stories launched in newspapers rather than the other way round. However, a radio news story which is quoted and followed up in the newspaper and television media has huge value to radio journalists' peers. Another story that is greatly valued is one where the radio journalist has exclusive access and challenges the journalist's courage and bravery. This may be due to good fortune, bad fortune, and/or initiative and investigative persistence. It seems the result is more important than the method to achieve it. An example of bad fortune concerned the South Australian radio journalist covering the Black Friday bushfires and describing the scene and his feelings as he witnessed the destruction of his own home. Radio journalists on the taxi rank of shift working could be lucky enough to be sent to cover the Falklands War as was the case with Robert Fox and Brian Hanrahan of the BBC and Kim Sabido of IRN. Journalists sent to catastrophic international events enjoy the syndrome of 'Foreign Correspondent in Adventure' kudos. The reporter in this context can normally quickly build reputation and fame, particularly among colleagues.

On the other hand, how difficult is the role of covering disasters and responding to international news events compared to investigative specialist work back in the home country? The glamour of fast travel and the adrenaline of intense human historical experiences combine a sense of individual exhilaration with a basic response to events which do not challenge the fundamental skills of story telling. Somebody once said 'travelling does nothing to improve the world except the ego of the foreign correspondent'. Investigating a sensitive social and political issue with a complex nexus of establishment intimidation and cover-up is equally stressful and more problematical. The firefighter reporter is a journalist sent anywhere around the world to cover any story. He or she can 'crash in' and 'crash out' of foreign beats without suffering the consequences of repression, intimidation and discrimination. An arrest or detention can turn the correspondent's presence into a story that centres on the journalist. Quite a bonus when it comes to self-promotion. In any event something will be done to secure release, and then the journalist can sell the book rights and appear on chat shows when returning home. In Britain there is even the prospect of a Royal award such as an OBE, CBE or even a

Knighthood! It is worth bearing in mind that OBE stands for Order of the British Empire at a time when Britain has long since lost its Empire. Should journalists be accepting such establishment seals of approval which are really relics of the past?

I do not intend any hint of cynicism. The horrendous experiences of journalists such as John McCarthy held hostage in the Lebanon for several years could not over-amplify the risks of working abroad. In 1995, BBC radio journalist John Schofield was killed covering the war in the former Yugoslavia. But the fact remains that qualitative, painstaking and risky journalism close to home in unglamorous contexts does not receive the same 'allure' from the point of view of radio journalists' peer assessment. There are more accolades for dodging bullets in a war-zone compared to trying to expose corruption on the part of a police detective in England. The UK libel laws would probably result in censorship or financial penalties for the dogged reporter, coupled with a request to find alternative employment. Meanwhile, the war-zone reporter would probably win a Sony Radio Reporter of the Year Award and be profiled by a national newspaper.

I believe that greater credit should be given to the radio journalist who considers the needs of the listener and the many listeners who make up the community which lives in the catchment area of the broadcast station. Generally, citizens want their news journalists to warn them of imminent physical danger from nature, public disorder, and other sources. Parents are strongly concerned about anything which is happening or could happen to their children. Usually, citizens appreciate information which helps them improve their economic and political position. They are also concerned about any threats to individual freedom and news of developments which can extend life expectancy or the quality of life. Another factor which is worth bearing in mind is the need to be entertained. This is why human interest stories involving strong and colourful characters enjoy appreciation. Good story telling has been with us from the very beginnings of our civilisation. And the ingredients of a good story in fiction are the same in the field of news. People like to hear about the drama of conflict with interesting characters undergoing fundamental changes. It is even better if the audience is in a position to identify with the characters who feature in the story.

A sociological view of the factors which determine the modern news agenda is that it is like a gate. The gate is represented by columns and beams of upbringing, education and social mores by people in the media. Social and political prejudices inherent in journalists are more important than the social and political dynamics of a real news event. Another theory is that the process of evaluating the news agenda in the broadcast media is wholly determined by the traditional approaches of the newspaper media, and the national press continues to seize the initiative. Another factor which is ever present in considering news priorities is the law of diminishing distance. This requires that a news event has less importance the further away it is from your own doorstep. The law of diminishing returns also applies to the ethnic origin of the people involved in news events. The death of 2,000 Asians in a railway accident in New Delhi receives less prominence than the death of a Guildford lawyer and his wife in a private plane crash on the M25, London's outer ring motorway. Subjects for news coverage have a disturbing habit of falling in and out of fashion and it is impossible to find a logical or rational explanation. Impetuous judgements are made about listeners becoming bored with the same 'running story'. Sometimes a moral agenda emerges so that an entire news corps retreats from the scene of an internationally significant news event. This was certainly the case in Dunblane, Scotland in 1996 after the mass murder of sixteen infant children. The media withdrew following a moral entreaty from politicians, church leaders and bereaved relatives that their overwhelming presence was distasteful, insensitive and intimidating.

In the early 1980s crime stories were explored and broadcast in depth and in volume. Protest marches in London on Sundays were always current news fare. By the late 1990s economic and environmental stories which had been previously consigned to specialist programmes are at the top of the news agenda. Is there any sure system of evaluating and applying a sound and reliable news agenda? There is a strange symbiotic and parasitic relationship between the media. On one day a broadsheet newspaper will reveal something new and significant and the rest of the media will ignore it. The story could relate to allegations of government corruption or 'sleaze' in parliament. Meanwhile a show business story about two TV presenters making insults about each other is on the front page of a tabloid and it is followed up enthusiastically by the electronic media. There would be something narcissistic about this, but it is not an uncommon occurrence in Britain. On another day a serious political story on the front page of a broadsheet will resonate heavily throughout the broadcast media. The other challenge to radio news is the issue of whether the medium will cover a story that is vitally important according to many criteria of a majority of listeners, but is dreadfully complicated and cannot be illustrated by interview or actuality.

As a conclusion, what is the best advice that can be offered the individual journalist to maintain the initiative in the news agenda and to continue seizing it? There are probably four useful questions that you need to ask. First, I would only consider newspaper stories for their follow-up and improvement potential. It is much better to develop from a small newspaper story into something original and startling. Second, it is wise not to rely exclusively on the news agency services and to be forever tied up rewriting other journalists' work. Third, place yourself as close as you can to original sources. Talk to people at the very grassroots of an issue rather than depending on political and pressure groups who are trained and skilled in 'spin doctoring' the way the media represents and evaluates the subject. Finally, always evaluate how valuable the story is to your listeners and continue this evaluation throughout the entire process of reporting the story.

In the end, what are the contrasts between a good radio journalist and a bad radio journalist? I could portray them as two distinct characters. The good radio journalist would make an immediate impression because of his or her sociable type and personal charm. Their desire to analyse and be nosey with curious enthusiasm is combined with a sense of public duty and responsibility. I would expect a good radio journalist to be able to grasp subjects that were previously completely unknown and to find ways of investigating these subjects. I would prefer a good radio journalist to be sceptical about conventional wisdom and traditional values, to be thick skinned and to maintain persistence in the search of truth. The good radio journalist should be an enthusiast about people and be able to understand people and their feelings. The ability to sympathise and empathise is invaluable. Understanding other people can be an exercise of imagination. Better still if it is based on experience because the better journalists tend to have a wide experience of life and the world. The good radio journalist is someone who would make each story as interesting as possible, with a desire to convey truth impartially and fairly. There should be respect for facts and a clarity of thinking and communication. The good radio journalist should be anxious about checking and rechecking and ensuring that the story is accurate. Ability should be combined with integrity and these qualities should be applied with a sense of freedom and responsibility. The good radio journalist will always be busy, using the telephone productively, using the potential of multimedia technology, taking care with accurate observation and working fast and accurately to deadlines. The good radio journalist should enjoy working under pressure and have an unfailing pride in meeting every deadline and an intense shame and disappointment at missing any deadline. The good radio journalist should be able to think laterally so that a combination of imagination, originality and persistence grabs the story and lifts the mundane and banal into something exciting and new. The good radio journalist has a good sense of humour. You are going to need one if you want to survive the modern world of radio journalism.

The bad radio journalist is the opposite of everything I have outlined. The bad radio journalist arrives at work lethargic, with a hangover, and a series of moans about the world. The poor radio journalist waits to be given ideas or told what to do. The bad radio journalist is more interested in using the television at work for entertainment rather than research. The bad radio journalist would use a computer to play games on rather than to write a news story. The bad radio journalist will be forever looking at his or her watch to check how long it is to go before the end of the shift. The bad radio journalist will accept freebies, junkets and favours in return for not pursuing a story. The bad journalist will say 'never let the facts spoil a good story'. The poor radio journalist will observe that colleagues who have good shorthand are dinosaurs. He or she will go for the obvious angle rather than the original. The same would apply to sources for a developing story. The bad radio journalist will make only one check call to the emergency services in an hour and would rather have a cup of coffee and a chocolate biscuit before a news bulletin instead of making final check calls. The bad radio journalist will always blame colleagues when things go wrong and will always point out other people's mistakes rather than pay attention to their own. The bad radio journalist will be pretending to be working extremely hard in order to give a false impression to management and will unhesitatingly claim credit for stories and successes he or she had nothing to do with.

The bad radio journalist will have a cold and rather brutal attitude to the feelings of others. He or she will have contempt for the intelligence and dignity of listeners. They will be referred to as 'the punters', or 'the great unwashed'. He or she will revel in other people's misfortune. The poor radio journalist will have a parasitic relationship with the other media and fellow radio journalists. The bad radio journalist will exhibit no signs of anxiety if there are major inaccuracies in his or her reporting. The priority will be style over content, affectation and impression over depth. The bad radio journalist will be motivated by money, fame and sexual attraction, and not necessarily in that order.

Chapter 5

Objectivity and theory

One of the most difficult conundrums in journalism is to find a clear and reliable working definition of objectivity. It seems working journalists have an instinct about what this means, but when they are strongly challenged for an explanation, the result is confusion and *non sequitur*. There are various dictionary definitions. Philosophically there can be no such thing as true objectivity in radio news. In the end you can only achieve a certain standard of subjectivity. If you as a radio journalist seek to be impartial, fair, equitable, neutral, detached, dispassionate and disinterested, then your approach has to be determined by some context or framework of criteria. If we are all trapped by our subjective experiences which guide the way we think and frame our approach to news gathering, then there can be no such thing as objective truth. Can you have a fair-minded approach to reporting the views and actions of an IRA activist if there is a clear distinction between you and the subject according to the catch-phrase 'them and us'?

The news media readily report actions by the IRA in Britain as acts of terrorism. However, there are many members of the Irish Republican community in Northern Ireland who would not use the word terrorist, but speak in terms of military action, freedom fighting, fighting for the cause. Equally, there are many Catholics in Ireland who are politically republican, but are bitterly opposed to the IRA and its tactics of arguing with the bomb and the bullet instead of the ballot box. The shades of opinion in the modern State of Israel are similarly complex. You can be a Zionist and implacably opposed to occupying Palestinian territories on the West Bank. The British media has always had problems of perception with respect to minority interests such as gay people, people who are HIV, and people who are not members of the majority white community. There is a famous

Yiddish saying that racism is no different from gossip. It is 'like feathers blown in the wind'. You have no idea of where they go and you can never retrieve them. Gossip as a form of human communication is very much a cornerstone of modern journalism.

The British media and government authorities now regularly fall into the trap of speaking in terms of 'ethnic minorities' and referring to race issues as 'problem' issues when the problem is quite clearly perceived as the existence of non-whites rather than the attitude of whites to non-whites. The relative perception of understanding is wholly dependent on the range of experience and communication that a radio journalist has within a given society. In Britain, the white middle-class journalist who has never read the leading black newspaper *The Voice* and has never socialised or worked with non-white people will have a different perception of a wide range of race-related stories compared to the radio journalist educated and brought up in a multi-cultural environment who reads widely when it comes to news sources.

The BBC in Britain is not controlled day by day through the exercise of statutory power. The existence of the Corporation owes itself to a bizarre and rather eccentric quirk of history and constitutional convention which is known as a Royal Charter. This means that the BBC can define its own standards of objectivity. Every few years the Corporation publishes a weighty tome called *Producers' Guidelines*. In an annexe to the Licence and Agreement the BBC accepts a duty to:

> ensure that programmes maintain a high general standard in all respects (and in particular in respect of content and quality) and to provide a properly balanced service which displays a wide range of subject matter . . . (and) to treat controversial subjects with due impartiality . . . both in the Corporation's news services and in the more general field of programmes dealing with matters of public policy.

> (BBC 1993)

The *Producers' Guidelines* also state that the BBC can express its own views on broadcasting issues but is forbidden from broadcasting its own opinions on current affairs and matters of public policy. This interesting contradiction might account for the soft pedalling seen in the coverage of media stories involving the BBC despite an infrastructure of media correspondents. A significant example of this is debate over the licence fee which compared to other countries is an undiscriminating tax on anyone who wants to watch television within the UK. The sum of £172m is spent every year enforcing it, tracking down those who have not paid the £90 tax, and then prosecuting them through the courts. When a leading association of probation officers complained about the instance of nearly 2,000 defaulters on licence fee fines being sent to jail every three years with a high proportion of single and Afro-Caribbean mothers, the BBC was rather silent.

There was clear evidence of self-censorship when covering this story. While many broadcasters abroad respect the freedom and independence the licence fee gives the BBC, many are somewhat doubtful about its democratic value and appropriateness in funding a state-controlled system. The Australian Broadcasting Corporation is controlled by a specific Act of the Federal Parliament in Canberra. The ABC produces a much slimmer and less pompous booklet on editorial policies which pays homage to presenting news and information which is:

> accurate and impartial according to the recognized standards of objective journalism . . . ABC journalists will not allow their professional judgment to be influenced by pressures from political, commercial or other sectional interests or their own personal views.
>
> (ABC 1995)

In 1984 the ABC Board adopted a nine-point Charter of Editorial Practice which places an obligation on its journalists to maintain the following standards:

1 The ABC takes no editorial stand in its programming.
2 Editorial staff will avoid any conflict of interest in performance of their duties.
3 Every effort must be made to ensure that the content of news and information programs is accurate and in context. Demonstrable errors will be corrected with minimum delay and in a form most suited to the circumstances.
4 Balance will be sought through the presentation as far as possible of principal relevant viewpoints on matters of importance. This requirement may not always be reached within a single programme or news bulletin, but will be achieved within a reasonable period.
5 Impartiality does not require editorial staff to be unquestioning, or the Corporation to give all sides of an issue the same amount of time. News values and news judgments will prevail in reaching decisions, consistent with these standards.
6 In serving the public's right to know, editorial staff will be enterprising in perceiving, pursuing, and presenting issues which affect society and the individual.
7 Editorial staff will respect legitimate rights to privacy of people featuring in the news.
8 Authority for editorial directions and decisions will be vested in editorial staff.
9 Editorial staff will ensure that coverage of newsworthy activity within the Australian community is comprehensive and non-discriminatory.

(ABC 1995)

National Public Radio in the USA, which is very much an admirer of the BBC, has adopted two principles concerning 'Journalists as Opinion Makers':

1 Our journalistic standards are the same when we are reporting on NPR's air as they are when we speak in other public settings. As part of those standards, we assure our listeners that we do not take sides in matters of public policy and that whatever opinions we may have do not introduce bias into our reporting.

2 As NPR staff members, our primary professional obligation is to NPR. Among those obligations is to contribute to and maintain NPR's reputation for impartial journalism and to do nothing that will detract from that reputation.

(NPR 1996)

The funding status of NPR is substantially different to that of the BBC and ABC. It is, in effect, a programming service provider to NPR stations and affiliate stations throughout the USA which are in turn funded by grant from the Corporation for Public Broadcasting. The CPB receives its money as a result of a vote from Congress. The Congress debate and vote on funding occurs in four-year cycles. But each NPR station needs to raise between 70 and 80 per cent of its annual budget by membership contributions from listeners or forms of sponsorship and outside foundation grants. The ABC depends on a funding grant from the federal parliament and the BBC is in the unique position of collecting its own tax or licence fee from television viewers as a result of a sanction from the House of Commons. The sanction is in the form of a licence agreement and linked to the continuation of a Royal Charter. The Monarch does not exercise any real influence or control. The Royal Charter is similar to a Statutory Instrument – a decision by a government minister which has the force of parliamentary authority.

NPR stipulates that its news personnel should not create a conflict of interest or the appearance of a conflict of interest by working for other news organisations. Public exchanges of personal opinion on political matters are strongly discouraged. They are reminded that they are 'reporters, not pundits'. NPR journalists are obliged to respect a number of guidelines which include 'sticking close to the facts, so that your analysis and conclusions clearly emanate from what you have gathered as a reporter, and not from your political opinions, prejudices and allegiances'.

Despite NPR's enormous respect for BBC radio journalism, the American network is very wary of the risks of absorbing BBC reporting of Northern Ireland into its output. NPR's production guidelines state:

Programs produced by NPR do not use reports from news organisations funded and administered by a foreign government when those reports concern that government. For example, we would not use BBC reports covering Northern Ireland or anywhere else in the British Isles.

(NPR 1996)

Having touched on the bureaucratic burden of good practice for journalists in the BBC, NPR and ABC, three highly reputable and well established radio news organisations, is there a general conclusion about how radio journalists can achieve good equitable practice? I think there is. If we can wriggle ourselves free from the politics of public sector broadcasting organisations such as the BBC and ABC, there are some simple ground rules or tricks of the trade that can help build respect from all areas of the community. I believe radio news organisations should think about their aims and objectives rather than becoming twisted in definitions and applications of an idea of objectivity. If a news organisation has an aim to broadcast news which is believed by its listeners because it is true, this is a good starting point. Credibility depends on accuracy, fairness and a good understanding of listeners' requirements and needs in news coverage. And these are probably constantly changing. The interesting challenge to any news organisation is to broadcast an item that challenges the majority of the audience's prejudices and understanding of 'truth'. What happens when the radio journalist recognises the need to report and broadcast a story that the editor, fellow journalists, and the audience would rather not hear?

The rules are very simple. Always attribute the opinions of people involved in a story. When using actuality edit the material in a way which identifies the author of the opinion and does not change the original meaning. Surveys and evidence from published reports should also be properly identified. Statistics should always be sourced and contextualised. The facts should be presented with simple, unemotional language which is also free of adjectives and adverbs that tend to cast an implied or charged meaning. If there is a difference of opinion in a story then it is the journalists' duty to report it. Never include your own opinion in radio news reporting. Listeners should be able to form their own opinion.

Sadly, these standards which were inculcated in me during my training and early years have been slipping. The BBC is developing a culture of editorialised opinion among its specialist correspondents. They are being developed as 'experts' whose analytical judgement and guidance are being preferred to the views and opinions of the protagonists in news stories. A recent example of this occurred in the BBC television and radio coverage of the collapse of the murder trial of white youths accused of the racist killing of a talented 18-year-old black student, Stephen Lawrence, in South East London. He was stabbed to death while waiting for a bus. The first police enquiry resulted in the state prosecution service, the CPS, stalling the process of prosecution by the dropping of charges at magistrates court level. The eventual trial was the result of a private prosecution by

Stephen Lawrence's parents. Two BBC legal correspondents stated explicitly that the collapse of the trial at the Old Bailey had vindicated the original decision by the CPS. This was an expression of opinion on a matter of enormous controversy.

The conduct of the CPS had been strongly questioned and so had the original police enquiry and first attempt at prosecution. The collapse of the Old Bailey trial was the result of a complex combination of factors and it is highly arguable whether the withdrawal of the private prosecution and formal 'not guilty' verdicts amounted to a vindication of the Crown Prosecution Service. An inquest jury has returned a verdict of unlawful killing and the *Daily Mail* newspaper has published the photographs and names of five white youths which the paper alleges are the murderers of Stephen Lawrence. They had refused to give evidence at the inquest. A television documentary on Channel Four has presented more allegations against the Metropolitan police and Crown Prosecution Service. Mrs Doreen Lawrence has made further allegations which have led to an enquiry by the Police Complaints Authority.

This tendency towards editorialising on the part of radio journalists is not limited to the reporting by BBC journalists. It has become a fashion throughout all areas of broadcasting in the UK. I was once told by an editor in one commercial talk station that he only wanted reporters who 'could say what they think with strong passionate opinions and no pussyfooting'. However, at the BBC any risks in inviting specialist correspondents to express opinion are more than balanced by a thriving culture of scoops and BBC originated stories that set an independent news agenda rather than simply following up stories published in the national newspapers. John Birt's reforms and the huge increase in investment in news and current affairs have earned substantial dividends in the quality of BBC journalism despite controversies about political pressure from Conservative governments during the 1980s and 1990s.

Where does the working radio journalist stand in the continuing debate by theorists about the function and imperatives of journalism in any type of society? The debate between theorists and practitioners in the context of training and industry recognition has become somewhat strained in Britain over the past few years. There are some editors and highly experienced journalists who have become academics, who are highly critical of the intellectualising of journalism and the academic ideology that is being enmeshed into the consideration of journalism practice in media and communications studies. This debate is not helped when working journalists dismiss theoretical courses as superfluous and irrelevant to the practice of journalism. The debate is further disabled by the arrogance of some theoreticians who assume an all-knowing judgement of working journalists that seems to be patronising and intellectually elitist. Working journalists, who struggle against the constant pressure of deadlines, frequent cost cutting, and relentless attempts to manipulate the news agenda by political and commercial interests, do not take too kindly to being told that they are mere 'social actors', attempting to dominate ideologically, creating social problems and moral panics, promoting conflict and negativity, and deceiving themselves with false assumptions and myths of objectivity.

In the middle of this lively debate is a real crisis in terms of standards and training infrastructure. I have observed a major decline in standards in radio journalism in the UK. It is based on personal evaluation and the experience of working with succeeding generations of radio journalists. Whilst expansion through deregulation has widened the choice for listeners, there has not been a concomitant expansion of experience, depth of resources and quality of remuneration. Downsizing and the chase for profits in the commercial sector means that most radio journalism is reactive and restricted to the packaging of outside sources. Experience and talent has migrated to television or to the BBC which has downgraded the status of radio journalism through a bi-media management philosophy and an obsession with maintaining a top-heavy hierarchy of specialist correspondents struggling to find stories to put to air. Training opportunities are limited and subject to budget restrictions at BBC radio and virtually non-existent in commercial radio. Entry into newsrooms is now nearly wholly dependent on one-year training courses validated by the Council for the Training of Broadcast Journalists. But the training and supervision ends when the trainee has to swim or flounder in a real newsroom.

My perception is also shared by Mike Meckler in the USA who declares on his 1997 'Writing For Radio' web site that:

> Journalism education has greatly declined over the past decade as colleges and universities have either closed journalism programs or transformed them into 'Communications Departments.' Radio journalism has been especially hard hit, with diminished teaching resources given over to television instruction because TV is the more attractive broadcast medium . . . cutbacks and downsizing in radio have reduced news staffs to the point where news directors can afford little time to training those new in the profession. In this sink-or-swim environment, far too many radio journalists have figured out only how to float.
>
> (www.newscript.com)

Mike Meckler maintains a no-nonsense and extremely helpful web site discussing contemporary American radio news and outlining the principles of good radio news writing. Talented young recruits to radio journalism see their role in a radio newsroom as a stepping stone to the apparently more glamorous and influential world of television. This was not the situation in the late 1970s and early 1980s when radio journalism was a career that was well remunerated. A starting salary for a 'rookie' radio journalist in commercial radio can be as low as £9,000 or £10,000 a year. I was receiving £8,000 a year as a local radio reporter in 1980!

The freelance rate for a 30-second news wrap on Independent Radio News at the time of writing was £28.87, the same rate that was being paid in 1987. I have learned that a leading international news agency employs radio journalists at its London broadcast centre on long shifts for a basic fee of £50 which can only be topped up on a productivity rate of stories packaged for transmission. If downsizing was not enough, the financial downgrading of the profession will leave radio journalists open to bribes and unethical compromises, and the profession will no longer be attractive to the well-motivated, well-educated and ambitious young graduates considering a future career. It is also apparent that equivalent jobs in public relations command salaries that are fifty, sometimes several hundred per cent higher. An examination of the UK *Guardian*'s media recruitment page reveals the disturbing vista that there appear to be many more openings and appointments available in public relations than in journalism. If UK journalists are substantially outnumbered by public relations personnel, is it any wonder that journalists find they have to struggle to obtain information necessary for publication and transmission on controversial subjects?

Contemporary media theorists can evaluate broadcast radio journalism with three main approaches which are grounded in the sociological discipline. These could be defined as:

1   Politico-Economic Approach;
2   Organisational Approach;
3   Culturalist or Culturological Approach.

I will endeavour to explain the thinking in the context of radio journalistic practice. The Marxist would be able to understand the Politico-Economic Approach rather easily. It depends on the idea that the radio news organisations are concentrated in the hands of a minority of elitist people through corporations or individual ownership, and that the media proprietors use their power to determine the style and output of the news services in a way which is favourable to them in the commercial as well as political sense.

The Organizational Approach says that the content of radio journalism is dependent on the infrastructure of the news organisation, the limitations of the broadcast form and output, the reality of news-gathering budgets and programme deadlines and the day-to-day operation of journalism. This approach also takes into account the idea that journalists perform a 'strategic ritual of routine professional practices' to achieve credibility and acceptance from the audience. At present the concept of 'objectivity' is linked to presenting both sides of the story or seeking representation from the broad spectrum of opinion.

The Culturalist Approach links Organizational and Politico-Economic theories together and places the imperatives determining journalistic practice in the overall culture of a given society. This means the causes and effects are not restricted to issues of media ownership and professional practice but the interaction of radio news organisations with the powerful elites, political, constitutional and industrial organisations and institutions which control a society. There is a distinguished and formidable international community of academics who continually debate and discuss these theories and also create various permutations and theoretical adjuncts. Is there any point in radio journalists taking up valuable time to consider the writings of Professors Stuart Hall, James Curran, Philip Schlesinger, Gaye Tuchman, Daniel Hallin, Noam Chomsky and Ed Herman? I think there is, but only if the practising journalist can place these theories in a practical context.

Radio journalists are continually subject to imperatives which are Culturalist, Organisational and Politico-Economic. I can recognise these imperatives in relation to my own career. Editorial independence becomes a very fluid concept when commercial radio stations regard radio news as an expensive luxury which is no longer a statutory necessity. When radio network and station proprietors expect newsrooms to be run by single journalists who have to report, write, edit and present regular bulletins, the opportunity for in-depth reporting and responding to news events is very much restricted to the art of the possible. Some proprietors believe in employing radio journalists with the expectation of achieving the art of the impossible. One radio journalist covering an entire US state or British county is going to depend on the existing structure of sources previously constructed by the radio station. He or she will have to depend on telephone and ISDN lines for acquiring actuality and reports. There will be a heavy reliance on correspondents if the station has a budget to take in freelance contributors' work. National and international news will arrive either pre-packaged or with components for wrapping from a network news provider. The opportunity to leave the station to check out the grassroots of a news event will depend on time and distance from the radio station and the rota of bulletins. News coverage will be restricted to events and stories which fit into the time frame of the journalist's shift.

Commercial stations or networks which rely on advertising or sponsorship are open to intimidation from advertisers, institutions and organisations with considerable financial muscle. Radio journalists may have editorial independence to pursue vigorously a story critical of a company which places a considerable amount of advertising with the station. However, in the author's experience any significant falling off of advertising revenue will result in lay-offs in the newsroom which cannot necessarily be attributable to a reprisal, or threat of reprisal from the advertiser. In my experience, proprietors can covertly control the political agenda and slant of news coverage outside election time by hiring and firing the reporters according to coded criteria. Union activists tend to be discouraged and discriminated against in job selection procedures in the UK and USA.

The UK libel laws place a heavy burden on commercial news organisations from the point of view of legal jeopardy. This means that radio stations tend to avoid investigative programmes which have a larger potential for justifying libel-lous assertions. In the UK the burden of proof for justification depends on the defendant news organisation. Investigative documentary projects require time, human resources and money and have a poor return in terms of 'product output'. I spent four weeks of my spare time as a junior reporter in 1980 producing a documentary on the impact of unemployment as a result of the first manufactur-ing and industrial recession precipitated by Margaret Thatcher's first Conservative government. The programme was networked when official unemployment figures hit the two million mark for the first time since the 1930s. The news editor could only offer a short driving holiday in Ireland as compensation. This would have been in return for producing a feature for the station's holiday programme. The offer had to be turned down because I did not have a car at the time. Ethical considerations about reviewing a 'blueprint' holiday package in this way were therefore postponed.

The documentary project sought to make sense of a developing social pattern of unemployment that hitherto had only been reported in terms of daily announcements of factory closures and redundancies. The station's daily news operation could not articulate the significance of a dole queue that now stretched the entire length of a street. Yet the station did not have the resources to widen the nature and style of its journalistic coverage. IRN/LBC in the UK during the 1980s would assign staff reporters to devote an entire week to originate and research half-hour documentaries under the title of *Decision Makers*. The reduction in economies of scale and desire for greater profits saw the cancellation of the programme. The programme's demise was also determined by a changing fashion among UK commercial stations. The priority was music format over speech. Half-hour documentaries had no place in these formats. In Britain only the BBC and the occasional commercial station will embark on properly funded and resourced documentary projects. IRN is still capable of producing high quality documentar-ies linked to very large scale stories such as the conviction of Rosemary West, the wife of Britain's notorious serial killer Frederick West.

Has the media become another self-perpetuating elite? We would be able to answer this question if the majority of radio journalism staff were drawn from the public school and Oxbridge university system. The make-up of British society has changed substantially in the post-war period. Waves of immigration from Africa and Asia have created a substantial non-white community. One in twenty of British citizens is now non-white. It is quite clear that the media has become an attractive field to work in during the last twenty years. A British MP and high-profile politician once told me that in his opinion broadcast journalists have more power and influence in a democratic society than democratically elected represen-tatives to the country's legislature. I recall an intriguing conversation in 1984 with a fellow correspondent in the IRN/LBC newsroom about the educational background of colleagues. Out of twenty journalists present during a day shift, 60 per cent had been educated privately and 40 per cent of personnel had attended Oxford or Cambridge Universities. At that time there were no non-white journalists present, despite the fact that London was by then a cosmopolitan city with large second- and third-generation Asian and Afro-Caribbean communities.

This pattern of recruitment and social background is similarly reflected at the national and international newsrooms of the BBC. There is no doubt that the maintenance and self-perpetuation of a privately-educated middle-class media elite will narrow the range of social perception and inevitably distort and influence the evaluation of news events. The last twenty years have also seen a considerable shift in distance between journalists and primary sources of information. In the 1960s and 1970s most trainee journalists entered the field through local newspaper training schemes with mentoring from experienced journalists. There was an emphasis on originating news stories through personal contact with ordinary citizens in the community. Most radio journalist entrants are emerging from one-year training schemes where the scope for social interaction is limited to well educated student communities. The experience of different social strata is wholly dependent on individual initiative. Social contact in first reporting jobs is determined by the operation of articulate and media literate sources and the needs of daily news operations. Any experience of communities and social conditions unknown to the middle class radio journalist will be fleeting and superficial. To this extent the academic J. Alexander has a point when observing that:

> to the degree that the news media is tied to religious, ideological, political, or class groupings it is not free to form and reform public events in a flexible way. Without this flexibility, public opinion becomes 'artificial' and 'biased': it will be keyed to a part over the whole.
>
> (Alexander 1981 and McNair 1994)

I recall the severe dislocation of understanding and communication between the media elites and black community on the Broadwater Farm Estate in the aftermath of the 1985 riot in which Police Constable Keith Blakelock was killed. The media reported the riot itself from behind the police lines and some journalists received injuries from petrol bombs and shotgun pellets. The riot was portrayed as a breakdown of law and order, with destruction of property, and murder and attempted murder committed by a rampaging mob of mainly black youths. Public discontent had emanated from a clumsy police raid on the home of Cynthia Jarrett. The officers were looking for one of her sons, but Mrs Jarrett suffered a fatal heart attack while they were searching her house. The incident was dramatised in a musical called *Raggamuffin* that toured the country and was broadcast on the first BBC Radio Five network. The tension between black and white youths and local police forces erupted into violence. The horrific murder of PC Blakelock as the result of multiple stabbing by a group of twenty to thirty youths became the focus of media interest.

A number of youths were arrested, prosecuted and convicted of the constable's murder. Little attempt was ever made by the mainstream media to seek the opinions of the local black community. The police viewed Winston Silcott as the ringleader of the riot and murderer of the unarmed police constable. He was effectively demonised by national newspapeers. There was negligible reporting of the severe criticism by the trial judge of the oppressive and inappropriate interrogation of one of the 13-year-old defendants who was detained with inadequate legal representation and questioned naked apart from a paper suit which he was obliged to wear while his clothes were being forensically examined. The judge discharged the young man, but the jury had been informed of his invalid statement which claimed that the rioters had planned to murder the policeman, sever his head and parade it on a pole in front of the police lines. Several years later, the Appeal Court quashed all the murder convictions. A *prima facie* case had been made out that the police statement taken from Winston Silcott had been fabricated. Two police officers were subsequently acquitted of perjury and perverting the course of justice after their defence lawyers effectively 'retried' Winston Silcott with unsubstantiated allegations and maintained the accusation that he had been the murderer. I was castigated by white journalists for mentioning in my trial reports that the only black person attending the trial of the two officers had been Winston Silcott's brother, who left the courtroom shouting that it had been a sham. This fact had been omitted from the reports of many mainstream media organisations. In April 1997, the *Daily Mail* reported that Keith Blakelock's widow and 20-year-old son were planning to bring an action for civil damages against Winston Silcott over the killing.

Two years after the original riot, the Metropolitan Police continued to portray the Broadwater Farm Estate as a den of iniquity, nest of drug dealers, and concrete beehive of muggers. The police planned a high profile raid with van loads of officers clad in riot protection equipment, accompanied by specialist firearms units. The police invited established and accredited news organisations to provide reporters who could join the raid in the police vans. I heard a radio reporter 'charge out' of the police transit van, shouting in an excited fashion behind the tumbling boots of police officers as though he were running into a war-zone. This ad-libbed sequence was broadcast. It gave the impression of danger. The reality of the event was somewhat different. No arrests were made because the police could find no muggers, drug dealers or thieves. In fact the estate was utterly peaceful apart from the police and media presence. I had discovered previously that the high rise estate had been demonised by the media and London police. The majority of residents were content with living there. Crime had been exaggerated.

The media coverage of the Dunblane massacre in Scotland by gun enthusiast

Thomas Hamilton is an excellent demonstration of the moral panic syndrome outlined by sociologist Jack Young in 1971. One man armed with licensed firearms created carnage and selected victims regarded as the untouchables in a supposedly civilised society. Hamilton decided to murder young children and he challenged the raw nerve of every parent's essential insecurity. Young has stated that the media can:

> create social problems, can present them dramatically and overwhelmingly, and most importantly can do it suddenly. The media can very quickly and effectively fan public indignation and engineer what one might call a 'moral panic' about a certain type of deviancy.

(Young 1971 and McNair 1994)

In this instance, the media had no need to begin the ripple of moral panic. Hamilton's actions were sufficient. When an individual decides to act in an evil and destructive manner, any society would find it difficult to explain or account for the event. The questions raised by journalists were fairly obvious. But the media withdrew from Dunblane and effectively shut down debate and investigation of the events leading up to the mass murder. A public enquiry criticised the failure of the local police to recognise that Hamilton was a risk. But a pressure group called Snowdrop supported by bereaved relatives campaigned for the statutory banning of all firearms. It became a political issue. It can be argued that the media has contributed to a moral panic about firearms and school security.

Anyone who shoots for sport has been effectively demonised as a potential Thomas Hamilton. Schools have begun to erect physical security barriers against the surrounding community. Local authorities have been pressured into supplying security patrols, and in some cases infra-red and razor wire fences. Is the cost justified when compared with the actual risk? The government has been prompted to pass laws which will result in the destruction of hundreds of businesses. Public money has to be spent compensating gun owners who are denied any sense of credibility. Previously legitimate and responsible gun owners have been converted into an anti-social morally alienated community. Not even the words of the Duke of Edinburgh, in an interview on the BBC Radio Five Live Network can be tolerated. His concern that the statutory ban amounts to an over-reaction is 'politically and morally incorrect'. His observation that a determined killer armed with a cricket bat could have committed a similar murder, but cricket bats are not banned, is met with universal and unanimous condemnation by the media. It can be argued that the media's moral outlook and support of the Snowdrop campaign is justifiable. However, the scope for public debate has been restricted and people who wish to argue rationally that there is nothing to stop a psychopath committing a similar crime with an unlicensed firearm are keeping their heads below the parapet of moral outrage.

The exercise of taste and judgement in journalism has become entwined in a complex web of public opinion formers, political pressure and quango regulation. In Britain non-elected public bodies have been set up to 'police' programming on the grounds of taste and decency. The media's unprecedented withdrawal from Dunblane was a moral judgement. In a sense the media had created their own moral panic about their presence. Bereaved families did not wish to be harassed by the hundreds of sympathetic journalists present in the small Scottish town. However, an interesting point that could be raised is that journalists did not have to harass the bereaved families. To what extent did news editors consider whether they had a public duty to continue investigating the background, implications and ramifications of this catastrophic event?

The behaviour of journalists when interacting with people suffering from grief is the subject of continuing public controversy in most countries. Script writers and dramatists have a tendency to mythologise a negative stereotype of the heart-less, ambitious journalist who will trample over people's feelings and sensitivities in the quest for a story. The reality is significantly different. Isolated examples of 'ratpack' sieges of bereaved families have become the focus of professional enquir-ies and justifiable soul-searching.

However, in my experience, contact with grieving individuals has been a con-structive and purposeful experience. I recall an assignment for a local radio station in 1980 when a new university-educated reporter had joined me for 'shadowing'. A 9-year-old boy had been crushed to death underneath concrete fence blocks. The tragedy had resulted from the failure of the local authority to repair a middle fence block that had been vandalised. The victim had been crawling through the hole while watching an amateur football match. Another child climbing on the upper fence block caused it to drop down, trapping the child who died. I had been given a tip-off by the local police that the family of the victim was angry with the local council for its failure to act on requests by people in the community to repair the fence or cordon off the hazard. The 'rookie' journalist refused to accompany me to the home of the bereaved family on the grounds that my actions were distasteful and an intrusion into their private grief. He insisted on staying in the car. As soon as I entered the street in this poor working-class community I was greeted warmly by local residents and they took me to the house of the unfortunate family whose son had died. The parents were grateful that I had taken an interest and recorded a dignified and important interview on a matter of public interest. I believe they appreciated my genuine sympathy and respect for their position. The 'rookie' journalist has since gone on to be one of the highest profile political broadcast journalists of his generation. In subsequent years I have found that the vast majority of journalists show respect and sensitivity to their fellow human beings. The myth of the exploitative and parasitic journalist feeding off people's misery is problematic and needs challenging.

Part II

Radio journalism history

Origins to 1939

Chapter 6

The origins

In 1899 H. G. Wells created the idea that at some time in the future there would be large speaking machines chattering out news and propaganda into people's homes everywhere. His novel *When The Sleeper Wakes* established the image of 'Babble Machines'. The author only had to wait another thirty-nine years to see millions of babbling boxes generating panic and alarm with an historic adaptation of another of his novels *The War of the Worlds.* It was on radio forty-two years later that H. G. Wells met and discussed with the author of the most famous media scam of the century – Orson Welles. At the turn of the twentieth century, sound was being translated into electrical patterns for recording and radio transmission. One of the greatest horror novels, *Dracula* by Bram Stoker, featured the idea of a journal being recorded onto Edison's Phonograph. *Dracula* was published in 1897. This gothic classic dramatised the idea of using sound technology to create a record of an event. In this case Dr John Seward was keeping a regular diary of observations about a deranged solicitor called Renfield who was a patient at his lunatic asylum in Purfleet near London. Renfield had been turned insane after visiting Count Dracula's castle in Transylvania. In 1878, Edison originally marketed a tinfoil cylinder phonograph which was succeeded by the wax cylinder model. These devices remained hugely popular until the 1920s. The mechanically powered machine used a moving needle to convert sound into electrical impulses and then back again through an external speaker. Hand-cranked models meant they could be used before the widespread distribution of electricity.

The origins of radio journalism are, therefore, not to be found at the time of the first radio broadcasts. The development of recording technology created a market for discs and sound playing machines which seemed to expand from 1896 onwards. Sound archivists have preserved the first sound advertisement. This is a promotional message that was sold with the Edison phonograph in 1906. Consumers could hear the voice of Len Spencer saying:

'I am the Edison Phonograph created by the great wizard of the New World, to delight those who would have melody or be amused. I can sing you tender songs of love. I can give you merry tales and joyous laughter. . . . The more you become acquainted with me the better you will like me. Ask the dealer!'

(Spencer on the Edison Phonograph, recorded 1906, Edison Studios, West Orange, New Jersey and distributed in *Great Speeches of the Twentieth Century* 1991)

The phonograph recording gave the nascent radio journalist a power that would not be available through electromagnetic transmissions. He did not have to seek the permission of any tribunal, government committee or minister to distribute the sound of the recording on a phonograph disk. He was in the same theoretical position as any group of journalists who wanted to publish books, pamphlets, newspapers and periodicals. The only obstacle to publishing in Britain, Australia and the USA was access to the capital needed to launch such a venture. In contrast radio journalism became a regulated and licensed activity. Government controls the right of journalists to broadcast and continues to manipulate the power of broadcasting in Britain, Australia and the US to this very day. The argument against a free for all has always been that there is limited space in the sky for radio services. It is a specious argument to justify censorship and control. Scientific developments and discovery open up the possibility of a vast range of frequencies in digital and analogue wavebands. The political history of broadcasting in these three countries has always been dominated by restrictions on access and opportunity.

The phonograph method of communication had the effect of establishing a permanent form for listening to music and spoken word. Of course, radio broadcasting eventually reduced a lot of news and speech communication to an ephemeral status. In the 1920s it nearly succeeded in destroying the recording business. People discovered that if you bought a radio set and that was combined with a licence fee in Britain and Australia, all the music and the information babbling out of it was free. Why pay extra for recording discs which were fragile and worn down after too many plays? Virtually all the early radio broadcasts were live. The end of the twentieth century has seen the return of live, ephemeral broadcasts being recorded and sold in a growing 'spoken word' cassette and compact disc market.

The first licensed broadcast in Britain was made on 11 May 1922 by a station called 2LO in London, which became the precursor for the British Broadcasting Corporation. The first permitted radio broadcast in Australia was from a building in Sydney's Phillip Street and consisted of a recital from the St Andrews Quartet. 2SB stood for Sydney Broadcasters Ltd and continued with a light programme of orchestral music and singing. The Australian Federal Government began with the strange system that a radio receiver could only be tuned into a single station and then sealed. When the Australian Broadcast Tribunal adjusted the frequencies of radio stations in the 1970s by giving them slightly different positions, several complaints were received by the ABC from listeners who had literally glued their car radios to their favourite station and now found it annoyingly 'off station'. The early system of single station reception enabled the commercial stations such as 6WF in Perth, 3AR in Melbourne and another Sydney station 2FC to set their own licences. The system was soon changed to enable radio stations to sell advertising and take sponsorship. 'A' stations continued to charge a licence fee and 'B' stations were allowed to survive on advertising and sponsorship. The 'A' stations were eventually amalgamated in 1932 into the Australian Broadcasting Commission and the licence became superseded by direct government grant approved by the Federal Parliament in Canberra. January 26 1925 is a critical date in Australian broadcasting history. It is Australia Day, a national holiday to remember and celebrate the creation of the Federation. It also marks the first broadcast of the country's oldest commercial service, 2UE, which now runs one of the leading news networks and commands the highest share of audiences.

In the USA in 1920 a Pittsburgh station, KDKA, owned by the Westinghouse Corporation transmitted the presidential election results. This is described as the first scheduled radio transmission in the USA. We have to be more sceptical than the academics about so called 'historical firsts'. The world of academia has shamefully neglected radio as an area of serious study. It does seem that radio services were being broadcast in other parts of America on a regularly scheduled basis before the KDKA election results. John Schneider researched the history of radio in San Francisco in the 1970s and because no publisher has been bright enough to make it available as a book he has generously placed the fruits of his work on the Internet for educational purposes. The detailed stories of the early radio pioneers demonstrate that with characters like Doc Herrold in San José regularly broadcasting from 1912 and founding the station KQW, radio has beginnings which are earlier and richer than previously reported. It is an enormous shame that John Schneider's work could not be duplicated throughout the world. Our knowledge of radio would be so much more reliable.

It is also intriguing that the first officially approved transmission by the British Broadcasting Company's London station 2LO on 14 November, 1922 was a news broadcast about the general election presented by Arthur Burrows using material supplied by news agencies which were credited on air. But of course the airwaves had been crackling with a myriad of unofficial and commercial transmissions some years before as soon as the pioneers in radio technology had established the method of broadcasting signals to a wide area of the population. The American entrepreneur Lee De Forest broadcast election night returns in 1916. On 15 June 1920 in England a shed-like construction owned by the Marconi company at Writtle near Chelmsford broadcast the Australian soprano Dame Nellie Melba and the signal was picked up and recorded by phonograph in Paris. The event was sponsored by the *Daily Mail* and she was heard singing in English, French and Italian. Her rendering of 'God Save the King' could be heard as far away as Newfoundland. The sponsorship was the result of enthusiasm shown for radio by the *Daily Mail*'s proprietor Lord Northcliffe. These broadcasts were the first true pirates of the airwaves. They were quickly outlawed by legislation and regulation, which appeared to be much more stringent in Britain. Prior to a special charter in 1927, which turned the BBC from a private company into a public corporation, monopoly broadcasting in the UK tolerated very few sponsored programmes. There was a feeling that Britain should avoid the perceived confusion of the American system where it was thought there were too many radio stations shouting each other out like gaggling cuckoo chicks screaming for food.

The Postmaster-General – a government minister responsible for the postal services and the telephone industry – had the power in Britain and Australia to grant and regulate licences. Initially the executive power over radio in the US rested with the Navy. This was soon transferred to an authority appointed by Congress.

One of the more intriguing early broadcasting histories and almost entirely neglected in the study of radio by UK, US and Australian universities and training bodies, is the early development of broadcasting in South Africa. Regular licensed broadcasting began on 1 July 1924. The first three licences were given to the Cape Peninsular Publicity Association, the Durban Corporation, and in Johannesburg, the Association of Scientific and Technical Societies which was a club whose members came from the management of mining and other industries. These radio stations were commercial and independent, but they depended for their income on a a bizarre system of licensing. The South African Post Office issued a licence to consumers for their receivers. The broadcaster also issued another licence for receiving the programmes which was very difficult to collect. The first stations were, therefore, not financially viable. I. W. Schlesinger, a mogul in the fields of insurance, theatre and film, improved the prospects of the radio industry by persuading the government to cede all three existing licences to his company, the African Broadcasting Company. But the ABC continued to operate at a deficit, until retailers of domestic receivers agreed with the ABC to create the 'Blue Free Voucher Scheme'.

This was an ingenious deal divided into three sound commercial decisions. The ABC stopped hiring receivers to listeners. The retailers agreed to charge more for the radio sets and pass that on to the ABC as a subsidy for programming. Instead of spending this money on concerts and plays, the ABC used it as prizes for on-air competitions. At a time of depression and with cash prizes of £250, sales of radio sets and licences took off. Radio was booming.

The early programmes reflected the urban English elite which controlled broadcasting and formed most of its audience. English South Africans controlled business, government, and the leisure industry in the urban areas where the first licences were first allocated. Afrikaners were entirely excluded because they were poorer and lived in the less densely populated rural areas. Programmes in Afrikaans were first introduced as half-hour sequences in 1931. The news was supplied as copy items for straight read bulletins from Reuters. This meant that the news agenda of early South African radio was determined by the British press which owned and controlled Reuters.

This confusing hybrid of British and American models of broadcasting created a demand for more state control. South Africa was experiencing an emergence of Afrikaner nationalism with an explicit apartheid ideology. Afrikaner Nationalists resented the propagandising of British cultural heritage through the existing ABC company. At the same time, English South Africans did not appreciate the commercial model of maximising the audience through popular programmes at the expense of highbrow programmes. The BBC's Director-General, Sir John Reith, toured South Africa in 1934 and supported the concept of a centralised state broadcasting system, but I do not think he appreciated the risks of state censorship and the implications of excluding and discriminating against South Africa's majority black cultures. The SABC was created on the 2 August 1936, but the first broadcasting to black communities did not start until 1949.

An event in 1938 had the effect of stimulating improved technological communication within the recently formed national network as well as improving coverage of Afrikaner affairs. FAK – the Federation of Afrikaans Cultural organisations – staged a re-enactment of the Great Trek. The SABC began by covering the departure of the wagons from Cape Town and did not envisage any further reporting apart from written bulletins from correspondents witnessing the event along the way. Demand from Afrikaans listeners was so great that the SABC had to assign a radio reporter to provide daily news features via landline, and local telephone connections.

Although the SABC was meant to be an independent broadcasting organisation, these good intentions evaporated as a result of the statutory requirement to present an annual report to the government. The SABC even controlled the development of commercial radio in South Africa with the advent of Springbok Radio in 1950. The story of broadcasting in South Africa is unique, not least because the advent of television was delayed until 1976. The first truly independent stations were not licensed until 1979 and 1980. Now the country is witnessing an extraordinary liberation of commercial and cultural changes as a result of the ending of apartheid and the dismantling of state controls which promulgated the dominance of white English and white Afrikaans culture and ideology.

The dominance of English culture within the SABC was so great that SABC's first short-wave receiving station near Panarama outside Johannesburg was used to record and re-broadcast foreign and chiefly BBC programmes. The BBC radio news was relayed from this station and transmitted by the SABC network for a ten-year period between 1940 and 1950. This reliance on an outside source for news broadcasting substantially stunted development of a home grown culture of radio journalism. 1950 saw the appointment of a new Director-General of SABC, Gideon Roos. He was sensitive to the ascendency of the Nationalist Party and growing demand for a South African focus in terms of a broadcast news agenda. This was also accompanied by the international isolation caused by formal implementation of apartheid ideology. He scrapped the BBC radio news relays and created SABC's own news section. Even in 1950, the SABC experienced the same vested opposition that the BBC in Britain, the ABC in Australia and large American networks had discovered when trying to establish news gathering and transmission independence.

The English and Afrikaans newspapers targeted radio for criticism, ridicule and political opprobrium. The press was primarily concerned about the poaching of newspaper advertising by the SABC's new commercial stations. SAPA – South Africa's Press Association, the equivalent of AAP in Australia, and Britain's Press Association, increased its charges so that the SABC's fledgling news section could not afford to use its material. These hindrances meant that SABC's Springbok commercial station founded in 1950 did not have its own dedicated news section until 1957. The South African broadcasting system was reflecting the same features of its economy – a form of 'state capitalism'. The lines between the public and private sectors became blurred or disappeared altogether and consequently created a centralisation of power greater than was possible in either sector.

From these humble beginnings the SABC news department has grown to a position where it now rivals the BBC in terms of its power and influence within its own country. This is despite deregulation and the granting of independent radio station licences. More than 300 bulletins for twenty-three radio services are prepared each weekday. There are thirty editorial officers, and 1,300 correspondents covering home news, with twenty strategically placed foreign correspondents and a BBC Caversham-style news monitoring section covering world news.

Chapter 7

The political
and journalistic
use of early
recording
technology

It is interesting that many licensed radio services began with a news bulletin. But deep in the sound archives of countries all around the world and also hidden away in private collections it is possible to find the evidence of radio journalism's original voice.

The recording of flat discs and cylinders had a considerable propaganda value and offered the chance to communicate opinions, values and ideologies that would not be given a platform in the existing mainstream media. This was especially true of the suffragette movement. On 8 December 1908, Emmeline Pankhurst's daughter Christabel outlined the cause of women into a microphone and left her message for posterity. Occasionally she stumbles or repeats a word, suggesting inexperience with the recording process, a poorly written script, or no script, and an insight into live, off-the-cuff speech making. Raw and natural political oratory from another age can, therefore, be heard by future generations:

> The militant suffragettes who form the Women's Social and Political Union are engaged in the attempts to win the parliamentary vote for the women of this country. Their claim is those women who pay rates and taxes, who fulfil the same qualifications as men voters, shall be placed on the parliamentary register. The reasons why women should have the vote are obvious to every fair-minded person. The British Constitution provides that taxation and rep-resentation shall go together. Therefore women tax-payers are entitled to vote.
>
> (Pankhurst, 'Suffrage for Women'. Recorded 8 December 1908. Mat. 276f: G. C. 01016. Distributed *The Blaze of Day* 1992)

It was to be another twenty years before women were equally enfranchised with men in the UK. A similar fight was taking shape in the USA. By 1915 women had the vote in fifteen states but in that year Mrs Raymond Brown and Rabbi Stephen Wise had to use recording technology to spread their message and campaign for enfranchisement in New York State.

> MRS BROWN   The most important question before the country today is women's suffrage. It is not only votes for women but the entire question of democracy which is at stake. Ever since our government was founded men have been so claiming a government who would not be of benefit for any man or class of men but where everybody should have equal representation. [sic]
>
> (Brown, 'Why Women Want to Vote'. Recorded 1915. Mat. M65288-29: USA Pathé 30305. Distributed *The Blaze of Day* 1992)

> RABBI WISE   I believe in equal suffrage because I believe in the fundamental rightness of democracy. . . . Suffrage is a duty and obligation of a woman as truly as a man. It is not a right to be waived, or a privilege to be foregone, but a duty to be met, an obligation to be accepted.
>
> (Wise, 'Women and Democracy'. Distributed *The Blaze of Day* 1992)

The story of women's rights was different in Australia and New Zealand. The state of South Australia granted women suffrage in 1894. The Federal Government and all the other states followed suit by 1908– the time Christabel Pankhurst's speech was recorded to further the British campaign. The Pankhursts were brilliant publicists and the militant style of their campaign turned the media focus onto their Women's Social and Political Union. The use of the phonograph is a symbol of the sophistication of their campaigning techniques which overshadowed the exhaustive work of thousands of working-class women who had tirelessly fought for women's suffrage many years before. Historians need to be careful about attributing full credit to a small group of articulate and creative middle-class women. The Manchester Suffrage Society was formed in 1867 and there is plenty of research evidence to show that other women were working as tirelessly and effectively to win the vote for women. Any phonographs they may have recorded have not survived.

In 1916 Corporal Edward Dwyer VC recorded this remarkable account of his experience in the trenches of the First World War:

> They tell me you would like to hear something of what our boys are doing at the front and although I am only a youngster and a soldier still I've seen about as much fighting as is good for any man and I think there's still a bit of fight left in me yet if I get the chance to go out again. I was already in the army when the war broke out and went to France on August 13 1914, nine days after the declaration of war.

The first big scrap we had was at Mons, at twelve o'clock Sunday noon, and the Germans don't take any account of Sundays. You people over here don't realise what our boys went through in those days. That march from Mons was a nightmare. Unless you've been through it you can't imagine what an agonising time it was. We used to do from 20 to 25 miles a day. . . . The longest march we had . . . was after we had marched on the Mons and started to push the Germans back to the Aines.[sic]

There was only one thing you [sic] could cheer us up on the march. That was singing. We used to sing Tipper . . . Gippy choruses invented by some of the chaps. Tipperary wasn't in full swing then. And they'd all go on to something they'd invented themselves. It used to buck us up and we would march all the better for it. . . . Sometimes we'd sing some of G. H. Elliott's songs. You know, 'The Chocolate Coloured Coon'. But we'd always go onto something we'd invented. I don't think I've got much of a voice to sing, but I'll try and sing one or two of the choruses we used to sing.

We're here because we're here, because we're here, because we're here. We're here, because we're here, because we're here, because we're here. We'd be far better off, far better off, far better off in a home . . . Here we are, here we are, here we are again. Hello! Hello! Hello, hello, hello. Here we are, here we are again, here we are again. Hello! Hello! Hello, Hello, Hello, Hello, Hello. Oh!

This remarkable recording contains all the value and power of documentary speech. We do not know how Corporal Dwyer from the First Battalion East Surrey Regiment presented his account. It has all the rhythms and cadences of spoken English. There is the suggestion that much of what he said may have been regularly presented to meetings and recruitment rallies. But it sounds spontaneous and from the heart. It is also a sobering lesson that more than seventy years ago English soldiers sent into the nightmare conditions of First World War trench warfare sang demeaning minstrel songs by the *The Chocolate Coloured Coon* to comfort them. Racist and apartheid values in English-speaking broadcast systems throughout most of the twentieth century have been ignored and only lightly touched upon in academic research. I believe it is an important nettle that needs to be grasped. In recent years there has been a more visible presence of black and Asian reporters in British radio news but, like most areas of society, positions of power and influence are dominated by a white middle-class male culture. There are only three stations providing a local news service specific to Afro-Caribbean and Asian communities in Britain and they were only licensed in 1989. The civil rights movement in 1960s America has gone some way to dissolving discriminatory practices, and there is a greater awareness of the contribution that Australia's native community can make to its broadcasting culture. But the story of the past needs greater investigation and evaluation to enable the journalism cultures in all three countries to perpetuate reforms that bring about change and greater equality. The Black Radio Series produced in 1995 and funded by the US Corporation for Public Broadcasting and James Smithson Society has at last made some contribution to marking the history of Black American radio broadcasters and services. *Passing It On* was another black history series aired in 1995.

The recording of Corporal Dwyer is now available on cassette and compact disc along with other songs and sounds of 'The Great War'. Journalistically, the recording has limited value. It says nothing about the appalling waste of human life in a war which killed three times as many combatants as the Second World War. Further research needs to be conducted. What happened subsequently to Corporal Dwyer? Why did he take part in recruitment rallies? How has his contribution to the Great War been remembered by his family, regiment and community? Some of these answers are to be found at the Museum of the Queen's Royal Surrey Regiment, in the public records of the Imperial War Museum and in research carried out by contemporary historians. It seems the young soldier died during the Battle of the Somme, leaving a young widow. His grave can be found in a military cemetery called Flat Iron Copse at the back of Mametz Wood near Amiens in the Somme region of France. Newspaper interviews with him while he was alive indicate that he addressed recruitment events in Trafalgar Square and was something of a London celebrity. His life was reviewed in a fascinating newspaper article written by Stephen Bates and published by the UK *Guardian* newspaper to coincide with Remembrance Day in November 1996.

The recording tells us nothing about the futility of military tactics. However, it does supply a sub-text of the horror of this soldier's experience which was absent from the heavily censored press reporting of the period.

The content of the recording gives us an important indication of the value of sound communication in journalism. When you hear Corporal Dwyer's voice trying to sing the soldier's marching songs you begin to feel the haunting loneliness and suffering of his comrades. Something is communicated which is not stated in the words of his speech. His series of cries *Hello, hello, hello* reaches out to us through the many decades in a way print journalism cannot do.

We do not know the extent to which the recording was produced and edited in content. A radio journalist would have encouraged him to describe how he won his Victoria Cross. The citation reads for 'conspicuous bravery and devotion to duty at Hill 60 on the 20 April 1915 . . . dispersing the enemy by the effective use of his hand grenades . . . whilst subjected to a hail of bombs at close quarters . . . leaving his trench under heavy fire to bandage his wounded comrades.'

So in 1916 we find the foundations of the radio interview. The opportunity given to witnesses of history and news events to describe their experiences. This is, of course, a description of an experience after the event. Most of a radio reporter's role is to interview people to obtain their accounts of a news story and the reliance is on the interviewee's memory, individual perception and sense of priority.

'The Great War' sound collection contains another remarkable recording which may well be radio journalism's first 'actuality' of a news event. A sound recordist for the Gramophone Company (HMV) called Will Gaisberg set up his equipment during the bombardment of Lille on 9 October 1918. The recording captures the sound of the Royal Garrison Artillery shouting out instructions and measurements and then giving the order to fire gas shells. We hear the cries 'Fire Four! . . . Fire Two! . . . Fire One! . . . Fire Three!' punctuated by the weird whizz-bang sound of gas shells being propelled into enemy lines. Finally the recording ends with the pompous homily 'Feed the guns with war bonds and help to win the war.' This is a clue to the recording's commercial purpose. It was produced as a marketing aid, or advertisement for fund-raising in the war effort. It is also an archival testimony to the courage and risks taken by generations of sound engineers and radio journalists in the field of battle and human conflict. Will Gaisberg inhaled some of the gas during this assignment and the damage to his lungs led to his death from the deadly Spanish influenza epidemic which laid waste millions of lives in Europe that year.

In the United States phonograph recordings were used to record presidential campaign speeches and in 1918 the commander-in-chief of the American expeditionary forces in Europe, Major-General John J. 'Black Jack' Pershing, recorded this address for the families of the soldiers under his command. He used a phonograph machine at Allied Headquarters in Chaumont France. The phonographs sold back home boasted that the recording had been made 'from the battlefields of France':

> Three thousand miles from home an American army is fighting for you. Everything you hold worthwhile is at stake. Only the hardest blows can win against the enemy we are fighting. Invoking the spirits of our forefathers, the army asks for your unflinching support so the end of the high ideals for which America stands may endure upon the earth.

> (*Great Speeches of the Twentieth Century* 1991)

The Pershing speech was also distributed with a bigoted and jingoistic attack on people of German descent by the former US ambassador to Berlin, James Gerard Watson. This recording was responsible for an ugly wave of anti-German prejudice throughout the country. Since many immigrants had been German-Jewish, the anti-German hysteria was combined with anti-Semitism. Businesses and shops with German-sounding names were attacked and burned. There were even reports of dachshunds being stoned by demented mobs. The speaker's terrifying reference to lynching spies on lamp-posts has an appalling resonance in American history. The culture of white racial superiority in the American South involved regular lynchings of innocent blacks. The disgusting practice of so-called 'nigger lynching' continued in the years before the Second World War and President Franklin D. Roosevelt's reliance on Southern Democrat political leaders meant that attempts to outlaw the practice through Federal legislation were filibustered in the House of Representatives. James Gerard Watson's speech is a poignant reminder of the way the modern media can fan the flames of racial prejudice and xenophobia:

> the time has come when every citizen must declare himself American or traitor. We must disappoint the Germans who have always believed that the German-Americans here would risk their property, their children's future and their own necks and take up arms for the Kaiser. The foreign minister of Germany once said to me: 'Your country does not dare do anything against Germany. The cause we have in your country, five hundred thousand German reservists who will rise in arms against your government if you dare to make a move against Germany.' Well I told him that that might be so but that we had five hundred and one thousand lamp-posts in this country and that that was where the reservists would be hanging the day after they tried to rise. And if there are any German-Americans here who are so ungrateful for all the bene- fits they have received, that they are still for the Kaiser there is only one thing to do with them and that is to hub-tie them. Give them back the wooden shoes and the rags they landed in and ship them back to the Fatherland. I have traveled this year over all the United States. Through the Alleghenies, the White Mountains, and the Gap Hills, the Rockies and the Bitter Root Mountains, the Cascades, the Coast Range, and the Sierras. And in all these mountains there is no animal that bites and kicks, and squeals and scratches that would bite and squeal and scratch equal to a fat German American if you commence to tie him up and told him that he was on his way back to the Kaiser.
>
> (Watson, 'The German Peril'. Ladies Aid Society of St Mary's Hospital, New York City, 25 November 1917. Distributed *Great Speeches of the Twentieth Century* 1991)

Chapter 8

Early radio
journalism

The development of sound and broadcast technology was first exploited as a means for military and commercial communication. 'Wireless Telegraphy' was used to secure the arrest of murderer Doctor Hawley Harvey Crippen who sought to flee from Britain on a liner bound for Canada with his mistress Ethel LeNeve. They were disguised as father and son, but the ship's captain telegraphed his suspicions to Scotland Yard. It was also used in 1912 to rebroadcast the SOS signal from the sinking *Titanic*. The Great War was a key factor in accelerating the application of wireless technology in the same way that the Second World War provided a social and political impetus in developing the practical skills of radio journalism and portable recording facilities.

The level of state control of broadcasting substantially hindered the choice and range of broadcast services in Britain. The story in Australia and the USA was very different. An aggressive market-driven economy, combined in the USA with a written constitution and the first amendment guaranteeing basic rights for the press, led to a rapid and exciting expansion of radio stations, networks and news services. It is important to recognise that the first wave of enthusiasm for radio in America was generated by universities. The first issue of *Radio Broadcast* in May 1922 heralded radio as 'the people's university'. Funding for broadcasting initially came from public, civic and religious bodies. In 1922 seventy college and university stations began broadcasting. Even the expensive, progressive school Orson Welles was sent to at Woodstock, Illinois in 1926 had a radio station where he could develop his dramatic talents. Todd School enabled him to experiment and explore the medium. He wrote a radio adaptation of one of the Sherlock Holmes stories when he was only 13.

David Sarnoff, the first commercial manager of RCA, which stood for the Radio Corporation of America, argued that broadcasting 'represents a job of entertaining, informing and educating the nation, and should therefore be distinctly regarded as a public service'. In 1922 American Secretary of the Department of Commerce, Herbert Hoover was warning the first American Radio Conference of the dangers of allowing this new service 'to be drowned in advertising chatter'. The WEAF station in New York City, which was owned by the AT&T telephone company, pioneered the concept of the 'toll broadcast'. When a property developer discovered an increase of $127,000 in sales after spending $50 on a ten-minute spot, the world of radio commercials was born. Commercial stations were granted frequencies free from interference and permitted to use powerful transmitters. The educational stations were left with inferior local frequencies. In 1927 only ninety out of 732 stations were educational. By 1929 forty-four of those had broadcast their last programmes.

The history of US radio before the Second World War was dominated by a complex battle between network commercial interests and 'public broadcasters' who protested vehemently against somewhat cynical tactics employed by the Federal Radio Commission to downgrade the frequency power and broadcast times of college and university stations. The developing commercial networks were underwritten with investment from the leading US telephone companies. Public broadcasters could not hope to effectively challenge these lobbying interests. Canada had analysed the commercial imperatives of US radio development and in 1932 the Canadian Prime Minister R. B. Bennett supported a non commercial and non profit broadcasting system. He declared that no government would be 'warranted in leaving the air to private exploitation and not reserving it for the use of the people'.

The difference in expansion can be explained by the difference in the scale between the UK, USA and Australian economies. Britain and its empire were exhausted by the massacre of a generation in the trenches, and the cost of fighting the Great War. The US economy was characterised by growth and an increasing confidence in its influence and power in the world. Even when the recession made millions jobless and hundreds of thousands homeless, radio remained a growth industry. The appeal for radio in Australia lay in the isolation of many communities over a vast continent. The sound medium proved to be a fast method of communication and as many local stations in the 1920s and early 1930s had presenters reading the newspapers as a way of providing a news service, many listeners could hear the content of the press before it had been physically distributed to their communities.

The major differences in culture and politics resulted in a suffocation of commercial marketing of radio in Britain and a contrasting explosion of the advertising potential in the medium in America and Australia. When the BBC was a private company between 1922 and 1927 there were some sponsored broadcasts. The famous Knightsbridge department store, Harrods, underwrote a concert in 1923 and a further series of broadcast concerts were sponsored by *Daily Graphic*, *News of the World*, *Evening Standard*, *Titbits* and the *Daily Herald* newspapers. This potential was never exploited and evidence of the practice is difficult to find in official BBC histories.

The foundations of radio news journalism are to be found in the culture of national news agencies developed in the early part of the century to provide news services to the newspaper industry. They had to follow a neutral and balanced approach to reporting in order to be marketable to the greatest number of outlets. The press and news agency interests were clearly worried about the threat that this new wireless medium posed to their very existence. The relationship between broadcast services and the news agencies in Australia, the USA and UK is charac-terised by disputes, ultimatums, and boycotts. This relationship has now developed into a symbiotic one as we near the end of the century. It could also be argued that the BBC now has the resources to compete with established news agencies such as the Press Association and Reuters and market the reporting of BBC journalists to the newspapers and foreign media.

But in the 1920s the power of the news agencies was such that 'a seven o'clock rule' was imposed on the BBC. This absurd restriction meant that the BBC could only transmit news between 7 p.m. and 1 a.m. The BBC had no news-gathering system. The bulletins were provided by a consortium of news agencies. Hence the preface before every early news bulletin: 'Copyright News from Reuters, Press Association, Exchange Telegraph and Central News.' Presenter Arthur Burrows on 2LO in London along with the presenters at 2ZY in Manchester and 2IT in Birmingham advised listeners that the bulletin would be read 'first of all rapidly and then slowly, repeating on the second occasion, wherever necessary, details upon which listeners may wish to make notes'.

The restriction on broadcast times for bulletins only began to melt slightly as a result of the General Strike in 1926 which silenced the country's presses. In the USA radio news origination was almost entirely dependent on news agencies and news programming was very slow to develop an independent infrastructure.

The threat to US newspapers from radio was much greater because they perceived the new broadcast medium as a leach on their advertising. In Britain the licence fee guaranteed a separate source of funding and the BBC became less of a direct threat in terms of news provision. In 1933 US news agencies imposed a blackout on providing services to radio. The press/radio war could be said to have been raging since February 1922. In that year Associated Press asked its member newspapers to prevent the new industry of local commercial stations using their stories. At this stage the newspaper industry had not quite realised the threat that radio posed to its advertising revenue. This instruction was motivated more by a desire to ensure that their own product was actually paid for rather than transmitted free of charge. The embargo appeared to have little effect since the developing radio networks could obtain their stories from AP's competitors. Petty tactics were employed when the press industry realised that this was becoming a fight over the advertising dollar. Some papers refused to give publicity to sponsored broadcasts.

The black-out of 1933 stemmed from the enormous success of the CBS and NBC networks in reporting the Hoover-Roosevelt election night in 1932. They proved that the radio medium was faster and more immediate than the press which could only publish an election extra more than an hour after citizens had heard everything. The embargo helped radio news directors enhance the developing resources of the news operations at the two main networks, NBC and CBS. They had to fend for themselves without the traditional reliance on the wire services. The established networks of affiliated newsrooms proved that they could succeed as a news-gathering system. Radio scoops and originated stories were even picked up and credited in mainstream newspapers such as the *New York Times*. America's three main news agencies United Press International, Hearst's International News Service, and Associated Press and the radio networks CBS and NBC decided to end the boycott with a 'peace treaty' in March 1934. The agencies were missing the subscription revenue from radio services and the radio networks realised that the large press associations had a service that they needed. The terms of the agreement had a positive and negative effect on the development of radio news. The setting up of a Press-Radio Bureau funded by the networks led to a refinement of the art of writing news for radio. The sub-editors recruited from newspapers had to think about writing for the ear. However, the agreement imposed a scheduling strait-jacket in that the morning news summary could not be broadcast before 9.30 a.m., well after the peak time breakfast audiences. There was a 30-second guillotine on the length of news stories, and the evening news summary could not go out until after 9 p.m. To add insult to injury, the news bulletins had to come out with the back-announce: 'For further details, consult your local newspaper'. This rather shabby system collapsed in the face of competition from agencies set up by entrepreneurial journalists who realised that one of America's fastest-growing industries needed a product – networked radio news stories at all times. By the end of 1935, the big agencies began to consider developing their own tailored services for radio.

In Australia a similar war developed when newspaper proprietors began hearing broadcasters on the new stations simply reading out information and stories from their own papers, and they were not paying for it. There had been no conception in early Australian radio that the medium could develop its own method of originating and communicating news stories. Radio was regarded as a 'newspaper of the air'. The USA had the American Newspaper Publishers'

Association. Australia had the Australian Newspaper Conference and it did its very best to restrict radio's use of news broadcasting. In 1932 the newly formed ABC was cajoled into an agreement which limited news broadcasts to the rate of only five a day and each bulletin could not exceed five minutes' duration. However, unlike in Britain and America, Australian radio listeners could at least hear news between 7.50 a.m. and 8 a.m. ABC also signed an agreement with Australian Associated Press which meant that radio could only use a maximum of 200 words in its overseas news per day. That is just over one minute of material.

The antipathy between press interests and broadcast news continued up until the Second World War. It was only in 1939 that the British Broadcasting Corporation could broadcast news bulletins before 6 p.m. and then it was to announce that Britain was at war with Germany. It could be argued that the reported impact of Orson Welles' production of *War of the Worlds* on Halloween night 1938 was accentuated by sensational and hysterical exaggeration by the press which saw an opportunity for blaming radio for the irresponsibility of generating mass panic by representing drama as reality. In press conferences after the famous broadcast, newspaper reporters actually accused Welles and other members of his Mercury Theatre of the Air of being responsible for murdering people by causing road traffic accidents and precipitating suicide.

A landmark year for the BBC's responsibility to the nation in providing news and information was 1926. The General Strike meant that UK citizens only had a choice between Winston Churchill's *British Gazette*, which was no more than a government propaganda sheet, and the BBC's monopoly service of radio. Sadly there had been no opportunity in the preceding years for the BBC to develop an independent news culture and tradition. The current concept of impartiality was not applied. The government prevented the BBC from allowing the opposition Labour party leader Ramsay MacDonald from broadcasting a reply to the Prime Minister, Stanley Baldwin. The BBC's Managing Director John Reith also acquiesced to government pressure to delay the Archbishop of Canterbury presenting a peace-making speech expressing the hope that the private mine companies and the miners' unions could reach a settlement.

A number of analysts have identified both the positive and negative aspects of this unhappy episode in broadcasting history. Philip Schlesinger in his outstanding textbook *Putting 'Reality' Together* makes the point that the General Strike enabled the BBC to manage the generation of its own news bulletins without the shackles of a press agreement. This is, of course, a valid judgement on logistical development of style and resources. But all the evidence points to the fact that the BBC as a private monopoly company was inextricably an arm of the state with no real editorial independence.

We have here the beginnings of a sharp philosophical debate about the editorial purpose of 'public sector broadcasting institutions'. For the radio journalist working in such an environment the facets of this debate are extremely perplexing. Britain still does not have a written constitution. Radio news development in the USA had clear reference points to an existing and healthy journalistic culture which derived its independence and confidence from the First Amendment. Australia also had a written constitution and a very aggressive press which had little desire to doff its hat to authority and government.

The BBC developed without any competition, and no constitutional reference points concerning freedom of the press. The story of the BBC throughout the twentieth century is characterised by changing definitions of the national interest. The relationship between the BBC and central government has been an on-going tension between individuals who have different perceptions of when the national interest, state interest and imperatives of executive government combine.

Professor Asa Briggs in his brilliant histories of the BBC presents a very sympathetic account of the trapeze artist-style balancing act that the BBC's first Director General John Reith performed during the General Strike. If judged by our modern standards, the BBC failed to maintain basic democratic principles of balance in broadcasting. But when judged against the circumstances of the time, Reith laid down the foundations for an independent role in news communication. This tall, intimidating, high-principled Scot was a moderating spirit during a frightening time in British social history. Winston Churchill's name for the 6ft 6ins BBC supremo was 'Wuthering Heights'. Churchill represented the force of reaction in the British cabinet. They did not get on and Reith referred to his first meeting with Churchill during the strike in the following terms: 'He said he had heard that I was badly wounded in the War. I said that was so, but that had no bearing on my actions at present, which embarrassed him.' Any study of the history and culture of the BBC's journalism will inevitably lead the researcher to the personality of Reith described by Jean Seaton in *Power Without Responsibility* as 'pompous, humourless, arrogant, and, like most megalomaniacs, paranoid and self-pitying'. He ran the BBC as a dictatorship. Dissension, protest and any manifestation of risky creativity tended to be met with dismissal or exile to the regions. One of the paradoxes of journalism in so-called liberal democracies is that the individual journalist may work in a society which has a democratic constitution and civil rights for the citizen, yet his or her professional environment is almost entirely totalitarian. This has certainly been the experience of the journalist in private and public corporations in Britain, USA and Australia throughout the twentieth century. There is the amusing story of one of the BBC's most brilliant feature producers Archie Harding being carpeted by Reith after the Polish government protested about the content of one of his programmes. Reith is alleged to have told him 'You're a very dangerous man, Harding. I think you'd better go up North where you can't do so much damage.' London's loss was inevitably Manchester's gain. More serious injustices were represented by the shabby treatment of the distinguished engineer and programme maker P. P. Eckersley who was forced to resign. The editor of *The Listener*, R. S. Lambert, was compelled to drop a libel action. The BBC expected conservatism and conformity from its employees. This policy was combined with hypocritical boasts about equal opportunities. In 1934, the BBC believed there was 'a good proportion of women to men on the staff'. The only problem was that most of the women were secretaries. A similar delusion emerged during the 1980s and 1990s with respect to so-called 'ethnic minorities'. Initially internal surveys suggested that the BBC had an egalitarian approach to recruitment. This was somewhat punctured when it was discovered most of the corporation's Afro-Caribbean staff worked in food preparation and cleaning. Policy decisions to contract out catering and cleaning services to reduce staffing levels resulted in a further decline of black representation within the corporation.

Reith is a controversial figure. A recent biography has dwelled on evidence that he was a closet homosexual, but the fact remains that despite having a dictatorial character and an element of moral hypocrisy, he is responsible for laying down the foundations of BBC radio journalism. He was a force of moderation during the General Strike. This is undoubtedly an editorial stance, but it is the beginning of the idea of balance in broadcast reporting. The middle way must inevitably give way to a consideration of all sides of an argument. This may not have been achieved in 1926, but it was certainly set out as an objective for the future. Reith persuaded Prime Minister Baldwin to insert the following words during a broadcast: 'I am longing and working and praying for peace, but I will not surrender the safety and security of the British constitution'. When the strike ended it was Reith who recited Blake's famous poem *Jerusalem* to the nation. The BBC was on the threshold of becoming a Corporation by Royal Charter funded by a licence fee collected from the buyers of radio sets. Reith was politically astute enough to realise that compromises made during a General Strike in 1926 would guarantee a status quo holding out the promise of greater editorial independence from 1927 onwards. The BBC's commonwealth sister in Australia, the ABC, would be subject to a regular grant from government and face more intimidating forms of political blackmail and economic sanctions in the years to come.

The General Strike of 1926 represented 'a rites of passage' process in newscasting. The BBC had been given an alarming prelude about the dangers of irresponsible broadcasting four months before in January 1926. Father Ronald Knox was permitted to broadcast a fictional description of an unruly unemployed mob attempting the demolition of the Houses of Parliament, trench mortars bringing Big Ben to the ground, the hanging of the Minister of Traffic from a tramway post and the burning of a well-known philanthropist in Trafalgar Square. His story ended with the destruction of the BBC's headquarters at Savoy Hill. Newspapers and police stations were besieged with calls from frantic listeners. The panic was not on the same scale as Orson Welles' Halloween Boo in 1938. But it demonstrated the danger of story telling and commentary being confused with news.

During the General Strike the BBC was enjoying its highest ever audience. Five bulletins a day were being broadcast. An emergency news staff bureau was set up to filter and evaluate information coming in from Reuters and the Admiralty. BBC employees actually went out collecting news. The first bulletin was not particularly distinguished by the following homily:

> The public should understand that the sudden change from the bulky newspaper to the short bulletin cannot be perfected in an instant. Moreover, the world has been asleep and not active for the last eight or ten hours and therefore there is bound to be comparatively little news in the first bulletin. In cooperation with Reuters, we are endeavouring to secure that at any rate a bare minimum of information essential to the community shall be available in spite of the suspension of ordinary means of communication.
>
> (BBC News Bulletin, 4 May 1926. Briggs: 1961, 1995)

The bulletins did improve and were free of fabrication and distortion. The content had a high degree of accuracy. Gladstone Murray provided what was described as an 'appreciation of the situation'. The nickname 'BFC' standing for British Falsehood Company stemmed from what was not included in bulletins rather than their actual content. Not many people realised that Reith himself read many of the actual bulletins including the announcement of the General Strike. On 12 May somebody ran down with an agency report that the strike was over while Reith was reading a bulletin. Rather than break the news immediately Reith insisted on confirmation from Downing Street. He did not announce the end of the strike until he had obtained the necessary confirmation. He was sowing here the seeds of proper sourcing in broadcast news gathering.

Licensed commercial radio did not arrive in Britain until 1973. Up until that point the history of radio had always been defined and written by the BBC. Even now the BBC enjoys a considerable political and cultural dominance that not even the pressures of eighteen years of radical and market-driven reforming Conservative Government had been able to weaken. The development of BBC Enterprises into BBC World Wide, now a powerful multi-million pound business on the back of monopolistic control of national radio broadcasting and television and radio listings, has given the BBC significant commercial muscle. The monopoly position has been ended recently, and it remains to be seen whether the BBC can maintain its cultural and political power in the face of widening competition in television and radio.

Chapter 9

The political
dimension of
sound
journalism

In the early part of the twentieth century, phonographs became an effective method of spreading political campaign messages in the USA. At 75¢ a disc, presidential candidates and other political figures could spread their voice across the country without all the travelling. Republican William Howard Taft won his bid for the presidency in 1908 and the farming vote in the Northeast and the West was critical. Taft used the new medium of recording to full advantage. He told the farmers in this recorded message:

> As the Republican platform says, the welfare of the farmer is vital to that of the whole country. The prosperity of the country rests usually upon the prosperity of agriculture. Just now one of the strongest hopes of returning good times is based on the business which the farmers' crops are to afford. . . . It is difficult to see how, with his intelligent appreciation of the threat to business prosperity involved in Democratic success at the polls, he can do otherwise than give his full and hearty support to the continuation of the policies of the present administration under Republican auspices.
>
> (Taft, 'The Farmer and the Republican Party'. Midwestern Campaign tour, Kansas City, Missouri, October 1908. Distributed *Great Speeches of the Twentieth Century* 1991)

This oleaginous rhetoric helped Taft win the election by a landslide. He even won in New York City which was a traditional Democrat stronghold.

Official US radio news broadcasting opened up with the excitement of the 1920 Presidential election battle between Republican Warren G. Harding and Democrat James M. Cox. The following transmission came from KDKA's transmitter on the roof of a six-storey factory building owned by the Westinghouse Electric Company in East Pittsburgh, Pennsylvania. On 2 November 1920, a few hundred radio listeners using individual headphones attached to their crystal sets were able to hear this landmark in radio news communication:

> Just one moment now. KDKA in cooperation with the *Pittsburgh Post* and *Sun* will present the latest presidential election returns. It is now apparent that the Republican ticket of Harding and Coolidge is running well ahead of Cox and Roosevelt. At the present time Harding has collected more than 16 million votes against some 9 million for the Democrats. We'll give you the State vote in just a moment. But first we'd like to ask you to let us know if this broadcast is reaching you. Please drop us a card addressed 'Station KDKA, Westinghouse, East Pittsburgh, Pennsylvania'.
>
> (Distributed *This Was Radio* 1990)

Warren G. Harding was the victor in that election race and he became the first American President to broadcast on radio. It was an inauspicious start for political participation in this new form of mass communication. He meandered unconvincingly with the following pledge to the nation which was also broadcast overseas:

> America's present need is not heroic but healing; not nostrums, but normality; not revolution, but restoration; not agitation, but adjustment; not surgery, but serenity; not the dramatic, but . . .

Calvin Coolidge took over the presidency in August 1923 after the unfortunate Harding died in office. Coolidge was a natural for radio and he knew it. He said: 'I can't make an engaging, rousing or oratorical speech . . . but I have a good radio voice, and now I can get my message across without acquainting the public with my lack of oratorical ability'. In the 1924 presidential election race, Calvin Coolidge's Republicans realised that radio changed the style of campaigning. Short messages were best. The long, rhetorical speech was a turn-off. A contemporary political commentator observed: 'Silent Cal's broadcasts went straight to the popular heart'. They also won the popular vote. The Republicans spent three times as much on radio advertising as the Democrats. Coolidge's final campaign speech was networked by 26 stations. The Republicans even set up and ran their own station in New York for the campaign. Coolidge used radio during his second administration and became the USA's fourth most popular radio personality.

The 1928 campaign between Republican Herbert Hoover and Democrat Alfred Smith showed a more imaginative use of radio, but both candidates were poor radio performers. The Democrats spent money on a radio play dramatising their candidate's life story. The Democrats also spent more money on radio than the Republicans this time round, but still lost the election.

Franklin D. Roosevelt was to discover that radio was a powerful political tool in changing public opinion and fighting the psychological battle against recession. He began with an inaugural speech in March 1933, which was transmitted to the American nation through the medium of radio:

> President Hoover, Mr Chief Justice, my friends, this is a day of National consecration and I am certain that on this day my fellow Americans expect that on my induction into the Presidency I will address them with a candour and a decision which the present position of our people impels. This great nation will endure as it has endured, will revive and will prosper. So first of all, let me assert my firm belief that the only thing we have to fear is fear itself.

He used radio to contribute another famous political maxim:

> To some generations much is given. Of other generations much is expected. This generation of Americans has a rendezvous with destiny.
>
> (Audio: This Was Radio 1990; Text: Maidment, 1994)

His 'fireside chats' are legendary largely because he realised that radio was an intimate and personal link to the individual imagination. He took advantage of a medium which allowed his voice to enter people's living rooms so that he could explain his administration's policies in a friendly style rather than with the bluster of tub-thumping oratory. It was a critical factor in reconstructing the country's confidence in a discredited banking system.

Radio played an important role in disseminating the philosophy of fascism in Germany and Italy. Adolf Hitler will always be remembered for his aggressive and thundering style of oratory somewhat characterised by the tendency to roar in the manner of a dictator. But recordings exist which demonstrate that he was also the master of the friendly, intimate conversation with the listener. His engaging and avuncular attitude in a recording made in 1932 highlights a reasoned approach to national socialism. It has a chilling plausibility. Hitler was, of course, seeking to gain power by legitimate democratic means following his failed putsch in 1923. He almost purrs like a cat when complaining about the international conspiracy to 'play off people one against the other, the national government against the states, office workers against civil servants, manual workers against workers with intellect, Bavarians against Prussians, Catholics against Protestants and so on and vice versa'. Radio was to play a critical role in the development of the Nazi totalitarian state and there remains little research in this area. Certainly the sound of Adolf Hitler and Benito Mussolini became a familiar motif for American radio audiences. The main news networks would transmit keynote speeches live on a short-wave link with analysts and commentators translating and assessing the rising power of fascism in Europe.

Britain's war-time Prime Minister Winston Churchill utilised radio's potential to raise the morale of his country's citizens. But it is worth considering that throughout the 1930s Churchill was denied access to the BBC when he was regarded as a political maverick, opposed to appeasement and repeatedly calling for rearmament. He was able to find a voice on US radio. He challenged the position of appeasement with forthright views about Hitler in an NBC broadcast in October 1938. Through the 1930s he came to detest the BBC for joining in the ostracism of his political position. At the same time he was carefully studying the influence of President Roosevelt's fireside chats and appreciating the power of radio to bind the nation's moral and psychological spirit.

While America's landmark radio news broadcast could involve a democratically elected president, the BBC responded by transmitting the stiff and awkward words of King George V on 23 April 1924. He was speaking at the British Empire Exhibition from Wembley and set a precedent which eventually led to the British monarch's annual Christmas address to the nation.

Politicians were heard for the first time on the BBC during the October General Election in 1924. Three uncensored speeches by the Liberal, Conservative and Labour party leaders were allowed to be transmitted by the Postmaster-General. He turned down a request to broadcast the 1926 budget speech with a right of reply from the opposition. The BBC's managing director John Reith scribbled on the ministerial notepaper, 'Isn't this absurd?' The Conservative leader Stanley Baldwin proved to be the best exponent of the art of talking to radio listeners. He was praised for his 'naturalness'. He took the trouble to arrive early at the studio and sought the advice of Reith who was a regular broadcaster himself. He was the only party leader who agreed to go to the BBC's then headquarters in Savoy Hill and 'talk' to the voters. Labour's Ramsay MacDonald stuck to his old tub-thumping manners. His speech was transmitted from a public meeting in Glasgow. The techniques of public speaking were inappropriate for radio. Listeners became irritated by the oratorical habit of raising and lowering the voice. The habit of turning from side to side and strutting about the platform away from the microphone did not help him at all. Reith described his performance as 'hopeless'. The BBC also discovered that great speakers in parliament and at live meetings did not make good broadcasters. David Lloyd George always proved a disappointment in front of the microphone. Stanley Baldwin kept ahead of the rest. Journalist Hamilton Fyfe made the following observations in the *Radio Times* about the 1935 election broadcasts. He said Stanley Baldwin talked and the others orated:

They wrote out speeches and delivered them in a platform tone. From a platform they would have sounded well. The audience would have collaborated. Cheers and laughter and interruptions would have helped the speakers out. Without such aid they sounded lamentably thin and dry. Attlee read his at breakneck speed, as if he feared he might not get it in – and finished five minutes before he need have done. Mr Greenwood was too statistical. Mr Lloyd George too emphatic, Mr Herbert Morrison too cocksure, Sir John Simon's tone was conversational, but his manner was not.

(Briggs 1985)

The BBC became the mechanism by which Edward the VIII announced his abdication. It began with a bulletin reporting the breaking of the news to the House of Commons.

This is London. A quarter of an hour ago, the Prime Minister came to the Bar of the House and handed to the Speaker a message from His Majesty the King. Here is the text of the message which was read by the speaker. 'After long and anxious consideration, I have determined to renounce the throne and I am now communicating this my final and irrevocable decision'.

(BBC Radio Four, *The Friend in The Corner 1936* 25 November 1992. Producer: A. Wilson)

The King spoke about his decision personally through a special broadcast on 11 December 1936:

SIR JOHN REITH [*in the style of a sombre radio announcer*]: This is Windsor Castle. His Royal Highness Prince Edward.

EDWARD   At long last I am able to say a few words of my own. I have never wanted to withhold anything. But until now it has not been constitutionally possible for me to speak. But you must believe me when I tell you that I have found it impossible to carry the heavy burden of responsibility and to discharge my duties as King as I would wish to do without the help and support of the woman I love . . . I now quit altogether public affairs and I lay down my burden. It may be some time before I return to my native land but I shall always follow the fortunes of the British race and Empire with profound interest. . . . And now we all have a new King. I wish him and you his people, happiness and prosperity with all my heart. God bless you all. God Bless the King!

The surprise and shock of this broadcast was the result of a paternalistic attitude concerning what ordinary citizens should be told about their reigning monarch. A combination of censorship and obsequious reverence for the monarchy had prevented free reporting and discussion of his developing relationship with American divorcée Mrs Wallis Simpson. The refusal of the then Prime Minister Stanley Baldwin to countenance a marriage had created a constitutional crisis which had been widely reported in the US and foreign media for many weeks. Britain's national newspapers and agencies were as much a part of this bizarre cover-up as the BBC which by this time had resisted developing a news-gathering structure.

The Australian Broadcasting Commission actually had a representative in London sending cables to Australia which marked an independence from newspaper accounts. Controversy still surrounds the real reasons for the abdication. Contemporary histories cited the constitutional embarrassment of the reigning monarch marrying a divorcée. Investigations in recent years point to the growing concern and sympathy shown by King Edward VIII for Hitler's Nazi regime and his social links with fascists. In 1939 within weeks of the outbreak of the Second World War, the Duke of Windsor broadcast a message of appeasement on American radio. The broadcast was neither carried nor reported by the BBC. At the time of the King's abdication in 1936, Richard Dimbleby had joined the British Broadcasting Corporation as a 'Topical Talks Assistant' only two months previously. He was to revolutionise the BBC's radio news culture in the coming years, but it was not without a considerable struggle.

The Royal Broadcast became a broadcasting institution always controlled and distributed by the BBC. It appears to continue to exercise authority on the rest of the British media even when the reported extramarital affairs of Queen Elizabeth's children have brought the monarchy into disrepute.

The *Sun* newspaper, published by Rupert Murdoch's News International Corporation, had to apologise and pay a considerable amount of money in damages for breaching the Queen's copyright when it broke the embargo and published the content of the Christmas speech in advance of the broadcast in 1992. The BBC's broadcast of a *Panorama* programme interview with Diana, Princess of Wales in 1995 was followed by the ending of the BBC's monopoly on distributing the Queen's Christmas message. The interview had been severely critical of the royal family.

Chapter 10

Sport

A springboard
for spontaneity

In the USA sports broadcasting highlighted the ad-libbing opportunity for radio commentators to build pictures in the mind by describing the colour and detail of sports action set against the roar of spectator crowds. Sportscasting of boxing, baseball and American football generated huge audiences and made stars out of the broadcasters. Former American president Ronald Reagan made a living out of sportscasting before the war. Here are a few examples of live US sports broadcasts which were instrumental in developing the craft of spontaneous communication of news through an outside broadcast microphone. They also had separate cultural and political value. The first is by Ted Husing, broadcast on WHN New York, 1934.

> TED HUSING   Here he is on the motion, there's the wind-up. Here's the pitch, it's a slow curve, low, and the Babe swings. [*loud cheer*]. It's a long one, a long one, going out towards right centre. Slinger's backing up against the wall. He can't get it. It's in there. [*loud cheer*]. Another holds onto the Bambino. . . . So the Babe hits his second boom of the day.
>
> (Audio: *This Was Radio* 1990)

This is just one of the broadcasts which helped turn Babe Ruth into a legend and consolidate the popularity of baseball as America's leading sport. George Herman Ruth was known as 'The Sultan of Swat'. He hit a record 714 home runs in a career which began in 1914. He tossed a record twenty-nine consecutive scoreless innings in a World Series. Radio broadcast his accomplishments and through his inspiration created dreams for youngsters who sought fame and fortune by following his example. He retired in 1947 and died shortly afterwards. His farewell to baseball in the Yankee stadium in New York City on 27 April 1947 is one of the most moving broadcasts ever made. His voice could not conceal the cancer which had racked his body. His tribute to society and the emotional warmth of the crowd has been recorded for posterity.

The black fighter Joe Louis was more than a world-ranking sportsman. He was a symbol to blacks in America that they had a figurehead who could achieve success on an equal footing with whites. In the late 1930s racism and fascism were developing into powerful political movements in the USA as well as Europe. The battle between Louis and German fighter Max Schmelling therefore became a political issue as well as a sports contest. After the German snatched the world heavyweight title from Louis with a knock-out, the rematch in 1938 became charged with emotional and political conflict. Black-Americans had watched with dismay as Italy's Benito Mussolini invaded Abyssinia – one of the few independent African nations. The failure of the League of Nations to intervene was also perceived as a failure of the isolationist United States to prevent tyranny crushing one of the few independent black states. This meant that radio listeners had many reasons for listening to Clem McArthy's commentary, broadcast on CBS in 1938, as Joe Louis managed to knock the German to the floor of the ring in only the first round:

CLEM MCARTHY [*growing uproar*] Five . . . Six . . . Seven . . . Eight . . . The men are in the ring. The fight is over on a technical knock-out. Max Schmelling is beaten in one round. The first time that a World Heavyweight Championship ever changed hands in one round. Ed Ferguson . . . I want you to have a chance on this broadcast . . . [*sound of ringside bell being rung*]

Get in there and describe the scene. I'm going up to the ring to get the winner. Ed!

ED FERGUSON Everybody's been taken by surprise here. The ring is all . . . eh . . . There's bewilderment all around . . . and here is Clem McArthy!

CLEM MCARTHY They said it would take you two rounds. Do you know how long it took you?

JOE LOUIS No I don't . . . I . . .

CLEM MCARTHY I imagine about a minute and a half.

JOE LOUIS Well, that's fine. Well, I won't be [*catching his breath*] getting mad for less than a round.

CLEM MCARTHY Joe, which punch if any, do you think was the one that started him downhill?

JOE LOUIS I think the right hand one to the ribs.

CLEM MCARTHY Right hand to the ribs?

JOE LOUIS Yeah.

CLEM MCARTHY I saw it going in there Joe . . . it looked terrible. Congratulations!

JACK BRACKBURN [*interruption*]   I wouldno' been no good if Joe hadn't got this second turn with Mount.

CLEM MCARTHY   That was Jack Brackburn, the man who has made Joe Louis the champion of the world. Max come over here! Bring him over! Max! Max! He came to very quickly but he was a badly beaten man and it was all Louis. And here is the distinction of the world's fastest broadcast on a fight. [*background sound of loud announcement*]. This was faster than Joe Louis and Charlie . . . and now I turn you back to Ed Ferguson.

(Audio: *This Was Radio* 1990)

US sports radio quickly established the professionalism required in ad-libbed broadcasts; the need to bring in background information when the line of sight for commentary was blocked physically, or stopped by an interruption of play.

The sports broadcasters quickly learned the value of highlighting detail, colour, form and movement. American networks and local radio stations were beginning to appreciate the excitement generated by live news broadcasts. Australian radio charted a similar growth in popularity and demand for live radio sports commentary. The immediacy of the medium and the background sound of horses' hooves and cricket balls clicking was music to the ears of sports fans. Radio sets would be marketed in major campaigns shortly before the cricket season.

The beginning of radio sports journalism in Britain was probably the use of a Marconi wireless telephone set to transmit the result of the Derby in 1921. This was an experiment with a very limited audience, but it was probably the first ever outside broadcast since the equipment was accommodated in a large bulky van. While 2LO, under Marconi's control, continued experimental broadcasts before the official formation of the BBC, a running commentary of a prize fight at Olympia between Kid Lewis and George Carpentier went out on 11 May 1922. The press soon put a stop to any attempt at live broadcasting of sports events and attempts in 1925 by John Reith to organise radio coverage of an England/Scotland rugby match, the boat race, the FA Cup Final and the Derby from Epsom were all frustrated.

The transformation of the BBC into a public corporation controlled by Royal Charter in 1927 meant that another attempt could be made to establish outside sports broadcasts. A special department was set up and a future radio drama producer called Lance Sieveking was given the task of finding commentators. He recorded this account of his approach:

I took likely people round to watch football games played by amateurs and small boys and asked them to describe to me what they saw. Many were entirely flummoxed. But one chap looked quietly on for a few moments and then plunged headlong into a cataract of words which never stopped for an instant. He was Captain H.B.T. Wakelam. It was something like this. It was brilliant. 'I don't know who they are but there's one little boy with the red hair. Oh yes . . . he's going to pass, he's going to pass to the little boy in the red jersey. Oh a fine shot! Now. Going on down the line with the little boy with the red hair . . . Oooah! Go on! It's magnificent. Shoot! Shoot! It's a goal'. So I engaged him.

(BBC Radio Four, *Arena Night* 'Back to Square One', 18 December 1993. Producer: D. Barlow)

Captain Wakelam had his first chance to show his talents at the England–Wales Rugby International at Twickenham on 15 January 1927. A special transportable shed-like structure was made to accommodate the commentator, a blind man who would be able to provide 'quality control' on the broadcast, and an actor whose mellifluous voice would provide an explanation of which square of the pitch held the action. Two words were written on a card inside the commentary box: 'Don't Swear!' Within the same month the BBC mounted the first ever commentary of a soccer match. The famous amateur side Corinthian Casuals were playing professionals Newcastle United in the fourth round of the FA Cup at the Crystal Palace. The *Radio Times* published a diagram of the pitch and divided it into squares so that listeners could have a visual aid to the commentary. According to the BBC, this is the origin of the expression 'Back to Square One!'. Live outside broadcasts of the Grand National, the Wimbledon tennis tournament and the Varsity Boat Race were to follow.

Chapter 11

Radio drama
A source of innovation and sensational treatment

The main inspiration to use real actuality, recorded speeches and events to illustrate radio news broadcasts could be said to have derived from the developing art of radio drama. Both Australia and the USA saw a fascinating growth in speech entertainment programmes in the 1930s which used the leading actors of the time to dramatise news events. CBS launched *The March of Time* in 1931. The earliest narrator was the broadcaster Ted Husing, who we have already referred to in the field of sports reporting. He had distinguished himself with a marathon broadcast performance for the presidential election results between Republican Herbert Hoover and Democrat Al Smith in 1928. He was based in the city room of the *New York World* newspaper and managed to anchor the presentation of the returns over a continuous ten-hour period. His on-air mathematical ability meant that he was able to calculate Hoover's victory nearly an hour before his newspaper host.

The March of Time programme pulled together an entertaining choreography of orchestral music, sound effects and acting. Orson Welles enjoyed his debut on this programme playing a baby in a news story about the Dion quintuplets from Ontario! The programme was exciting, sensational and dramatic. Actors would portray the voices of Emperor Haile Selassie of Abyssinia, Winston Churchill, and New York Mayor Fiorello LaGuardia. Trials were dramatised, wars re-enacted, and political assassinations recreated in the studio. And each programme would end with the immortal pronouncement 'Time Marches On!'. More importantly for the networks, sponsors and advertisers, this type of programme was a hit with the listeners and the money poured in. The commercial objectives in the programme are underlined by the fact that *The March of Time* was produced by a New

York advertising agency. It began as a promotion for *Time* magazine and the radio stations were given the programme free. By 1935 the pioneering news documentary show was sponsored by Remington Rand and then by Wrigley Chewing Gum. The programme starred acting luminaries such as Everett Sloane, Paul Stewart, Agnes Moorehead and Dwight Weist who found that he was rather busy in the role of the new Chancellor of Germany – one Adolf Hitler. Orson Welles found that his gift for impersonation and acting led him into playing the roles of King Victor Emmanuel, and Charles Laughton.

In Australia, radio audiences were working up a similar enthusiasm for dramatisations of contemporary news stories. In 1935, the ABC produced a recreation with actors and sound effects of the war between Italy and Abyssinia. Emperor Haile Selassie took centre stage with a resonant bass voice. ABC was pushing the frontiers of feature production. At the BBC, Lance Sieveking produced a special dramatised feature programme called *Crisis In Spain*. He used a creative mixture of telephone and radio ambiences to dramatise the abdication of the Spanish King in 1931. It was described as 'the first English example of the reporting in radio form of contemporary events'. The programme depicted the crisis in Spain before the Civil War in terms of news items printed and broadcast at the time all over the world. The BBC's features department was undoubtedly one of the most pioneering areas of production. But unlike *The March of Time* programmes in America and Australia, the BBC failed to establish a regular programme format which dramatised contemporary events. A recreation of the rebellion by Bonnie Prince Charlie and the battle of Culloden in 1745 was more in keeping with the BBC's programming philosophy. Commercial stations such as 3DB in Melbourne imitated the American *March of Time* with a programme called *Time Marches On*. The show was performed by an acting group called 'The Time Radio Players'. They followed this up with *Millions in the Making* – a series of dramatised biographies of living millionaires such as John D. Rockefeller.

Australian, American and British radio all indulged in 'stunt' broadcasts – taking the microphone into the outside world to record individual daredevil activities or significant events which were usually divorced of any political controversy. A remarkable recording was made of a diver at the bottom of Sydney Harbour. Australian radio microphones greeted Amy Johnson's arrival in Darwin and there was live commentary of the opening of Sydney Harbour Bridge in March 1932. However, some of the announcers failed to notice the fracas involving Captain de Groot, a leading member of the Australian fascist organisation 'The New Guard' who vandalised the ceremonial ribbon. The broadcaster Conrad Charlton was an exception. He was quick enough to see what was happening and described the event live and established a precedent in Australian radio news.

In the USA stunt broadcasts involved short-wave transmissions from planes. A naturalist broadcast from a bathysphere 2,200 feet under the surface of the ocean.

Transmissions were made from balloons, speeding trains, and reporters at KDKA in Pittsburgh were equipped with a touring radio car which they used to chase fire engines and police cars even though it weighed half a ton. In March 1931, airline passengers in England were able to watch and listen to the Boat Race from above the Thames at the same time.

The scale of radio journalism's development in the USA became obvious with two major stories of the 1930s. The first was domestic and concerned the kidnapping of Atlantic aviator Charles Lindbergh's baby. The infant's body was found in some nearby woods. The challenge to report the story of the kidnapping of the world's most famous baby produced a Herculean battle between CBS and NBC. A veritable media circus descended on Trenton, New Jersey. Newscaster and commentator Lowell Thomas fronted the NBC operation and Boake Carter represented CBS. The arrest of Bruno Richard Hauptmann led to what was then the most publicised murder trial in American history. The courthouse at Flemington was jam-packed with 150 reporters. The jurors shared accommodation in the same hotel with the attendant media and it has been reported that they could hear the radio reporters shouting their commentaries and reports into the microphones set up in adjoining rooms. When the jury retired a mob gathered outside the courthouse. The crowd howled 'Kill Hauptmann!'. Amid this highly prejudicial atmosphere it has been argued that a great miscarriage of justice took place and radio journalism cannot be absolved of its responsibility for contributing towards it. The Hauptmann trial prompted a continuing and sharply-drawn debate over the conflicting rights of freedom of expression and the defendant's right to have a fair trial. Hauptmann went to the electric chair and his last view of life contained a vision of thirty reporters waiting to dash out to describe his execution. But out of the chaos and sensationalism radio journalism did rescue its dignity with an extraordinary ad-libbed performance from reporter Gabriel Heatter. On 3 April 1936 he expected to be on air for five minutes. A delay forced him to communicate his knowledge and sensitivity for up to fifty-five minutes. This was recognised by over 50,000 letters of praise. He had refused to enter the death chamber himself and so spoke to his listeners from a hotel room opposite:

> There will be no reprieve, of that I am certain . . . I wonder what's going on in that room. It wouldn't be a confession . . . No. That silent fellow, lips pressed together would not confess.

He completed this remarkable broadcast with a simple and poignant sign-off: 'Ladies and Gentlemen, Bruno Hauptmann is dead. Good night'. The BBC would never have tolerated this style of coverage at that time. Consistent radio reporting of criminal trials only became a regular feature on UK radio news with the birth of commercial radio in 1973. The Independent Radio News Network and London's commercial news station LBC have maintained regular courtroom correspondents and despatched reporting teams to provide daily reports of newsworthy court cases supported by background reports and documentaries. The time chasm between concentrated broadcast coverage of legal cases in the USA compared with the UK might explain the fact that many American states allow television and radio recording of trials for broadcast. It is a criminal offence to take a tape recorder into any British courtroom with the intention of recording for broadcast. The UK had to wait until 1993 for the first experiment in broadcasting cases. This is actually being accommodated by the Scottish Judges who oversee a separate legal system from England and Wales.

Chapter 12

Appeasement and fascism

Radio's response through journalism

Hitler's rise to power and growing domination of central Europe was the second major story which established pioneering conventions and practices in US radio news. The two key characters in this episode were William Lawrence Shirer and Egbert Roscoe Murrow – Ed Murrow to his friends and audience. Again these developments were spawned as a result of competition between CBS and NBC. Hitler took totalitarian control of Germany in 1933, scrapped the Versailles Treaty in 1935 and in 1938 seized Austria. Prior to the Anschluss there had been an extraordinary propaganda battle between the Nazi-controlled German radio networks and Austrian broadcasting which sought to report objectively and critically the crushing of civil rights in Germany and the persecution of the Jews. Hitler's move into Austria was motivated by a desire to silence the weapon of truth as well as annexe another substantial German-speaking population.

William L. Shirer's experience of challenging the Nazi regime with truthful reporting for radio has been documented brilliantly in his autobiographical accounts. To his credit he made himself unpopular with the Nazi propaganda machine because he reported actions and events which were embarrassing to Germany's international reputation and asked awkward questions at press conferences in Berlin. Ed Murrow was the European Bureau chief for CBS and was based in London. He had recruited Shirer after hearing that he was out of a job as a result of the Universal Press Agency going bust.

When the German army marched into Austria on 11 March 1938 Shirer found that they would not let him use Austrian broadcast facilities to bounce a short-wave transmission to London and then across the Atlantic via the BBC's Broadcasting House. Shirer and Murrow conceived an extraordinary plan. Shirer would find any way to fly to London so that he could provide an uncensored and objective account beyond the reach of the Nazis. Ed Murrow who was in Warsaw setting up a broadcast of a famous boys' choir would travel to Vienna. It is difficult to understand now that US radio news was compelled at the time by regulation to transmit reporters' despatches live. There was a block on broadcasting prerecorded sound and eye witness accounts apart from a few exceptions. So at 1 a.m. London time William L. Shirer had to anchor an extraordinary half-hour news programme involving live contributions from Murrow in Austria and American newspaper correspondents in Rome, Paris and Berlin. The CBS team only had twenty-four hours to organise a technically complex link-up between the main capitals of Europe. One cannot underestimate the significance in radio journalism history of this broadcast. When Ed Murrow went on the air from Vienna he was introducing the first radio news round-up of an international story:

> I arrived here by air from Warsaw and Berlin only a few hours ago. . . . Young stormtroopers are riding about the streets, riding about in trucks and vehicles of all sorts, singing and tossing oranges out to the crowd. Nearly every principal building has its armed guard, including the one from which I am speaking.
>
> (CBS Anschluss 1936)

The broadcast also demonstrated that American news network staff in Europe were not just arrangers and producers who would find commentators to communicate the news of events. The tradition of the radio foreign correspondent had been established.

In Australia the first radio journalists were being hired and started broadcasting. The recruitment of P. C. Murphy by the ABC was an important landmark. A curious voice of news commentary began in Melbourne entitled *The Watchman*. As we will learn later, editorial comment on news events in Australia would stimulate a lively debate about partiality and bias in radio broadcasting.

As the BBC had Richard Dimbleby, the ABC had Frank Dixon and Charles Moses. In the 1930s Dixon believed that radio could do what the newspapers had failed to achieve; create a homogeneous national news service for Australia. In a letter to Moses he pointed out that the ABC could foster a national culture and identity. In 1935 Dixon was brought in as a federal editor to develop news broadcasting with copy written specifically for the medium. Moses talked about the need 'to paraphrase, or rewrite, the news into spoken English, and to make it a good deal easier to listen to'. Charles Moses directed the acquisition of news cables for the coverage of the Japanese invasion of China which apparently had been neglected by the Australian press. The Munich affair and the German takeover of Czechoslovakia resulted in the ABC re-broadcasting radio despatches received by short-wave from Europe. Short-wave radio was the 1930s equivalent of the satellite services of the 1990s. Commercial services such as 2UE in Sydney were made to feel very insecure because Moses and Dixon were stealing a march on radio news developments.

Dixon and Moses sought help and guidance from the BBC in London. In 1935 a request for a BBC style sheet was met with the pompous riposte that no such document existed because 'trained journalists are supposed to know'. By 1938 the ABC had drawn up a booklet entitled *Hints for the Guidance of ABC News Compilers*. This has become something of a bible in Australian Radio News philosophy. The concept of 'Where, What, When, How' was defined. A news culture for the ABC was established so that news directors were guided by priorities such as 'impartiality in our presentation of news' and the idea that 'reliability needs to dominate everything in the ABC news'. Charles Moses and Frank Dixon were stressing the need to avoid sensationalism and the maintenance of good taste. These points have their modern echoes in the BBC's editorial guidelines. News judgement was to be determined by 'public interests'.

The late 1930s saw a growth in radio journalists' recruitment. A Sunday news service was set up when it was realised that this day had not been covered by the agreed restrictions with the Australian press. The 'national interest' was maintained by avoiding references to the various Australian states in news bulletins. However up until the Second World War the ABC resisted suggestions and pressure to include actuality and news cuts from the people in the news. The opportunities certainly arose when British Prime Minister Neville Chamberlain returned from Munich with the notorious *Peace In Our Time* document. The 1930s were clearly a period of dominance by the ABC in the field of radio news development. There was an emphasis on straight presentation and the voice of authority. However there were signs of innovation from the commercial sector. Sydney's 2UW introduced the concept of telephone reports from the scene of news stories to provide instant information. The foundations of 2GB's *Eye Witness News* and 2UW's *Flash News* were being laid down, and unlike the august Australian Broadcasting Commission, the commercial services took the lead in drawing on actuality and taking the listeners to the scene of news events.

Meanwhile, US radio networks found the Munich crisis demanded not just dramatic up to the minute news reports, but some form of explanation and interpretation. John Birt's essays published in *The Times* in the 1970s on the philosophy of 'bias against understanding' and 'mission to explain' have mistakenly been identified as original ideas and viewpoints on the purpose of news broadcasting. The Americans had experienced this way of thinking forty years earlier. H. V. Kaltenborn was perhaps the most famous of American radio news analysts. He came into his own during the eighteen days of the Munich crisis and transmitted eighty-five talks on CBS. He was later to move to NBC and his performance for WEAF in New York during the D-Day landings matched that of the Munich crisis. Munich also locked NBC and CBS in a fierce and competitive battle. If CBS won on resources and depth of coverage, NBC won on nerve and scoop value. NBC's Max Jordan simply walked up to British diplomats who had just emerged with draft press releases on the text of the agreement. He explained that his microphone was live and ready for broadcast in the studio set up in Hitler's headquarters. William L. Shirer admitted that this was 'one of the worst beatings I've ever taken'. It is a lesson on the speed and immediacy of radio. Max Jordan had only to reach a microphone to tell the world his story.

Ed Murrow's and William Shirer's reporting of the events in central Europe demonstrated the ability of radio to report events quickly after they had occurred. Most radio journalism is reactive. Journalists interview and research in order to build a picture of a news event after it has happened. However, recording technology offers radio the chance to be present at the events which shape our lives. The experience of a young Chicago reporter just before the war demonstrated the real potential of the medium to make the listener share in the horror of a disaster.

On 6 May 1937 the German airship *Hindenburg* was arriving in Lakehurst, New Jersey, having made the Atlantic crossing in less than forty-eight hours. American radio journalist Herbert Morrison was broadcasting a live account of the airship's arrival to his Chicago station WLS. What happened during his report left an indelible imprint on the minds of radio listeners throughout the world:

> The ship is riding majestically towards us like some great feather. And these giant flagships standing here, the American Airlines flagships waiting to . . . to all points in the United States when they get the ship moored. It's practically standing still now. They've dropped ropes out of the nose of the ship. It's starting to rain again . . . The rain has . . . eh . . . slacked up a little bit. The back motors of the ship are just holding it . . . ah . . . just enough to keep it from . . .[*Sudden cry.*] It burst into flames. [*Explosion, microphone dropped.*] Get out of the way! Get out of the way! . . . [*Picks up the microphone.*] Get this started! Get this started! [*More screams.*] It's craa . . . And it's crashing . . . It's crashing . . . Terrible! . . . Oh my! Get out of the way please! . . . It's running . . . bursting into flames [*Loud whooshes of gas explosions.*] an . . . and it's falling onto the mooring masts and all the folks in between . . . This is terrible . . . This is the worst . . . one of the worst catastrophes in the world. [*More screams and shouts.*] . . . Oh! . . . This is flashing twenty . . . oh four or five hundred feet into the sky . . . It's a terrific crash ladies and gentlemen. [*Commentator breaking down.*] The smoke and the flames now . . . and the plane is crashing to the ground not quite to the mooring masts . . . Oh the humanity . . . and oh the persons screaming around me . . . I don't even . . . [*Commentator now crying.*] . . . I can't even talk to people whose friends are on there . . . It's . . . It's . . . It's . . . Oh! I can't talk, ladies and gentlemen. [sic]
>
> (Morrison for WLS, 1937) Distributed *The Aviators* 1991

Herbert Morrison's broadcast demonstrated radio's power to convey the emotional impact of the events that make news. He was unable to hide his grief at seeing a human disaster unfolding around him and he was able to immediately identify in an emotional way with the relatives of the people dying in the inferno.

The transcription represents only a few minutes of a series of dramatic recordings. Morrison ran out to the scene to interview fire officers and survivors. He and his engineer Charley Nehlson filled forty minutes of discs with live commentaries, explosions, screaming and interviews. Morrison found a German passenger who had jumped from the airship's cabin unscathed and whose personal account was translated live by a friend at the aerodrome. NBC invited Morrison into their studios the following day to reflect on what he had witnessed and the entire recording was networked across the country. Fortunately, the unexpurgated record of that broadcast survives and can now be obtained on compact disc.

More than a year later Orson Welles remembered the impact of this broadcast when directing the adaptation of the *War of the Worlds* by H.G. Wells. He instructed the scriptwriter Howard Koch to build the story around a contemporary broadcast and to reproduce the contemporary sound motif of music programming being interrupted by urgent live news broadcasts. On 30 October 1938 many millions of Americans tuned into the CBS network and heard a convincing and almost too real account of a throbbing phenomenon that had descended into a pit of a field in New Jersey. A reporter called Karl Phillips appeared to be at the scene of a major incident at Grover's Mill Farm:

[*Background sound of sirens and crowd noise.*]
KARL PHILLIPS Ladies and Gentle . . . May I? . . . Ladies and Gentlemen . . . Ladies and Gentlemen. Here I am – back of a stone wall that adjoins Mr Wilmot's garden. From here I get a sweep of the whole scene. I'll give you every detail as long as I can talk and as long as I can see. More state police have arrived. They are drawing up a cordon in front of the pit. About thirty of them. No need to push the crowd back now. They're willing to keep their distance. The Captain's conferring with someone . . . I can't quite see who. Ah yes. I believe it's Professor Pearson. Yes it is . . . Now, now they've parted and the Professor moves around one side studying the object while the Captain and two policemen advance with something in their hands. I can see it now. It's a white handkerchief tied to a pole. A flag of truce if those creatures know what that means. What anything means. [*Loud electronic type noises.*] Wait a minute. Something's happening. Some shape is rising out of the pit. I can make out a small beam of light against the mirror. [*Throbbing sound continues.*] What's that? It's a jet of flames springing from that mirror and it leaps at the advancing men. It strikes them head on. Oh lord, they're turning into flames.

[*Loud screaming.*] By the fields. . . . The gas tanks of the automobiles. It's spreading everywhere. It's coming this way now. It about twenty yards to my righ. . . .

[*Silence.*]

(Script published in *Cantril* 1966)

Orson Welles had instructed his actor to study very closely the Herbert Morrison commentary on the *Hindenburg* disaster. A disc recording was repeatedly played to the actor in a CBS news booth to help him rehearse for the live drama broadcast. This dramatic script captures some of the basic truths of effective and immediate radio news communication. It underlines the need to communicate in the bunches of words that make up spoken English. It's a vivid pastiche of the value of describing the specific detail and painting the picture for the mind of the listener through words. It also demonstrates the emotional relationship between the radio news broadcaster and the listener.

This is very personal. It means that the reporter's feelings are almost invariably experienced by the listener. Orson Welles proved that this great medium could be used to fool and manipulate. The world forgave him and hailed him a genius after a twenty-four hour period when it had accused him of being a charlatan and a criminal.

A few years earlier a frustrated newspaper reporter called Richard Dimbleby was trying to tell the BBC how to get its act together with radio news reporting. He was bumptious enough to send his advice to the BBC's Chief News Editor Mr John Coatman after the BBC had informed him that they would not be needing his services 'for some time'. Richard Dimbleby set out in 1936 some of the basic principles of radio news gathering and they are as pertinent today as they were then:

I suggest that a member or members of your staff – they could be called 'BBC reporters, or BBC correspondents' – should be held in readiness, just as are the evening paper men, to cover unexpected news for that day. In the event of a big fire, strike, civil commotion, railway accident, pit accident, or any other major catastrophe in which the public, I fear, is deeply interested, a reporter could be sent from Broadcasting House to cover the event for the bulletin.

At the scene, it would be his job, in addition to writing his own account of the event, to secure an eyewitness (the man or woman who saw it start, one of the survivors, a girl 'rescued from the building') and to give a short eyewitness account of the part he or she played that day. In this way, I really believe that News could be presented in a gripping manner, and, at the same time, remain authentic. . . . The principle of enlivening news by the infusion of the human element is being followed in other spheres, as you know.

(Dimbleby 1975)

Six months later Dimbleby joined the BBC in the lowly position of an assistant in the Talks Department. The BBC had made little progress developing a news-broadcasting system. Six years earlier the national press and two leading agencies – The Press Association and Exchange and Telegraph – had allowed the Corporation to transmit a 6 o'clock evening bulletin.

Two editors and two sub-editors were allowed to prepare the bulletins from a direct supply of agency tape rather than material edited and packaged by the news agencies. But there was an appalling lack of journalistic values in an unself-consciously amateur operation. The BBC's Review of the Year in 1930 was happy to declare:

> When there was not sufficient news judged worthy of being broadcast, no attempt was made to fill the gap, and the announcer simply said 'There is no news tonight.'

This reference was to the immortal declaration one Easter holiday:

> Good evening. Today is Good Friday. There is no news.

The BBC was held in contempt by Fleet Street journalists.
Major news stories affecting the course of Europe were conveyed in slow ponder-ous tones by dinner-jacketed announcers who sounded like the ushers at a funeral:

> German troops made a formal entry into the dimilitarized zone on the left bank of the Rhine. [*Pause for 3 seconds.*] Berlin states that no reoccupation in force is intended and that only small detachments have marched in as a symbol that the last shackle of the Treaty of Versailles has been broken.
>
> (BBC Radio 4, 'The Friend in the Corner 1936' broadcast
> 25 November 1992. Producer: A. Wilson)

Throughout the 1930s, news bulletins continued to be credited with their agency source and a typical news broadcast for 1936 would begin in this way:

> FIRST VOICE The second news copyright by Reuter, Press Association, Exchange Telegraph, and Central News.
> SECOND VOICE Fighting in the University City of Madrid appears to have gone on more or less all night. Fighting has also been resumed west of Madrid in the Casa del Campo and directly south of Madrid. In the south the insur-gents' success is considerable.

Not many people realise that the first full-time employee responsible for news at the BBC was a woman. Vita Sackville-West described Hilda Matheson as 'a sturdy pony'. Dr Fred Hunter makes the poignant observation that nowadays she normally, 'appears in books about other people's lives where she features, usually, in a lesbian relationship with someone better known than herself'.

Dr Hunter observes that she helped develop the concept of the scripted talk and was instrumental in putting the voices of the outstanding writers of the 1930s to air including James Joyce. She had a background in MI5, not unlike many employees of the BBC from the past to the present day. (Investigative journalist David Leigh exposed the permanent presence of an MI5 security intelligence officer at Broadcasting House who vetted all employee applications, advised on intelligence matters and monitored the activities of BBC staff. The story was splashed across the front page of the *Observer* in the early 1980s and any discussion of links between BBC journalists and the intelligence agencies is still an extremely sensitive subject.)

Hilda Matheson was not a journalist. She was determined that the BBC should be committed to the avoidance of sensationalism. There was a painfully slow accumulation of resources. In 1927 the Exchange Telegraph news agency, which later became known as 'Extel', allowed one of their tape machines to be installed at Savoy Hill. By 1930 the 'newsroom' clattered to the sound of all the main news agency machines. She did secure the agreement of government departments to supply information direct to the BBC instead of via Reuters and the PA although it made BBC bulletins sound utterly boring. They began to resemble a sort of government press release gazette. Her decision in 1928 to commission a former assistant editor of the *Westminster Gazette*, Philip Macer-Wright, to assess the potential of an independent BBC news section was a fundamental development which has been rather overlooked by many published researchers. His eleven-page document emphasised the need for 'accredited experts' on financial, sporting, scientific and legal matters. In this regard he was sixty years ahead of John Birt. If John Birt had ever cared to read this document he would have done well to note Macer-Wright's observations about the appeal of human interest news which is simply and attractively conveyed. He also recommended news bulletins written for the ear and Hilda Matheson did everything she could to adopt his suggestions.

Despite her establishment credentials Hilda Matheson was left wing for the period. She believed in the League of Nations. She had sympathy with socialist experiments and she was an advocate of the avant-garde in art and literature. She was an early feminist. John Reith began to resent her 'red credentials'. He was relieved when she departed after a row over his refusal to allow Harold Nicolson to eulogise James Joyce's *Ulysses* in a radio talk. Matheson was followed by a 31-year-old Oxford intellectual with no journalistic experience called Charles Siepmann. In 1932 Edgar Holt arrived. He at least had worked on a newspaper. But it would be decades before a woman again had so much responsibility for news and current affairs within the BBC chain of command.

Richard Dimbleby was fortunate in joining the BBC shortly after news had been separated from the Talks department. The new boss, John Coatman, had been professor of Imperial Economic Relations at the London School of Economics, but his lack of journalistic background did not prevent him increasing the number of bulletins broadcast and recruiting journalists from national newspapers such as the *Manchester Guardian* and the *Belfast Telegraph*. The News Section also had one full-time woman – Elizabeth Barker, the daughter of a Cambridge professor. Twenty-seven-year-old Ralph Murray joined from a Bristol newspaper and his linguistic abilities meant that he was sent to cover the Saar plebiscite where the German-speaking population was being asked if it wanted to join the German State. During the 9 o'clock news he hoped to stick his microphone out of the window where he had arranged a group of demonstrators to repeat their yelling of the slogan: 'The Saar is German'. This was achieved in a live transmission even though his 'rent-a-mob' did not begin chanting when they were given their cue.

Dimbleby was joined by Charles Gardner and David Howarth and they formed a subversive group committed to breathing life into the BBC's news-gathering operation. They developed a technique of sending reports back to Broadcasting House by telephone. Dimbleby also developed an unofficial network of stringers out of the petty cash fund.

The burning down of Crystal Palace in November 1936 offered Richard Dimbleby the chance to put his principles into action. The story broke after London's *Evening News*, *Standard* and *Star* had put out their last editions. The BBC's outside broadcast unit was set up in Sydenham. Dimbleby's lively, urgent voice was one of many struggling to communicate the detail and scale of the disaster. Here is a flavour of what listeners to the BBC could hear that evening.

FIRST REPORTER   It's a pretty clear sky and a moment ago it was almost a full moon looking straight at me across this blaze of smoke and ruins. It's a fairly strong wind. I'm up on top of a house here. There's somebody got an umbrella behind me trying to shield the microphone and I don't quite know how much wind on the microphone you may be getting, but I hope you can hear what I am saying. [*Noise of a fire engine bell.*] There goes one of the bells. I don't know what that means. By the North Tower there . . . there's eh . . . the . . . the . . . um . . . building just between me and the South Tower. . . . It's beginning to blaze up and I can see smoke coming through all the tiles on the roof. . . . What? . . . They tell me there's something wrong about my position by the microphone. I must find out. . . . There's a dickens of a lot of wind on the microphone but eh . . . I don't quite know what I do. Hold on a minute. I'll try and open my coat and see if that'll protect it. Not that there's a great deal more to tell you because eh . . . unless I keep you here all night. . . . It's still blazing all over. The whole framework. But I don't know if it's much good keeping you up to hear about that. . . . I think the only thing to say is that so far as I know and I haven't . . . eh . . . bothered the experts because it seems to me on an occasion of this sort. . . . [*Sound of a voice in the background saying*] 'Oi, oi oi!'. . . . Hello! Here is an expert.

SECOND REPORTER   Not at all an expert but I've just come round from the other side of the building right in the gardens and the brick . . . the wind is blowing huge clouds of great acrid smoke right across and sparks that are travelling a matter of two hundred yards and there's glass all over the grass and those strange shrouded females that inhabit the parks are being peppered with flying sparks and flying glass. . . . Ah!

FIRST REPORTER   Well, I don't know if there's very much more to say. I'm told that the first part of the broadcast was probably missed. I might as well explain to you that this was just fixed up at very short notice. We're on the top of a roof on the West Terrace of the Crystal Palace. [*Sound of people coughing from the smoke behind.*] So . . . unless . . . Oh . . . There's something more to be said. . . .

SECOND REPORTER   Just let me tell you one more story and that is that the South Gallery, the flames are moving at the rate of about a yard in every five minutes and the roof has come crashing down in sections. The floor is getting under . . .

FIREMAN   Get away from the hose please!

SECOND REPORTER   . . . and is beginning to heat up under the fireman's boot . . .

[*Pause. First reporter off-mike can be heard saying* Are you ready. . . . Have you got any more?]

FIRST REPORTER ON MIKE   Well, I don't think we can keep you here any longer. I suppose this will go on blowing through the night. There'll be policemen here on duty all night. There'll be the firemen working. And so . . . we'll now leave the Crystal Palace and go back to Broadcasting House.

(BBC Radio 4 'The Friend in the Corner 1936' broadcast
25 November 1992. Producer: A. Wilson)

This is a very quaint and rather amateurish outside broadcast. Occasionally, the BBC's reporters succeed in homing in on some interesting detail, but there is a rather awkward, apologetic and very English upper-middle-class attitude to a major news event breaking out before their very eyes. With hindsight it is an enormous pity that Richard Dimbleby and David Howarth were held up in traffic jams and so could not be the observers providing this report for BBC listeners.

This broadcast betrays the lack of experience and confidence in the British broadcasters. The second reporter completely dries up at one point. He has not even been introduced properly, largely because the BBC had a bizarre policy of avoiding giving names to their observers. The description lacks concrete geographical perspective and any communication of the news story. There is no report on casualties or the scale of the firefighting operation, and there is a complete lack of human interest. We can hear the shout of a firefighter telling people to get away from one of the water hoses, but we are not told why. We have no clear idea how far away the observers are from the blaze. Clearly this is a story that would feature heavily in radio's natural breakfast broadcasting position. But all the efforts of the BBC's first major outside broadcast operation are going to be frustrated by the moratorium on news broadcasts from 1 a.m. until 6 p.m. the following day.

The language used by the observers is quite peculiar. 'Those strange shrouded females that inhabit the parks' is presumably a reference to stone statuettes which were part of the garden furniture at Crystal Palace. Given the appalling sexism and discrimination against women that was part of the culture of early broadcasting, the expression becomes a very apt description for the prevailing attitude to the role women played in broadcasting. They were very much a case of being 'strange shrouded' creatures that only 'inhabit parks' and the domestic environment. As has been mentioned, they also made very good secretaries.

The BBC began by recruiting from Oxford and Cambridge universities. The self-perpetuating elitist nature of recruitment remains a current feature of BBC staffing. The majority of senior management are still drawn from the public schools and two universities. Richard Dimbleby was an exception having spent all his working life prior to joining the BBC working in newspapers.

The BBC had no permanent correspondents in Europe during Hitler's rise to prominence. Here William L. Shirer of the American CBS network became a pioneering voice bouncing his reports by short-wave to Ed Murrow in London who would use BBC facilities at Broadcasting House to retransmit by short-wave across the Atlantic to New York. BBC observers would accompany government ministers to international conferences.

Here is the script of another delicate and rather quaint broadcast from a BBC reporter attached to foreign secretary Anthony Eden's delegation at a League of Nations conference on the future of Danzig in 1936:

> Will you excuse your observer from Geneva tonight for some hesitations or stumblings. But today has been a long day of much negotiation and moreover in the Council Chamber from which I have just run to the studio there has just been a most unfortunate incident . . . an incident in which the President of the Senate at Danzig after a passionate speech as he was going out and after saluting with the Nazi salute . . . Mr Eden . . . which caused some slight laughter in some quarters of the press, made a very rude gesture indeed at the international press. An incident at which Mr Eden presiding over the Council found it in him to say: 'We did not see any incident and if there was one it would be more in keeping with our dignity if we did not notice it.' It was an incident

with which the corridors of the League of Nations are even now buzzing.

(BBC Radio 4 'The Friend in the Corner 1936' broadcast
25 November 1992. Producer: A. Wilson)

This flapping BBC observer minces through the broadcast rather like an amateur actor playing Lady Bracknell in Oscar Wilde's *The Importance of Being Earnest*. The affected delicacy undermines the authority and purpose of what is supposed to be a critical report on the status of the League of Nations and the threat to the stability of Europe from Nazi ideology. The late 1930s were a painful time for the BBC and nothing underlines the need for professional broadcast values more than the notorious commentary by Lieutenant Commander Tommy Woodroofe on the illumination of the fleet at Spithead in 1937. The long and short of this disaster was that Lieutenant Commander Woodroofe was thoroughly drunk by the time he reached the microphone:

> At the present moment . . . the whole fleet is lit up. When I say 'Lit up' I mean lit up by fairy lamps. It's fantastic. It isn't a fleet at all. It's just. . . . It's fairyland. The whole fleet is in fairyland. Now if you'll follow me through . . . if you don't mind . . . the next few moments you'll find the fleet doing odd things.' [*Pause lasting 11 seconds.*] I'm sorry, I was telling people to shut up talking. [*All the lighting on the fleet is switched off to provide a black backdrop of darkness so that the firework rockets could have a suitable contrast.*] Oh. It's gone. It's gone. There's no fleet. It's . . . It's disappeared. No magician who ever could have waved his wand could have waved it with more acumen than he has now at the present moment. The fleet's gone. It's disappeared . . . I was talking to you in the middle of this damn . . . [*Cough*] . . . in the middle of this fleet and what's happened is the fleet's gone and disappeared and gone.

(Pile 1979)

Broadcaster Commander Stephen King-Hall criticised the lack of resources for news gathering in a *Radio Times* article in 1937 entitled: 'If I Ran the News'. He advocated the setting up of a team of permanently-based foreign correspondents. He talked about the BBC asserting 'its duty and its right to give its listeners the best news service in its power, and a news service of a character which cannot be given by any other medium'. Coatman's reply was headlined: 'I Do Run The BBC News.' His rather hysterical riposte that the previous article amounted to 'impossible policy, impossible finance, and impossible technique' probably sealed his doom. Like most BBC employees who were out of favour, he was exiled to the North Region. This meant that BBC Radio News was at last edited by a real journalist. R. T. Clark took over. He was a military historian and classical scholar who had cut his journalistic teeth on the *Manchester Guardian*.

The necessary professionalism in radio news broadcasting did arrive and much of the drive came from and was being provided by Richard Dimbleby and his colleagues in the news division. By the end of 1938 the news department had 31 staff, 95 minutes of broadcast time between 6 p.m. and 1 a.m. and Dimbleby's philosophy was beginning to bring some life to the news broadcasts. His reports of the Fen Floods in East Anglia were recognised in press reviews and the quality of his detailed, descriptive writing began to be recognised. However the progress in news gathering did not extend to controversial industrial, economic, social or political issues.

The BBC's Director General Sir John Reith disliked any notion of controversial and sensational news coverage and he was terrified of offending the political establishment. His conservative tastes in broadcasting and belief that the BBC should dictate the cultural agenda resulted in a collapse of BBC audiences at weekends in the face of the more popular commercial services of Radio Normandy and Luxembourg being broadcast from the Continent. Radio Normandy was owned by the International Broadcasting Company which in 1937 occupied 100,000 square feet of office space at number 37 Portland Place, only a few doors down from Broadcasting House. The company also had three garish outside broadcast vans with the words 'Radio Normandy 274 M' emblazoned on the side. These were used to travel the length and breadth of Britain and Richard Dimbleby must have looked upon them with enormous envy and frustration. It does seem strange that these excellent broadcast resources were not used to compete with the BBC in the field of news coverage. They appeared to be used exclusively for light entertainment, music and personality programmes. In fact the broadcast schedules for both Radio Normandy and Radio Luxembourg suggest that neither service was interested in developing a radio news policy.

Sir John Reith was succeeded as BBC Director-General by F. W. Ogilvie and there had been a brief temporary leadership by the deputy Director-General Sir Cecil Graves. Between 1936 and 1939 the BBC failed to send a reporter to cover the two most important international stories of the decade: Mussolini's invasion of Abyssinia and the Spanish Civil War. This is despite the fact that the national newspapers and news agencies had sent reporters. The BBC's news policy was directed by the home editor, R. T. Clarke, who faced continual political pressure and his resistance to this at one point provoked his dismissal. This was reversed after a campaign for his reinstatement. The British government was hoping for a Franco victory. BBC news terminology changed the description of Franco's forces as 'rebels' to 'insurgents'. Just as the Civil War was about to end with Franco's victory the BBC despatched Richard Dimbleby to the French–Spanish border in the Pyrenees.

This was Dimbleby's first exposure to the miseries and deprivations of war. The experience stimulated the awakening of a substantial and significant talent in radio journalism which is timeless in its elegance and dignity. He demonstrated an extraordinary flair for broadcasting coherently and movingly without a script. He established a tradition and standard which has been emulated between 1992 and 1995 by the BBC's correspondent in the former Yugoslavia, Martin Bell.

The distinguished BBC broadcaster Wynford Vaughan-Thomas said:

> His reporting of the Spanish Civil War was to bring home perhaps for the first time to many ordinary listeners what war now meant to ordinary people just like ourselves. The suffering was no longer confined to a battlefield in some far away country.

> RICHARD DIMBLEBY   There was an old woman at the international station at Cerbere last night, the colour of deep sunburn with dirt, and with dried blood on her face from a deep gash in the cheek. She told me how she and her children, and eight other old people, lay down in the open to sleep. It was, she said – and for this I can vouch – bitterly cold. In the morning, three of the group, one of them her daughter, were dead.
>
> Everyone is agitated. The headquarters of the Prefect are like a beehive day and night and Sunday included. I've had to wait a total of nearly nine hours for two special permits. I've shown them altogether exactly forty-seven times. I've been asked if I carry arms six times and searched for them twice. And once last night someone mistook me for a refugee and tried to push me into a cattle truck. Perhaps that sounds vaguely amusing, but the whole refugee problem here is intensely serious and . . . and pathetic is the only word I can think of. Perhaps tragic is better. There are thousands of them, mostly women and young children coming over the three main entrances. Cerbere, Le Pethus and Beau Madame. Some of them are in the last stages of exhaustion. They are hungry, starving many of them. And numbed with cold. In spite of the work of the relief organisations and the scheme of evacuation which the French authorities have put into operation quite successfully, many of them have died.
>
> (Dimbleby 1975: 85, and audio: 'The Voice of Richard Dimbleby' 1966, introduced by Wynford Vaughan-Thomas)

Richard Dimbleby accomplished another, live ad-libbed recording on the border with the sound of battle reverberating in the distance:

> Since early today, early this morning when we got here, there have been crowds, masses, lines of wretched torn and tattered soldiers going by, throwing down their guns, their rifles, and their pistols at the guard at the frontier. . . . There are machine guns by the dozen stacked up just behind me. I'm sorry I'm pushing my way past the Garde Mobile in order that I can get well onto the frontier line. He didn't like it very much. . . . Now here comes another procession of lorries. I'm going to stop for a moment and let you hear it go by.

The first one is a Russian lorry piled high with soldiers. . . . The second carries a heavy gun . . . and behind it is another lorry with two soldiers in it, four or five sheep and a cow piled up in the back of the lorry. This would be almost comic if it weren't such an appalling tragedy to watch down here.

(*ibid.*)

In these reports Richard Dimbleby began to define the basic tenets of excellent radio journalism: the ability to write journalistically with an eye for concrete detail and a feel for spoken English; the ability to present in clear, human style with a voice which is pleasing to the ear; the ability to think and speak with fluency and honesty; the ability to use sound to convey the images and atmosphere of the world around you.

During the Italian invasion of Ethiopia the American network CBS had a correspondent called Robinson McLean sending despatches from a broadcast facility set up by Swedish engineer Ernest Hammar. However the reporting was not particularly distinguished. The following example betrays racism and partiality: 'So far as I can see, it doesn't really matter much when men, women, and children die, whether they are killed in a real war or merely a glorious little expedition to bring civilisation to a savage tin pot kingdom lost in the African hills'. Emperor Haile Selassie used this facility in Addis Ababa to communicate to the rest of the world and on one occasion appealed to American citizens to boycott Italian products.

Richard Dimbleby's work for the BBC was only on the periphery of the Spanish Civil War. H. V. Kaltenborn achieved the first action war report in an abandoned farmhouse between Franco's forces and the Republican army on the outskirts of Irun. An incredible link by telephone line to Bordeaux, Paris, London and Rugby in the British Midlands and then a short-wave transmission to New York carried a fifteen-minute ad-lib during the thick of a battle:

In a moment or two, when the machine gun which has been barking all evening sounds again, I will stop talking for a moment in order that you may get something of the sound of this civil war as it continues even through the night.

(CBS, 3 September 1936, Bliss 1991: 79)

Kaltenborn went on to be one of the most famous on air radio analysts. The radio commentators of the 1930s such as Elmer Davis, Fulton Lewis, Junior, and H. R. Baukhage have been described as 'the oracles' of broadcasting. They included Dorothy Thompson who broadcast anti-Hitler, anti-dictator commentaries with passion and elegance:

When the dictators commit what to the rest of the world are crimes, they say there is a higher justice. They claim the justification of national necessity and emergency. We do not think that such justice is higher. We think it low.

(CBS, 3 September 1936, Bliss 1991: 61)

However, the radio became a platform for right-wing opinion as well, and two broadcasters have been credited for making a charismatic impact on listeners which alarmed liberal politicians. Former Louisiana governor Huey Long used biblical language and a colloquial style to develop his huge following. He was nicknamed 'The Kingfish' which had something to do with his call-sign or slogan 'Every Man A King'. Here is an example of his direct style of communication:

What is the trouble with this administration of Mr Roosevelt's and of Mr Johnson, Mr Farley, and Mr Ashworth and all their spoilers and spell-binders? They think that Huey alone is the cause of all their worry. They go gunning for me. But am I the cause of their misery? Well, they're like ol' Davy Crockett who went out to hunt a possum. He saw in the gleam of the moonlight that a possum in the top of the tree was going from limb to limb. So he shot him. But he missed. He looked again and saw the possum. He fired a second time and missed again. Soon he discovered that it was not a possum that he saw at all in the top of that tree. It was a louse in his own eyebrow. And now it is with the PWAs, the GWAs, and the MRAs, the HAAs, JUGs and the GIMs and every other flimsy combination that the country finds its affairs has been entangled and no one can recognise. More men are out of work than ever. The debt of the United States is going up ten billion more dollars. There is starvation. There is homelessness. There's misery on every hand and corner. But mind you in the meantime, Mr Roosevelt has had his way. He's one man that can't blame any of his troubles on you at all. He's had his way. Back down in my part of the country if any man has the measles he blames that on me. But there's one man who can't blame anything on anybody but himself and that's Mr Franklin Delano Roosevelt. [sic]

(NBC 1935, This Was Radio 1990)

His broadcasting career was ended by assassination in 1935.

Father Charles Coughlin began preaching on the radio from a little Detroit radio station in 1926. By 1936 his broadcasts were being networked to an audience of millions from a power base in the Midwest. His opinion on one issue led to the White House receiving 200,000 telegrams. He was something of 'a prophet of doom' filling the vacuum of insecurity caused by the Depression. Here is a flavour of his extreme rhetoric:

FATHER COUGHLIN   We have endeavoured to teach you time and time again that there can be no coming out of this Depression until what you earn goes to sustain your wife and your children. But somehow an' another you are satisfied to sustain the wives and children of those who do the coining and regulating of money, who live in their palaces and travel in their yachts. You want that. You voted for that. You have that and it's time you take that. Good evening. God bless you.

ANNOUNCER   You have just listened to a broadcast address delivered by Father Charles Coughlin of Royal Oak Michigan.

(WJR Detroit 1936. CBS networked, *This Was Radio* 1990)

Father Coughlin became discredited after making a series of anti-Semitic remarks, and by 1940 neither sponsors nor radio stations were interested in accommodating his oratory.

Alistair Cooke, a former English journalist on the *Manchester Guardian*, who became a naturalised American, has maintained the world famous 'Letter From America' to BBC audiences in Britain and ABC audiences in Australia over several decades. (In 1990 the commercial London speech station, LBC, opened up an editorial position for former *Sunday Times* editor Andrew Neil during the peak breakfast-time period. He would present live by ISDN link from his home.) The radio editorial remains an important component of broadcast journalism.

The 1930s saw a considerable amount of censorship and political interference in Australian radio news commentaries by the minister responsible for broadcasting – the Postmaster-General. It has been argued that the PMG assumed the role of moral guardian of listeners' homes. Broadcast organisations exercised self-censorship and found themselves castigated by the free press. One of the most celebrated rows in 1938 concerned Judge Foster who wrote a commentary for the ABC attacking the 'organised church', government, censors and 'military officers'. The speech was anti-establishment, controversial and it was banned. It condemned the government's handling of the anti-war and anti-fascist speaker Egon Kisch who was declared an illegal immigrant when he tried to enter Australia. Another storm blew up when the left-wing commentator Constance Duncan was dropped by the ABC. A confidential report was uncovered in later years describing her as being 'anti-British' and believing in some form of 'Christian Communism'. The Sydney commercial station 2KY was taken off the air in December 1938 after the PMG objected to a series of allegedly biased commentaries. 2KY was styled as a station of the labour movement. The PMG himself was compared to Hitler for his 'anthropoid idea of thrusting all women back into the kitchen and making them have children'. 2KY was able to resume broadcasting after making a suitable apology.

The BBC in Britain was also responsible for clumsy censorship of mainly left of centre speakers. In 1932 communist trade unionist William Ferrie strayed from his written script during a live talk on working class conditions. He began to reveal to the general public that the BBC had censored his talk. Engineers and producers quickly faded him out. He wrote later: 'I was particularly incensed at their demand that I should put across that the slogan "Workers of the World Unite" is not a revolutionary slogan. I also refused to drop my h's and talk as they imagine a worker does.' Here is a classic example of the patronising force of BBC middle to upper-middle-class culture which derives some frisson at the idea of giving a broadcast opportunity to 'workers'. The BBC imposes its preconceived notion of the identity of working-class language and values. Blatant political censorship is dressed up as 'trying to improve the language . . . so that it meets BBC professional standards'. Blacks and Asians in contemporary Britain have a similar problem. Actors find they are typecast in the role of rioting, drug dealing, delinquent teenagers, or the 'victims' of arranged marriages. Racial Equality awards are collected by white, middle-class, Oxbridge-educated programming executives. Black and Asian reporters find they rarely rise beyond the newsdesk or reporter level of career advancement. There are a few exceptions but the number in the higher chain of executive command and decision making does not reflect the proportion of non-white population in contemporary British society.

The BBC completely buckled under political censorship in 1935 when they objected to the idea of left-wing politician Harry Pollitt responding to the leader of the British black shirts Sir Oswald Mosley in a series on the British Constitution. The government regarded Pollitt as a revolutionary subversive. The BBC, through its governors, tried to exercise editorial independence, but the Postmaster-General reminded Sir John Reith that the licence fee was due for renewal and it would be sensible to go along with government demands. In August 1939, Labour leaders Hugh Dalton, Harold Laski and the TUC general secretary Walter Citrine wanted to broadcast a special message to the German people. They were blocked by Director-General F. W. Ogilvie who had been a Conservative MP.

The Spanish Civil War was an experiment by the German Nazi regime in the exercise of the military tactics of Blitzkrieg. It was the prelude for the Second World War which provides the next section of this book charting the development of international radio journalism. It represents the Golden Age of radio before television replaced sound as the pre-eminent medium of mass communication. It can be argued that the Golden Age of radio journalism has never really come to an end. Listening surveys continue to demonstrate that people turn to their radios for the first news of the major events which affect their lives.

Part III

Practice skills and contemporary practice

Chapter 13

The voice and the A to Z of presentation

An examination of the history of radio news broadcasting demonstrates that a good voice and an ability to communicate with authority is a vital prerequisite for progress in a highly competitive profession. Radio news journalists need to be almost obsessive about improving voice presentation. There is never a justifiable time to be complacent and there would be few current practitioners who could not gain by continued training and education.

The radio journalist uses all the skills and attributes of the actor when broadcasting and this book recommends that the radio trainee achieves a radio actor's standard of presentation. The voice should be regarded as a Stradivarius violin. It can be played beautifully after years of technical and creative training. In the wrong hands it can sound like a cat on heat at the beginning of summer. The clarity and quality of vowel, consonant and diphthong sounds need to be improved and polished all the time.

There are two excellent acting training manuals written by Cicely Berry for Virgin. Cicely Berry has been the Voice Director of the Royal Shakespeare Company. *Your Voice and How to Use It Successfully* and *The Actor and His Text* would be worthwhile investments. The broadcaster who can project and perform Shakespeare on the stage will be able to communicate the events of the world with authority and dignity.

I would recommend students and professional broadcasters taking up acting and speech classes. If this is not possible, the voice mechanism needs to be exercised and trained regularly. At least an hour each day needs to be set aside for voice exercises. Breathing and voice control need to be natural skills which require no mental preoccupation during live broadcasting.

In the early days the radio journalist should learn to concentrate and deconstruct a script that is to be broadcast live or prerecorded. The first thing to do is simply to read and understand it. This process should not be silent. It should be done as if the broadcast were actually taking place. The journalist should psychologically absorb and evaluate the significance of the script and its mood. As in radio acting the key factor is the thought in the presenter's mind and not the mere fact of vocal enunciation. The journalist should make a mark for key words and expressions which are vital to the communication of the story. These are the points which need emphasis. At this stage the journalist will have to make quick decisions on changing the script to make it more natural and appropriate to the style of spoken English. Live radio news broadcasters need to learn the habit of reading ahead so that while the voice is enunciating certain bunches of words, the mind is taking in and preparing for the following bunches of words. It is not a difficult skill and gives the radio news broadcaster control over any script that has been thrust in front of the microphone without any time for preparation. This is quite common in radio news with breaking stories. Word-processing mistakes are common when typing under pressure. I was caught out on one occasion when my failure to read ahead resulted in the delightful expression 'Streaking Style-workers' instead of 'Striking Steel-workers.' I also remember the time when a local radio news broadcaster was caught out on April Fools' day morning. He had a habit of arriving late for the early morning shift. The 6 a.m. bulletin was, therefore, not properly prepared. At about 5.50 a.m. he raced into the teleprinter room to tear off the overnight bulletin sent by the local Cleveland Constabulary in north-east England. He had no time to rewrite it and decided to present it live. It seemed like a lead story . . . something about a man run over by a roadworks machine and in hospital with serious injuries. The broadcast proceeded in this way:

> [*Sound of the news jingle.*] And now the local 257 news. A 37-year-old man is being treated for serious injuries at Middlesbrough General Hospital this morning after an accident during the building of Grangetown's bypass. Robert April from Norton was in collision with a one-ton steam-roller and is now recovering in wards 4, 5, 6 and 7 . . . . Ah . . . . Shit!
>
> (Radio Tees 1979)

At this point the news presenter had realised too late that he had been well and truly taken in. His incompetence was compounded by an on-air expletive.

The A to Z of Presentation

What are the mistakes that radio news presenters tend to make?

A   They speak too fast. This leads to the mouth running away from the brain and inevitable stumbles and fluffs. All you have to do is slow down. When you slow down consciously you will find there is more time to establish control over the material. While it is good to be nervous, try not to allow your nerves to subconsciously turn your presentation into a race to get it finished.

B   Authority is not conveyed by shouting. News may be urgent but it is not so much of an emergency that you have to scream into the microphone and spread emotional panic as well as burst ear drums amongst your listeners. The idea of authority is established through a measured balance of speed of delivery and tone of interpretation.

C   You are in fact reading, but presentation is not reading. The communication style is the same as if you were talking to a friend. This is the way you 'lift the words from the page'.

D   If you do not understand what you are presenting it will not work. Even actors train themselves to pretend to understand what they are performing so that gobbledygook sounds dramatic and truthful.

E   Always read aloud your scripts to try them out even at the risk of turning the newsroom into a tower of Babel. Most newsrooms have an affectionate atmosphere of human madness. More people apparently talking to themselves is not going to make any difference.

F   Do not mumble. Stretch the mouth, hit your consonants and articulate your vowels, but watch the plosives such as ps and bs which can pop the mike. Heavy, close microphone breathing can also cause 'popping'.

G   We think in phrases. So think in phrases and present in phrases. Phrasing is the key to effective presentation and pacing.

H   Always write out figures to avoid the brain having to translate numerals into words. It is easy to confuse a million from a billion when it is in numerals. I once heard a disastrous news bulletin when the news presenter started by saying fifty thousand people had died in a cyclone. He corrected himself and then said it was five hundred, but then corrected himself again and said it was a thousand. By the end of the bulletin he had gone back to his original figure of fifty thousand. The figure was in fact fifty. Zeros can be confused with the letter O and this could lead to embarrassing misunderstandings.

I   Deeper, lower bass voices carry more psychological authority. This is why Baroness Thatcher had voice training to lower her voice when she was Prime Minister. When we panic and lack a sense of control the pitch of our voice is raised and we can sound like Donald Duck inhaling laughing gas. To achieve lower base authority you only need to experiment with practice runs by varying the tone of your voice and reducing the musical register for more serious stories. You do not need to maximise the base frequencies on the equalisation facility. You do not need to smoke forty cigars a day washed down with buckets of malt whiskey. Smoking is bad for the voice because it can cause cancers at all points along the breathing mechanism, the carbon dioxide reduces the amount of oxygen getting to the brain, and your listeners are not going to appreciate a news programme interrupted by a coughing fit.

J Add the diaphragm to your conscious breathing style. It is a wall of muscle towards the bottom of your torso. If you contract it at the same time as using your chest muscles you will find that your breathing is better.

K Do not forget to have a positive attitude to communicating on the radio. You have to enjoy talking to people and listening to people. You must be interested in what you are talking about, or people will switch off.

L You may admire other presenters. You may want to talk like them, but never, ever try to be somebody else on the radio. When I started out I happened to think that another broadcaster had an excellent style of presentation and I spent months trying to copy it. During the interview for my first job I did rather well because I was so nervous I could be nobody but myself. But when I started trying to sound like my hero, the results were risible. The news editor called me into the office and said 'Whatever you're doing, stop it now, or go back to London'.

M When you are being yourself, always remember that you have to be at your best. You may be facing a divorce, the house may have burned down, the cat may be sick, and you might be one number away from winning the lottery, but listeners do not want to be infected with your angst. They want to hear somebody who is involved in communication and interested in talking to them. If you turn up for work in broadcasting and the first thing you think about is how long it is before you can go home, then you should be doing something else.

N Variety is the spice of life. Communicating news involves a variety of ideas, human experience, and emotion and if your voice does not have variety, the monotony of listening to you will mean that your presence on the air waves with be a monopoly of one. You and no listeners.

O Make sure you know how your equipment works. If you are self-operating and your mind is preoccupied or worried about how the mixing desk works, you will be setting up an artificial barrier between you and your listener. The same rule applies to conducting interviews with a portable recording kit. Before going on air, you should always do a full studio check and verify that every item of equipment that is going to be used operates properly and you know how to operate it properly. I know this might sound a bit like a doomsday approach, but take the trouble to identify the things that can go wrong and how you would recover. For example if you talk and nothing can be heard in your headphones and there is no response from the PPM, it is likely:

1   Your mic fader is not up.
2   Your mic switch is not on.
3   Your channel has been switched to line or an alternative broadcasting mode e.g. from transmission to post or pre-production.
4   You are on pre-fade.
5   Your headphone monitor control has been switched to zero.
6   There has been a massive power failure in the studio.
7   Your Peak Performance Meter is broken.
8   You have gone deaf.

P   Why do people listen to voices on the radio? What are they hoping for? What do they appreciate? And how do they listen? You need to understand that listening is an individual experience. Community listening is a thing of the past. The radiogram or wireless set stopped being the main focus of domestic entertainment from the middle 1950s onwards. Car radios and the tranny, Walkmans and the fact that many households have several radios dotted around the kitchen, bathroom, bedroom, living room, mean it is a moving source of communication. It travels with people as well as resting on the pillow in people's bedrooms. But in the end presentation is a personal relationship with one person. Of course, the essence of journalistic communication is to give information. Not surprisingly this is still an important reason why people listen to the radio. However, radio is still a hit in media terms because it provides companionship and entertainment. This helps people to relax and enjoy themselves. This is why most people are listening. So your attitude has to respect and participate in the idea of being a companion and a source of informative entertainment.

Q   Play with the full potential of the microphone. Practice speaking softly and loudly and moving within its pick-up field while talking. Know your microphone well. It is one of your best friends in the studio. You need to know if it is uni-directional or cardioid. Uni-directional mics will mean that if you carry on talking while picking up a pile of newspapers from behind you, you will effectively 'drop out' of the pick-up field. You could imagine that the microphone is the face or ears of your companion, the listener. Use the full array of facial expressions when communicating to it. Smile, frown, or look enquiringly. I tend to draw the line at kissing the microphone. It is taking intimacy too far and will make an unpleasant noise.

R How to relax; otherwise known as warming up. You do not need to yodel from the top of the Matterhorn, or for that matter memorise Hamlet and recite it in Central Park. You do not need to run twenty-five miles every morning and undertake fifty press-ups before going to bed. But there are a few things you could do to help. For example, ten deep, relaxing breaths using the diaphragm and loosening up the neck, chest, jaw on exhalation. Try not to hyperventilate. If you are into meditation, that always helps. But do avoid picking up a mantra while on air and dissolving into a meditative state during a news programme. Dropping the head and rolling it very gently clockwise and anti-clockwise is a time-honoured and rather effective relaxation exercise. Have a go at singing expressive ballads. I do not recommend screaming Janis Joplin style. A ragged, sore throat is a hindrance and leads to coughing or voice failure. Little voice exercises are a good idea. Practice ad-libbing around the subjects in your programme. It is not a good idea to do live presentation with low blood sugar levels and a deep sense of hunger. The voice will be dry and the mouth smelly which is not good for your reputation in a dual presentation programme. It is also important to avoid going on-air immediately after a *grande bouffe*. An over-fed stomach bubbling with gases can lead to burping, strained swallowing, and drowsiness.

S Never, ever drink alcohol prior to or while on-air. The same applies to soft and recreational drugs. Alcohol does not stimulate, it depresses and separates the brain from the voice in an alarming cascade of dislocation which can be disastrous for a station. In any event, listeners can normally detect both consciously and sub-consciously when someone has had a tipple. Muscles in the mouth and voice box lose their tightness.

T Avoid eating toffee or tough, syrupy chocolate immediately before transmission. Hard or soft cheese sandwiches are not a good idea because the cheese tends to stick between the teeth and any 'gluey'-type food affects the texture of voice communication, since it takes time for the enzymes in the mouth to break down the food cells for digestion. Still water is fine, fizzy drinks have their obvious dangers. Baked beans or meals that stimulate bowel activity can lead to embarrassing sounds emanating from another human orifice. Not only is it unpleasant for your fellow presenters and guests, it can lead to corpsing (uncontrollable giggling) and undermine credibility as well as severely embarrass the station if this is combined with a sombre newscast.

U Never swear anywhere near a radio studio or recording environment. When things go wrong there is always a temptation to use expletives. But it is a temptation which will lead to instant dismissal. If you fluff, find an inoffensive way of stopping and starting again. I well recall the colleague who had a habit of always using the 'f' word when tired and fluffing towards the end of his shift. He let out a roaring 'f' when completing a prerecorded news package on the affect of bad weather on traffic and transport one Easter Monday. The expletive even penetrated the soundproofed walls of the news booth. Unfortunately, in the rush to complete the package for transmission, he accidentally left in this out-take which was broadcast throughout the London area on a religious holiday. Within minutes newspaper reporters had contacted Mary White-house (a leading UK campaigner against violence and sex on radio and televi-sion) and the Archbishop of Canterbury and were queueing up outside the radio station's entrance with their photographers. I think a two-week suspension for the offending radio journalist was a rather lenient penalty.

V   Pronunciation is vital. Get it right. Do not offend your listeners by getting it wrong. There are good pronunciation dictionaries. The BBC publishes a guide to good pronunciation. Foreign names need to be researched by contacting the embassy of the country concerned and producing an accurate phonetic representation of the word or name which can be read easily by yourself or a presenter.

X   When you fluff, do not draw attention to it. It does no harm to apologise but, if it is really unimportant, just ignore it and carry on with the programme.

Y   Avoid blaming other people for making you look foolish when things go wrong. The listeners do not want to know that your news bulletin editor is a wally and that is why the story you have read does not make any sense. Equally, they do not want to hear that your programme is not going so well because the station bosses are skinflints, who have cut your fee and do not replace equipment which is breaking down. The station bosses do not like hearing this sort of thing and that is why you will probably be looking for new horizons if you do.

Z   Zero tolerance for indulgences really. You are being self-indulgent if you spend more time expressing your opinions about music, or the subjects of your phone-in programme instead of listening to the callers. It is also self-indulgent to burden your programme with endless pally chats with fellow presenters. The listeners will begin to think your radio station has aban-doned them. Of course, such discussion is justified if your colleague has just been cast in the latest Robert de Niro film, been rescued while adrift for two weeks in the South Atlantic, or become engaged to Diana, Princess of Wales. Another indulgence to avoid is babbling aimlessly during talkback programmes. You might like the sound of your own voice, but listeners will be irritated by it, particularly if it is voicing banalities and nonsense.

Chapter 14

Using portable equipment

The radio journalist needs to invest in basic portable recording equipment and the recorder and microphone need to be the journalist's third arm; always there and ready to be used at any time. The two leading professional cassette-recording machines are the Sony Professional Walkman and Stereo/Mono Marantz. The Walkman has the advantage of being small enough to slip into a handbag. The Marantz is bulkier and heavier. These machines need to be fed with a high quality microphone which is robust and does not have any problem handling noise. The microphone cable leading to the machine needs to be thick and insulated against 'cable rattle'. I would recommend spending money in this area. Beyer, Shure, AKG, and Electro-Voice manufacture excellent outside broadcast mics. If you are buying the Sony package, I would recommend spending more money on a portable stereo microphone rather than settling for the ECM-909. At the time of publication such an investment for both recorder and microphone was in the region of £350 in the UK. There are major differentials around the world because of the relative value of currencies.

Radio journalists should know the characteristics of their portable recording equipment so well that they can operate 'blind' and in the dark. The mic and recorder should always be ready for recording. Radio journalists are never off-duty. Anything might break before them. The opportunity to record and describe news stories as they happen will always be there and you would never forgive yourself if you had not been equipped to operate properly. Lindsay Taylor was working for Independent Radio News in London in 1987 when returning home after a long shift. As he began to drop off amid a packed rush-hour train, he noticed that it trundled through King's Cross without stopping and smoke was billowing down from the empty staircases. He jumped out at Euston Square and ran back to the scene of a major disaster. He was able to describe the brave attempts of firefighters to save lives. His non-stop reporting that night won him the UK Sony Reporter of the Year Award and a job as a senior correspondent for ITN's Channel Four News.

The expansion and development of digital technology has created a market for portable digital recorders. Sony sell a version with a UK price of around £500. Whilst the quality of the recording will be superior to cassette and reel-to-reel, there should be a note of caution that digital recorders are more delicate machines and can easily develop circuitry problems after the rough and tumble of a news story assignment. Sony have also developed an impressive 'mini-disc' facility in both portable and flat-bed components. Denon have also manufactured a professional mini-disc rack for studio operations. The mini-disc technology appears to be more stable than DAT. It is a digital recording and playback process using laser tracking which avoids the problem of dust, contamination, and poor head alignment which tend to create the unusable digital squelching sound feared by all those radio producers who depend on digital mastering via DAT machines. A mini-disc can store up to seventy minutes of stereo sound in a huge number of files which can be individually titled and read on a small display. There is an excellent software programme which provides useful back tracking and parameter information about the tracks. Cueing is not as instant as reel to reel playback and high speed computer hard disk operations, but it is a useful addition to the repertoire of audio equipment. The portable mini-disc machines record a beautiful digital stereo sound for documentary and creative projects or soft news stories but I am still wary that they would not be robust enough for the rough and tumble news scrum scenario. A little bang on the side can upset the laser recording process. In my experience door-stepping situations can result in a lively succession of heavy bangs on portable recording units from bodies, cameras and other moving and stationary objects. However some of my students recently reported that several UK independent radio stations were using these machines for actuality news gathering and no technical problems were reported. In addition they noticed the BBC local radio reporters enviously observing the tiny mini-disc machines which are light and can fit into the palm of a hand while they were struggling with a condition known as 'Uher shoulder'. This is a stoop downwards caused by the weight of the old and very heavy reel-to-reel machine combined with the pain of the leather shoulder strap cutting into the skin.

The sturdy Uher reel-to-reel tape recorder may be rather old-fashioned, but it still has its appeal as a versatile outside broadcast machine. I think by the beginning of the new century, Uhers are likely to be consigned to recording technology history and will be affectionately remembered by the old timers in the same way that veterans of Second World War journalism can recall the charms and hazards of the BBC midget units which cut sound onto discs using a needle. At the moment the main advantage of the Uher is the quality of the record and playback heads. The origination of a good quality quarter-inch recording in this way means that you have something with a higher broadcast standard than cassette. Uhers are likely to be cheap secondhand fare as soon as the broadcast industry becomes fully dedicated to digital operations. There is a time-honoured technique of editing on a Uher using a splicing block, razor blade and chinagraph pencil. You will need a little Philips screwdriver to remove the metal plate covering the heads. At the time of writing many BBC local radio stations still used Uhers and reel-to-reel technology. Fast and immediate news reporting requires the transfer of sound recordings quickly to broadcast. If the on-air studio is geared up for quarter-inch tape transmission, a reel of Uher recorded tape can simply be slapped on the studio tape machine ready for immediate transmission. Cassette and digital recordings have to be copied and edited. The pause facilities on many cassette machines are not nearly as accurate as on reel-to-reel recorders. However, digital software editing is developing so fast that broadcast stations now have access to computer hardware and software combinations which can achieve higher sound quality and equal cueing standards.

What are the things you need to avoid and watch out for when operating portable recording units?

A It is amazing how many people embark on assignments without taking cassettes, tape and recording supplies with them. It is embarrassing to endeavour to 'take level' from an interviewee only to discover that the cassette chamber is empty.

B Another common mistake is that operators do not check their machines before they leave the station. You need to check the batteries in the recording machine and the battery supplying the microphone. The check has to include a full recording and playback of sound. You might discover that the microphone cable is frayed and a wire is about to disconnect from the plug or microphone. You need to check that the machine is calibrated according to the type of cassette you are using e.g. chrome dioxide, ferric or metal oxide. You need to make sure the microphone attenuation is at zero and not minus 20 decibels which is a setting for recording in very noisy locations. Make sure the vari-speed is not switched on and operating.

C Before you go out check that you have 1) the recorder, 2) the microphone, 3) headphones for monitoring while recording, 4) cassettes or recording units, 5) some spare batteries, 6) any necessary audio leads for specific connections you are likely to make when covering the story, e.g. output from PA system, pooled audio source such as the facility supplied at New

Scotland Yard by the Metropolitan Police in London, or audio feed from closed-circuit television panel at US state court centres which allow broadcasting of legal proceedings, 7) pen and paper.

D   Always record one minute of 'wild track' or atmosphere at the scene of interviews. This gives you flexibility in editing or a cross-fade bridge to hide untidy edits, and difficult inflections.

E   Always monitor on headphones because you will be hearing from the play-back head exactly that which is being recorded through the record head. You will be able to make adjustments to the recording level and position of the microphone. Trusting your ears is probably more important than trusting the VU meter which you should always be monitoring to make sure the record level is not too low and not too high.

F   Keep the microphone in a sensible position so that there is a minimum ratio of three to one between direct sound (voice of interviewee) and indirect sound (atmosphere and background sounds).

G   Maintain a consistent position of the microphone in relation to the interviewee's mouth. Try not to ram the mic up your guest's nostrils or wave it in front of your guest in an intimidating manner. Three to four inches (approximately 10 centimetres) is normally a good distance between mic and subject. If you double the distance the diminution in quality will be a multiplication of four rather than two. This is the inverse rule of physics.

H   Never leave the scene of a news story or interviewee without checking that what you need and recognise as story actuality has been recorded. If it has not, then you may have the chance to do it again and you have to try.

I   In media scrums do not be shy – 'get in there'. Your job as a radio reporter is to acquire the news. You are a failure if you fail to record it adequately when television and radio competitors were more successful. Where there is heavy competition between the electronic media, I would recommend using a boom monophonic uni-directional mic with specific pick-up characteristics of anything between 6 and 12 feet.

J   Where there is competition for interviews you have to be assertive and ask the questions that you want to ask. It is irritating when reporters all ask different questions at the same time. But there is a way of catching the eye of a news protagonist by asking questions they want to answer and then hitting them with questions they do not want to answer last. In this way you can maintain a stream of questions and answers which the TV news organisations have to use. Make sure your microphone has a station identification/ call sign block so that you achieve free advertising for your station. You will find that as soon as you ask the question that the subject does not want to answer they have a habit of ignoring it and inviting alternatives from your competitors.

Chapter 15

Writing radio news

Glossary of Radio News and A to Z of Vocabulary and Principles

Introduction

This is a fairly lengthy module but it is rather crucial to the craft and practice of radio journalism.

Language is everything. Here are the principles which are germane to the practice of radio journalists throughout the English-speaking world. I have drawn on the knowledge of experienced radio journalists in Britain, Australia, Canada, USA, South Africa and New Zealand as well as from my own background. I have also attempted to cover the practice in state-funded, public and commercial news organisations.

You have to understand that radio news is a different language from written English. Radio English is spoken English. It is the way we speak the language as opposed to the way we write it. This does not mean that we have to abandon the discipline of correct spelling, good writing and communicating essential grammar. But because one of the primary aims of radio news English is clarity and precision, you have to understand that people generally communicate more clearly with the voice than with the pen. If you remember to keep your writing style in the way that people talk rather than the way people write you are on your way to winning the battle. There are lots of time-honoured maxims about writing radio news which I will gladly trot out because there is a considerable amount of truth in all of them.

KISS stands for 'Keep it simple, stupid'. Do not write your story, tell it. Or if you are writing radio English you should be saying and writing 'Don't write your story, tell it'. Spoken English involves eliding words in expressions such as 'he'll', 'we'll', 'he's' 'they're' and that is how it should be written for radio news. Bear in mind that eliding negatives may not necessarily be such a good idea. With a fast pace in presentation it is possible that some listeners may not pick up the 'nt' sound in such an elision and as a negative meaning can be hugely significant in communication, the potential for misunderstanding is such that it would be wiser to always state the 'not' in radio news English. A simple conversational style using the idiomatic flavour of the English language, but not vulgar expressions, is what you should be aiming for.

Another well-known maxim that relates to the idea that you should tell your stories rather than write them in a literary way is this:

'Tell'em you're going to tell'em.
Tell'em.
Tell'em you told'em'.

Short sentences are best. People communicate in short 'bunches of words' not in long meandering sentences with sub-clauses divided by commas. You might like to try out a little experiment. Record some natural conversation and then transcribe. Analyse the grammar and sentence construction. It will prove my point. This is a principle that will help you to write well in radio news. You will find that clarity and effective phrasing can be achieved by breaking up the longer sentences into shorter ones. It is a good idea to express one idea with one sentence.

In spoken English you will find that people tend to use simpler, shorter words whereas in written English there is a tendency to use multi-syllabic, Latinate words. There is a useful trick of the trade to judge quickly the style of vocabulary you have used in your radio news writing. Turn the page upside down. Look at the length of the words rather than the content. A pattern of long words will reveal itself. Simple, straightforward words are the ones which people will readily understand. Avoid adjectives and adverbs. These words can over-gild the lily. They can also exaggerate, sensationalise and eventually cheapen the method of communication. You want to avoid the verbosity of prose, poetry and academic writing at all times. It is not a good idea to begin radio news stories with prepositions or 'inverted sentences'. By the time the listener gets to the point of the story, he or she will have forgotten the opening sub-clause.

Always use the present active tense. Radio news and journalism is about what has happened, not 'was' or had happened. No radio news story should begin with 'Yesterday'. The better style of sentence construction is subject/ verb/ object. The active mood is present, urgent and authoritative rather than abstract, vague and often belonging to the past. That is for historians and not for journalists.

One of the basic rules of radio communciation is that if you bore the listener and fail to generate interest, the listener will find better things to do. So it is vitally important that you should think of a style of writing which provokes thought and images and holds the listener's attention. One very experienced radio news editor from New Zealand once told me that in radio news you must avoid the 'Ah, Shit!' point. That is what some listeners will exclaim when they are hearing rubbish on the radio, and while uttering this expletive they will be twiddling their radio dials to hear a rival news service.

I have mentioned the need to be exciting and interesting in the way you paint images in the mind of the listener. This requires a style of writing which emphasises the concrete rather than the abstract. Think of building pictures in the mind of your listener. It is advisable to look at the way you develop the story with concrete points so that the flow is both logical and moving the story on in a way which is easily understood. Radio news is different to the bottom end of the pyramid structure of newspaper news English which involves a descending scale of the hierarchy of importance. The Who, What, Why, Where, When, How syndrome applies to radio news as much as it does to newspaper news, but in radio there is no question of subbing out the less important facts from the bottom upwards. In whatever time frame you have, you need to have written succinctly and with a structure that expands the story deftly and clearly.

Remember that your audience is only one. The one listener and not Wembley Stadium, the Sydney Opera House, or Madison Square Garden. Avoid any risk of being patronising and underestimating the intelligence of your audience. Respect for your listener is vital for a continuation of the relationship of trust between listeners and a radio news service.

A common mistake made by many people when they start writing radio news is to overload the story with too much information. Too many numbers and statistics are difficult to take in quickly. Try and aim for a precise backbone of factual structure rather than an overweight flabby mass of information. Only use abbreviations that are readily identifiable. If there is an organisation with a long title that is also known by an abbreviation, then it is good practice to state the proper title once and then the abbreviation follows.

The intro is undoubtedly the most important part of any radio news story. This is the first bunch of words the listener hears and it should contain the essential angle and point of the story whether it is the beginning of a cue for a voice report, a piece of radio news actuality or a 20–30 second piece of copy. I would recommend that you concentrate on this aspect of the writing. Consider carefully what is the latest information which is the foundation of the news story and then find a quick and precise way of telling it. Imagine that you only have 5 or 10 seconds to tell a friend some urgent news. Under this pressure how would you express yourself? Try your intro out with colleagues. Discussion and crafting leads to better writing.

Once you have found the nucleus of your story you only need to follow with a paragraph with additional information that brings more clarity and precision to the intro. In Australia, the intro is sometimes referred to as 'a lead'. The next paragraph or bunch of words is a development from the first two paragraphs and could contain a final point to indicate the end structure of the news piece if your copy time is limited to 15 or 20 seconds. Another paragraph, or bunch of words can provide extra illuminating detail. I referred earlier to the pyramid image in news writing. Newspaper handbooks sometimes talk about the 'inverted pyramid' so that you have the idea of the mass of important information at the top with the more peripheral 'tapering out' to an unimportant tip at the bottom. With this image the newspaper sub-editor is encouraged to lose the less important paragraphs at the bottom of the story text. It could be argued that with radio you need to look at the pyramid image 'right way up' with the tip at the top demonstrating a shorter, concise and concentrated point of intro writing. The larger body of the story is developed with points of relevance and background adding layer after layer. Whatever way you look at the image of the pyramid you must not forget the qualitative approach you need for intro writing.

A good writing style in radio news is one that avoids clichés and 'journalese'. A well-known British journalist Keith Waterhouse once talked about endemic journalese – which he defined as using pompous vocabulary to give stories more gravitas and 'tabloidese' – which he defined as a sort of 'selling' English. You must remember that when people communicate to each other with spoken English they do not speak in the style of the British *Sun* and *Daily Mirror* newspapers. Has a friend ever said to you: 'Shock, horror, my last ditch bid has been slammed by an evil tot who exposed my sleaze and probed my tragedy'? A BBC style guide for regional television and radio once stated 'Avoid clichés like the plague'. Good advice.

I have attempted to arrange an alphabetical sequence of key words and expressions in the language of radio journalism and I have also included some subsidiary topics such as 'War reporting', and 'Sexism'. A living language is constantly changing and you have to bear in mind that spoken and written English transcends many different countries. Some theorists are speculating that at the change of the millennium the most potent resource in the world will have shifted from natural resources, industrial and manufacturing output, and military strength to the communication of information. Communication depends on language. George Orwell recognised in his novel *1984* that political control depends on the use of language and its linguistic, semiotic connection with thinking. It is in this context that the selection and style of language in broadcast journalism is of the utmost importance.

A, an A is the indefinite article before consonants and before aspirated h's such as 'hunt' and 'hotel'. However, you need to use **an** before vowels and unaspirated h's in words like 'hour' and 'honour'.

Abbreviations As indicated earlier there are a few well-known acronyms which can stand on their own in terms of first appearance, but you need to be careful when the audience changes in knowledge and background. In the UK, abbreviations such as NATO, the IRA and the BBC are recognisable and established shorthand for their proper titles. This would not be the case for an international audience. MP can represent Military Police or Member of Parliament. NPR in the United States has a similar policy. CIA to Americans is obvious. But to citizens of another country it might be better to say 'Central Intelligence Agency' and then continue using the acronym. The BBC World Service does not like its journalists saying US and UN instead of United States and United Nations, but Independent Radio News in Britain would have no qualms.

Abortion Abortion is a highly charged moral, religious and political subject. It is easy to betray your personal views with the language you use. So you should say 'aborted foetuses' rather than 'unborn babies'. How do you describe people who campaign for a woman's right to an abortion? Do you say 'Pro-Abortion' or 'Anti-Life'? Of course not. Women who have to have abortions are in a position whereby they are not necessarily promoters of abortion. Their circumstances are such that they feel they have no choice. People campaigning on their behalf feel they should still have the right to this distressing medical operation. 'Pro-Choice' would be better. 'Pro-Life' relates to anti-abortion campaigners, so you must be careful to define the sides in this debate very carefully. NPR cautions the avoidance of labelling. The organisation that anti-abortion campaigners belong to is called 'Pro-Life', but it does not make them any more pro-life than the women who wish to preserve the right to abortion.

Absolute farce I have never seen an absolute farce. Are you sure that you have seen one?

Acid test This is a specific chemical test to discover the presence of an acid. It is being over-used in the description of important events or challenges.

Active Active is always preferred to passive mood. For example 'The plane has crash-landed'. Not 'The plane crash-landed five minutes ago'. Not 'The plane had crashed five minutes ago'. The passive voice in English is said to have a tendency to weaken the force and direction of news writing. Compare: 'The school children have been told to stay at home by the Head Teacher', to 'The Head Teacher has told his pupils they have to stay at home'. There are instances when good writing style would accept the passive mood. This is true when the object is more important than the subject, when the subject is unknown, when the action is more important than the subject and object, or when the style of writing requires delicacy and diplomacy. The perfect tense is better than the past historic.

Additional In radio news you want to reduce the number of syllables in your words, so it is much better to say 'more'.

Adjectives Use sparingly because of the danger of creating a charged meaning. Descriptive values may give colour and unfortunate sub-text to a news report which would be unacceptable to many listeners who had other opinions on the subject.

Admit It is not a good idea to use the word 'admit' instead of 'said', because it could be implicit that the subject has been trying to hide something.

Adverbs Like adjectives, they should be avoided where possible. They can imply biased meaning. Your listeners may disagree with your assessment that a speech has been 'brilliantly made', or the package of 'severe' reform proposals was 'implemented harshly'. Little adverbs like 'up' and 'out' are being added to verbs such as 'rest', 'sound' and 'try'. Leave them out.

Adverse, averse 'Adverse' means unfavourable, and 'averse' means being opposed to something. You can be averse to joining the Republican Party but the polls can have an adverse showing for the Democrats.

Advocate People do not advocate for better employment conditions, they advocate better employment conditions.

Affect/effect It is intriguing how many journalists confuse the noun with the verb. You can influence people by affecting them. If there is a plan of action which you want to implement, you can effect it. Your influence may have effects. The effect is the outcome.

African-American/Afro-Caribbean The acceptable and polite way of describing black Americans and black Britons. 'Nigger' and 'negro' are widely regarded as pejorative and insulting words even though 'negro' was in use by Black Americans themselves until the 1970s. The famous 'dream' speech by Dr Martin Luther King in Washington DC in 1963 is peppered with it. In Britain black citizens do not like being called 'coloured'. 'Afro' or 'African-Americans' and 'Afro-Caribbean' are interchangeable with 'black'. People with an Asian origin prefer to be called 'Asian Americans' or 'Asian Britons'. Words like 'Paki', 'chinky' and 'brown-skins' are insulting and demeaning.

Age There are many news organisations, particularly the BBC and NPR who do not like the age being stated before the person's surname. 'John Brown, who's twenty-five' is preferred to 'twenty-five-year-old John Brown'. No radio news organisation should tolerate the newspaper style of 'John Smith, forty-nine, has lost his job as president of the County Water Company.' It is worth being cautious about adjectival values of age such as 'girl', 'old', and 'middle-aged'. Some can cause offence.

Agreement Plural nouns can cause problems when combined with plural verbs. You need to appreciate the distinction between: 'The jury has decided on a not-guilty verdict' and 'but the jurors were not unanimous'. The confusion can be extended with pronouns that do not agree with plural nouns. For example 'The team has won', should not be joined with the expression 'but they were not jubilant'. You should write 'It is not a jubilant team tonight'. Beware of nouns such as 'number' and 'public' which should be followed by singular verbs. There are also some commonly-used plural nouns that are incorrectly given singular verbs when they should be plural: You should be writing 'The data are' and 'the media are'. Finally, on the subject of agreement, remember you agree 'on a' proposal or 'to a' proposal, but you do not 'agree a proposal'.

AIDS This is becoming one of the world's most well-known acronyms. We do not have to say 'the disease AIDS'. It stands for acquired immune deficiency syndrome. This is a disease which weakens the body's immune system and it is caused by the human immunodeficiency virus or HIV. So this means that HIV virus and AIDS disease are redundant. The most important *faux pas* in news language is to refer to people with AIDS as 'victims of AIDS'. It is better to write in terms of AIDS sufferers or AIDS patients. There is also a danger in talking about 'innocent victims of AIDS' when you are overwhelmed with a sense of pity for children or people who have contracted AIDS through a blood transfusion. Bear in mind that AIDS tests are for the presence of antibodies that the body has developed to fight the virus. A positive test is only an indication of infection with the virus and does not mean people have AIDS. This means there is a distinction between people who are HIV Positive and people who have AIDS.

Air raids It has been said that there are many English languages. This is certainly true in relation to the difference between American English and British English. The BBC does not like the Americanism 'air strikes'. 'Air raids', 'air attacks' are preferred, although commercial newsrooms in the UK tend to absorb and adopt a wide range of Americanisms.

Al In Arabic 'Al' means 'the'. So there is a redundancy when saying 'the al Aqsa mosque'. The same applies to the owner of Harrods, Mohammed Fayed, or the Fatah Palestinian organisation. There is still a tendency for journalists to refer to Mr Al Fayed or the Al Fatah organisation.

Alcoholic You sometimes hear the bizarre expression 'reformed alcoholics'. Anyone unfortunate enough to suffer from this condition would prefer the idea of being a 'recovering alcoholic'. 'Reformed' implies some criminal past.

Alibi You need to remember that this word has a specific purpose in relation to a defence in a criminal case. It is evidence that when something took place the defendant was elsewhere. Avoid the informal use of the word in terms of an excuse, or justification.

Alleged This word is never a way of ensuring a defence to libel in the UK and you must be cautious by not using the adjective to saturate your copy with a sense of suspicion. The word is only two syllables. It has been known for some people to use the affected pronunciation of 'uh-le-jed'. 'Allege' is over-used when combined with a verb which already conveys the sense of a charge or allegation. If a suspect is accused of murder, there is not much point saying he turned up at the courthouse charged with 'allegedly murdering' his business partner. When your story concerns accusations that have been denied, it is good practice to ensure that follow-up stories are balanced with the fact of accusation and denial. You should also remember that people are accused of a crime and not accused with a crime.

All out effort If the cricket team is all out, I suppose they would make a special effort when bowling the other side's innings. I am sure you can find a better adjective to describe the effort.

Alternate and **alternative** When Abigail and Beatrice take turns to present the *News at Ten*, they have agreed an alternate arrangement. When the news editor can choose between Abigail and Beatrice then they become alternatives rather than alternates.

Ambassador If you are fortunate enough to have this job, remember to remind people that you are Ambassador to Papua New Guinea and it is only a job and not a title. Frown when they call you Ambassador Crook, and smile when they call you Mr Tim Crook, the ambassador to Papua New Guinea based in Bougainville.

Ambulances Ambulances do not rush to the scene of the accident. The same can be said of police cars and fire engines. They are not exactly strolling when answering an emergency call and in any case, the word rush can imply a lack of preparation or panic.

America In Britain, news journalists should be precise about the United States and Canada. North American is given to understand that you are including both these countries.

Americanisms These are sometimes spoken of as 'a plague'. I think there is a danger that it becomes a somewhat paranoid preoccupation of British people who have never forgiven the American colonists for rebelling against King George III towards the end of the eighteenth century. The 'English dialect' which emerged after the Revolution is dismissed as ignorant, sloppy and vulgar. But this attitude belongs to a certain kind of person. They are snobbish and pompous and, like the poor, will always be with us.

This means that you might be advised to avoid stretching words when writing radio news in Britain. Say instruments instead of instrumentation. Try not to 'ize' everything and if you do, make sure you do it with an 's'. Americans tend to turn nouns into verbs. There are many people in Britain who would prefer to use 'pure' verbs. It has been said that English English is the product of a rich mixture of Latin, Anglo-Saxon, Norman-French, and Scandinavian influences, whereas American English is 'a dynamic expression of individuality'. Australian English is sometimes relegated to the status of a sheep shearer's or bushwacker's vernacular spiced with slang and familiarities. My feeling is that there should be respect for all forms of dialect and the British, North American, New Zealand, South African and Australian traditions of English usage are equally valid. Radio journalists working in New York should take the trouble to say 'sidewalk' instead of 'pavement', and write 'the casualties were taken to the hospital' instead of 'taken to hospital'.

The same need for respect applies to pronunciation. It does not take a British radio journalist much trouble to say 'skejool' for schedule if presenting an American news bulletin as opposed to 'shedule' when presenting a bulletin in London. The radio news journalist should be sensitive to public opinion on usage and have an instinct for when an imported word is gaining in popularity and current use. You can 'meet with' your American friends or you 'can have a meeting with' your British friends, but there is no need to get worked up about the issue of saying 'you met' your Australian friend yesterday or whether you will 'meet up with' your South African friend tomorrow. In recent years there has been a considerable expansion and use of Afro-American and Afro-Caribbean English among young people of all backgrounds and I do not think there should be any more reason to resist their popular current use (or should I say 'usage')?

So when you are visiting the United Kingdom you visit your friends, whereas you visit with your friends in New York where the Democrats are on the stump, while Labour are campaigning for victory in the General Election. In New York you move to do something, whereas in London you just do something and if things do not go so well in New York you will be hospitalised, but in London you will just enter hospital. When you are travelling you get on an airplane in New York and get off an aircraft in London. On the sidewalks you might bump into a heist, but on the pavements in Westminster, London, you will come across a robbery. At the time the traffic will be congested, but in New York there will be gridlock. The robbers may have gunned down a security guard in Harlem, but in the City of London the gang simply shot the unfortunate guard. You could find that your publisher is headquartered in the Trump Tower whereas in London it is based in Canary Wharf. Your trip has been prompted by that latest book that you have authored in New York but written in London. You could be in central London, but in the centre of New York you will be downtown. Your publisher may well host you a dinner, but in London you would be given a dinner and when in New York you meet with them and in London you meet them, you can discuss your American pay hike and your British pay rise. In London you would be currently, but in New York you would be presently hoping that the publishing company had in New York sanctioned, but in London approved the huge increase in your fee. When negotiating your payment you should try to avoid slating your editor in New

York, but you might like to criticise the editor in London. Keep your rhetoric in New York polite and your language in London courteous. In New York you will be using moot points. In London they would be debatable. So your aim is to beat your rival authors to the highest advance in London, whereas in New York you would be handing your fellow authors a stupendous defeat. The fall in New York is probably the best time to impact on your finances whereas in London, the autumn is a better time to affect your financial position. Ousters in New York are to be avoided because there you need all the proponents you can get, whereas in London you need to avoid dismissal and look forward to as many supporters as you can find. In New York you will be throwing rocks in Central Park, but in London's Hyde Park you will be throwing stones. But if you lose you could be sick as a parrot in New York, ill as a parrot in London, and crook as a parrot in Sydney.

Amid Some editors in the BBC feel this word is not at all idiomatic and has become redundant and clichéd in expressions such as 'amid tight security'. You should always avoid 'amidst' which really belongs to the age of Shakespeare.

Among When you are talking about 'being between' you are normally considering two concepts or two people. But when it is a question of 'being among people' you are talking about a number which is greater than two. You can also apply the word 'between' in another context. This can be a comparison between one person or concept and several others.

Analysts I am very sceptical about this description. Who on earth is an analyst? This is a question I often ask myself when they pop up as geeky-looking experts on a myriad range of subjects. Are they journalists? Are they journalists who have been given a more professional-sounding description to improve their credibility? Are they academics who have been drawn into a media organisation to become specialist correspondents? If this is the case, why are they not called specialist correspondents? If they are analysts from an outside policy organisation or 'think tank', it is important that listeners know where they are coming from.

Another This word tends to be over-used. If fifteen commuters have been killed in a coach crash, there are twenty wounded not 'another twenty wounded', because another twenty killed commuters cannot be wounded and still alive. 'Another' suggests an addition to the number of people who have been affected within a particular period. But the time factor can become irrelevant. What would you mean if you wrote that 'another soldier has been killed in Northern Ireland'? Is this in relation to thirty years of violent conflict or a recent campaign by the IRA?

Anticipate Many journalists use this verb as an alternative to expect. They are different. To 'anticipate' means dealing with or forestalling an event, although it has to be accepted that the meaning of 'waiting for' and 'looking forward to' is becoming more commonly used even though it was not the strict original meaning of the word.

Antisocial Antisocial behaviour harms society. If you are unsociable you simply do not like being in the company of others and the word 'unsocial' relates to the idea of unsocial hours or working pattern. Some journalists inadvertently swap these words around thinking that they mean the same when they clearly do not.

Anxious Some journalists have a habit of confusing 'anxious' with 'eager'. You should bear in mind that 'anxious' is more appropriate in a context of worry or apprehension and 'eagerness' relates to a more positive and enthusiastic desire for something. For example: 'The Police Chief's family anxiously waited for news of the outcome of his operation', and 'The Police Chief is eager to return to work'.

Anybody's guess I am not sure that it is necessarily. Why do you not simply say 'I don't know and I would be surprised if anyone else does.'

Apparently Apparently this is becoming one of the most over-used redundancies in common English usage. Apparently we rarely think about why we use the word. Apparently it just goes on and on until a radio news journalist has the good sense to ask 'To whom is it apparent?' Then perhaps we shall be hearing less of this word in the years to come.

Appraise, apprise When senior civil servants inform the Prime Minister that the country is going bankrupt they are apprising him or her of the situation. When people are considering their redundancy package so that they can assess its financial value, they are appraising the offer, or proposal.

Argentina is not 'the Argentine'. The BBC prefers to describe Argentinians as Argentines.

Arms Remember the difference between being owned and made. If you are in the habit of disclosing the origin of the weaponry in terms of manufacture you need to be careful about how even-handed you are. Emphasis on the Russian-made weapons could betray bias if you do not also identify the western-made arms. It is a little like emphasising that an alleged murderer or rapist is black, when white alleged murderers and rapists are referred to by their trade or profession.

Around the table Better to sit at a table since tables are generally oblong, or square.

As sick as a parrot I would not know myself as I have never been a parrot or asked one what it is like. You could be as sick as a dog, but I am not sure whether you or the dog would know what that means.

Assassinate This is a verb which should be reserved for the killing of heads of state or governments. Lesser mortals are merely 'murdered' or 'killed'.

Assistance There is a tendency to over-use the expression 'render assistance'.

This comes out of 'emergencyalese' which is the language of the official police, fire and ambulance services.

Astonished There is a tendency to interchange the word 'astonished' with the word 'surprised'. How can you tell the difference? It is simple. Consider this story: 'Surrey Police say they are astonished to discover one of their officers in a gang of armed robbers arrested on the M25 motorway this morning. The gang was surprised by a police raid at the Box Tree service station.'

At this point in time You could always say 'Now' and you would save yourself more than a second of time and four words.

Attribution It is bad style to leave your attributing clause hanging at the end. Not only is this 'newspaperese', but you can leave the impression in the mind of the listener that a controversial statement has been made by your radio news organisation, before the qualification sinks in. An example of a misleading intro would be something like this: 'Inflation is set to go down by 2 per cent because of successful government economic policy, according to the Chancellor of the Exchequer'. It would be better style to start with the expression 'The Chancellor of the Exchequer says . . .'. Many news editors believe that building trust with an audience requires continuous attribution in all news reporting. This is vital when you receive your information from a country, organisation or state security force which has a specific agenda and political position. If the internal security police of a country says four of their officers have been killed after being ambushed by terrorists you will be stating this as fact with the intro: 'Four members of Russia's Internal Security Police have been murdered after being ambushed by Chechen terrorists.'

This copy is laden with problems. To begin with, you have not sought or received any further independent corroboration. Second, you have used the word 'murdered' which is more charged with moral value than 'killed'. It also implies that you are on the side of the Russians, if in other news reports you say that 'Russians kill Chechens' instead of 'murdering' them. Third, you have described the Chechens as 'terrorists'. Their argument would be that they are patriotic soldiers fighting for their freedom and independence. Fourth, by using the word 'ambush' as a statement of fact you are precluding an alternative account of the incident. Attribution is the solution. This is safer: 'The Russian Internal Security Police says that four of their officers have been killed in a fight with Chechen fighters.'

Axe A bit of a cliché when used to mean 'reduce', 'dismiss', or 'cancel' a service.

Backward National Public Radio (NPR) does not like people going backwards.

Bad and **badly** Some people have a habit of confusing their adverbs with their adjectives and it is common to make a mess of the difference between 'badly' and 'bad'. You can be 'bad'. But what happens when you do not feel so good?

Do you feel 'badly'? Yes, if you mean that you do not have a very good sense of touch. No, if you are talking about bad health. You should really be feeling 'poorly' which is in relation to health more than it is in relation to finances.

Bail and **bale** The difference is simple. You can be granted bail in a court hearing. You can bail out a boat or a business which is going bust. Apparently, you bale out of an aircraft. But in radio it does not make any difference because they sound the same.

Balanced on a knife edge This is a rather painful and very delicate operation which leaves one prone to serious injury. Better to leave it out.

Bankruptcy It is easy to get into difficulties with this word journalistically. It is possible for a company to sue for libel so you must be aware of using the right terminology. A company only becomes 'bankrupt' when a court has formally declared it as such. You need to be aware if the bankruptcy proceedings have been the result of a voluntary liquidation or forced by the creditors who are owed money. The appointment of an official receiver or administrators does not mean that a company has gone bust or bankrupt. It means the court has appointed an official or accountants to manage the company with a view to finding further investors, a buyer or to realise the debtors' assets through trading or selling goods and equipment. You also need to be aware that terms such as liquidation, bankruptcy and insolvency have different legal implications depending on the country you are reporting on. In the USA companies can 'make a Chapter 11 application'. This is a move to achieve legal protection from creditors and does not mean the winding up of business operations.

Banks Avoid the cliché of putting banks in the High Street. The expression 'High Street Banks' is used too much in UK broadcast stories about interest rates and mortgage increases. There are main banks and minor banks and merchant banks and banks that used to be building societies, and they are not necessarily always sited in High Streets.

Banned The BBC World Service is unhappy about radio journalists using this adjective in the context of an outlawed or prohibited organisation. For example, 'The banned IRA' sounds like a pop group.

Basically A despairing phone-in caller to one of my shows recently complained that whenever he heard broadcasters using this word or 'absolutely' when all they wanted to say was 'yes' he felt he was having pins stuck into sensitive areas of his skin. Ninety-nine-point-nine per cent of the time you can cut 'basically' from your scripts and live presentation and there is no loss of meaning.

Basis BBC World Service does not like the expression 'On a regular basis'. They have a point. Is it not more straightforward to say daily, or regularly?

Battledress This is a uniform and it is not good English to say that the Highland regiment fought the action in 'battledress'.

Beat a hasty retreat A rather quaint expression concerning Napoleonic military tactics and relating to the battlefield before the advent of radio communications. It would be better to leave it in its proper period.

Because, since 'Because' belongs to cause and effect relationships. 'Since' belongs to expressions where one event follows another. How does this work in practice? 'The giant crushed the dwarf to death with his foot because he was small and ridiculous'. 'Since he was on his way to the circus, he turned into a garage and filled his tank with petrol'.

Bedouin Remember that this is a description for a desert Arab and remains the same whether singular or plural.

Beg the question Many radio news journalists have a habit of using this expression during Q and As when they want to mean that somebody has evaded a difficulty, or posed and invited the question. The proper meaning would be that somebody has assumed the truth of an argument. It is the same as arguing in a circle.

Belarus Byelorussia or Belorussia is no longer accurate.

Belgium It is important to remember that people from Belgium do not speak Belgian. They speak French or Dutch and those that speak Dutch are in fact Flemish.

Between Often confused with 'among'. What is the difference? Generally, 'between' distinguishes between two people whereas you should talk about being 'among' three or more people. 'Between' can also be used in a comparison between one concept/person/thing and several others. It is good style if the word 'between' is always followed by 'and'. This is particularly true when making a comparison between year descriptions.

Biannual/biennial Some style books recommend saying 'twice yearly' and 'every two years' in order to avoid the possibility of confusion.

Bid Another tabloid word to avoid. It is a conversational noun. You can always say 'try' or 'attempt' instead.

Billion There is the interesting point that a listener could easily confuse hearing 'a billion' with 'a million' because making the sound of 'm' and 'b' involves using the lips. So it is advisable to describe the exact number of millions and ensure that you know when you are referring to an American billion as opposed to an English billion – a thousand million.

Bitter end Whether the end is bitter or sweet is really a matter of opinion. This is a threadbare expression. Do not use it.

Biweekly Danger word. This can mean twice a week or once every fortnight. The confusion means that it would be better not to use this word.

Black This is an acceptable description of non-white people in most parts of the world. 'Negro' is regarded as offensive to African-Americans and Afro-Caribbeans. 'Coloured' is out of fashion and not appreciated, although 'coloured' does have a special legal connotation in South Africa.

Black radio journalism Racial discrimination and systems of apartheid have been highly oppressive for non-white communities in Britain, the USA, Australia, New Zealand and South Africa throughout much of the twentieth century. Non-white journalists have been unfairly excluded from the significant history of radio journalism development. Research is very scarce. The USA saw a significant growth and cultural importance in the Black Press, represented by newspapers such as the *Chicago Defender*, *Pittsburgh Courier* and *Baltimore Afro-American*. Black papers in the south faced the threat of fire bomb attacks and violent reprisals from the Ku Klux Klan. Yet the contribution of the Northern Black Press such as Robert Abbott's *Chicago Defender* demonstrates the historical importance of Afro-American journalism. The *Defender* championed the cause of equality and promoted northward migration. It also foreshadowed modern American journalism techniques by compartmentalising news into sports, editorials, women's news and state news. It would appear that William Worthy was the first black American network reporter in that he made a freelance report for CBS from Moscow during the height of the Cold War in 1954. He was employed by the *Baltimore Afro-American*. Two years later he obtained a visa to enter Communist China and defying a State Department ban broadcast by shortwave to CBS from Beijing. ABC's first black reporter was 54-year-old Mel Goode who was hired in 1962 having been a *Pittsburgh Courier* reporter since 1948. A significant acceleration in recruitment occurred after the race riots of the 1960s. The Harlem radio station WLIB lost five of its black radio journalists to mainstream New York outlets. A similar rise in recruitment of black journalists occurred in Britain after equivalent race riots in the early 1980s. The UK Radio Authority set about licensing 'incremental' stations to serve the non-white communities. Stations such as Choice FM and Sunrise in London produce news programming with a different agenda which matches the news priority you would find in the black newspapers such as *Voice* and the *Asian and Caribbean Times*. ITN's Trevor MacDonald is an outstanding icon for UK black journalists having progressed from local radio in the West Indies, to the BBC World Service and mainstream reporting for ITN from 1973. He now newscasts on ITN's flagship *News At Ten* programme. Up until now there have been no developments to establish news networks serving the non-white communities in Britain. The USA saw the establishment of the National Black Network in 1972 with a presentation of five minutes of black-orientated news on the hour and live coverage of public affairs and sporting events. MBS set up the Mutual Black Network in the same year which served more than fifty affiliates and was bought by Sheridan Broadcasting in 1979.

Blaze This word tends to be an over-used substitute for fire.

Blind You need to put this disability in the right context. People are blind if they are completely without sight. You would be more accurate in many situations to say that a person has partial vision or their sight is impaired.

Blow Back to unacceptable tabloid English again. Although these words have more syllables, it is more precise to say disappointment or setback.

Bolt from the blue A rather colourful expression to describe lightning. But remember that lightning does not strike twice.

Bombshell It becomes rather ridiculous when you report that the breakdown in talks was 'a bombshell' for the Prime Minister when the talks broke down because of a bomb explosion in Belfast.

Boost Are we talking about rockets or increases in medication? 'Boost' is becoming an over-used word.

Bosnia-Hercegovina There has been a lessening of the conflict in the former Yugoslavia, but if you are running reports from this part of the Balkans make sure that you use the full title when referring to the entire political country. Bosnia was the northern region and Hercegovina was the southern region. Do not fall into the trap of describing the Bosnian government as a Muslim government. It may be Muslim-dominated but Bosnia is still a multi-ethnic country and Sarajevo always had Serbs, Croats and Muslims living together, even at the height of the civil war.

Boss This is something of a tabloid word rather like 'boffin' or 'tot'. It has a pejorative, almost political connotation. The term 'Mafia bosses' has become acceptable but 'boss' should be restricted to informal contexts.

Both This word is often used to establish a tautology. The sides agreed. But you should not say that 'Both sides agreed'. It is also unnecessary to say that 'President Clinton and President Yeltsin were both talking to each other'.

Boycott What is the difference between 'boycott' and 'embargo'? An 'embargo' is a legal, usually UN ban on trading with a particular country. A 'boycott' relates to a group of people refusing to buy a product or have any business or community relations with an individual or group of people. The word 'embargo' is also used in relation to the time that press releases and Treasury documents can be released.

Brainchild The more you think about this word, the stranger it becomes and the more reason there is not to use it. If you are talking about somebody having an idea, why don't you just say so?

Britain There is a difference, is there not, between the United Kingdom, Britain, Great Britain and the British Isles? Remember to apply each description to the meaning that you intend. The United Kingdom includes Northern Ireland, but if you are talking about the mainland then you need to say 'Britain'. People in England sometimes forget that Britain consists also of Scotland and Wales. Here is some clarification. 'British Isles' is a geographical and not a political description. They include the Republic of Ireland, Isle of Man and Channel Islands. The 'United Kingdom' comprises Britain and Northern Ireland.

British law This can never be correct. There are two legal systems in Britain. English and Welsh Law and Scottish Law.

British royals You do not need to get too hung up on the proper etiquette of addressing and referring to members of the Royal Family, particularly if you are working in North America, Australia or New Zealand. Even British public opinion is no longer uncritical and deferential to the idea of royalty. However, the BBC does maintain important rules on language and you do need to bear in mind the BBC is constituted by Royal Charter. In news stories the monarch is referred to as 'Queen Elizabeth' and then 'The Queen'. Expressions like 'the British Queen', 'Her Majesty' and 'the Queen of Britain' are somewhat awkward and inappropriate if you are working for a BBC news service. The BBC prefers journalists to refer to Prince Philip as 'the Duke of Edinburgh'. The BBC still avoids being familiar about 'Diana, Princess of Wales'. She should not be called 'Princess Di'. Since the Queen's sons divorced, their ex-wives have lost some of the gravitas of royal connection. The Duchess of York has become plain Sarah Ferguson. BBC newsrooms tend to frown on the familiar tabloid nickname of 'Fergie'. Neither women are referred to as 'Her Royal Highness' any more. An American journalist about to interview a member of the royal family visiting New York once informed me that 'Americans bow to no one'. At the BBC, the Queen's eldest daughter is referred to as 'The Princess Royal' to begin with and then as Princess Anne in copy that follows. Prince Charles and Prince Andrew can also be referred to as the Prince of Wales and the Duke of York.

Britons The BBC World Service prefers 'British people' or 'British citizens' rather than 'Britons'.

Brutalize Be careful about this American verb. A dictator can brutalize his people by being brutal to them. He cannot make his people brutal, which is what drug addiction can do to a young generation.

Brutal reminder Ouch! Dreadful cliché. Do not use. An example of its use is this: 'The latest bomb explosion in the City of London is a brutal reminder to the government that the Northern Ireland conflict goes on'. The more you think about it, the more ridiculous it becomes. The IRA does not set out to remind the government of anything. Depending on the nature of the incident, the adjective 'brutal' may be inappropriate.

Bungle Not to be confused with 'blunder'. When you 'bungle', you mismanage or fail in your work. But when you 'blunder', you make a rather important and foolish mistake.

Burgeoning The real meaning tends to be a botanical observation about shoots growing rapidly. A growing company or organisation should be described as such unless it is also developing off-shoots of its activities.

Burglary In Britain this is a simple criminal term meaning to enter premises unlawfully and steal something while you are there. 'Theft' is unlawfully and permanently depriving an owner of property. 'Robbery' is doing this with violence. 'Blackmail' is doing this by threatening violence or menaces. 'Stealing' and 'theft' in non-legal language can mean robbery and burglary. In the USA, there is another word to contend with – 'larceny'. This means 'theft'. 'Burglary' in the USA means entering a building unlawfully with the intention of committing a crime which includes theft.

Burmese names Like the Arabic 'Al' the Burmese 'U' is the equivalent of Mr. Daw means Mrs. This means you should not say Mr U Phat.

Bus Do understand well the tautologous meaning of 'passenger bus'. If a bus carries passengers, why the need to give it the adjective 'passenger'?

But 'But' can stand on its own without 'despite', in the same way that 'despite' can do without 'but'. They do not go together.

Calm before the storm I think it is time to restrict this expression to reports of the build-up to a hurricane.

Calm but tense What utter nonsense people speak!

Can Remember that 'can' means that you are able to do something. 'May' means that you are permitted to do something.

Capable There is a danger of tautology when saying something like 'having the capability of launching'. 'A bus can carry fifty passengers'. Not 'a bus is capable of carrying fifty passengers'.

Careen and **career** Those of you ignorant of the art of sailing should know that you careen a ship by turning it on its side to clean the hull. To 'career' means to move rapidly.

Cash boost Blasts of financial rocketry are ridiculous.

Cashier As a verb it means to dismiss or sack a member of staff and tends to be used in the context of military matters. The noun is a description of an employee of a financial organisation who dispenses money.

Caution Avoid confusing the use of this word with 'warn'. For example, 'The United Nations are warning journalists to avoid travelling into the war zone'. This can be contrasted with 'The police are cautioning motorists arrested for drink driving'.

Celebrant, celebrator If you are at a birthday party and you are enjoying yourself then you are among a group of 'celebrators'. But a 'celebrant' is an official at a religious service.

Censor, censure Another source of confusion for radio journalists. 'Censor', with clear pronunciation of the second syllable as 'sor', relates to the correction of communication. 'Censure', with clear pronunciation of the second syllable as 'shure', relates to the criticism or admonishment.

Centred around Gobbledygook and nonsense. You centre on, do you not?

Chaos Are you sure? Is it really utter confusion out there? Can you observe pandemonium? If not, find another word.

Character, reputation Try not to confuse the difference between these two words. If you are writing a report about a politician accused of 'sleaze' then when you use the word 'character' you are analysing his personal moral qualities, but when you use the word 'reputation' you are considering how he is regarded by his peers and voters.

Chauvinism Many radio journalists wrongly think that a chauvisnist is a male with contempt for the other sex. They are wrong. Chauvinism is having an irrational commitment to one's own sex, race and country while at the same time believing in superiority over others. The word is rooted from the surname of a Napoleonic soldier who was famous for backing lost causes. This means that a man with a misogynistic attitude to women has to be 'a male chauvinist'. You could say that the Bosnian Serbs had 'a chauvinistic attitude' to Bosnian Muslims.

Chequered career I rather like this cliché because the image thrown up is that of the person in the news sitting on a big draughtsboard with black and white squares and it looks like he has lost from the position of the pieces. Some stylists think it is over-used.

Chiefs Transport chiefs. Football chiefs. Army chiefs. Sounds horrible. You could say transport ministers, football managers and army generals and you would be more specific.

Chronic This word belongs to medicine. It loses its relevance and power if it is always used as a substitute for 'very bad'.

Circumlocution This is a flabby expresssion which is inflated with meaningless and repetitive vocabulary. This is something you must avoid. For example, you do not need to say 'horns of a dilemma' when you can say 'dilemma'. Rather than saying 'people went to the polls' you can simply say 'people voted'.

Claimed Do not use this word in news reporting. This is because it suggests that the author of the assertion may not believe in its veracity. In addition, if you are reporting people's comments then the use of the word 'claimed' suggests that you as the journalist do not necessarily believe in the truth of the statements.

Clampdown Very painful. Exactly which parts of the human body are being placed into a 'vice-like grip'. Oh dear, here is another cliché.

Clash What are you really talking about here? A battle? A fight? A conflict? It has come to mean many things, but in its regular usage it tends to relate to the sound of metal objects being struck together, or to a collision of forces.

Climax This word can only apply to a process of ascending strength or movement. This means that there cannot be a climax at the bottom of the ladder or at the end of a major reduction in fortune or finances.

Clichés These are the expressions and words that you should not use, particularly if they lead to exaggeration. Expressions such as 'stamp-sized country' and 'oil-rich sheikhdom' are patronising and inappropriate. The more unacceptable cliché expressions are included throughout this radio news alphabet.

Collective nouns When you use plural nouns such as 'family', 'company', 'class' or 'group', they all take the singular verb. The same applies to 'team', 'jury' and 'political party'.

Collision Avoid using the expression 'in collision' in a context indicating blame. For example: 'The freighter collided with the fishing vessel and five seamen died'. It would be safer to say that 'The freighter and fishing vessel collided'. It is also important to remember that two moving objects have to collide. The freighter cannot collide with a harbour. The bus cannot collide with a lamp post.

Colloquialisms Radio English is of course conversational English which reflects the idiomatic method of communication rather than the formal literary form. However, you should avoid slang and language which is too informal.

Commence An unacceptable substitute for 'begin'.

Common Market This description is now out of date. You should say 'European Union'.

Communiqué A communiqué is an official announcement. So make sure you never write or say 'official communiqué'.

Comparisons Some journalists make the mistake of not comparing like with like. Time cannot be compared with length and a human condition cannot be compared with the weather. Comparisons have significant crevices when you compare months which have varying lengths or statistics which have different parameters between countries. 'Compared with' has more general usage than 'compared to' which compares similarities rather than differences.

Complement and **compliment** Remember that it is nice to receive a 'compliment', but it might be more useful to be 'complemented' if there is a missing component in your personal resources for a project. There is a difference here in pronunciation which can be effectively enunciated.

Compose, comprise Great Britain is composed of three countries – England, Scotland and Wales. Great Britain comprises three countries – England, Scotland and Wales.

Confrontation Becoming long-winded and over-used when words like 'dispute' and 'clash' are shorter and can be more precise.

Consensus It is common to hear some radio journalists say 'general consensus' when the word consensus connotes a general expression of opinion.

Contagious, infectious Remember that these adjectives do not mean the same. You can catch a contagious disease by merely touching and infectious diseases are spread by water droplets or germs suspended in the atmosphere.

Continual, continuous Know the difference. 'Continual' has a sense of frequency and repetition. 'Continuous' is a process not being interrupted.

Contrasted to, contrasted with Contrasted to is only used in a contrast of opposites, whereas 'contrasted with' can contrast differences or similarities.

Conurbation Many journalists use this word to mean 'urban area'. The precise meaning of 'conurbation' is an aggregation of towns.

Convince, persuade It is very simple. You never convince anyone to do something, because that is the function of the word 'persuade'. You can convince someone of something rather than to do something.

Court martial The verb is 'court-martial' and the plural is 'courts martial'.

Crackdown Very nasty if your imagination can hear the bones cracking.

Credit, responsibility We are in the realms of cliché when talking about the IRA or HAMAS 'taking responsibility' for bomb incidents. 'Taking credit' is an inappropriate expression since it has nothing to do with credit cards or merit.

Credibility, creditworthiness You will not be solvent with the former, nor will people necessarily have trust in you with the latter, but it is better to reserve the word 'credibility' when you are reporting about confidence and integrity in a story and reserve the word 'creditworthiness' for stories about financial viability.

Crescendo I frequently hear radio journalists writing and announcing that 'a row has reached a crescendo'. This is sloppy broadcasting because crescendo means a passage of music gradually increasing in loudness. In the emotional context it can mean a progress towards a climax.

Crimespeak Crime reporters are notorious with their canon of clichés and coded language. Even the more respected broadsheet newspapers in the UK descend into what I call 'Crimespeak'. Here is an example:

> 'John Smith *looked impassive* as he was led away from the dock after being convicted of the *brutal murder* of Janet Smith. He had carried out *a frenzied attack* and despite *an emotional appeal* to the jury when giving defence evidence, they found him guilty. He was *a Jekyll and Hyde character*. A killer by night, a respectable businessman by day. The community is *still coming to terms with his rampage and catalogue of evil*. It now emerges that he lied about his qualifications and it would appear that at work he was *something of a Walter Mitty character*. Neighbours say *he kept himself to himself*. Hopes are now fading about the fate of his first wife whose body has never been traced. The jury acquitted him of murdering his second wife. Detective Chief Superintendant Jim Jones said afterwards that they *were not looking for anyone else in connection with their enquiries into her death*'.
>
> (Created by the author to include the worst crimespeak clichés)

You should be able to count at least eleven clichés in this agonisingly awful report.

Crisis Crisis? What crisis? So said British Prime Minister James Callaghan when he returned from the Caribbean during a severe run on the pound sterling in the international money markets. Or did he? This was a newspaper headline and he did not actually use these words. Ask yourself is it a really dangerous time? Can it truly be said that you are reporting a significant turning point in the history of a long running story? In the end it is better to allow other people to say they think there is a crisis and then report what they say.

Crucial Reserve this word for the very important rather than the important.

Currently This is generally an unnecessary word when talking about the present. If you say: 'The Ukraine has twenty destroyers in its navy' it is clear by the verb mood that you are talking about the present. 'Currently' is a good word to use when making a comparison between the past and the present.

Cyprus Do not fall into the mistake of making a distinction between the Greek Cypriot and Turkish Cypriot regimes. There is the legitimate and recognised government of Cyprus, and the Turkish Cypriot administration which has only been recognised by Turkey who invaded the northern part of the island in 1974.

Damage, damages Damage is what happens when fire destroys a building. Damages are what are paid out by the local building company which caused the fire when repairing the flat roof.

Dangling participle Reuters do not like them, and nor should you. The problem is caused by an opening participle sub-clause which could be related either to the subject or to the object. Here is an example: 'Having been disarmed, the right-wing protesters fought the left-wing group with bare hands.'

Or another: 'While on the way to the hospital, the police car overtook the ambulance'.

Data This takes a singular verb. You should say 'the data is unreliable'.

Dead on arrival This is the language of the paramedics and ambulance service. What does it mean precisely? Well it means that the victim's body is dead when it arrives at the hospital. It does not mean the victim died on the way to the hospital or that the victim died in the accident or incident. So avoid this expression since it can cause confusion.

Deaf This description has a similar loading to 'blind'. It would only be accurate to describe someone as 'being deaf' if he or she is totally without hearing. It is recommended that you use a more accurate and sensitive expression such as 'hearing difficulties' or 'impaired hearing'.

Death-toll This has become a cliché. No bells are tolling. Why do you not just say how many people are now dead?

Debtor nations The BBC World Service correctly recognises that this sounds like detonations and could lead to confusion.

Decimate This is very often misused. The common mistake that people make is that it is used to mean 'a virtual wipe out' or 'largely destroyed'. Some pedants also mistakenly assert that it precisely means 'reduce to one tenth'. I am sure you are rather anxious to know the proper use and meaning. The mathematic reduction factor is in fact only by one tenth. Loosely you might be able to get away with the meaning 'to reduce heavily'.

Defensive, offensive How do you know which side and which action is defensive and offensive? Better to keep those terms in the context of attribution.

Delhi This is Delhi and *not* New Delhi.

Demolish, destroy Many radio journalists have a habit of over-dramatising a news event by reporting that 'the town was totally destroyed' or 'the city hall has been completely demolished'. The words 'totally' and 'completely' are unnecessary.

Denial Some journalists have a habit of adding adjectival qualifications so that denials are either 'categorical' or 'flat'. When you think about it a denial should stand on its own. Saying someone has 'refused to comment' implies that there is an obligation to respond to the enquiries of the media.

Deprecate, depreciate If you are using these words, it is safe to assume you are not really communicating in radio spoken style English. You 'deprecate' when you deplore something and you 'depreciate' when you disparage or belittle.

Derry A city in Northern Ireland. The Protestants call it Londonderry and the Catholics call it Derry. Is there a way of wriggling out of the sectarian divide? It might be helpful for you to know that the official name for the City and County is Londonderry, but the local council is called Derry City Council. Take your pick.

Described as Nice 'get out' expression. But try not to use it if you cannot say who it is who is doing the describing.

Devastated When a football manager is 'gutted' or 'devastated' by the fact his team lost one nil what words have you left for the father who has just learned that his wife and children have been killed in a car crash?

Developing The better word to describe countries we used to patronise by calling 'Third World'.

Dictator This word is as charged as 'terrorism'. There are some people on the very left of British politics who would say that Margaret Thatcher behaved 'like a dictator'. However it would be highly contentious to assert that Mrs Thatcher was a dictator when she depended on elections in the Conservative Party and General Election for her position as leader of the Conservative Party and Prime Minister of the country.

Different The effects of organo-phosphate poisoning are different from the effects of arsenic poisoning. You do not say 'different to' or 'different than'.

Dilemma A dilemma is not a problem and a problem is not a dilemma. It is possible that you may have the problem because you are faced with two or more unpleasant choices. Your problem is that you have a dilemma and your dilemma may be an unfortunate choice between problems.

Disabilities It is now accepted that it is fair and polite to avoid mentioning a person's sex and race unless they are relevant to the story. The same applies to disabled people. Disabled people do not like being exposed to patronising and condescending attitudes. In Australia there is a convention to use the expression 'people with disabilities' rather than 'disabled people'.

Disassociate Quite a difficult word if you have badly-fitting false teeth and a big whistling gap between the front two. Dissociate means exactly the same and is easier to say. It means to become disconnected and separate.

Disaster When you report a disaster stick to proper sourcing guidelines for early reports both official and unofficial. Always attribute and be cautious about letting something go to air if you have an instinct it might be wrong and there is a way and time to check. There is always confusion and the capacity for human error during the shock and aftermath of a disaster and you will need to take this into account.

Disclose Similar problem with the word reveal. It suggests that something has been hidden.

Disinterested This is a word often confused and misused. Disinterested does not mean uninterested. It simply means impartial. This means that you can be uninterested in a speech because it is boring or because the subject does not interest you. You can also be a disinterested listener to a political speech because you are a broadcast journalist.

Down's syndrome It is no longer acceptable to use terms like mongol or mongoloid to describe sufferers of this form of chromosomal mental retardation. The word 'spastic' is also now regarded as pejorative. The charity described until a few years ago as 'The Spastic Society' has renamed itself 'Scope'.

Downtown People outside America have been confused by this American word which means central to the city.

Dozens and **scores** Britain is such a quaint little place that it has a habit of using esoteric words for non-metric quantities such as 'dozen' meaning twelve, and 'score' meaning twenty. British radio journalists broadcasting internationally should be sensitive to this fact.

Draconian Derived from the laws of a severe and rather cruel ancient Greek legislator called Draco. It is supposed to mean a severe or very harsh measure and should not be used to describe strong measures.

Dramatic All journalists would rather that their stories were 'dramatic'. However saying an event or story is dramatic does not achieve that effect. One news editor once told me that it was better for the facts of a news story to establish the idea of drama rather than depending on adjectives and adverbs.

Duped This has a slightly different meaning to having been cheated. It connotes being made a fool of as well.

Economic, economical Some journalists have a habit of interchanging these words as if they have the same meaning. They do not. When you are being economical with the truth you are being thrifty with your honesty in the same way as having an economical approach to your weekly budget means that you would be spending less. However, you can be an economic minister and have a responsibility for finances, but you may not necessarily be economical with your policies.

Either . . . or The trick in using these connecting words for comparison is to ensure that the verb agrees with the subject closer to it. Constituency boundary changes mean that either the Labour party, or the Liberal Democrats and the Conservatives are likely to win by-elections this year. Either the Liberal Democrats and the Conservatives, or the Labour party is likely to win a by-election this year.

Emotional words There is a tradition in radio journalism that emotive language belongs to the people you report and not to you as the reporter. In most style books you will find a common concern about words like 'terrorist' and 'insurgent'. The twentieth century has seen people condemned as terrorists later rehabilitated as freedom fighters and statesmen. Menahim Begin of Israel, Robert Mugabe of Zimbabwe and Jomo Kenyatta of Kenya are a few examples. The BBC found itself in considerable confusion about the use of the word 'insurgent' during the Spanish Civil War. General Franco led a military revolt against the legitimate and properly-elected government. There was a difficult debate about whether to describe Franco's forces as 'rebels' or 'insurgents'.

Emotive, emotional Issues are emotive and people are emotional.

Enemy Better to identify troops and forces with an alternative description. Whose enemy are we talking about? The BBC and other broadcast organisations were criticised in the UK Parliament for not referring to Argentinian troops, planes and ships as 'enemy forces' during the Falklands War.

Enormity This does not mean big. It suggests wickedness and evil.

Ensure, insure The difference is capable of being pronounced and they mean different things. You can ensure that the play is performed successfully. But you can only insure the actors against injury and you cannot insure the play against critical and artistic failure.

Epidemic Make sure that you have a source for the assertion that there is an epidemic. It is also worth understanding the difference between epidemic and endemic. If a disease is endemic it is found in a particular group of people.

Equally The expression 'equally as useful' or 'equally as bad' sends pinpricks of agony along the spine of grammatical purists. You only have to say equally bad or equally useful.

Escalate This is an over-used word in radio journalism. Keith Waterhouse would describe it as 'journalese'. It is a long word designed to create a false sense of authority which can easily be substituted with rise or increase.

Euphemism This is a technique used by bureaucrats and politicians to 'soft soap' the public into thinking something nasty is actually more pleasant than it really is. There is something anaesthetic about saying disadvantaged instead of poor. 'Colateral damage' is more digestible than 'blowing non combatant men, women and children to bits'. Radio journalists would be wise to judge the motivation behind official language and resist the manipulation of subtle propagandists.

European Do not fall into the trap of equating the idea of Europeans with being 'white Europeans' when covering a story with racial implications. It would be much more appropriate to say 'white' because of the multi-racial nature of Europe and the fact that centuries of immigration have substantially changed the racial profile of most European countries.

Evoke Do not confuse evoke with invoke. Evoke means to inspire or bring forth feelings. Invoke means to invite help with earnestness. Examples: 'Our foreign correspondent evokes the atmosphere of the inter-community conflict'. 'The President of the Republic invoked the members of the Legislature to protect the constitution from mass strikes and protests sweeping through the country'.

Exceeding the speed limit Police talk. You mean 'speeding'.

Exceedingly Mr Kipling makes exceedingly good cakes. But Mr Kipling is trying to sell his cakes. You only have to say very good cakes.

Exceptionable, exceptional I have heard some radio reporters get into a bit of a twist over this. Exceptionable has an entirely different meaning to exceptional. It means open to objection, and 'exceptional' of course means brilliant, superb and unique etc.

Excess of You do not need to say this when you can simply say 'more than'.

Execute Happens to people convicted of capital crimes. Execute is in fact strongly linked to the legal world. It means putting into effect a legal order.

Expel Remember the distinction between expelling and deporting. Britain deports foreign nationals or political refugees who are not welcome. Israel expels Palestinian Arabs from the occupied territories.

Extremist This word belongs to polemics and not to the language of radio journalism.

Facility What does this actually mean in the context of your report? Have you thought of being a lot more specific instead of using this superficial filling word when the actual noun would be so much more precise?

Falklands Well everyone in the United Kingdom knows that the Falklands are in the South Atlantic and the nearest country is Argentina. But in Argentina and many Latin American countries these Islands are called the Malvinas. Argentina and Britain went to war over the issue of sovereignty.

Famine-stricken This has become a cliché through over-use.

Farther, further The difference is very simple. Farther is all about distance and further is about time or degree.

Fears and **hopes** Bit of a cliché. What are we really talking about here? A fear is quite different from a hope and in what context can we justify joining the two words together in one expression? It would be bettter to talk about opinions when we mean opinions. For example: 'There are still hopes of saving the three divers trapped on the continental shelf'. 'There are still fears of another gas explosion on the plant'.

Feasible The correct use of this word is in the sense of 'practicable' or 'possible'. You should not confuse it with 'likely'. For example: 'It is feasible for the marines to cross the moor on foot and without any heavy equipment'. Not: 'It is feasible the marines will cross the moor in twenty-four hours'.

Fewer, less than It is quite simple. Fewer relates to the number of people or actual individual items and less relates to quantities. For example: 'Less than one hundred thousand US dollars have been stolen in the robbery. The Police Commissioner said that there were fewer patrol officers on duty because of cutbacks which were forced on him by the Mayor last year'.

Fighter jets Modern fighters are always jet planes.

Fighting for his life Was he really? What was he using? His fists? A semi-automatic machine gun? How could he fight for his life while unconscious and connected by tubes to a life support unit?

Figures In radio you should always write your figures out. You should not start your intros with large figures because this might be the critical core of the news story which may have been forgotten by the time you state context. Most style books recommend rounding off large complex figures. This means rounding off hundreds to the nearest ten, thousands to the nearest one hundred and millions to the nearest ten thousand.

Filipinos The right description for men from the Philippines. Women are Filipinas and anything pertaining to the Philippines is 'Philippine'.

Flout, flaunt Some journalists have an irritating habit of confusing these two words. You flout the law of good writing style by flaunting an excessive number of flowery adjectives and long words.

Following Some style books state that it is better to use the word 'after' in a preposition.

Football In the USA it is useful to make a distinction between American football and Soccer which is the football which originated in Britain.

For you and I This is the sort of mistake that a grammatical snob would make. It is 'for me' not 'for I'.

Forced Can you confidently say that the army was forced to open fire? You need to attribute a statement of this kind to a source.

Forensic Do not confuse this word with scientific. Forensic relates to the criminal process of investigation and trial.

Fortuitous I have heard some radio journalists use this word when they are trying to say that somebody or a group of people have been lucky or fortunate. Fortuitous means that something has happened by chance.

Fractions As with numbers, there is the risk of creating confusion and boredom in the mind of the listener. A number of style books recommend using fractions instead of decimals. I suppose the idea of saying 'one in three South Africans' is better to take in than 'thirty-three-point-three per cent of South Africans'.

Fresh I am delighted that the talks were fresh. The aroma must have been most pleasant. Are you sure you do not mean new?

Full-scale When have the police conducted a half-scale search and what is the difference between a police search and a full-scale police search? Is there something rather inferior about the plain enquiry held into Gulf War Syndrome and the 'full-scale enquiry' into the media coverage of the trial of alleged serial killer Rosemary West?

Fulsome Some radio reporters have been heard inadvertently using the adjective 'fulsome' as a way of saying somebody was being lavish. But the word is much more extreme and denotes excessive behaviour which is repellent.

Fundamentalist This word has almost as many problems as 'terrorist'. Most westerners are completely ignorant about the nature of Islam, Muslim religious opinion and Arab political groupings. 'Fundamentalist' is grossly misused. Try and find descriptive language which precisely matches what you want to say. It would be better to say that an Orthodox and committed man from Riyadh is a devout Muslim.

Gambit So many radio journalists use the expression 'opening gambit'. It is nonsense because gambit is always an opening move and it is also a gesture or action that involves a sacrifice.

Gay This word has now the accepted and well understood meaning of 'homosexual'. It has achieved this purpose through a successful political and cultural campaign to improve the status and respect of homosexuals. However, in the process the original meaning of the adjective has nearly been lost because of people's anxiety to avoid ambiguity.

General British military rankings have a scale which moves from brigadier to lieutenant-general and major-general. The equivalent US generals are one, two, and three star. The equivalent of a full British general would be an American four-star general.

Getaway Something that gangsters do after robbing banks. They are normally doing it in stolen cars or sometimes they run or jump onto motorcycles. Why do you not just say . . . the robber escaped?

Giant Nowadays anything big and growing is being described as 'giant'. This is a giant *faux pas*. Save the giants for the fairy stories.

Gift 'Free gift?' Think about it.

Girl There is a larger section on sexist language. But many women feel that they are being belittled when described, usually by men, as 'girls'. Whilst the debate on when a boy becomes a man and a girl becomes a woman is likely to engage intelligent minds for a long time, you would not cause too much offence by recognising that a girl becomes a woman at eighteen years of age. You might also like to bear in mind that 'girls' aged between fifteen and eighteen could merit the description 'young women'.

Global This is very much an 'in' word in the late 1990s. You might like to think about the distinction between 'world' and 'global'. A large corporation can trade on a world-wide basis but that does not necessarily mean it is 'global'. I think the idea of a global profile should encompass activities in all the trading and commercial centres.

Good 'Good news, bad news'. It all depends on what side of the fence you are standing. Your stories may have a strange slant if you emphasise that the news is good for one area of the community when it is bad for another.

Government Associated Press have clear distinctions between the idea of a government, a junta and a regime. A government is regarded as an established system of political administration. A junta is a group of people who rule after a military coup. In order for a junta to become a government the generals have to establish a system of political administration. A regime can be a democratic or totalitarian political system. Other style books have a different connotation for 'regime'.

Government descriptions You need to be cautious when saying 'The Paris Government'. Are you talking about the French Government or the local administration for Paris?

Guerrillas The BBC World Service does not use this word unless it is sure that it is a description of soldiers carrying out irregular warfare.

Gunman You should be shot (metaphorically speaking) if you ever say 'armed gunmen'.

Gunned down I suppose it would be all right if you were talking about Clint Eastwood in a Spaghetti Western. Are you sure that the victim has been shot while standing up and has actually been gunned down?

Gunshot wounds If the injured person has been fired on from a shotgun then they are 'shotgun wounds', and if a revolver was used they are 'bullet wounds'.

Gutted Its use is changing. It used to be misused in the description of a house or premises damaged by fire. Now it is being used to describe a feeling of grave personal disappointment.

Had to The Ulster Defence Regiment had to use plastic bullets to disperse the crowd. Immediately this news assertion demands the question why did they have to use plastic bullets? If you cannot answer the question confidently you should not use the expression.

Handicapped This word needs to be used with very great care. It should only be used if it is an accurate description and it is clearly relevant to the story. You should state the exact nature of the handicap and how much it interferes with the person's mental and physical overall function. Associated Press in the USA have a clear guideline on the way descriptions of disability should be used. 'Disabled' is relevant when there is a condition which interferes with a person's ability to do something independently. 'Blind' can only apply to people who have complete loss of sight. For others the term 'partially blind' is more appropriate. 'Deaf' should be reserved for those unfortunate people with total hearing loss. 'Partial hearing loss' and 'partially deaf' are the terms used to describe other categories. 'Mute' describes people who physically cannot speak, but others who have difficulty speaking are 'speech impaired'. 'Wheelchair bound' can be an unfortunate and inaccurate cliché. The person concerned may be using the wheelchair only occasionally.

Hang James Hanratty was wrongly hanged. And so were Derek Bentley and Timothy Evans. Their effigies might be hung in a museum devoted to the study of miscarriages of justice. People are hanged, objects are hung. Simple.

Harass, harassment Apart from the tendency to spell this word wrongly with two 'r's arguments always rage over the right point for the main stress. Is it the first syllable or the second? The Atlantic Ocean has come to the rescue. If you are writing and working in British English happily stress the first syllable and if you are writing and working in American English happily stress the second syllable. If you are writing and working anywhere else I think you are entitled to your own independent way of saying it. Why don't you stress the last syllable just to be different?

Helping the police with their enquiries Police talk. It implies that in reality the police have their suspect and he is not being particularly helpful. It would be better to provide more precise language such as 'questioned' or 'interviewed'.

Hit out I did not know that politicians and pressure groups use their fists and feet when they want to say something of importance.

His and **hers** It is only in the latter part of the twentieth century that attempts have been made to adjust language to recognise the existence of women. Culturally billions of people have been brought up to cite generic examples in terms of the male sex – 'his'. Stylists do not like the expression 'his, or her'. They suggest you should revise the sentence to include an antecedent which could be male or female and if this is not possible you should say 'his'.

Hispanic, Latino These terms are not considered derogatory. Hispanic denotes Spanish origin and Portuguese origin. Latinos can be of mixed racial origin.

Historic, historical Most journalists want to be reporting events which are so important and dramatic that they are genuinely historic. But historical is something rather different. It is simply an event which is part of the narrative of history and it could be undramatic and unimportant in terms of news values. This means it would be sensible to use the word 'historic' with discretion.

Hoax Always amusing when it happens to somebody else. However, it is rather easy for radio journalists to be taken in with extended resources and the pressure of deadlines. April Fool's Day and Halloween are obvious times to be on guard. There are people in Britain who have made an art out of running hoaxes which have ended up on the front pages of national newspapers as well as the lead items on broadcast bulletins. Political and pressure groups are not beyond creating 'a flyer' to test the gullibility of the media.

Hoi polloi This is not French or Norman French. It is Greek and hoi in Greek means 'the' but you are going to sound a bit strange saying 'Hoi Polloi blocked the motorway with a sit-in'. I do not think it would be appropriate to call anyone you are reporting about 'hoi polloi' which means the common people.

Holland The official name for this country is the Netherlands. But in Britain most radio journalists say Holland.

Holocaust The dictionary definition before the Nazis applied 'The Final Solution' against European Jewry was massive destruction and killing by fire. The policy of Nazi extermination is always represented by this word and with a capital 'H'. Avoid applying this word to any other large-scale story of human killing. It would be wholly inappropriate to state that 'three hundred and thirty-eight passengers died in the holocaust of fire and destruction when the plane crash-landed.'

Homosexual Try and avoid any pejorative subtext in the way you pronounce this word. It is also worth bearing in mind that a homosexual can be a man or a woman.

Hopefully Hopefully you will not be using this adverb in this way. I would much prefer that you embarked hopefully on your radio journalism career. It is better to be optimistic rather than pessimistic in your approach to ambition.

Hurricane Meteorologists have a habit of giving hurricanes names. But for the purposes of news reporting a hurricane is an 'it' and do not use 'he' or 'she' even if they are given names such as 'Archibald' or 'Mabel'.

Hypocrisy This word is not commonly misused but hypocrisy is very much what I can be accused of. Having carefully considered Tim Crook's guide to an improved method of communicating in English you may find that the text elsewhere is sprinkled with examples which offend against the proscribed laws in this section. There is a simple and humble explanation. I wanted you to spot the 'deliberate mistakes'. If you believe that you will believe anything.

Ilk I think most radio journalists outside Scotland will be astonished to learn that this word only correctly relates to the possessions of a Scottish lord or 'laird'. This means that it is always misused in expressions like 'Donald Duck and politicians of that ilk'.

Immigrants, aliens In America there is the term 'undocumented immigrants' but it is not in use in Britain. The problem with 'illegal aliens' is that the word alien connotes something from outer space and is regarded as having a dehumanising effect. In addition in normal usage the word as an adjective can mean 'unacceptable and hostile' which is not necessarily the case with immigrants. I would recommend you simply use the word 'immigrant' and avoid old-fashioned legal jargon and modern politically correct phrases such as 'newly arrived'.

Impact This is very much an Americanism since it is an attempt to turn a noun into a verb. But some American stylists feel that its function as a verb should be restricted to dentistry. Most British writers on style would agree.

Impeachment Belonging to and arising out of the US constitution. There is a distinction between the constitutional process of the House of Representatives and the Senate. The House of Representatives impeaches whereas the Senate tries. The idea of impeachment received international prominence during the Watergate Affair and the events leading up to President Nixon's resignation.

Impedance, impediment It has been known for radio journalists to use one for the other. 'Impedance' is a specific electrical term concerning the flow and strength of electricity so unless you are talking about wiring this is the wrong word for you. Impediment is the word that you want if you are talking about a hindrance or obstruction.

Imply/infer Sometimes confused by radio journalists writing in a hurry. Here is a good comparison: 'The President implied that he was unhappy with his finance minister's budget' and 'The President inferred from the four-hour debate that he would not win the vote of no confidence motion'. This is a simple matter of knowing the difference between insinuating something and drawing a conclusion from a speech which may or may not contain insinuations. Imply is an implicit communication. Infer is a process of interpretation or analysis.

Inchoate Some radio reporters have been heard to use this word to mean chaos or 'difficult to understand'. I am not surprised. It is not an everyday word used in spoken English and it would suggest your writing and communication is too elaborate even if you use its proper meaning which is 'in the process of starting, or under-developed'.

In the event of All you have to say is 'if'.

India In India the foreign secretary is a civil servant. The politically appointed figure is called the External Affairs Minister. 'The Indian sub-continent' used to be a common expression but caused offence to Bangladesh and in particular to Pakistan. It is now advisable to say 'Asian sub-continent'.

Industrial action A clumsy expression if you mean strike, but you may have to use it if trade union members are 'working to rule'. This means withdrawing services they are not contractually obliged to provide.

Inferno This idea belongs to Dante's famous poem and you should simply say 'fire'. Four letters and one diphthong syllable are better than seven letters and three syllables.

Inflammable, flammable, non-flammable The days when radio journalists and the emergency services knew how to use these words properly seem to belong to the distant past. If your blue suede shoes are inflammable or flammable it means it is easy to set them alight. Anything which is not easily set on fire is non-flammable. It is common for many people to say inflammable when they mean non-flammable. This could be a matter of life and death.

Inform Save yourself a fraction of a second and say tell.

Ingenious, ingenuous These words are often confused by radio journalists and the people they interview who do not know what they are talking about. You would not be ingenious if you tried to say you were ingenuous, unless you wanted to say that you were naive and straightforward in your attitude to other people which is what ingenuous means precisely.

Initiate Save yourself half the time with begin or start.

Injuries, wounds Is there a distinction? Indeed there is. Brent Sadler was wounded in Beirut when a piece of shrapnel hit his wrist. Kate Adie was injured in Bosnia when she fell over and broke her ankle. Wounds are what you get when in battle or hit by gunfire and injuries happen in an accident. I am not sure that you would be too bothered about the semantics if you were sustaining them.

Innocent Is there a difference between being 'not guilty' and 'innocent'? There is a well-established principle in western adversarial courts that the defendant is innocent until proved guilty. However, there are verdicts returned by juries in England and Wales which are based more on technical grounds for acquittal or because the prosecution has not 'proved' the case beyond reasonable doubt.

Scotland has a very useful 'not proven' verdict which does not grant the defendant the privilege of an implied declaration of innocence. As a conclusion it would be good practice to say that somebody has pleaded not guilty and when they give evidence you can say that they maintain their innocence. This adjective does have a troublesome usage when sloppy journalists make a sub-conscious judgement on the moral culpability of victims.

During the notorious Yorkshire Ripper crime story in Britain, the serial killer Peter Sutcliffe's non-prostitute victims were referred to as 'innocent victims'. A similar moral distinction has been wrongly made concerning homosexual people who are infected with HIV and people who become HIV positive as a result of blood tranfusions or heterosexual relations. The latter are sometimes referred to as 'the innocent victims' of HIV or AIDS. This is a dangerous turn of phrase. It implies that anyone else becoming HIV is some-how culpable. The use of the word victim may well be inappropriate in this context.

Intense, intensive People and students can be intense but a course which covers a huge amount of ground in a short period of time is intensive.

Interment, internment If the British government introduced a policy of 'interment' for members of the Provisional IRA in Northern Ireland you would be covering a much more important and dramatic story than you origin-ally imagined. 'Interment' means burying a corpse, whereas 'internment' is the right word for detaining prisoners.

In the wake of Restrict it to its proper use. The wake of a destroyer or ocean going liner makes it difficult for sailing boats to stay afloat. Although metaphorical it has become threadbare through over-use.

IRA Although this point is somewhat academic now, it is a fact that the Irish Republican organisation committed to achieving a united Ireland by violence was a breakaway group from the Official IRA in Dublin. The proper title for the new organisation which was initially funded and supported by the intelligence service of the Republic of Ireland is 'The Provisional IRA'. The original Official IRA is virtually defunct.

Ireland Eire is rarely ever used in radio news reports. Journalists should nor-mally say 'Republic of Ireland' or 'Irish Republic'. Ulster arguably contains counties which are in the Republic so it is better to use the term Northern Ireland to describe the northern part of the island which is still in the United Kingdom.

Irony You do not need to point out irony and if you do it probably is not really ironic. Ironic does not mean paradoxical, or coincidental. If you are reporting something ironic, it is good policy to allow the listener to appreciate it rather than to spell it out. Irony is the expression of meaning by the use of language of a different or opposite tendency. It is often an ill-timed or perverse arrival of an event which is in itself desirable and it is also the use of language with one meaning for a privileged audience and another for those addressed or concerned. This means that there is nothing particularly ironic about a goal scored by penalty or the Charge of the Light Brigade at Balaclava.

Irregardless The more you think about it, the more doubling will be your sense of the negative.

Jail, prison The Americans make a distinction between jail and prison. In Britain the words are interchangeable. Associated Press defines 'prison' as maximum security institutions officially entitled 'penitentiaries' and medium security institutions which are officially named as 'correctional institutions' or 'reformatories'. These 'prisons' accommodate people convicted of US 'felonies' – the more serious crimes. A 'jail' normally detains people convicted of the lesser crimes known as 'misdemeanours, defaulters of fines and contempt of court, and people awaiting trial'.

Jargon This word has several meanings. It swings from 'jibberish' to the 'language or vocabulary of a particular group or profession'. It is easy to be influenced by the expressions and coded language of the legal profession, the military, or officialdom. The radio journalist has a responsibility to translate and avoid the euphemistic expressions created to conceal the reality or truth of an idea or practice.

'Fowler's English' has always been something of a bible in determining the basic principles ensuring good English style. Although published eighty-five years ago Fowler's principles are still good. Short words are better than long words. Single words are better than circumlocutions. Anglo-Saxon words are better than Latin, Greek, or European words. Choose the concrete image and word over the abstract. Go for the idiomatic and well-known word rather than the erudite, obscure and not so well known.

Jet You do not need to say jet airliner since most airplanes nowadays are jet-powered. The distinction only has to be made if the engines are piston-powered.

Jokes Difficult to run during radio news bulletins. You could create an unfortunate juxtaposition with something very serious. If the joke is not universally appreciated you could cause offence. Puns are liked by news people but seldom enjoyed by listeners. Step out into the raging currents of humour with great care.

Journalese The language and words that journalists love using and seem incapable of giving up. The expressions frequently originate in the compressed cliché-style language of headlines in tabloid newspapers.

Joyriding This is becoming something of a charged word. There is nothing particularly 'joyful' about having your car stolen or finding that your daughter has died in a car stolen by one of her friends which has crashed into a lamp post at high speed. The word tends to trivialise and romanticise the activity as well as the crime.

Labels You need to be very careful about giving politicians labels which may well be a matter of opinion and offensive to the subjects. Some politicians are happy to be described as 'militant', others will be asking their lawyers to issue libel writs in the UK, and ordinary voters might be confused if the label is not accurate.

Lady Feminists began a campaign from the 1960s to substitute this word with 'woman' or 'women'. The argument is based on the concern that 'women' is neutral and accurate as a noun description for the feminine sex. The word 'lady' is old-fashioned, linked to the idea of an aristocratic title and implies a class, or value judgement concerning respectability.

Large-scale Go for the shorter word. It begins with b and has three letters.

Last ditch Not so common now as a cliché. It was used far too frequently during the industrial relations troubles of the 1970s.

Latter Do remember this has to be the second of two things and not the last of several things.

Laudable, laudatory These words are verging on the pompous. Laudable means commendable and you could say that a radio journalist working for a rival news organisation is laudable but if you wanted to criticise his habit of 'sucking up' to authority, you might choose the more polite expression 'laudatory' when describing the style of his reporting.

Launched Since it will be a long time before political parties hold news conferences in space you should leave launches to NASA and describe parties as 'announcing' their manifestos.

Lay and **lie** Ducks lay eggs, garçons in Paris lay the tables. There has to be an object for lay, but not for lie. The court jester lies down on the king's bed. Grammatical experts explain this difference by explaining that lay is a transitive verb and lie is intransitive. So if you do not feel like getting up in the morning what do you have? – 'A lie-in' of course. Not 'a lay-in'. According to Wynford Hicks, Americans get into a mess over this. I suppose 'I lay me down' is awful compared to 'I lie down'.

Leading question Some purists say this expression should be restricted to describing a style of question during adversarial court proceedings and should not be generally applied to awkward questions which people do not want to answer.

Leave There is this weird idea that earthquakes, volcanoes, infernos and disasters 'leave' something after they have done their worst. Go for the direct language. We are talking about killing here. The train crash killed four people. It did not leave four people dead. This is because the train crash is not going anywhere else.

Lend, loan You lend a loan and do not loan a lend. Get it?

Liable Again some language purists strongly believe that this word should remain in the legal arena concerning an obligation to pay fines, and meet punishment and responsibility. Nowadays it is commonly used in this type of expression: 'He was drinking so much that he was liable to crash his car.' It is used to mean that something unhappy is likely to happen.

Like Pretty straightforward. Like makes the comparison and 'such as' gives the example. A very colloquial use of spoken English contains an overuse of 'like'. So much so that 'like' appears at the end of the sentence and in place of any pause 'such as' 'I went down the pub like. Like I was drunk already like. I tell you I felt like I was out of it like'. I do not like this way of talking. It makes editing very difficult.

Literally Most radio journalists use this word without thinking what it actually means. If it means word for word or verbatim, it is nonsense when you say 'the league champions have been literally destroyed by the home team's three goals in five minutes'.

Locate When you are speaking strictly you should not use this verb if you mean to say that you have found something. 'Locate' is appropriate for when you want to say that you have discovered a geographical position.

Long words Do not use them. Examples: Many is better than numerous. Show is better than demonstrate, and rise is better than escalate. Reduce the syllables. People speak with shorter words.

Loyal Loyalist is something of a resonating description in Northern Ireland. The word loyal can have a charged meaning in other contexts. I would recommend you use an alternative word such as supporter or follower.

Luxuriant, luxurious If you are running a story about the high life and opulence of an exploitative dictator, notorious and or colourful criminal you would say that your subject had a luxurious lifestyle rather than a luxuriant one. 'Luxuriant' is normally used to describe somebody's garden or a country's landscape. It means prolific and lush.

Maintain This is as dodgy as 'claim'.

Major Becoming almost a cliché adjective. Do remember that it is not a superlative so do not place 'The' before expressions such as 'The major violinist in the world'.

Majority In Britain majority means the difference between the winning candidate and the candidate who came second. The majority party has more votes than any other individual party and the overall or absolute majority refers to having more than half of all the available votes.

Manhunt The police are normally searching for somebody specific or they are carrying out a murder enquiry and are seeking a suspect.

Massive Tends to be used in relation to security and heart attacks. You may well see a large amount of security but is it necessarily solid? Can the same be said of a heart attack?

Masterful, masterly 'Masterful' tends to be used properly to describe the person, and 'masterly' is a more appropriate adjective for the actions or achievements of somebody who may well be 'masterful'.

May and **might** Not selecting the right tenses for these verbs can create serious ambiguity when you are out in the field reporting. For example: 'The 747 may have avoided the risk of disaster by allowing time for the de-icing service provided at Milan airport'; 'The 747 might have avoided the risk of disaster by allowing time for the de-icing service provided at Milan airport.' The first statement implies by the use of 'may' that the jet has been de-iced and it is possible that it has avoided disaster. The use of the word 'might' indicates the disaster has come to pass.

Meanwhile Surplus to speech and radio news requirements. Cut it out.

Media The media always are and never is.

Medical stories It is easy to fall into the trap of making a speculative assertion about a cure or medical development. These stories need to be balanced, attributed, and extensively checked with a range of medical opinion. I always advise huge scepticism and constant questioning of scientists. They have the aura of expertise, but are as egotistical, opinionated and unreliable as journalistic pundits on any specialist area. A minority have been proved to have falsified research, exaggerated and distorted research analysis. You also need to bear in mind that professional specialist groups regularly propagandise about the superficiality of the media and exaggerate the excesses of journalists.

Metaphors When original and precisely stated, they can electrify radio news communication with bright imagistic language. Be careful about using metaphors which are inadvertently insensitive. For example: 'John Smith has at last been able to stand on both feet in the paraplegic marathon'.

Midnight Why do radio news presenters often say 'twelve midnight'? Probably because they do not know the time. The same can be said for saying 'twelve noon'. Midnight always means twelve a.m. and noon always means twelve p.m.

Military bases In the United States the different services use different words to describe where they are permanently 'encamped'. The navy and marines have 'stations', the army has 'fields' and the air force has 'bases'. In the UK the army is permanently quartered in barracks, the navy has shore installations with names such as 'HMS Elizabeth' or 'HMS York'. The RAF call their bases 'RAF Wittering' or 'RAF Woodbridge'. You must also beware of military jargon which tends to come up with euphemistic expressions to cover up the unpleasant result of military action particularly against civilians. The Gulf War spawned expressions such as 'smart bombs' and 'collateral damage'. The only collateral thing about some of those operations was the death and destruction caused to non-combatants. The military may well think that this damage was additional and subordinate, but for the victims it was somewhat predominant.

Militate, mitigate Radio journalists sometimes confuse these words. For example: 'The new law passed by Parliament is designed to militate against the growing trend of convicted criminals presenting inaccurate and distorted accounts of their past record.' 'This new law will mean that when defence lawyers mitigate for their clients, there will be no room for deceiving the court over previous convictions'. In conclusion 'militate' means to create or establish a force which is normally applied against something and 'mitigate' means to reduce the severity of something or somebody.

Minuscule A French word meaning very small. 'Tiny' would be better and shorter.

Miraculous If you have really observed a miracle you should contact the Vatican but not report it as such to your listeners.

Missing So many radio journalists talk about somebody 'going missing'. A missing person is missing.

Mob In America this word often means Mafia or organised crime. Its ordinary meaning connotes an unruly and violent crowd. You have to be careful to make a distinction between a crowd and a mob and it would be a good idea to avoid using the word mob if it is synonymous with organised crime.

Modifiers We can do without them. What do you actually mean by 'actually' and if I finished the sentence properly what do you mean by using the words 'ultimately', 'probably', 'entirely' and 'inherently'?

More than This is a more precise phrase when paraphrasing numbers. The word 'over' can mean six bowls of the ball in English cricket and have a geographical connotation when you say 'over there'.

Mortar It is common for radio journalists to misunderstand the true nature of ordnance. Mortar bombs are fired from mortars, not shells. This means that mortars or mortar bombs fell on the market place in Sarajevo. They were not 'shelled' in relation to these incidents.

Move to Action can be verbal and physical. However, if you 'move to' do something this is undoubtedly a physical action. This means that politicians do not 'move to' meet political challenges with words.

Muslim Different style books have different recommendations about whether you say Muslim or Moslem as a description of worshippers of the Islamic faith. I do not think it matters.

Myriad The word stands on its own and it means countless. So you only have to say myriad incidents . . . myriad references . . . myriad examples. Do not say under any circumstances 'myriads of references'.

Names The BBC is very careful about maintaining politeness in its news broadcasts. People of all nationalities are accorded the courtesy of Mr, Mrs, Miss or Ms. People accused of crimes receive this courtesy during the trial until convicted and sentenced. Sports personalities and description of sporting events create an exception. They are identified properly to begin with and then can be referred to by their surname subsequently. The BBC also prefers the more formal 'The British Foreign Secretary Malcolm Rifkind' rather than the IRN, popular radio style of 'British Foreign Secretary Malcolm Rifkind'.

Nationwide Government leaders always broadcast nationwide. You risk writing a tautology by over-using this adjective.

Neither, nor This can only be used when referring to two concepts, or two named subjects/objects.

New Can be over-used. If the City of London decided to build another cathedral next to St Paul's, there is not much point in saying it is a new St Paul's Cathedral.

News conference Always better than press conference which seems to imply an exclusion of the presence of broadcast and non-print journalists.

Nicknames These have the potential for being very prejudicial when reporting crime cases in Britain which are being tried before a jury. You also need to appreciate whether the nickname is negative or positive and whether the subject is happy to answer to this name.

Nobility For those of you who are interested this is the descending scale of hierarchy: Dukes are above marquises, and marquises are above earls, and earls are above viscounts and barons. Life peers are barons and women peers or peeresses are baronesses. The wife of an earl is a countess, the wife of a viscount is a viscountess, and the wife of a marquis is a marchioness. You might be intrigued to know that the sons and daughters of dukes and marquises are lords and ladies. Baronets and knights are Sirs and Ladies. A dame is a woman honoured in her own right and she would be called Dame such as 'Dame Peggy Ashcroft'. The wife of a baron, peer, or knight would be called Lady Smith, but you would not use her christian name Penelope. However, the daughter of an earl or higher aristocratic rank would be called Lady Penelope Smith.

Non-controversial issue Over-used and not well thought out expression. As all issues are by their very nature controversial then an issue cannot be non-controversial. Furthermore you do not have to say controversial issue because the controversy is implicit in the word issue.

Non sequitur Linking two ideas together when they bear no relation to each other. For example: 'The Second World War ended because there was a hurricane in South East Asia.'

Normality In the United States things return to normality, but in Britain they return to normal. Although I would be delighted to know what normal or normality really is.

Northern Ireland The BBC has strict rules about terminology and coverage. It is the army in Northern Ireland and not the British Army. There are two main parties which support the maintenance of the union between Britain and Northern Ireland. They are the Ulster Unionist Party and the Democratic Unionist Party. The Alliance Party is very small and attracts support from both Catholic and Protestant communities. The Social Democratic and Labour Party campaigns for a united Ireland through peaceful negotiation. Sinn Fein is the political wing of the Provisional IRA. The party tolerates violence in order to achieve a united Ireland, but it stresses that it does not advocate violence. It is interesting that NPR in the USA will not use BBC reports on Northern Ireland. The BBC World Service Newsroom and Radio 4 do not use Press Association copy on Northern Ireland without consulting the Belfast newsroom which is staffed twenty-four hours a day.

Notorious Famous for being not very well liked or appreciated. So do not accidentally use it as a synonym for famous or well-known when you do not intend a negative meaning.

Numbers Always say them on the radio. 'Two thousand and twenty-nine' is better than 'two oh two nine'.

Obscenity Even in the context of a violent and catastrophic news event, obscene language is not only capable of being very offensive to many listeners, but could also be unlawful if it offends against statutory broadcasting codes. Radio organisations tend to have their customs concerning the handling of offensive language. These techniques could include 'bleeping out'. You need to reference the chain of editorial command if a leading politician is responsible for the language or the obscenities are in the background of significant and newsworthy actuality.

Observance and **observation** Know the difference. There is one. Observation is what you see. But observance is following a custom or duty. For example 'Remembrance Day observance'.

Old Bailey Old Bailey is in fact the road in the City of London where the Central Criminal Court is situated.

On the increase, decline Clumsy expressions. Simply say increase or decrease.

Ongoing It is an ongoing habit to use this word to emphasise that a human process of activity is continuing. You do not need to use it in most instances.

Only You should only use this word if you place it immediately before the word it qualifies.

On the heels of Keep this expression limited to the description of animals. 'On the heels of a 20 per cent increase in manufacturing output' sounds ridiculous.

One and **you** I do not think it is appropriate for radio journalists to communicate with the impersonal pronoun 'one'. 'You' is more friendly. In Q and As it sounds as if you are a member of the Royal Family by responding: 'One really does not know what to think in these circumstances as one is in a dreadful quandary about what one should do.' Much better to say 'You really do not know what to think in these circumstances as you are in a dreadful quandary about what you should do.' And never mix your yous with your ones.

Others There is a tendency to use this word in a redundant way. If three people have won the lottery and ten missed out by one number you do not have to say ten others missed out by one number.

Oust Old-fashioned word meaning to expel or drive out. Not appropriate in sport or politics. Do not use it.

Overseas Try not to confuse the idea of being overseas when you simply want to denote that something is foreign. If you are living in France, Barbados is overseas, but Germany is foreign.

Pall of smoke Tending to become a cliché. The exact meaning of pall is a dark covering like the cloth placed over a coffin. Since smoke tends to rise in columns your use of this expression may be inaccurate.

Panacea Not many people know that a panacea is the remedy for all ills. So it cannot be the remedy for piles, road traffic accidents, drug addiction and shoplifting.

Paramilitary Always take care to remember that paramilitary police or forces are not soldiers or troops.

Paraplegia I have heard journalists confusing paraplegia with quadraplegia. The first means the paralysis of two legs while the second encompases paralysis of all four limbs.

Parliament How do you explain the eccentric workings of the British Parliament? Whips are not into sadomasochism, well not in public. They are the business managers of the political parties in Parliament and are responsible for ensuring their members vote effectively for their parties. The Shadow Cabinet is the government in opposition. It consists of the senior parliamentary men and women in opposition. Three-line whip means that MPs have been ordered to cast a vote in line with party policy. A second reading in the Commons means that a government or private member's bill is well on its way to becoming law. The House of Commons has approved it. The House of Lords, whose members are not elected, cannot reject a finance or tax revenue bill.

Participate A word of four syllables which can be reduced into two words.

Phenomenon Do not forget that the plural is phenomena.

Practicable, practical When something is practicable it can be done, but when something is practical it is simply useful. Some radio journalists do have a habit of saying practicable when they mean practical and practical when they mean practicable.

Pre- The pre- suffix is sometimes redundant when added to words such as 'pre-planned' and 'precondition'.

Predictions Do not make them in radio journalism. Always hedge your bets and use expressions such as 'is expected to', or 'is due to'.

Predominant, predominate The first is the adjective and the second is the verb.

Premier, Prime Minister Interchangeable titles for top government person. In Britain Prime Minister is preferred. In France and some countries in Asia they prefer 'Premier'. In Austria and Germany they prefer 'Chancellor' and in Canada and Australia the Federal government chief is known as 'Prime Minister' but the heads of states are called 'Premiers'.

Prescribe, proscribe It is the difference between ordering and prohibiting. The minister would prescribe a series of road building projects to relieve the congestion on London's outer ring road. The minister could also proscribe vehicles over two tons in weight on the outer ring road.

Presently In America it means at the moment, but this is not the case in Britain where it should mean soon.

Prestigious Do not make the mistake of saying something is prestigious when such a description is open to dispute. Furthermore you could be using a superfluous adjective when the subject is already prestigious.

Prevaricate, procrastinate You may well be prevaricating when an idiotic and unfair radio presenter has asked you a question which you cannot answer. So you may well speak evasively. If you are a procrastinating radio journalist then you may find yourself out of a job. No news editor wants a radio reporter who is always postponing and putting off his assignments.

Prior to This is an old-fashioned expression with three syllables when 'before' has only two and is modern.

Probe Something doctors tend to do with medical instruments. Police officers, tax inspectors, MPs, and customs and excise officers are not as well qualified.

Protagonist I have often heard radio journalists talking about leading protagonists. But a protagonist by definition is the leading actor or figure in a story. If you want to say somebody is advocating something you could call them a proponent.

Protest Do remember that you cannot 'protest against your innocence'. You 'protest your innocence' and 'protest against your conviction' after the jury has returned a guilty verdict and the judge has sentenced you to twenty years' imprisonment. In the USA Americans protest a decision. In Britain we protest against a decision.

Purchase Not a word you need when it is easier and shorter to say 'buy'.

Quip This a verb which relates to telling jokes. In recent years some radio journalists have been suggesting that politicians 'quip' when trying to say something witty or amusing. Sadly when a politician attempts a joke not everyone thinks it is much of a laugh.

Quit Slightly American. In Britain you could say resign.

Quiz This is a competition on the radio or television and is not a police interrogation.

Race You must avoid mentioning race, colour, sex and religious affiliation unless it is strictly relevant to the story. When I first started reporting criminal trials at the Central Criminal Court in 1980 it was common practice for print journalists to highlight the racial origin of black and Asian defendants. The practice ended as the result of repeated Press Council complaints by a black Londoner from Tottenham. Eventually offending newspapers became fed up with having to defend the indefensible.

Raised and **reared** All creatures bright and beautiful, dull and ugly are raised. But human beings are reared and we are the only ones.

Random sample That's what you think you do when you go out on the street to record vox pops. But the strict scientific definition says that every constituent in your sample must have an equal chance of occurring. This is impossible on the street. So you should find something else to call it. How about 'rough poll', 'very small survey' or 'unscientific survey'?

Ravage, ravish Ravish is a word which connotes abduction, rape and violence against the person. Ravage has a wider meaning and encompasses devastation to property as well as people.

Raze This can be confused with raise so avoid it.

Reassure This word has a limited meaning. It only means to give another assurance.

Rebel This is a charged word like loyalist and should be avoided unless attributed.

Rebut/refute It is quite common to find confusion with the use of these words. They are sometimes wrongly used to mean deny or reject. The proper definition is disprove or reply with argument.

Recent How recent? This morning, last week, last month, last year? Why do you not simply describe when with precision?

Record Remember that you do not create a new record, because a record is new.

Recourse, resource and **resort** These words are often confused. Recourse is a possible source of help. Resource is a facility or asset. Resort as a noun is a tourist location. You resort to something when everything else has failed. Something could be your last resort.

Refuse, declined Most people have a right not to take part in a live programme, not to be interviewed and not to give their names to the authorities. This is a matter of declining the invitation. You can refuse to cooperate with the

IRS or the Inland Revenue. You can refuse to give evidence. You do so at your peril.

Refute This word should be used when you are describing somebody disproving something.

Regime It would be unwise to use this word because it is generally pejorative. It implies a dictatorship and lack of democratic accountability.

Regularly Many radio journalists do not know the difference between regularly and frequently.

Reluctant, reticent I often hear radio journalists confusing these words. You are reluctant when you are unwilling, and you are reticent when you would rather not speak.

Rendered To say that doctors 'rendered first aid on the airplane' is rather clumsy. Just say 'gave first aid'.

Repetition It is good style to avoid using the same vocabulary and to vary your use of language, but at the same time avoid repeating the process of variation.

Responsibility I have mentioned the inappropriate use of the expression 'have taken credit' for the bomb explosion. To say that HAMAS took responsibility for the Tel Aviv bus explosion can be interpreted as a boast. This would be most offensive to the relatives of the victims. Try and find a more specific expression such as 'HAMAS says they placed the bomb on the bus and intended to cause an explosion'.

Reuters The largest news-gathering media corporation in the world. You say a Reuter correspondent rather than a Reuters correspondent.

Reveal This is a highly-charged verb and you must understand that when you use it you are saying that the news organisation accepts the information as true facts and that it had been kept secret.

Reverend In Britain some clergymen get very upset if you say 'Reverend Geoffrey Jones' when you should be saying 'the Reverend Geoffrey Jones.'

Robbery Try to avoid giving tacit approval or admiration for a crime with expressions such as 'brilliant Knightsbridge Safe Deposit Robbery', or 'bold raid on Security Express Headquarters'.

Row Try not to use this word every time you are reporting a debate, or dispute among politicians. Row tends to mean a fierce quarrel or dispute and should be reserved for this kind of disagreement.

Rumours Rumours are to be handled with critical rigour. You must avoid putting them to air unless they have been checked and substantiated as a credible story. The expression 'unconfirmed rumour' is tautological. Remember that reckless publication of rumours can cause irreparable damage to money markets and reputations, and serious public disorder. I remember that during the 'Great Storm' of 1987 in Britain a local radio service reported that an entire building had collapsed with scores trapped inside, the roof of the police station had been blown off, the army were travelling from a nearby garrison to help rescue the trapped and injured, and an oil tanker had broken its moorings in a large harbour threatening a massive explosion. I spent the morning discovering that no building had collapsed in the seaside town, only two tiles had been blown off the police station's roof, the tanker had not broken its moorings, and I found that the army were following me because they assumed I knew the way and were only travelling to the seaside resort because they heard about the collapsed building on the radio!

Sanction Keep it as a noun rather than using it as a verb. There is the risk of confusing the meaning since you can punish by sanctioning as well as approve when sanctioning.

Scenario Scenarios belong to plots for Hollywood films and dramatic productions and should not be an alternative description for situations.

Scene Part of paramedics' and firefighters' language. For example: 'Ten pumps and four paramedic mobile units attended the scene.' *Mise en scène* belongs to the world of directing Hollywood movies and not news stories.

Scheme Be careful when you use this word. It could connote dishonest dealing. Stick to words like plan.

Schizophrenia Utterly misunderstood psychiatric illness. Contrary to myth, 99 per cent of schizophrenics are not violent. Schizophrenic does not mean 'split personality'. The condition is a serious personality disorder where the individual suffers a breakdown in the relation between thoughts, feelings and actions.

Sensual, sensuous If you want sexual overtones use 'sensual'. 'Sensuous' is more innocent and relates to aesthetics rather than physical, sensual experiences.

Sentences They should always be short, but not with the same repetitive rhythm. Staccato style writing is as irritating as long meandering sentences with complex sub-clauses.

Set So you are set to return to radio journalism are you? Would it not be better simply to say you are coming back? Thank you.

Sexist It is only in recent years that progress has been made in adjusting everyday language to stem the sexist and discriminatory assumptions inherent in radio news coverage. There are many areas of the community which have been subjected to linguistic exclusion, ridicule and trivialisation. There is a large edifice of language which perpetuates a stereotypical image of women as the inferior, weaker sex.

Job description nouns with the component 'man' exclude the idea that women either do or can do these jobs.

People, not man explore space, although primates were up there before human beings. A ship is crewed not manned. An office is staffed not manned.

Police not policemen set up roadblocks. Firefighters not firemen deal with a blaze. Armies have troops and soldiers and not legions of men. We have journalists and reporters and not newsmen. It's 'one person, one vote' not 'one man, one vote'. Workers, prison officers and flight attendants are better than workmen, warders and stewardesses. There is no point in identifying someone's gender unless it is relevant. For example if a woman police officer is injured during a riot is the fact that she is a woman relevant? It is common for many male radio journalists, although I have also heard women commit the same sin, to write 'woman policeman'!

Think the next time you write or say 'Gentleman's agreement'. How can Baroness Thatcher have a 'man-to-man' chat with the President of Eire Mary Robinson? The risk of unnecessarily highlighting a woman's gender is that it reinforces the idea that women are female and are without skill and ability. Why do many women prefer the prefix 'Ms'? The argument here is that the prefixes 'Mrs' and 'Miss' delineate a woman's marital status whereas 'Mr' does not. Are we asking 'the man in the street' for his opinion or are we vox-popping a sample of people in the street?

It is not too difficult to replace outmoded sexist language. 'Man-made' can be 'handmade' or 'synthetic' and 'man hours' can be 'working hours'. 'Man-power' can be 'labour force.' 'Cleaning ladies' can be 'cleaners'.

Sexual orientation This should not be a relevant factor in many of your stories and there is the ethical consideration that you should not reveal people's sexual orientation against their will. Avoid language which is demeaning and implying shame. For example: 'suffering from homosexuality'.

Ships In Britain they are feminine. Naval ships and liners have captains. Cargo and merchant ships have masters and trawlers as indicated elsewhere have skippers.

Shootout If you were reporting the OK Corral then ok.

Shot in the arm It is not a good idea to use this expression if you are saying, for instance, 'the government is giving a shot in the arm for addiction clinics by increasing funding for health practice referrals'. This is another cliché to avoid.

Should, would Should implies obligation and would expresses a regular action. 'We should be excellent radio journalists. We would bundle our belongings into a small rucksack.'

Sieges Radio journalists need to exercise great caution when reporting sieges which inevitably attract considerable news value. The broadcast medium offers the opportunity for hostage-takers to use radio to disseminate demands and because it is fast moving there is the risk that communication of news material could place lives at risk. The US Society of Professional Journalists report on the Waco siege in 1993, which ended with so much loss of life, made significant recommendations that are relevant to all countries. The cult leader David Koresh conducted live interviews with KRLD radio in Texas and the report suggests that more could have been done to consult with negotiators in stand-off situations where lives are at stake. The report also criticised the talk show host for KGBS, Ron Engleman, who broadcast messages of support for Koresh and very likely interfered with the delicate negotiations taking place. The report alleged that he had abdicated his ethical responsibility. The Society made practical recommendations which included always assuming that hostage-takers have access to media reports, resisting the temptation to telephone a gunman or hostage-takers, avoiding description of security tactics and positions, and avoiding becoming a player in the event itself. All radio newsrooms should have a strategy for dealing with calls from hostage-takers. The BBC newsroom received such a call from the gunmen in the Iranian embassy in 1980. It was in an immediate position to record the call.

Single out What a groan of displeasure rumbles through the radio newsrooms of the world when the hapless radio reporter says 'The road protesters have singled out the Transport Secretary, Devon County Council and the Devon Constabulary in their campaign of protest'. How can you single out three people and organisations?

Skipper This word should only be used when referring to the master of a fishing vessel. Say captain for every other type of ship.

So-called Implies a heavy amount of scepticism. You should use another expression as this has become a well-worn cliché. 'Widely known as' or 'well known as' would be preferred.

Some About two million people instead of some two million people when your figures are an approximation.

Sophisticated This word has five syllables. If you are observing the use of complex weaponry you should use a shorter word like 'modern'. You would save yourself a good part of a second.

Sound-bite Television can keep its sound-bites. In radio we have 'cuts' or 'actuality'. We also avoid eight- or nine-second spurts of staccato opinion. In radio news reporting the cut or actuality should contain a fully expressed and interesting point of view.

Source material I do find it frustrating that my continuous homilies to students and trainees about the value of their notebooks are frequently ignored. There has been a recent multi-million pound fraud case in which well-known foot-ballers have been accused of throwing matches for a betting syndicate. The prosecution has been relying on the evidence of two national newspaper reporters, but both journalists had to express regret that their original note-books were no longer available. Notebooks should be kept like general practitioner medical records. Notes should be timed, dated, and 'slugged'.

The word 'slugged' means giving the story a short title which matches any other record concerning this story in the news gathering and transmission system. All journalists should avoid making any scribbles or doodles which could be critical of the people being interviewed and the subjects being explored.

Sourcing You must source everything. This is vital in order to enable your listeners to form their own opinions and to develop your news service's credibility which would be undermined by proven evidence of partiality. Be careful to indicate that you have a single source and avoid saying something like 'diplomatic sources' when you have spoken to only one diplomat. It is important to be specific.

Spark off Fine if you want to cause an explosion. Otherwise leave it out.

Split infinitive In conversational English infinitives are frequently split, but try not to get too obsessional about it. Sometimes splitting infinitives can ensure a more fluid and natural style of English communication.

Spokesman, spokeswoman and **spokesperson** Some news organisations call for a specific identification of gender, and others prefer the neutral spokesperson.

Sprayed with bullets Machine guns fire bullets not paint.

Spurn A weird word to use when you may only want to say 'reject'. Do bear in mind that spurn has a connotation that you are turning down with 'disdain and contempt'.

Stadium, stadiums Never stadia.

Stand-off Nothing is happening. That is it. So you do not need 'Stand-off'.

Standstill The weather can cause all sorts of problems and so can strikes. But do they really create a standstill? Are people standing still? No. Do not use it. News organisations regularly ban its use. Try not to provoke another ban.

Stepping up This is an expression more suited to describing the process of receiving an honour from the Queen, or moving onto the ballroom floor for a dance.

Storms Like generals, and the English aristocracy, there is a hierarchy or gradation of storm strengths. Storm descriptions are also linked to their geographical origin.

A storm is stronger than a gale, and a cyclone is stronger than a storm.

Cyclones belong to the Indian and Australian oceans.

Typhoons are the same as cyclones but occur in the China Seas and West Pacific.

Typhoons and cyclones on the East Coast of the United States and Caribbean are called hurricanes.

Tornados are violent and narrowly-funnelled windstorms mainly occurring in the USA.

So in Britain the ranking begins with a light breeze which is Force 2 with a wind speed of 4 to 6 knots. You then move up to gentle breeze, moderate breeze, fresh breeze, strong breeze, near gale, gale, strong gale, storm, violent storm and hurricane which is Force 12 and a wind speed of over 63 knots.

Strategy To apply a strategy you should be conducting some kind of military campaign and your tactics need to be in the context of an enemy whom you presumably wish to outmanoeuvre.

Strikes Quite a rare occurrence in Britain in the 1990s. But when a company gives you statistics about losses, analyse them with care. Twenty-million-pound losses a day may only relate to lost turnover of goods and sales. The actual losses to the company would be much less because the company has no over-heads during the time of the strike.

Sufficient, adequate When you are sufficient you have enough. When you are adequate you are ok but it is a matter of being barely sufficient or fair to middling. Many radio journalists do not think about the difference.

Summit Limit the application of this word to meetings of heads of state.

Superlatives Most superlatives belong to the world of public relations hyper-bole. They should be attributed to a clearly identified source and any radio journalist should be very wary of saying something is the biggest, the first, or the oldest. Can you be sure? Another very dodgy expression is 'makes legal history'. How do you know it 'makes legal history'? And what do you mean by 'making legal history'?

Surgery In Britain we are operated on, but in America we undergo surgery. Does it make a difference?

Sustain fatal injuries What a long-winded euphemism for dying.

Sweeping changes I cannot see anyone with broomsticks.

Swoop I never knew that the police could fly. Well pigs can't either. But neither can they swoop like hawks not that I have ever seen.

Technical Esoteric technical terms can build up into a complete language of jargon. You need to strike a balance between using accurate words to describe a technological process or breakthrough and defining and explaining what these words mean.

Temporary respite Respites are always temporary.

Terminate It is easier, is it not, to say end?

Terrorism This is one of the most highly-charged words in the vocabulary of radio journalism. One of my students hit the mark when he said it depends on whether your gunman is on your own doorstep. If you or your community is the target, the gunman is a terrorist. But his community might regard him as a freedom fighter. When you are covering a civil war, if one side committed to overthrowing the established though undemocratic government sanctions a guerrilla attack on a train killing forty people is this a terrorist attack? How would you describe a reprisal operation by the government which involves a napalm attack on a rebel village killing ninety unarmed people? It might be advisable to use neutral terminology and avoid using the word terrorist.

That, which That is what defines and which is what informs.

Think Yes radio journalists are paid to think. But they should not be paid to editorialise by expressing opinions and views not rooted in the facts of the story. All radio news organisations should know when they depart from the traditional reporter's role of reporting facts and other people's opinions rather than their own. I have spoken elsewhere about the dangers of asking radio journalists 'what do you think?' when the question should be put to the protagonist of a news story.

Third World How would you like your country to be relegated into the third division of international political and economic status? It might make you think twice about using this term without discretion. How would you make a distinction between second and first world countries? 'Non-aligned' is not a clever synonym for 'third world'. The country has to be a member of the political grouping of non-aligned countries.

Throughout Do you mean everywhere and all the time?

Today If you are listening to radio news you are listening to today's radio news. You do not have to remind your listeners.

Told reporters Has been elevated to the status of a cliché. The expression should be used when an important source has briefed reporters, but not given a news conference.

Top level I am sure it is and there is another way of saying it.

Tortuous, torturous You may want to say that a radio news service is excruciating and it is like 'torture' to listen to it. In this case you say 'torturous'. If you have a route which is full of twists and turns and is somewhat 'circuitous' then it is 'tortuous'.

Total Meaningless unless it is your favourite petrol station.

Tracker dogs An unusual breed. Are you sure that they have been trained to track? Why do you not simply say police with dogs?

Trademark Trademarks are registered product titles or brands and are designed to prevent other producers from raiding the product's reputation. You must also be careful about any publications which are both libellous or maliciously false about the named product. You could be receiving a libel writ in Britain. *UK Press Gazette* and trade publications in other countries regularly publish an update on currently used tradenames. Try choosing another description. For example instead of saying 'Hoover' why don't you say vacuum cleaner?

Tragedy Shakespeare wrote many good tragedies. The Greeks started it. It was always a story depicting the downfall of a central character through his own actions. In the end one inappropriate use of the word tragedy in relation to death, destruction and misfortune will leave you lost for words at another time. Well I suppose you could call it a tragedy again. But will people believe you?

Transpired Occasionally misused. This word means proved to be the case, or came to be known. It should not be used to mean 'what happened next'.

Trigger off Another attempt to cause an explosion. Stick to radio journalism. It is safer.

Trillion Means one thousand billion or a million million. A billion is a thousand million.

Triumphal, triumphant If you are saying somebody is victorious then they are 'triumphant'. But if there is a festival to celebrate the successful military campaign it is a 'triumphal festival'. A monument may well be erected and this would be triumphal as well.

Troops This word should be used for large numbers of soldiers.

Try and Better try to avoid using this expression at all times.

Unique This is an absolute concept and cannot be qualified. There is an independent production company in Britain called 'Unique'. Shame really. They preclude themselves from being described as the good unique company, the brilliant unique company and the very unique company. They were not even the new and original unique company.

Unrest Is this a strike, a demonstration, a rebellion, or a civil war?

Utilise Do not use it.

Valued at, costs were Presenting a news phone-in programme gives me the opportunity of comparing newspapers and news agencies. The different estimated costs of police enquiry and trial process varied from six million to fifteen million pounds. How did this come about? The information was arrived at by a combination of guesswork and unattributable sources.

Some journalists decided to agree on one figure. Hence there were three newspapers that said the cost was six million. Another two climbed to ten million. I think it was the *Sun*, Britain's biggest selling tabloid, that had the highest figure. I suppose thinking big, and selling big means they had to have the biggest claim. You must be cautious about value and cost figures when there is no readily available scale for calculation. It is always better to attribute assessments. This is rather difficult in Britain where officials have to work in a culture where you never help the media if you can help it.

Vast This word relates to geographical area and not to quantity or numerical values. It can be a vast country, but you cannot have vast numbers of students.

Vital It is vital that you do not overuse this word.

Vogue words Language is fluid and always changing. In any year you will find a new generation of words and expressions many of which do not make a lot of sense. 'Downsizing' and 'downshifting' had become 'buzzwords' in 1997. The world of computers has introduced a lot of vogue words, 'becoming wired or connected'. Human intelligence is being measured in terms of 'RAM'.

Volatile The true meaning of the word is a liquid which evaporates quickly. It does not mean explosive.

Vowed If you are thinking about becoming a priest you might find this a useful word. Otherwise say promised or said.

Walkabout We can thank the Aborigines for this word. The Queen 'went walkabout' during her first visit to Australia. Now everyone does it. Boring.

War reporting If you are a trainee or student do not go to war zones. You do not have the experience and you do not have the backup. What is the point of getting seriously injured, killed or arrested for a story you have not even sold? The recent war in former Yugoslavia was a nasty civil war which was no respecter of journalists. Many very doubtful 'journalists' turned up in Sarajevo and some did not return in one piece. Accredited and professional radio journalists needed protection, infrastructure, backup and insurance. Even somebody of Martin Bell's experience and judgement was badly injured. BBC Radio's *World Tonight* reporter John Schofield was shot dead despite all the BBC's outstanding training, resources, experience and protective equipment.

Radio journalism can be a dangerous business, but your duty is to cover and report and placing yourself at risk is a dereliction of that duty. This is not a job for people hooked on *schadenfreude*. This is not a profession for adventurers who get a kick out of the rush of close survival. It is a little stated fact that most radio journalists can effectively cover a war without placing themselves in the middle of the danger zone. Interviews, distant observation and recording from a safe distance does not undermine the drama or power of the reporting.

You must always stay in contact with your office and you must always seek permission and provide information about your movements.

When you move into the danger zone, do not go alone. Ensure there is more than one vehicle in case of breakdowns. Use your common sense about the advisability of marking the vehicles. You must have a trustworthy interpreter and guide who knows all the local customs. You must be able to understand the meaning of hand gestures, signs and flags.

It is vital that you have proper identification as a journalist, that your role and identity could not be confused. If you are on unfamiliar ground take advice from other correspondents who have learned how to stay alive. You must never carry a gun or any other weapon. Think about your body movements and the way you use objects such as a portable microphone and tape recorder. Could your movements be interpreted as the pointing of a weapon? The wearing of body-vests and helmets may be a good idea, but you must avoid looking like a combatant. Always re-evaluate your lines of communication and medical assistance. Never agree to do part-time work for non-journalistic government agencies. British journalists working as intelligence gatherers or messengers for the UK foreign office's intelligence service, MI6, create very serious risks for other journalists.

It is generally wise not to report both sides of the conflict at the same time because of the risk of creating suspicion and inadvertently passing on sensitive information from one side to the next. When you are threatened, get out. Running is a vital technique of survival. Always protest politely, and keep enough money and provisions, such as cigarettes, to bribe your way out. Too many maps and a small camera when you are not a declared photographer could give the impression that you might be a spy. A satellite phone is a very useful service to offer to intransigent and belligerent soldiers. You should be trained in first-aid and have a decent first aid box, white flag and short-wave radio.

You should also avail yourself of any training you can obtain about the techniques of evaluating the risks of warfare in urban and rural settings. You need to know about the power of bullets and ordnance. You need to know what kind of protection the thin metal of a car, or a wall of bricks might provide. You need to know how you can tell the direction of fire and what are the best things you can do when faced with a mortar bomb attack.

The rules of war reporting change when you are accredited as a war correspondent with a rank and obligation to wear special dress. You are subject to censorship and the orders of the army you have joined. In the end precautions are not going to be as useful as sharp wits and the ability to negotiate with a friendly smile when soldiers threaten you with loaded weapons. The International Press Institute, the Press Division of the International Committee of the Red Cross in Geneva and Reporters Sans Frontières are useful organisations which provide advice in relation to the wars which break out anywhere in the world. Ideally you should seek direct advice from journalists who have recently returned from the war location.

Warships Warships do not 'steam' to the battle zone. Now that they are powered by diesel, oil turbines or nuclear power, 'steam' is inappropriate. But captains like to continue saying 'sail' when the only flapping cloth is the small ensign.

Weather When you are writing your weather reports you could advise of good weather on the way, but you should not say 'good weather conditions on the way'.

Wed When do you ever say to anyone: 'Ever think of wedding again?' Have you ever said 'Bob is to wed Rita'? No, just use the right expression – get married. Leave the tabloidese for the tabloids.

Which This is the right pronoun when you are talking about governments and countries.

Widescale Does not make any sense. Say widespread instead.

Widow The widow of the late mayor is a tautology. You should either say ' the wife of the late mayor' or 'the widow of the mayor'.

Women's clinics With the growing incidence of murders and bomb explosions at US abortion clinics you need to check if the predominant activity is the carrying out of abortion operations. It may be the case that only ten per cent of medical services are abortion related.

Zoom You can only zoom up. You cannot zoom down.

Part IV

The Second World War

From adolescence
to adulthood

Chapter 16

The phoney war
and the fall of France

The Second World War dragged radio journalism out of its adolescence into adulthood. The most catastrophic conflict of the twentieth century was responsible for destroying any innocence radio news broadcasting ever had. Radio journalists were faced with the biggest 'stories' ever to involve the human race. The world had never before seen a war on such a global scale. The world had never seen such an evil and scientific annihilation of so many millions of people in what became known as the Holocaust. The world had never witnessed the awesome power of nuclear weaponry. The world had the chance to hear about it all on radio.

National Socialism in Germany used radio as propaganda. The Nazis were ahead of the British and Americans in technology and the use of radio in war. During the first two years, the Americans were ahead of the British in the quality and breadth of their journalism. The USA was neutral until the Japanese attacked Pearl Harbor. In the beginning American reporters could outmanoeuvre incompetent and First World War-style censorship in France by basing themselves on the German side. They were assisted by Dr Goebbels who was a brilliant tactician in the field of propaganda. When the USA became an ally, American radio journalists became subject to strict censorship and government control. Australian radio was similarly shackled. In war the purpose of journalism became synonymous with the national interest. But in radio, governments and listeners found that reporting through sound was more immediate and had an enormous potential for presenting a sense of what was going on. Radio sustained the emotional link between the fighting soldiers and their communities back home.

It is a story of success and failure. The BBC's *9 o'clock News* followed by the War Report became a national and cultural institution. Radio journalism developed with war correspondents capturing the sounds of conflict through actuality and ad-libbed commentary. Legends in radio journalism were created. In Britain Richard Dimbleby, Wynford Vaughan Thomas, Frank Gillard, Alvar Liddell and many others became household names. In America the CBS reporters Ed Murrow and William L. Shirer became stars.

Australia's Chester Wilmot also became an icon through his reliable and dramatic reporting from Tobruk and other major campaigns. In a matter of only a few years the ability to record programmes had been changed from the clumsy Blattnerphone with huge wheels of deadly steel wire to the portable midget recorder that could record two minutes of sound on an acetate disk. The German pioneering developments in reel to reel tape technology were discovered in the Allied advance through Europe and exported by US servicemen to Hollywood and BBC engineers in London.

Through the fog of victory and defeat radio journalism was manipulated by government control. Lies were told. Disasters and incompetence were covered up. Foreign Office interference controlled the way the BBC covered 'The Final Solution'. Ethnic cleansing in the former Yugoslavia has become a frightening echo of European history more than fifty years earlier. By studying the failures of radio journalism in the past, perhaps we might begin to find a perspective on our attitude to modern events and the role journalism should play.

During the First World War the Germans used radio to send out a Morse Code service of news from Berlin to neutral countries such as the USA (before 1917), the Netherlands and Scandinavian countries. In the battles over the trenches Zeppelin crews would use radio to communicate the disposition of allied forces beyond No Man's Land to their artillery positions on the ground. In Russia the Bolsheviks used radio as a political weapon during the Revolution. Lenin had a message sent to the people of St Petersburg. It was transmitted from the Russian cruiser *Aurora*. Morse Code messages and eventually voice broadcasts were transmitted to the outside world to counteract the increasing international hostility to the formation of the Soviet Union. Britain, France and the United States financed, sent arms and even despatched their own troops to fight on Soviet soil in support of the White Russian forces opposed to the Bolsheviks.

It would be good to say that the BBC World Service was created as a result of a spontaneous and well meaning intention to spread British culture abroad. In fact the development of BBC External Services was a desperate response to the growing success of German, Italian and Soviet broadcasts in foreign languages. Britain felt threatened by foreign broadcasts to areas of the world under the British Imperial sphere of influence.

In 1933 the Nazis used a short-wave station in Zeesen near Berlin to target German populations abroad. They fomented German nationalism particularly in

Saarland which later voted to join the German state, and anti-Semitism in North America which had been the destination of many German emigrants. Foreign language services included Hindustani to foster rebellion against British rule, Afrikaans in South Africa and even Gaelic in Scotland.

Mussolini's fascist state in Italy undermined British influence in the Middle East with Arabic services from Bari in Southern Italy. One of the more sensitive areas was Palestine where the indigenous Arab population felt threatened by waves of Jewish immigration generated by pogroms in Russia and Nazi tyranny in Germany. From 1938 the Nazis started Arabic broadcasts. Both the Germans and the Italians built up popular services in Latin America where they exacerbated tension and paranoia about 'Yankee imperialism'. These activities were highly professional and innovative. They involved the setting up of listening clubs and competitions, effective marketing of programmes, transcription services and syndicated news services so that programmes could be re-broadcast in targeted countries by their own radio services. The Italians pioneered language courses. Texts of important speeches by Mussolini would be included for translation and dictation. The BBC World Service has shamelessly copied these audience-building techniques to this very day. The British government was painfully slow to respond to this aggressive and impressive growth of external Axis radio services. In 1937 a typically British solution to the problem was put forward. The Foreign Office would provide the money and the BBC would provide the services. The BBC would be responsible for straight news and not propaganda. The question of who was boss was left to an unwritten gentleman's agreement between Director-General Sir John Reith and the Foreign Office. Like the British Constitution which is unwritten, the terms of reference for journalists at the BBC World Service have been developed by convention and precedent.

A good example of this was the controversy over the first Arab Service news bulletin in January 1938. It led with an accurate report of the hanging of a young Arab at Acre prison in Palestine. He had been tried and convicted by a military court after being arrested for possessing a rifle and ammunition. Acre prison is a notorious symbol of British Imperialist rule. Before the war the gallows there hanged young Arabs who fought against the British administration of the United Nations mandate. During the war and afterwards the gallows were used to hang young Zionists for similar offences. Trial would be by military tribunal, or a single judge sitting without a jury. Under current UK law the unlawful possession of a firearm with ammunition would attract a non-custodial or short prison sentence. In 1938 the Foreign Office and MI6 were rendered apoplectic by a piece of news which was hardly going to endear the British Empire to the Arab nations of the Middle East. In time-honoured BBC fashion the head of the Empire Service wrote a memo. The words of J. B. Clark have become a sort of precedent. He said:

> There is no question about the object of the service: it is to serve the best interests of Great Britain and the Empire. But there may be different ways of achieving this object. . . . Selection of news is of great importance and needs expert knowledge of an audience and background . . . but the omission of unwelcome facts of news and the consequent suppression of truth runs counter to the corporation's policy laid down by the appropriate authority.
>
> (BBC memo 1938, Walker 1992: 33)

The position does not appear to have changed. The 1988 edition of BBC World Service News Guide and Style book offers an interesting definition of the obligation and loyalty of their journalists. Under the heading 'Independence' it is stated that:

> Independence of the government is something we enjoy because the
> World Service is an integral part of the BBC, operating under the
> same Charter, Licence and Agreement. These stipulate that we
> should broadcast in the national interest, but the content of the
> broadcasts is left up to us. So though the government pays for
> the World Service and decides the languages and hours in which we
> broadcast, we alone decide what goes into our news bulletins.
> Broadcasting 'in the national interest' means just that; it is
> not necessarily the same as 'in the government's interest.
>
> (BBC World Service News Guide and Style Book 1988)

The language used here is more significant in what is omitted. It does not say that power of control ultimately rests with the government. The Foreign Office is at liberty to increase, or decrease the funding of the World Service. That is the ultimate editorial control in a capitalist society. The discussion of 'the national interest' is rather intriguing. The final sentence appears to be a charter for self-censorship. The national interest may not be necessarily the same as 'in the government's interest', but we can assume that for most of the time they are the same.

The beginning of the war was a shambles for the BBC. It is true that television was shut down. But the policy of closing places of entertainment and reducing the BBC to an information service from ministers and boring record programmes led to public outcry. Newsprint was being rationed. In fact if you look at copies published at the time you would be lucky to find a national containing more than two large sheets, printed on both sides and folded down the middle. The state had planned to feed the BBC news information from the Ministry of Information which the writer George Orwell later satirised in his novel 1984. Winston Churchill was First Lord of the Admiralty and he preferred a policy of complete silence. His resentment of the BBC was strong. He disliked the media. Meanwhile, the first Director-General of the BBC, Lord Reith, was a Minister of Transport and it was he who ordered all the country road signs to be uprooted to disorientate German parachutists. This consigned thousands of confused motorists to drive round and round in circles in the British countryside.

In London, the energetic Richard Dimbleby was 26 years old and bouncing between Dover and Paris with the BBC's recording car, and getting his uniform fitted, because war correspondents had the status of commissioned officers. The British Army and every other service was planning to ensure he had nothing to report.

America was at least a decade ahead in the attitude of general reporting and from the point of view of equality of opportunity. Women radio correspondents were in the thick of the action from the time of Munich. Sigrid Schultz worked for the poor relation of the American networks, MBS – the Mutual Broadcasting System. William Shirer, the brilliant radio correspondent for CBS in Berlin, observed in his diary that Sigrid was buoyant, cheerful, and always well informed. She had been educated at the Sorbonne and her journalistic track record included an interview with Hitler in 1931 when Dimbleby was still in his school shorts. Dimbleby and Murrow were to take the main credits for revealing the horror of the Nazi concentration camps. Her report from the Ravensbruck concentration camp for women is equal to theirs. In August 1940 she was wounded by the British in a bombing raid over Berlin.

Mary Breckinridge was hired by Ed Murrow for CBS and had assignments in Berlin, Holland and Paris. Betty Wason covered the German invasion of Norway for CBS. She scooped the rival networks with a report of how the Norwegian royal family survived a deadly bombing raid by the Luftwaffe:

> Down the road ran King Haakon, Crown Prince Olaf, the British and Polish ministers, and all the other government officials. They had to stand waist-deep in snow beneath fir trees while bombs crashed.
>
> (CBS, 12 April 1950, Bliss 1991: 110)

Mary Breckinridge was also very much 'on the case' two months before the German invasion of Norway. She managed to board the *Altmark* which was a German merchant ship conveying captured British seamen to internment. But the Royal Navy had successfully intercepted her. In a live broadcast she interviewed the ship's captain and dramatically captured the reality of war:

> I saw a line of frozen blood and a lump of flesh which fell through the slats into the snow where a German sailor was fatally shot. . . . So there lies the *Altmark*, grounded in a lonely little Norwegian fjord, its rudder and screw broken, some

of its men dead, the others confined to their ship, its captives gone, its future uncertain, and the ultimate effects of its adventure still unknown. I return you now to Columbia, New York.

(CBS, 21 February 1940, Bliss 1991: 110)

The BBC coverage of the Norwegian campaign was abysmal. News bulletin reports had consistently generated optimism when it was not at all justified. My father was in the ill-fated Narvik campaign. As Leland Stowe of the *Chicago Daily News* observed in an uncensored despatch from Stockholm, British troops were:

> dumped into Norway's deep snows and quagmires of April slush without a single anti-aircraft gun, without one squadron of supporting airplanes, without a single piece of field artillery.

(*Chicago Daily News*, 25 April 1940, Knightly 1989: 227)

Norway was in fact occupied by a German army of only 1,500 men without firing a shot in Oslo as a result of the treason and compliance of the Norwegian pro-Nazi party whose leader was Major Vidkun Quisling. Quisling soon became synonymous with the word 'traitor'. My father and his comrades were quickly despatched to Iceland on evacuation from Narvik to properly train in the art of Arctic warfare and keep private discussion of the military *débâcle* with their families to a minimum. Ed Murrow broadcast from London:

> the handling by press and radio in this country of the news from Norway in the past ten days has undermined the confidence of a considerable section of the British public in the integrity and accuracy of its news sources.

(CBS, 5 May 1941, Knightly 1989: 227–8)

In contrast, the German PK correspondents had generated nearly 300 despatches, hours of film and audio reports and hundreds of photographs published all around the world. PK personnel had suffered 20 per cent casualties. The failure of the Norwegian campaign led to Chamberlain's resignation. It prompted this report by Ed Murrow for CBS:

> This is London. I spent today in the House of Commons. The debate was opened by Herbert Morrison – one of the ablest members of the Labour Party. He doubted that the Government was taking the war seriously. Mr Morrison said that the Labour Party had decided to divide the House. In other words call for a vote. Mr Chamberlain, white with anger, intervened in the debate and accepted the challenge. In fact he welcomed it. He fairly spat the words. He said that he had friends in the House and he appealed to them to support him. When he had finished, Mr David Lloyd George rose and placed his notes on the despatch box and members surged into the room through both doors, as though the little square grey-shouldered, white-haired Welshman were a magnet

to draw them back to their seats. He swept the House with his arm and said: 'If there is a man here who is satisfied with our production of planes, of guns, of tanks or the training of troops, let him stand on his feet.' No one stood.

(CBS, 8 May 1940. Audio: Included in *Second World War* 1989)

This report is a magnificent example of radio journalism. It is written in short sentences with strong, clear images. The concrete narrative of the drama of the House of Commons chamber and the gestures of the leading politicians tell the story of a vote of no confidence and the downfall of a Prime Minister. It is devoid of editorialising and saturated with authority.

On 30 April 1940 CBS broadcast a news programme in which the only foreign correspondents were Betty Wason from Stockholm and Mary Breckinridge from Amsterdam. This is an admirable recognition of the equality of women in broadcast journalism. But it did not necessarily mean that equality was something which was guaranteed. CBS let Wason go because her voice was too feminine and Network bosses thought it lacked authority. Breckinridge had a deep voice but she left CBS and radio journalism for marriage and a future career in diplomacy. Meanwhile, over at NBC, Margaret Rupli became that network's first woman correspondent.

The USA was in a position of being a neutral country so apart from the censorship in both Germany and Britain, the quality of radio news coverage depended on the ability of their reporters and good fortune. CBS introduced much more rigorous rules concerning balance and fairness. American listeners had to be reminded that the news received from many sources was censored, possibly inaccurate and incomplete. News analysts were being directed that 'in a democracy it is important that people not only should know but should understand, and their function is to help the listener to understand, to weigh, and to judge, but not do the judging for him'. NBC applied similar rules. Since millions of Americans wanted to stay out of the war, the news networks were conscious of the need to achieve a standard of objectivity. This stipulated that broadcasts from democratic European countries had to be balanced by reports from totalitarian countries. The distinguished journalist Dorothy Thompson became a casualty of this doctrine when her denunciation of the Nazi invasion of Poland was broadcast on the NBC affiliate KWK in St Louis. She was taken off the air and prevented from making future commentaries. The networks set out standards of avoiding sensationalism in war coverage. No dramatics and an unexcited demeanour in front of the microphone were the order of the day.

Margaret Rupli covered the Nazi invasion of Holland. She had broadcast a live two-way a few weeks before, using a mobile transmitter provided by the state broadcasting service in Hilversum. The short-wave transmission included Dutch soldiers singing and an officer describing how they were using water to create a flood barrier. She was in Amsterdam on 10 May 1940 but Dutch censors prevented her from broadcasting during a bombing raid. She had to leave Holland immediately because she was married to a British citizen. As she was fleeing the Hook of Holland in a coal barge overloaded with RAF personnel and the Sadlers Wells ballet company, NBC managed to rig up a live interview with the wife of an American banker who described how German parachutists had been seen landing disguised in Dutch uniforms. The interview was terminated with a cacophony of air raid sirens and the immortal words: 'And now I have to get out of here. Goodbye.' Margaret Rupli's account of the invasion of Holland was later broadcast from London and earned Ed Murrow's admiration.

Helen Hiett was NBC's correspondent in Paris. She was well educated and multi-lingual. The American news networks also recruited far more women into their home news operations compared to the BBC. Writers were recruited from the Columbia Graduate School of Journalism in New York. Britain did not take journalism seriously at any university level until forty years later. There are still many academics and politicians who do not recognise Journalism or Media and Communications as a serious subject for academic study and enquiry.

American women also reached the highest positions in news network broadcasting long before a similar opportunity existed in Britain. Helen Sioussat was to succeed Ed Murrow as director of talks at CBS. By the 1950s, Margaret Cuthbert at NBC succeeded as the overall executive in charge of public affairs programmes.

After the invasion of Poland until May the following year the Western Front was in a state of 'Sitzkrieg' or 'the phoney war'. The British Ministry of Information expanded in personnel from twelve to nearly a thousand. Short-wave radio was regarded as a threat to national security. Military chiefs did not want any news coverage of hostilities. There is no evidence that the BBC provided any coverage of a demand for peace by seventy Labour Party constituency associations and a petition signed by twenty-two Labour MPs demanding an early armistice. Radio correspondents assigned to the British Expeditionary Force, BEF, in Europe, were subject to First World War-style restrictions. French censorship was even more severe and saturated with ridiculous disinformation.

The American radio news networks quickly realised that there was more information emanating from Germany where Dr Goebbels and his Foreign Press Department, run by Professor Karl Bonner, had been developing a much more sophisticated propaganda infrastructure. Most of the neutral radio correspondents along with their print colleagues migrated to Berlin after experiencing the oppressive banality and censorship on the Western Front.

The Germans had a much more dynamic and exciting approach to radio reporting in the war. Radio correspondents were part of the Propaganda Kompanien. They were expected to fight in action and train as soldiers. They suffered 30 per cent casualties. It is not surprising when you listen to the real life combat recordings that were made from dive bombers and submarines. PK broadcasters were sending back dramatic eye witness accounts of air raids, land battles and naval engagements to a country where virtually every adult citizen had access to a state-approved radio set manufactured to receive only German stations. PK radio engineers and producers set up a radio station in Dirschau, East Prussia, with the call sign 'Radio Warsaw' during the siege of Warsaw.

The German regime regarded distribution of wireless sets as 'an affair of national, even imperial importance'. This had the result that there were probably twice as many radio sets in Germany as in Britain during the war. German state radio broadcast nine news bulletins each day. They were known as 'Zeitgeschehen' (newsreels) and 'Frontberichte' (dramatic reports from the front).

At the same time draconian penalties in the form of long prison sentences awaited citizens listening to foreign broadcasts. The Berlin correspondent for CBS, William L. Shirer, reported in his diary the extraordinary story of the mother of a Luftwaffe airman who had been told that her son was missing and presumed dead. When eight friends and acquaintances told her they had heard the BBC announce his capture, she reported them to the Gestapo for listening to English broadcasts. On another occasion, the family of a U-boat officer had to continue with an official funeral even though they knew that the BBC had reported his safe capture.

The hesitation caused by British Ministry of Information censorship led to the embarrassing spectre of the Germans broadcasting the resignation of the British War Minister Hore-Belisha before the BBC. Deutschlandsender in Stuttgart and Hamburg Radio also transmitted other cabinet changes twenty-four hours before they were heard on the BBC. These disparities were undermining morale at the Front. Dr Adolf Raskin, director of Radio Saarbrucken, was an expert at combining propaganda Blitzkrieg with the real thing. The Germans developed the dissemination of false news stories to a fine art. Propaganda broadcasts saturated with apparently credible news stories on the eve of military campaigns sowed confusion and panic within countries about to experience the horror of invasion.

The Germans were also very much ahead in technology. The I. G. Farben company had created the first magnetic tape which was being manufactured by one of its subsidiaries BASF. The Allies were still struggling with disc acetates and optical film and wire recorders. German technicians were regularly using Magne-tophone audio tape recorders and players. The machines had high fidelity because of the constant speed transport, high frequency range and technical bias. The plastic tape, impregnated or coated with iron oxide, offered a more precise and speedier method of editing. The sound quality of German broadcasts was generally of a higher standard than that of the Allies.

The Germans were obviously skilled propagandists and they were supported by a handful of 'British traitors' willing to broadcast on the Nazi side. William Joyce joined Radio Hamburg and became popular listening for British troops as well as their families at home. 'Germany calling, Germany calling' was his call sign. He became known as 'Lord Haw Haw'. His voice had a nasal, mean, arrogant quality described by one commentator as 'Cholmondeley-Plantagenet out of Christ Church'. 'Charlie and his Orchestra' was a classic example of how effectively the Nazi regime combined propaganda with high quality entertainment. The musicians played popular tunes of the day with swing arrangements and satirical lyrics in English.

St Louis Blues

BAND LEADER   A negro from the London docks sings the blackout blues.

[Sung in minstrel, Uncle Tom-style English]

> I hate to see the evenin' sun go down,
> hate to see the evenin' go down,
> cause the German, he done bombed this town,
> Feelin' tomorrow, like I feel today . . .
> I'll pack my trunk, make my getaway . . .
> that Churchill badman with his wars and things . . .
> pulls folks 'round by his apron strings . . .
> Got the black-out blues, yeah, blue as I can be,
> that man got a heart like a rock cast in the sea.

(Hitler's Inferno 1990)

This approach to the Afro-American influences in popular music is particularly ironic considering the fact that the Nazis had outlawed jazz music on the basis that it was the decadent emanations of an inferior race. In 1925 a troupe of black American musicians, singers and dancers called 'the Chocolate Kiddies' had taken Germany by storm with a hugely successful tour which sent ripples throughout European music and established jazz as a popular music form. In a radio programme broadcast by BBC Radio 4 in 1997 surviving members of the tour recalled watching one of Hitler's early street marches unaware that a minority extreme political group would be responsible for another world war less than fifteen years later. Jazz influences underpinned another propaganda distortion by 'Charlie and his Orchestra'. The swing lyrics of 'Slumming On Park Avenue' turned into a satirical and moral denunciation of the Royal Air Force:

> Let's go slumming, take me plumbing,
> Let's go slumming on Park Avenue,
> Let us hide behind a pair of fancy glasses
> And make faces when a member of the classes passes.
> Let's go smelling where they're dwelling,
> Sniffing everything the way they do,

> Let us go to it, let's do it
> Why can't we do it too?
>
> (*ibid.*)

Then the band leader announces: 'And here is the song of the British airman'.

> Let's go bombing, oh let's go bombing,
> Just like good old British airmen do,
> Let us bomb the Frenchmen who were once our allies,
> England's fight for liberty, we make them realise from the skies,
> Let's go shelling, where they're dwelling,
> Shelling Nanette, Fifi and Loulou, Let us go to it, let's do it. . . .
> Let's go bombing, it's becoming quite the thing to do.
>
> (*ibid.*)

Other songs in the repertoire included: 'The Man With the Big Cigar', 'Bye Bye Blackbird', 'Found A Million Dollar Baby', 'I'm Putting All My Eggs In One Basket' and 'Boom'.

The radio correspondents in France were accompanied by an eccentric band of censors, many of whom consumed huge quantities of alcohol and appeared to be hired for the sole purpose of ensuring that journalists had nothing informative to send in their despatches. Some of the journalists predicted military disaster on the basis of what they could see and what they could not report. These remained private observations so the public in Britain and America were unprepared for the military disaster that followed. The farcical and chaotic censorship arrangements were not helped by the lack of coordination between the services. A row over an RAF ban on correspondents visiting air bases led to the BBC withdrawing its correspondent Charles Gardner.

Richard Dimbleby was acutely frustrated by this atmosphere. However, a recording of his does survive. It is poetic and masterful in saying absolutely nothing, but capturing the atmosphere and mood of the BEF's presence in Europe. It also includes an ad-lib timed with actuality sound effects of marching feet, singing and bagpipes and this is then combined with a 'voicer' link recorded in the radio truck or in a studio.

> We're standing in the pouring rain at the side of a French road – a road squelching with mud and lined with, right away over the plain to the far skyline with the inevitable double row of poplars. It is a grey cold dismal day. A few lorries only are splashing by to and from the forward areas. [*F/X feet. Growing sound of bagpipes.*]
> But coming down the road towards us is a battalion that I know to be of a famous Irish regiment. They're marching in threes. And in their full battledress and kit they blend with the dripping green grass of the roadside and the brown

of the haystacks. [*F/X Sound of bagpipes rises. Loud cheer from the men. Fading out of music.*]

[*Studio acoustic.*]   As they passed us on that road, their brown capes glistening and their tin hats perched on their heads, I thought how similar this must be to pictures of the last war. The road, the trees, the rain and the everlasting beat of feet. [*F/X Sound of marching feet and chanting by soldiers.*]

(BBC News Broadcast, 15 October 1939. Included in
The Second World War 1989)

Here is an example of evocative radio journalism painting powerful images in the mind of the listener and demonstrating that a radio correspondent can still communicate sub-text and mood if faced with suffocating censorship. Richard Dimbleby leaves us with a report which resonates in the mind and is emotionally engaging.

William Shirer's 'Berlin Diary' is a fascinating account of life as 'a neutral correspondent' in Berlin during the build-up to the outbreak of war and the period before Pearl Harbor. Whilst there was considerable censorship, skilful correspondents such as Shirer could push the boundaries. Shirer's account is the most outstanding journalistic description of the development of Hitler's regime between 1934 and 1940. Here were the foundations for his autobiography *The Nightmare Years* which was dramatised into a three-part television series called *The Wilderness Years*. His later success as an author demonstrates that radio journalism is a fine grounding for future success in literature. His entry for 22 September 1938 demonstrates how the eye of the radio journalist can illuminate the paradox of history in a way that no other medium can:

I was having breakfast in the garden of the Dreesen Hotel, where Hitler is stopping, when the great man suddenly appeared, strode past me, and went down to the edge of the Rhine to inspect his river yacht. X, one of Germany's leading editors, who secretly despises the regime, nudged me: 'Look at his walk!' On inspection it was a very curious walk indeed. In the first place, it was very lady-like. Dainty little steps. In the second place, every few steps, he cocked his right shoulder nervously, his left leg snapping up as he did so. I watched him closely as he came back past us. The same nervous tic. He had ugly black patches under his eyes. I think the man is on the edge of a nervous breakdown.

Shirer's postwar journalism career foundered after a quarrel with Ed Murrow at CBS, and blacklisting during the McCarthy period. He turned to lecturing and writing and became one of America's foremost historians of the twentieth century. He died on 28 December 1993.

His diary gives a graphic idea of the degree of pro-Nazi public opinion in America. On 16 September 1939 he could read a banner headline in the *Borsen Zeitung*: 'Colonel Lindbergh Warns Against The Agitation of the Western Powers'. Shirer had to share a hotel room with American fascist Phillip Johnson who claimed to be representing the American radio commentator Father Charles Coughlin who had set up a right-wing anti-Semitic 'Social Justice' movement. The diary also discloses the frustrations of being a radio foreign correspondent – at the mercy of technology and the whim of editors. Shirer was able to witness the brave defence by Poles of their garrison at Danzig, but his broadcast to New York did not get through.

The disparity between US neutral reporting from Berlin and the quality of information supplied to the BBC by government sources is well illustrated by the story of William Shirer's live and scripted interview with U-Boat Captain Herbert Schultze. The captain claimed that he had torpedoed the British ship *Royal Sceptre*, and had also arranged for the rescue of the passengers and crew by another ship, the *Browning*. But the BBC reported that the *Royal Sceptre* had been sunk without warning with all sixty of those aboard going down with her. Schultze also claimed to be the submarine commander who had sent a cheeky cable to Winston Churchill, the then First Lord of the Admiralty, informing him of where he had just sunk another British vessel. The BBC had reported Churchill telling the House of Commons that he had captured the U-Boat commander who was in a British prison. Shirer went about checking the conflict in information. Shultze was able to produce the contents of his log book showing that he was in fact the author of the cable to Churchill and he had made it back to Kiel without capture. Reuters also reported that the *Browning* had arrived in Brazil with the entire crew and passengers of the *Royal Sceptre*.

On 2 October 1939 the BBC reported that British planes flew over Berlin overnight. Shirer had heard nothing. Not even an air-raid alarm. He concluded that all sides were lying. Although Churchill had been in charge of the Royal Navy, the Norwegian campaign sealed Chamberlain's fate as Prime Minister and Churchill was given the mantle of leadership. No amount of First World War-style censorship would be able to keep the British public from the impending disaster of the fall of France. It is difficult to assess whether Britain's ability to snatch victory out of defeat in the Dunkirk evacuation was a brilliant stroke of propaganda or good radio journalism. The British rightly realised that now was the time to tell the truth consistently. American correspondents on the German side continued to be even-handed in their coverage. They had no reason to distort coverage for any national purpose. But another five years of exhausting and traumatic warfare were to test the boundaries of objectivity for US journalists. Pearl Harbor was not exactly Dunkirk. But the United States lost a large proportion of its Pacific fleet and a decision was taken to lie. Radio played a fundamental role in the construction of that lie.

Chapter 17

The Holocaust and other horrors

The Nazis' 'Final Solution' remains the most horrific story of the twentieth century. The implementation by Adolf Hitler's regime of persecution and genocide against European Jewry coincided with breathtaking developments in radio journalism techniques, professionalism and the relationship between the radio journalist and the listener. The first radio reporters acquitted themselves with dignity and sensitivity. However, the overall organisational and politico-economic pressures of the time leave us with a legacy of doubt and outrage about the motives and actions of Allied governments.

There are observers and bystanders and a lingering controversy remains that more could have been done to save the lives of millions of Jewish victims. But the growing charge that the BBC and the British Foreign Office deserve to be tried for moral neglect and cultural anti-Semitism is too simplistic. There is justifiable anger, but there are also myths that need to be dispelled. In Britain and the USA the cultural icons of radio journalistic coverage are Richard Dimbleby's BBC report of what he saw on the liberation of Belsen and Ed Murrow's CBS report of what he saw on the liberation of Buchenwald. There is more and it is equally valid. Reports and coverage by other radio journalists demonstrate a greater depth and success of communication than has hitherto been recognised. Radio, with its unique engagement with the imagination and poetic dignity of the human spirit, showed that it could report the unreportable. Sigrid Schultz reporting for the US Mutual Broadcasting System unlocked the horrors of the Ravensbruck camp reserved for women near Berlin and the BBC's Patrick Gordon Walker achieved news feature interviewing and production to which any contemporary BBC radio journalist would be proud to put his or her name.

It is also a shabby story of censorship. What the world heard in April and May 1945 it could have heard in July and August 1944. It is possible to assume that Richard Dimbleby and Ed Murrow buckled to the existence of cultural anti-Semitism by deliberately omitting reference in their reports to the fact that most of the inmates of Belsen and Buchenwald were Jewish and that the focus of the Final Solution was the annihilation of the Jewish nation. Anne Karpf, the UK *Guardian*'s radio critic has recently written a moving account of the experience of being the child of a concentration camp survivor. Her book offers a frightening account of the cultural anti-Semitism in Britain through the 1930s and 1940s. In a *Guardian* article published on 25 June 1996 she has pointedly highlighted the observation that Richard Dimbleby 'scarcely mentioned Jews' in his famous Belsen report.

Does Richard Dimbleby deserve to be criticised for his failure of emphasis? There is a risk that anyone researching this issue could be led into believing that he made no references to Jews at all because his original report has been dubbed and edited into so many secondary sources and the critical phrase 'thousands of them Jews' edited out. My own research with primary source interviews with survivors at Belsen appears to confirm that Belsen contained a ratio of roughly half Jewish and half non-Jewish inmates. I would conclude that eloquent and sensitive writers such as Anne Karpf are justified in challenging the indifference of a world which condemned her mother and family to the horrors of the Holocaust. The Holocaust leaves reverberating emotional footsteps which transcend generations and ripple into the history of the contemporary world, particularly in Israel and the Middle East.

Ed Murrow's report has no references to Jews. It could be that the population of Buchenwald was similarly divided into 50 per cent Jewish and 50 per cent non-Jewish detainees. The concentration camps sited within Germany tended to deal with Nazi dissidents as well as other categories which had become the target of extermination. It would be highly unlikely that Ed Murrow, nicknamed 'Bleeding Heart' by his friends, would have been susceptible to any tendency towards anti-Semitism or cultural self-censorship. We can only speculate about the omission of any identification of Jewish victims. Previous CBS despatches by Ed Murrow vigorously highlighted the immorality of Nazi actions against the Jews. He was emphatic in his reporting and in a better position to amplify reports of Nazi atrocities reaching London. BBC correspondents and contributors were subjected to censorship and policy strictures from the UK Foreign Office and Ministry of Information.

The world has rarely seen such an incredible acceleration of evil. It started with the banding together of a few individuals in 1920 around a former army corporal who had a predilection for anti-Semitism. In less than twenty years it mushroomed into an atomic cloud of nationalistic and racist political ideology. The brutal and expansionist force unleashed by Nazism occupied most of mainland Europe by 1940. At the Wannsee conference in January 1942, Hitler's cronies decided to exterminate an entire race. In less than three years they were very close to achieving this objective.

The origins of anti-Semitism are complex. There are chronicles of Jewish massacres going back to the eleventh century in England. Even the famous medieval writer Geoffrey Chaucer is responsible for a virulently anti-Jewish story in the *Canterbury Tales*. It recycles the old myth of Jews slaying a Christian child at Easter by cutting its throat and drinking the blood. 'Pogroms' or uprisings of violence against Jewish communities in Russia and Eastern Europe claimed tens of thousands of lives in the early part of the twentieth century. Anti-Semitism was common and deeply ingrained in Britain, America, France and Australia where thriving 'black-shirt' movements supported and recycled the anti-Jewish propaganda of Hitler's Brown Shirts. In the East End of London riots broke out as Oswald Mosley's Black Shirts attempted to march into streets populated by mainly Jewish and working-class communities. Germany's Jewish population was one of the most assimilated, metropolitan and middle-class in Europe. Mixed marriages were common. But the historical roots of anti-Semitism had been planted many centuries before when the German Protestant reformer Martin Luther had talked about a Jewish problem in 1543. He advocated that synagogues should be set on fire and 'whatever does not burn away should be covered or scattered with dirt so that no-one may ever be able to see a cinder or stone of it'. He echoed the jealousy engendered by Jewish enterprise in trade and banking by stating that Jews had 'extorted usuriously from us'. In European history, Jews had grown used to mass expulsions.

There is no evidence of radio documentary attempting to explain or analyse a generation of anti-Semitic writers and philosophers who were to provide the ideological impetus for genocide. The new medium failed the purposes of civilisation. In America the burgeoning power of right-wing radio broadcasters such as Father Coughlin and Huey 'Kingfisher' Long regurgitated the myth of an international Jewish conspiracy to dominate the world. This originated as a forged publication in Russia in 1905 called 'The Protocols of The Elders of Zion'.

Hitler's *Mein Kampf* drew its anti-Semitic inspiration from four key writers. French diplomat and social philosopher Comte Joseph Arthur de Gobineau laid the ground for belief in an Aryan, white race which was superior to all other races. His 'Essay On The Inequality of Human Races' influenced Housten Stewart Chamberlain. Born in Southsea, England, Chamberlain married the daughter of the German composer Richard Wagner and his 'Grundlagen des XIX Jahrhunderts' proclaimed the superiority of the German people on the basis they were descended from superior Teutonic or Aryan stock. The German philosopher Eugan Karl Dühring believed in a compatibility between capital and labour within a nationalistic and anti-Semitic context. Alfred R. Rosenberg was instrumental in fusing these theories into an intellectual and ideological framework of 'National Socialism'. He wrote *Der Mythus des 20. Jahrhunderts* in 1930 to 'prove' the racial superiority of Germans over all other peoples. He also became the editor of the official party newspaper *Völkischer Beobachter*.

Harassment, violence, and murder became a likely experience for Germany's half million population of Jews from the time Hitler achieved power in 1933. Laws categorising the race of German citizens were introduced in 1935. The Nuremberg Race laws exacted racial categories and effectively disenfranchised Jewish Germans. Extra-marital relations and marriage between Jews and 'German Aryans' were forbidden. Historical anti-Semitic myths were mutated into contemporary propaganda in Julius Streicher's *Der Sturmer* which alleged that Jews were rapists and 'polluters'. The CBS correspondent William Shirer wrote in his diary about a successful Jewish doctor and First World War veteran who had been tortured for several months in a Gestapo jail. Many Jewish families consulted him about ways of escaping to Britain and America. By 1938 all passports belonging to Jews were recalled for endorsement and stamped with the letter 'J'. Concentration camps built to punish socialists, communists and trade unionists were expanded to receive Jewish detainees. Thousands had fled the indignities of losing their possessions, jobs, professional livelihoods, the constant threat of arbitrary violence and murder. Hundreds of thousands remained. Some held onto the traditional Jewish optimism that 'it could not get any worse'. But it could.

William Shirer was on holiday in Switzerland writing his first play *Foreign Correspondent* when a young Polish Jew assassinated German diplomat Ernst vom Rath in Paris. Two days later the Nazis launched a terrifying national pogrom on the night of 9 November 1938. The shattered glass of synagogues and Jewish businesses littered the streets of German towns and cities. 'Kristallnacht' was a night of slaughter and humiliation. The Jews of Germany had become outlaws.

From this point on there was a need to expose the brutality and evil of the Nazi regime and campaign against it. An examination of the British press during the period 1933 to 1938 clearly indicates that there was accurate reporting of violence against Jews and the existence of concentration camps. Yet some British newspapers were sympathetic to Fascism with the result that news coverage of Nazi atrocities was muted. The *Daily Mail* and *The Times* newspapers employed journalists who were pro Hitler. The Australian radio journalist Chester Wilmot encountered anti-Semitism for the first time when trying to enter Austria while on a lecture tour with a Jewish friend from Melbourne. They had to wait three days before his Jewish friend was permitted entry. He recalled that watching the charismatic Adolf Hitler enabled him to 'understand how he got hold of the Germans in the way he did'. He was honest enough to observe 'I felt that if I'd stayed around too long, he would have got hold of me too'. I recall interviewing a

German woman who was in the Hitler Youth during the war. She had been brainwashed with the idea of Jews being sub-human and inferior. She was conditioned to say 'Heil Hitler' and raise her hand in salute. She said in this frenzied and hysterical political world of social control and totalitarian propaganda free thinking was not permitted.

The British authorities were receiving detailed accounts of Jewish persecution by refugees fleeing Germany. British consuls sent graphic accounts to the Foreign Office. British officials in the United Kingdom found it very difficult to believe the accounts. Refugees found that the English aristocracy was more interested in whether they 'had met the Goerings, or Ribbentrops'. BBC European producer Harman Grisewood had been in Germany in the weeks before the invasion of Poland. He returned to Broadcasting House to brief the then BBC Director General Frederick Ogilvie. He was rendered virtually speechless when Ogilvie explained that the BBC planned to broadcast a special recording of a nightingale singing and a cellist playing in an English wood to appeal to German sentimentality. Such apathy and complacency was to determine the BBC policy over the next six years. To be fair to BBC journalists they were subject to strict government control. The Ministry of Information, portrayed by George Orwell as the 'Ministry of Truth' in his novel *1984*, determined propaganda policy and the content of BBC programmes. The Foreign Office recruited much of its personnel from the Oxbridge-educated aristocracy. It is also important to bear in mind that the tension in the Palestine Mandate administered by Britain was an important factor in the formulation of attitudes and prejudices. Generally, the Foreign Office was pro-Arab despite the Balfour Declaration of 1919 expressing a policy commitment to establishing a Jewish homeland in Palestine. British foreign policy was determined more by economic considerations than by prejudice. Maintaining control over the Arab sphere of influence was critical in the battle for the access to the world's richest oil resources.

The German propagandists had two trump cards to play against the British: First World War propaganda had wrongly accused German troops of slaughtering Belgian civilians and bayoneting babies; and the British had herded thousands of Afrikaner women and children into 'Concentration Camps' where many died from disease and starvation during the Boer War. The Foreign Office responded by publishing a White Paper incorporating first hand accounts of Nazi atrocities against German Jews, socialists and political dissidents. 'Papers Concerning the Treatment of German Nationals in Germany' had an impact. But examination of public papers reveals that not all government civil servants were enthusiastic about the veracity of the accusations. 'Jewish voices' were described as 'always doubtful' and observations were made that persecuted Jews were not entirely reliable witnesses. Sir Alexander Cadogan wrote in longhand 'The Germans will only say this is further proof that the British Empire is run by

International Jewry and I am not sure that sympathy with the Jews has not waned very considerably during the last twelve months'.

The invasion of Poland in September 1939 significantly changed the scope and potential for Jewish persecution when the Nazis took control of Europe's largest Jewish population. William Shirer for CBS reported privately in his diary that the new Governor-General of occupied Poland was shutting off the Jewish ghetto from the rest of the capital. General Hans Frank regarded Jews as 'carriers of diseases and germs'. The Nazi policy towards the Jews in Poland was based on one objective – 'extermination'. Censorship prevented Shirer from directly reporting this to CBS listeners but his 'Berlin Diary' was published in 1941 and instantly became a bestseller. American diplomats knew that German Jews were to be sent to Eastern Poland to die. The British press carried many accounts of Nazi massacres of Polish Jews and in December 1939 the London *Evening Standard* cartoonist David Low somewhat prophetically depicted Jews being loaded onto a goods train. The BBC news bulletins did not reflect the depth of this press coverage.

To the BBC's credit, in November 1939 the talent of the Drama Department under Val Gielgud produced a remarkable series called *The Shadow of the Swastika*. It was an intelligent and effective attempt to dramatise the real nature of anti-Semitism in the Nazi party. The plot included the storyline of a Jewish surgeon in Berlin being called upon to operate on a member of the Hitler Youth. The surgeon was the only doctor available and skilled enough to perform the life-saving operation, but while in a state of semi-consciousness the patient mutters 'Down with the Jews, kill the Jews, the Jews – we've got to get rid of the Jews, kill the Jews'. The series ends with the poignant line from the surgeon: 'Curious isn't it, the things people say when they're under anaesthetic?' Marius Goring played the role of Adolf Hitler. The series was truthful, engaging and educational, but it was also regarded by the BBC hierarchy as controversial and provocative. It was broadcast on the Home Service, but not the German service. Jewish voices were kept off the air in broadcasts to Europe. The Foreign Office was concerned that moralising about Jews would alienate the German audience. Assessors and 'switch censors' were appointed to be present during live transmissions. They had the power to disconnect microphones amplifying Jewish voices and accents. *The Shadow of the Swastika* was not repeated and during the war nothing like it was produced or broadcast again. The BBC and Foreign Office feared stirring up 'latent anti-Semitism'.

The acceleration towards genocide began with the invasion of the Soviet Union. Einsatzgruppen SS units set about murdering Jews with guns and experimented with portable gassing trucks. The head of the SS security branch, Reinhard Heydrich, convened the Wannsee conference in Berlin on 20 January 1942. In a meeting lasting half an hour, the 'Final Solution' was put into operation. Systematic extermination would require industrial efficiency. New death camps were constructed at Auschwitz, Treblinka and Majdanek. At the same time eight governments-in-exile and the French National Committee convened in London but rejected an American–Jewish Congress request to condemn the Nazi crimes against the Jews. They obfuscated with the statement: 'reference might be equivalent to an implicit recognition of the racial theories which we all reject'.

The British Press began to report stories emanating from occupied Europe of Jewish massacres during the summer of 1942. Jewish groups always found it difficult for their envoys to be taken seriously. The Polish government-in-exile in London published a White Book of German atrocities. The Polish Socialist and Jewish activist Szmul Zygielbojm was the vital conduit for information coming from Poland. He had smuggled himself out of Poland in 1942 and had witnessed the horrors of starvation and murder in the Warsaw Ghetto where his wife and son were still living. He was the source of the *Daily Telegraph* report published on 25 June 1942 stating that 700,000 Jews had been murdered in Poland and that the Germans had developed a special gas to poison Jews and political prisoners in trucks. The BBC European Service permitted a broadcast by the Roman Catholic Bishop of Westminster which was based on the information supplied by the Polish government-in-exile. BBC news bulletins in July 1942 reported the process of mass killings but always waited for confirmation from its own channels. An anti-German British diplomat, Sir Robert Van Sietart, vehemently attacked the Nazi policy of Jewish extermination in an impassioned broadcast after the *9 o'clock news* in September 1942.

But the news media's coverage was not accompanied by an official condemnation or confirmation of the Nazi policy. The US State Department had the intelligence in August 1942. The official Allied confirmation of the plans for a Final Solution did not occur until December 1942 by which time at least one million European Jews had been slaughtered. Zygielbojm had to depend on the support of Labour MPs who organised a protest meeting in Caxton Hall, London on 2 September 1942. He and his supporters urged direct action. He suggested bombing railway lines and dropping leaflets on German citizens detailing the atrocities. By the end of 1942, 6,000 Jews were being killed every day. Most of the mass deportations from the Warsaw ghetto were over. Zygielbojm's close friend Adam Czerniakow had committed suicide rather than draw up lists for deportation to death camps.

The problem for Zygielbojm was that the Allied governments were reluctant to accept the truth of Jewish emissaries. The Polish government-in-exile had to sponsor a special observer and former army officer Jan Karski to travel to occupied Poland and bring back a first-hand account of the killings. He then had to personally travel to London and Washington DC to describe his agonising memory of visits to the Warsaw ghetto and the camps at Belzec and Treblinka to British and American government officials. Even in the 1980s and 1990s he would break down under the strain of having to recall the horrific scenes he had witnessed.

The Polish government-in-exile published another pamphlet on 10 December 1942 called 'The Mass Extermination of Jews in German Occupied Poland'. Combined with an Allied declaration of solemn protest on 17 December, coverage in both the press and on BBC radio was strong. Members of the House of Commons rose and stood in silence for two minutes after the declaration was read by the Minister for War, Sir Anthony Eden. At last there was official acceptance that the Nazis had a deliberate plan for mass extermination of European Jewry. But no action to stop it was to follow. The intensity of radio news coverage evaporated. Marius Goring made an impassioned broadcast on the German service. Earlier protocol to censor threats of recriminations against German radio listeners was postponed, but only for this short period. Ed Murrow broadcast from London for CBS:

> One is almost stunned into silence by some of the information reaching London. Some of it is months old, but it's eyewitness stuff supported by a wealth of detail and vouched for by responsible governments. What is happening is this: Millions of human beings, most of them Jews, are being gathered up with ruthless efficiency and murdered.
>
> (CBS, 1942. Bliss 1991: 163)

He stated boldy that the Nazis were exterminating the Jews. He said it was a vista of mass murder and moral depravity which was 'unequalled in the history of the world'. But from December 1942 the world was virtually silent until the BBC and American networks permitted broadcasts of correspondents entering liberated concentration camps in April 1945. Why did radio fail to maintain accurate and proper reporting of this appalling horror?

It was the application of a systematic policy to 'soft pedal' the entire story of mass extermination. There was no Jewish representation at executive and decision-making levels of the BBC, Foreign Office and Ministry of Information. The controller of the BBC Home Service, Sir Richard Maconachie, wrote in April 1943 that 'any direct action to counter anti-Semitism would do more harm than good'. The assistant director of the BBC's *Children's Hour* programme rejected a proposal to produce features on Jewish persecution because: 'If you give Jewish broadcasters an inch, they come clamouring for a mile'.

In April 1943, Jewish fighters were challenging eight hundred SS officers with home-made grenades, Molotov cocktails and their bare hands. It was a fight to the death. Szmul Zygielbojm's wife and son were now dead. He had pleaded with the London-based official of the US Office of Strategic Services to bomb the railway lines leading to the death camp at Treblinka. The US government declined.

The chill hand of complacency and prejudice was stalling desperate attempts by

Jewish organisations to ransom the lives of Jews, press Allied governments for military action to stop the extermination and even prevent Palestinian Jews from forming their own brigade to fight in Europe. The British Foreign Office obstructed attempts to broadcast threats and warnings to Germany throughout 1943 and 1944. Labour MP David Robertson was rebuffed by the Foreign Office when he asked for continual condemnatory broadcasts over a period of thirty days. On 11 May 1943 Szmul Zygielbojm returned to his lodgings in Porchester Square, London and killed himself. He left a note apologising to his landlady for the distress he had caused and another for the Polish government-in-exile. He said:

> By my death I wish to express my strongest protest against the inactivity with which the world is looking on and permitting the extermination of the Jewish people. I know how little human life is worth.
>
> (Levin, N. 1975: 354)

He hoped that his death would contribute 'to breaking the indifference of those who are able and should act to save the handful of Polish Jews, who are still alive, from certain annihilation'. His death was not reported by the BBC or American radio networks. Most of the British newspapers failed to report that his suicide had been a protest. In June 1943 Jan Karski arrived in Washington DC for a private audience with President Roosevelt. He had been disguised as a policeman so that he could witness the deportations and killings at Treblinka and Belzec. He informed the American President:

> I was instructed by the leaders of our underground to tell the British and American military authorities that only through direct reprisals, such as mass bombing of German cities, after dropping millions of leaflets telling the Germans that they were being bombed in reprisal for exterminating Jews, could this mass extermination be stopped or at least limited.
>
> (Karski 1947: 182: Levin, N. 1975: 696)

The Allies did drop leaflets in Germany in the summer of 1943 and these detailed the mass killings. It can be argued that the carpet bombing of German cities and the death and destruction of civilians at Dresden, Cologne, Frankfurt and Hamburg in firestorms could have been the manifestation of these reprisals. But it is a fact that at no time did the Allied governments ever make an explicit threat of reprisal and the Nazis' Final Solution continued. No systematic action was taken to bomb the railway lines leading to the camps. US media coverage was muted. Even the Jewish-owned *New York Times* failed to feature the killings as a front page story. Colliers and American *Mercury* did publish Jan Karski's chilling eye witness accounts in late 1944 after he became frustrated by the lethargy of President Roosevelt and the Allies and decided to go public.

Eight months before Richard Dimbleby entered Belsen, the BBC had three major sources for reports of the liberation of concentration camps by the Red Army. The BBC did not have an accredited correspondent in Moscow. It depended on contributors who were correspondents for national newspapers. Alexander Werth was a regular contributor. He had been born in Leningrad and worked for the *Sunday Times*. From 1942 his despatches were broadcast every fortnight by the BBC as *The Russian Commentary* after the nine o'clock news. They were presented by Joseph Macleod. The Russians created technical difficulties so that he was only able to make one direct broadcast from Moscow in June 1943. In July 1944 he arrived at Majdanek Nazi Extermination Camp. He saw an industrial plant of gas chambers and ovens. An estimated one and a half million people had died from shootings and poisoning from Zyklon-B. His report was suppressed by the BBC.

Paul Winterton, the *News Chronicle*'s Moscow correspondent, was another BBC contributor who also accompanied the Red Army into the deserted Majdanek. He filed a report which was shocking and detailed. He now says the BBC thought he was regurgitating Soviet propaganda. A clumsily-edited and shortened version of his report was later transmitted in August 1944 but only on the BBC's North American service. It prompted a call for a special war crimes commission, but the Foreign Office in London successfully stalled and deflected the outcry. The other source for the reporting of Nazi atrocities was the Russian Jewish writer and correspondent Ilya Ehrenberg. He felt very strongly about the Nazis and tended to stress their atrocities. But his despatches were only broadcast as weekly talks in French on the BBC's European services. The paucity of broadcast coverage compares badly with much more extensive coverage in the newspapers which were still subject to paper rationing. The *Sunday People* for 30 July 1944 consisted of one folded broadsheet with a single sheet inside. Columnist Peter Forbes started his week's peroration with the words:

> Recently came the shocking news of how the Nazis herded children into 64 trains – telling the wondering parents that the kiddies were to be 'exchanged for prisoners-of-war' – transported them to Poland and there put them to death in gas-chambers. After which the trains went back, loaded up the parents, and a similar process was carried out. Upwards of 400,000 thin, fearful, simple people died. And the children's ages were from two to six years; their 'crime' – they had been born into the Jewish faith!
>
> (*Sunday People* 30 July 1944)

The cover-up had been so effective that as the Nazi military machine and totalitarian government crumbled before the Allied advance in the East and the West, public opinion throughout the world was incapable of understanding the nature of this unspeakable crime against humanity. The first radio correspondents and their print colleagues were faced with an unbearable task – to write the unimaginable, to explain the inexplicable and to communicate a reality that was beyond belief.

I have interviewed twenty people who were educated teenagers or young adults in 1945 and they say that they had had no inkling at all from the radio and newspaper media in the years previously. Their first confrontation with the horror of this story was through the presentation of newsreels in the cinema. Radio news coverage was not saturated or particularly emphatic because reports of the liberation of the camps had to compete with the news of so many other aspects of the war.

Richard Dimbleby wrote a fourteen-minute report which does not appear ever to have been broadcast in its entirety. That was a mistake. If there was ever a justification for dispensing with the time-frames of programme structures this was it. Initially, the BBC refused to transmit his report. He broke down when attempting to record it for the first time. The BBC hesitated, ostensibly because they wanted confirmation from newspaper reports in the same way broadcast news editors hesitate before broadcasting a correspondent's exclusive because they would prefer to 'see the story on the wires'. Dimbleby had the courage of his convictions, rang Broadcasting House and informed his superiors that he would never broadcast again in his life if they continued to suppress his report. As indicated in an earlier chapter, the censorship and editing of Richard Dimbleby's extraordinary report has led to unfortunate misconceptions about whether he properly reported the number of Jewish survivors in Belsen. Of course he did. His original report has been repeatedly edited and shortened for different formats of documentary and published presentations. He did more than any other radio or newspaper correspondent of the time to marshall the resources of anger, disbelief and a courage in describing the truth. He challenged the very boundaries of what is acceptable from the point of view of presenting the reality of the war's horrors and human degradation. His contribution deserves much more respect than it has hitherto been given. His script is more than just a radio report. It has the testimony of historical truth and the poetic voice of somebody profoundly changed by what he has witnessed.

I wish with all my heart that everyone fighting in this war and above all those whose duty it is to direct the war from Britain and America could have come with me through the barbed wire fence that leads to the inner compound of the camp. Beyond the barrier was a whirling cloud of dust, the dust of thousands of slowly moving people laden in itself with the deadly typhus germ. And with the dust there is a smell sickly and thick, the smell of death and decay, of corruption and filth. I passed through the barrier and found myself in the world of a nightmare. The living lay with their heads against the corpses and around them move the awful ghostly procession of emaciated, aimless people with nothing to do and no hope of life, unable to move out of your way, unable to look at the terrible sights around them. It was as though they were waiting their turn. This is what the Germans did. Let there be no mistake about it. Did deliberately and slowly. To doctors, authors, lawyers and musicians, to professional people of every kind whom they turned into animals behind the wire in their cage. There was no privacy nor did men and women ask it any longer. Men and women stood and squatted stark naked in the dust trying to wash themselves and to catch the lice on their bodies.

(19 April 1945, BBC Sound Archives. Quoted from 'Richard Dimbleby Remembers Belsen', January 1995, BBC2)

He described a mother, mad with grief, handing her dead baby to a British soldier believing it was still alive, and the awful fact that in the frenzy of starvation survivors had removed the liver and kidneys of corpses to eat.

The BBC's coverage of this story was finally equal to the approach of the newspaper media. The *Daily Mail* for 24 April 1945 shed its anti-Semitic past by publishing the full-length feature by Rhona Churchill, *Education for Murder*. It was an extraordinary analysis of why so many Germans had been able to will-ingly participate in genocide against Jews: 'At 17, Hans Schmidt was in tears at his first murder . . . at 30, merely impatient at the slowness with which his last thousand-odd victims dug their own graves'.

As Richard Dimbleby moved on towards Berlin with Montgomery's Second Army, the BBC's European Services producer Patrick Gordon Walker stayed behind to record interviews and actuality and compile two reports that have an equal standing in the quality of communication and journalism. The BBC can be rightly criticised for the unjustifiable censorship of reports emerging from Eastern Europe of the Nazi genocide between December 1942 and April 1945. The biggest charge laid against the BBC, British Foreign Office and Allied governments is that this duplicitous policy contributed to the destruction of half a million Hungarian Jews in 1944. By this time the Allies were on the offensive. They had the military power. The British have never been able to explain exactly what were the 'certain technical difficulties' preventing Allied bombing of the death camps and railways leading to them. The Hungarians were terrified of the destructive power of air raids. And in April 1944 the BBC did broadcast the Allied threat that if a Jewish ghetto was created in Budapest, Allied planes would bomb residential areas as well as military targets. But the BBC was not used to carrying these threats to the other towns and cities of Hungary where Jews were being rounded up for deportation. On 11 July 1944, Winston Churchill wrote to his Secretary of State for War, Sir Anthony Eden:

There is no doubt that this is probably the greatest and most horrible crime ever committed in the whole history of the world, and it has been done by scientific machinery by nominally civilised men in the name of a great state and one of the leading races of Europe. It is quite clear that all concerned in this crime who may fall into our hands, including the people who only obeyed orders by carrying out the butcheries should be put to death after their association with the murders has been proved.

(Levin, N. 1975: 674)

Fine sentiments, but the backing of threats of this kind did not manifest itself in military action combined with the full power of broadcast propaganda and journalism which was in the command of the BBC.

In 1940 Winston Churchill also urged the formation of a Jewish Brigade in Palestine to fight the Germans but by 1944 even he became exasperated by the reluctance of pro-Arab and anti-Jewish civil servants and military chiefs to facilitate his command.

These are matters which hang heavily on the conscience of history and we find radio journalism wanting in its assistance to millions of victims of the Nazis' Final Solution who include gypsies, Slavs, homosexuals, the disabled as well as dissident Germans. But failure should be balanced with an acknowledgement that broadcasters used radio powerfully and effectively to tell the story of the Nazi killing machine as it collapsed in front of the advance of British and American troops through Western Germany.

Patrick Gordon Walker's two reports from Belsen had a significant impact on listeners in Britain and particularly in North America where radio stations regularly dubbed the short-wave transmissions onto acetate discs for rebroadcast. Patrick Gordon Walker interviewed the soldiers of the Oxfordshire Yeomanry desperately trying to save lives and struggling with their emotions. He recorded the first Kaddish or Jewish lament for the dead ceremony with the survivors. Their exhausted voices resonate with a sense of hope. He recorded rational and sensitive interviews with the survivors themselves. A woman described how she had been at Auschwitz and seven other camps before being marched to Belsen. Dutch and Russian orphans aged between nine and fourteen sang songs including 'The English May Live In Glory'. The reports have the quality and professionalism of a modern news package prepared for the BBC's *World Tonight* or *Today* programme. The writing and language of Patrick Gordon Walker is also thoughtful and intelligent. His broadcasts in May 1945 allowed people to speak for themselves and in some ways are more valuable than the single-voice accounts of the first correspondents to enter the camps. A Jewish soldier from London's East End described how he shared tears with women he had liberated. Driver mechanic Payne provided the first-hand account of the blackened dead baby handed to him by the demented mother who had been referred to by Richard Dimbleby. The soldier described how the mother died shortly afterwards with the dead baby in her arms. He said: 'I'm a British soldier and it's not propaganda. It's the truth.' Another soldier said he feared that the men, women and children of England would repeat the mistake he had made of regarding reports of the atrocities with 'a pinch of salt'.

Patrick Gordon Walker observed:

> One British soldier I shall never forget. I found him in the typhus block. Sick and dying people were lying crowded together in rags. Many of them on the floor. The stench brought me to a standstill at the door. There sat this British private hour-after-hour cheering up the sick, though they could not understand a word that he was saying and ceaselessly ladling out fresh milk.
>
> (BBC North American Service. Quoted from *Concentration Camp Horrors, Broadcasts heard in 1945*)

The report included the playing of 'God Save The King' by a French Jewish survivor on an out of tune piano in the SS canteen. Patrick Gordon Walker concluded somewhat prophetically:

> Already people are beginning to ask questions. Questions that we must answer. What is the meaning of these things? What are we to do about them? These questions are not easy to answer. I have seen at first hand the horrors you have heard and seen at second hand. Ever since I saw them my head has been full of them. And all the time I have been puzzling over the questions the world is now asking itself. One thing I am sure of. The world is up against something new here. Against evil in a new form. What I have seen is not just cruelty and oppression of opponents such as the world has known before in its history. No. These things were done by men who had their cruelty and sadism under control, who did these things knowing exactly what they were doing. They were, I am convinced, deliberately and calculatingly attacking the foundations of our civilisation. They were deliberately flouting the respect we have for individual human lives. They were deliberately flouting the distinction we make between human and animal. The men who set up and ran these camps delighted in arbitrary killing. They forced people in a planned way to live like animals. They made experiments on women and twins and deformed people as if they were guinea pigs. This manifestation of evil is particularly dangerous because it arose in the heart of civilised Europe, and because it commanded power over men's minds and actions such as we have never known before. These things are very near us. That's one of our strongest feelings. What are we to do? First we must revenge these things. We must in a great act of world justice punish and trample upon this evil. We must harden our hearts to mercy. We all feel that. But there is something else. We must not wreak indiscriminate

vengeance. I say that after having seen the worst horrors with my own eyes, because I have seen them with my own eyes. If our vengeance is indiscriminate we will be perpetuating the evils started by the SS and Gestapo. They wish in their lives and after their lives to destroy respect for human life. We must restore that respect. We have been brought down to the very foundations of primitive decency. One of these, I am convinced, is that there should be order, formality and proven guilt before any human life is taken away. Many lives must be taken away. Let us not flinch before that task. But let us beware how we do it. That to my mind is one of the lessons of Belsen.

(*ibid.*)

The proper chronology of liberation is that the Russian Red Army liberated Auschwitz in January 1945. In December 1944, the US Airforce had dropped a few bombs on the camp. The action did not prevent the SS marching 58,000 survivors west. Many died of hypothermia and starvation. Those that arrived at Buchenwald, Belsen and Mauthausen were to succumb to diseases such as typhus. A university professor left a poignant and everlasting image of the living dead of Auschwitz and other camps. Survivors found they became known as the 'Musselmen':

It was impossible to extract from their lips their names much less their date of birth. Kindness itself had not the power to make them speak. They would only look at you with a long expressionless stare. If they tried to answer, their tongues could not reach their dried up palates to make a sound. One was aware only of a poisonous breath rising out of entrails already in a state of decomposition.

(Témoignages Strasbourgeois, *De l'Université aux camps de concentration*, 1947: 89. In Levin, N., 1975: 701)

The Americans were the first to liberate a concentration camp on the western Front at Ohrdruf Nord and then they encountered the horrors of Buchenwald. Ed Murrow entered the camp and broadcast an unforgettable description of his experience by short-wave to CBS in New York. In seven minutes he had written a testimony which will remain an indelible chronicle of the Holocaust and which was printed verbatim in many US newspapers. A Frenchman came up to him at Buchenwald and observed: 'You will write something about this, perhaps? To write about this you must have been here at least two years, and after that – you don't want to write any more.' Ed Murrow concluded: 'I pray you to believe what I have said about Buchenwald. I have reported what I saw and heard, but only part of it. For most of it I have no word'.

Sigrid Schultz for the US Mutual Broadcasting System entered one of the last camps to be discovered by the Allies. Ravensbruck was reserved for women and situated north west of Berlin. Her report deserves greater emphasis and consideration:

MBS ANNOUNCER   According to reports from Germany women have fared no better than men at the hands of German prison guards. Among the huge camps that soldiers and correspondents now have a chance to inspect is the huge Ravensbruck concentration camp for women North West of Berlin. And here is Mutual's Sigrid Schultz now in Germany with an account of conditions there.

SIGRID SCHULTZ   One hundred and ten thousand women have passed through the Ravensbruck concentration camp until March of this year. I talked to more than thirty of these women who have managed to survive the harrowing ordeal of enslavement. Many of them have been dragged from prison to concentration camps and to labour concentration camps for years. The prisoners in Ravensbruck included society women and little seamstresses of France – Polish, Czech, Russian, Dutch, Belgian women. The guards in charge of the prisoners were Schutzstaffeln women in regular military uniforms wearing the buttoned jackets, the big cape and the high boots of the SS 'and those boots were hobnailed which we knew only too well because we were kicked around with them' said Ravensbruck prisoner number 42216. She was a cultured woman from Brest. She and her companions had actually seen one of their female Schutzstaffeln officers trample on a woman who had fainted from exhaustion. The SS women carried whips with leather clods and used them freely. Upon arrival in Ravensbruck, all women were given a sterility shot and now they fear they will remain sterile for life. The American among the prisoners of Ravensbruck who were sent to Leipzig was married to a French man. Her name was Countess Roberta de Monteuil. But she was known as Betty by her comrades. The day I talked to them, she had suffered a nervous breakdown and was unable to see visitors. The healthiest and most beautiful women of the concentration camp at Ravensbruck were segregated in an experimental station where veins were removed from their legs and grafted on other bodies while the wounds were infected with diseases which the Germans wanted to study.

(MBS Radio, May 1945. Quoted from *Concentration Camp Horrors*, *Broadcasts heard in 1945*)

How are we to conclude our assessment of the role of radio journalism in the coverage of the Holocaust? The real danger is to make a condemnation of individuals, countries, institutions and governments with the benefit of hindsight and the moral values and knowledge of a future age. Radio journalism undoubtedly lost its innocence as an exciting and delightful medium of communication. It had to reach into the very depths of the human soul to find a voice which could articulate an outrage to the human imagination. Actual censorship and self-censorship was undoubtedly the result of cultural anti-Semitism in all the English-speaking countries of the world. People did not have any idea what was going on until April 1945 because there was an overriding reluctance to allow the Nazi treatment of the Jews to be a central theme of German coverage both before and during the war. Now it is easy to underestimate the admiration for German growth, economic expansion and efficiency. Reports of atrocities were treated with scepticism because journalists had 'cried wolf' during the First World War. The British Empire had another agenda in the Middle East determined by oil interests and the expediency of maintaining good relations with Arab interests that were opposed to the idea of a Jewish homeland in Palestine. It would be comforting to be able to say that at the end of this century and the beginning of another the world has learned its lesson. Sadly it has not. Political and economic expediency, racism and the indifference of the most powerful countries in the world continue to condemn people to the horrors of genocide. The evils of the Nazi Holocaust have been revisited in Cambodia, the former Yugoslavia and Rwanda. Radio journalists with varying degrees of success struggled the world over to come to terms with the depressing cycle of history repeating itself.

Chapter 18

Dieppe, Pearl Harbor, D-Day and other campaigns

The German invasion of France through Belgium, Holland, Luxembourg and the thrust through the Ardennes quickly led to capitulation. BBC war correspondents were taken by surprise. Charles Gardner and Bernard Stubbs had been with the BEF in Belgium but by 24 May 1940 they had returned to London, and were only in a position to report the Dunkirk evacuation on the English side as the troops were landed by the armada of rescue ships. The suffocation of censorship during the phoney war left the BBC poorly represented during the rest of the campaign. It is easier for the victorious side to report with panache and German radio coverage was dramatic. But American neutral correspondents were in a position to report objectively and William Shirer for CBS found himself at the centre of one of the most spectacular scoops in the history of radio journalism. As he followed the advancing German troops into Belgium, he came across 'hollow-chested, skinny and round-shouldered' British prisoners of war who talked about being overwhelmed by dive-bombers and tanks. As he handed out cigarettes, a shell-shocked soldier told him that it was amusing to meet his first American while in German captivity.

On 21 June 1940, William Shirer witnessed Adolf Hitler reversing the humiliation of 1918 by forcing the French to capitulate in the same railway carriage at Compiègne where the First World War armistice had been signed. Hitler had wanted this event to be an exclusive propaganda victory which would be broadcast first on German radio. However, Shirer found a short-wave transmission vehicle nearby and used this to transmit his report during a half-hour window of opportunity. The NBC correspondent William Kerker was also there using the same facility. All the agency reporters stayed in Berlin expecting the news to emerge from the capital of the Third Reich. If the German technicians had used an ordinary telephone line, control and censorship would have been guaranteed. The use of a short-wave link from Compiègne via Brussels to Germany involved a wider transmission which may have been deliberately switched on by a German army technician. Technicians in New York were able to pick up the frequency on the other side of the Atlantic and broadcast the radio journalists' remarkable despatches before it was officially announced to the German people. Radio listeners throughout the USA heard Shirer describe a significant moment in history:

> Through the windows we could see them talking and going over various papers. At one-thirty p.m. there was a recess so that the French could contact their government in Bordeaux for the last time. And then came the big moment. At six-fifty p.m. the gentlemen in the car started affixing their signatures to Germany's armistice conditions. General Keitel signed for Germany; General Huntziger for France. It was all over in a few moments
>
> (CBS Radio, 21 June 1940. Shirer, W. L. 1987: 427)

Shirer's inadvertent scoop hardly endeared him to the German High Command and his days as a neutral correspondent in Berlin were now numbered.

American women radio journalists had been in the front line of the radio news coverage of this six-week period of invasion and surrender. Mary Breckinridge had scooped the news of the surrender of Belgium on 28 May. Helen Hiett reported the Nazi bombing of France's new provisional seat of government in Bordeaux and she then went onto Spain where she reported the bombing of the strategically vital British colony of Gibraltar.

After the *débâcle* in Norway, the Ministry of Information and the BBC were acutely aware of the dangers of distorting the reporting of another military disaster – the collapse of the BEF in France. An adjustment of propaganda tactics enabled Britain to 'snatch victory in the jaws of defeat'. This was achieved by poignant and truthful reporting combined with the brilliance of Winston Churchill and J. B. Priestley's ability to communicate in the medium of radio. Bernard Stubbs reported the arrival of dejected troops in the Channel ports, devoid of their equipment. J. B. Priestley had a Yorkshire accent. His language was simple. He focused on the emotive image of the little paddle-steamer *Gracie Fields* which had been part of the eccentric armada of ships that had saved entire armies from destruction and captivity:

> She'll go sailing proudly down the years in the epic of Dunkirk. And our great grandchildren, when they learn how we began this war by snatching glory out of defeat, and then swept on to victory, may also learn how the little holiday steamers made an excursion to hell and came back glorious.
>
> (BBC Home Service, 5 June 1940. Quoted from *The Second World War* 1989)

Priestley was a socialist writer and after he had served his propaganda purpose in 1940, he soon found that his critical comments about a changing society and creating a new Britain would not be tolerated by the establishment. His voice was silenced on the Home Service after his second *Postscript* series in 1941. However, he continued broadcasting on the North American Service where his popularity matched that of the American network correspondents. Ed Murrow's position as a foreign correspondent enabled him to echo the developing swell of opinion in Britain that society was being changed irrevocably by the war. He observed that people were asking the following questions:

> Why must there be eight hundred thousand people unemployed when we need shelters? Why are new buildings being constructed when the need is that the wreckage of bombed buildings be removed from the streets? What shall we do with victory when it is won?
>
> (Murrow, CBS Radio, 1 October 1940. Knightly, 1989)

Ed Murrow was sometimes critical of censorship and he feared that no one was being given any information about the Battle of the Atlantic. Winston Churchill had ordered that the loss of merchant shipping should not be reported under any circumstances. Murrow observed that 'nothing may be said either to the Americans or to the British public about this battle which, we are told, will determine the destinies of free men for centuries'.

The Battle of Britain offered a wide range of propaganda opportunities and controversies for radio news coverage. Charles Gardner broadcast live from 'Hell-fire Corner' which was the nickname for the narrow Straits of Dover and the scene of a continuing battle between RAF and the Luftwaffe above the convoys trying to bring much needed supplies to Britain. Nearly sixty years later Gardner's report sounds over-excited and old-fashioned. It was criticised as being too much like a dramatic sports report and insensitive to the reality of men dying in a ghastly air battle. But the listeners of today have to appreciate that the emotion of a man who said, 'Oh boy, I've never seen anything so good as this – the RAF fighters have really got those boys taped', is the voice of a man who has survived Blitzkrieg and is a citizen of a country that is standing alone against a war machine that had occupied most of Europe. He was not a neutral bystander. Ed Murrow was technically a neutral correspondent but there was little doubt where his sympathies lay and his reporting of the plucky Londoners surviving and battling against the Blitz is as much a version of propaganda as Gardner's gung ho excitement in seeing German planes smashing into the sea.

The reporting of the Blitz is a classic example of effective propaganda creating myths that were substantially removed from the reality. The Ministry of Information exaggerated the number of British 'kills' and reduced the information about losses, but the margin of error was ranged between twenty and fifty per cent.

German exaggeration was so outrageous it could not be believed. The British were able to create successfully the idea that Britain was outnumbered in the quantity of planes. The myth of the brave Spitfire was established when the most commonly used fighter plane was the Hurricane. The bombing of Coventry was established as an appalling civilian atrocity when, in fact, it was a legitimate military target since the most important engineering and arms manufacturing factories were situated in and around the city. The reality of human behaviour – panic and looting during air raids – was effectively covered up through censorship. The news media were not allowed to identify the location of major incidents involving civilian casualties. This means that the deaths of more than a hundred civilians, mainly women and children, in the crypt of the Church of the Holy Redeemer in Chelsea on 14 September 1940 went unreported until after the war. Court hearings of Auxiliary Fire Service men accused of looting were suppressed. There was no reporting of thieves plundering valuables from the well-to-do casualties killed when a bomb crashed onto the basement dance floor of the Café de Paris on 18 March 1941. A wedding and birthday party had been dancing to the jazz music of the black American 'Snakehips' Johnson who was decapitated in the explosion. It has been alleged that rings were removed from the dead and wounded.

The use of parachute mines by the Luftwaffe was kept a secret. The first evidence of V2 rocket explosions were also subject to severe censorship. At 6.45 p.m. on 8 September 1944 several houses in Staveley Road, Chiswick disappeared and a crater forty feet wide and thirty feet deep appeared in the street. A news blackout was imposed on the BBC and newspapers. Despite the deaths of a soldier in the street, a 65-year-old woman in her house, and a 3-year-old girl in her cot, officials claimed a gas main had exploded. The truth was not revealed for a further two months. More V2 rockets landed in Dulwich, Deptford, Islington, Luton and Aldgate. Churchill first announced that these high-speed rockets had been arriving without warning in London on 10 November 1944. Fifteen days later a V2 rocket destroyed the Woolworths' store in New Cross Road, Southeast London killing one hundred and eight people. We can question the nature of this censorship now, but at the time the War Ministry feared providing information which could help confirm to the Germans that they had hit their targets. There was always concern about undermining civilian morale particularly in the heavily bombed cities. A similar attitude operated in the USA where absolute censorship covered up the assault by Japanese paper balloons which drifted with the trade winds to bomb America. More than 9,000 were launched and each carried a small bomb. They landed all over the USA and killed six people.

However, one of the BBC's most distinguished war correspondents, Frank Gillard, has always berated himself over his role in covering up the true nature of the military disaster at Dieppe on 19 August 1942. He says he was forced to delay the reporting of the raid which had resulted in a massacre of Canadian troops.

Only 25 per cent had returned back to Britain. More than twenty-four hours after the event Gillard was forced to concentrate on the air battle and his report left him with an abiding sense of personal 'shame and disgrace'. But Gillard was not responsible for this distortion. It came from the commander of the entire operation Lord Louis Mountbatten who had reported to the war cabinet that the raid had been carried off 'very satisfactorily'. Even the Canadian correspondents had reported the positive aspects of the operation. This is because they were not neutral observers. They were subject to censorship and effectively 'onside' with their fellow countrymen.

It would have been impossible for them to have echoed the words of a German correspondent who had reported that 'the venture mocked all rules of military logic and strategy'. In the heat of a war how could it be possible for Frank Gillard to report directly that the operation was nothing short of suicide on a bloody beach for the Allied troops and for the defending Germans it was like shooting fish in a barrel? He was not the only radio correspondent assigned to cover Dieppe. NBC's correspondent John MacVane was there and subjected to the same censorship and control. The actual casualty list was 300 dead on the German side and 1,027 killed on the Allied side. Gillard was not the only journalist forced to distort the truth. The *Daily Mirror* reported the event with the headline 'Big Hun Losses in Nine Hour Dieppe Battle'. But the *Mirror* also printed the 'Nazi Version' on their front page including the assertion that more than 1,500 prisoners are in German hands and 'the enemy's casualties are very high'. The *Sunday Pictorial*'s use of German photographs two weeks later demonstrates the bizarre twists of slanted and propagandist reporting. The newspaper was still asserting that there had been 4,000 German casualties. The only tank to have actually moved from the beaches into Dieppe was supposedly 'destroyed by our own men to prevent it falling into enemy hands when they re-embarked for England'. Another extraordinary caption is placed next to a photograph of an Allied tank destroyed on the beach. A German soldier is actually piling up the bodies of dead Canadian soldiers, but the *Pictorial* unashamedly states 'another of our tanks has served its purpose and has been left, wrecked by its crew, on the Dieppe beach. By its side a soldier looks after wounded comrades'. Frank Gillard was not the only representative of the news media to allow truth to be the first casualty in war.

The USA was forced to enter the war because of the Japanese attack on Pearl Harbor on the 7 December 1941. The US radio networks frantically tried to establish links with their affiliate stations in Hawaii and the Philippines. Some got through but only for a short while. Connections were cut. Censorship prevented the world from knowing the truth about Pearl Harbor until after the war. Five American battleships had been sunk, three crippled, three cruisers and three destroyers severely damaged, 200 planes destroyed and 2,344 men killed. The world was deceived into thinking that only the older *Arizona* had been sunk and another battleship had capsized but could be righted. Ed Murrow's reputation was so high that he was granted an audience with President Roosevelt that very night. The Commander in Chief had indicated that virtually all US planes had been destroyed on the ground. Murrow decided that patriotism had precedence over his journalistic instincts. Some British newspapers gave the impression in early editions that Pearl Harbor was an American victory. On the whole the USA operated a successful system of voluntary censorship. The First Amendment could not prevent Congressman Melvin Mass complaining that the war was being lost in the Pacific. Congress was reported, but not broadcast live until 1979. The Australian Parliament in Canberra was broadcast live from 1947. Live radio transmission from the Houses of Parliament in Britain was not permitted until 1975. US censorship could not control this type of event, but it could prevent British correspondents from sending the information to London.

The veracity of radio reporting tended to be more successful where the radio correspondent had a neutral position or was an Allied representative in an event without a critical national interest. This meant that Britain's disastrous losses in the Far East were subjected to intensive and truthful reporting from Americans on the scene. CBS reporter Cecil Brown was on the British battleship *Repulse* when she and the *Prince of Wales* were destroyed by Japanese airpower. He survived the torpedoes and sent his reports from Singapore. He was never one to hold back his opinions and his tendency to challenge British complacency threatened his accreditation. He remained in Singapore to witness an ignominious defeat by Commonwealth troops who vastly outnumbered the Japanese in soldiers and equipment. Brown realised that the problems of censorship meant that the wider world was not prepared for the news of Singapore's fall. His battle with censorship continued in the States when in 1943 he was forced to resign as a CBS news analyst after expressing strong opinions which were perceived as 'editorialising'.

Chester Wilmot became one of the war's most distinguished radio journalists. He was the ABC's representative covering the Middle East war for nearly two years and provided evocative and accurate action reports from the siege of Tobruk. Wilmot along with the Canadian broadcast journalist Stanley Maxted demonstrated that Commonwealth reporters were in the same league as the BBC's leading foreign correspondents such as Richard Dimbleby. And Wilmot, like Dimbleby, had to come to terms with the politics of reporting as well as the logistical demands and skills required to do the job. Wilmot fell out with General Sir Thomas Blamey, the Allied Land Forces Commander and Australia's military Commander in Chief. Wilmot gossiped about Blamey's shortcomings and he began to imply Blamey was not doing enough to stamp out corruption. Blamey soon found an opportunity to effectively excommunicate the talented war correspondent from the Australian campaign in New Guinea. His accreditation was withdrawn. The ABC and Wilmot found that Australia's most powerful military man was short on forgiveness. He blocked attempts to have Wilmot cover the war from the Indian Front and any other area of the Pacific. Blamey was later promoted to Field Marshall and attempted unsuccessfully to scupper Wilmot's appointment as a BBC correspondent in the invasion of Europe.

Richard Dimbleby found himself burdened with the politics of the Middle East war and it nearly terminated his career with the BBC. There had always been tension within the BBC caused by his ebullient and extravagant personality. However, he was unaware that General Auchinleck's command in Egypt was being challenged by the war cabinet. General Rommel's skilled military tactics and capture of Tobruk led to a general perception that the BBC's coverage had been 'over-optimistic'. Dimbleby as the BBC's representative was in the firing line. Winston Churchill regarded the North African campaign as a priority. He was frustrated by the lack of success and he desperately needed victory against the Axis forces. Dimbleby was unaware that the BBC in London was acutely embarrassed by his despatches which had inevitably depended on 'the highest sources' in Cairo GHQ. Wilmot became a casualty of the poor relations with the military source he needed to cultivate. Dimbleby became a casualty of the good relations with the military source he had cultivated. Auchinleck was relieved of his command, and Dimbleby had to follow him back to London a few days later.

In Australia the heavy influence of newspaper interests prevented the ABC from fully establishing the power to collect all its own news and to broadcast it when it chose. An independent news service was not set up until June 1947. While the BBC in Britain and US radio networks developed pioneering techniques of using actuality for war-time coverage, progress was slow. But by 1944 the ABC was employing thirty-six full-time journalists including six war correspondents. In mid-1941 there were no women journalists on the staff rota. By the end of the war, the ABC had recruited female newsdesk and news reporting talent which included Marjorie Plunkett, Eve Falconer, Mary Lucy, Kathleen Vellacott-Jones and Dorothy Auchterounie who was responsible for covering Allied General Headquarters in Brisbane and a Brisbane newsroom staffed entirely by women. The BBC failed to promote any significant number of women radio journalists to work on the front line of reporting. Audrey Russell is the only journalist who appears to have made any progress. She reported on the bombing of British cities and took part in the coverage of the invasion of Europe but the cultural sexism and chauvinism of a male-dominated broadcasting profession prevented her from receiving the equivalent attention and opportunities of her male colleagues.

The D-Day operation and subsequent invasion of Europe represents a heyday in the history of radio journalism. Technology was at last beginning to support the immediacy of live reporting of dramatic events. BBC engineers had developed a portable 'midget' recorder. There was nothing particularly small about it, but reporters in the field could record their eye witness descriptions on flat discs and send them to transmission short-wave points for broadcast. The Americans had found a way of reducing wire recording technology into a portable unit. American radio reporters were now permitted to pre-record their reports. The logistical and technological strengths of Allied countries combined to create an astonishing level of broadcast coverage. Richard Dimbleby had been rehabilitated within the BBC largely through his courageous coverage of the bombing raids over Germany. He played a key role in organising the nature of the D-Day coverage. The BBC created a new programme *War Report* which, following the news at nine o'clock in the evening, enthralled British and North American listeners until Germany and Japan's surrender. Radio reporters flew with the parachutists and bombers, landed on the beaches in amphibious craft and sailed with the largest armada ever assembled for a military operation. A portable unit was even given to Air-Commodore W. Helmore who, in a Mitchell bomber, provided the first eye witness account of the invasion. The American networks maintained an extra-ordinary marathon performance of twenty-four hour rolling news coverage through the early days of the invasion. Veteran analysts such as H. V. Kaltenborn interpreted the continuous flow of written, recorded and live despatches on NBC's flagship New York station WEAF.

A mistake by the American Associated Press news agency led to a false report of the invasion going out for just two minutes on 3 June 1944. On 6 June they got it right with the following bulletin which depended on the monitoring of German radio:

> London Tuesday June 6 (AP) – The German news agency Transocean said today in a broadcast that the Allied invasion has begun.

NBC's John MacVane had a series of technical mishaps with his portable wire recorder. Interviews with soldiers embarking on the destroyers were unusable because his batteries had gone flat. He was the only American radio reporter on Omaha beach where enemy fire was the heaviest with thousands of casualties. It was the bloodiest beach of the invasion. He escaped bullets by millimetres, he saw floating bodies passing by and for hours under the steep cliff shared the terror of mortar and machine-gun fire. He was wet, exhausted and the following day found a mobile transmitter and sent his report to London. He thought he had the scoop of the invasion, but his report had not been recorded or distributed. Two days later he broke his ankle. He was the first radio correspondent into liberated Paris, but not the first to report the story because he waited for censorship approval while others did not.

The life of the radio war correspondents was exciting and dangerous. After Normandy their reports covered the drama of Arnhem, where Stanley Maxted recorded remarkable ad-libbed accounts of the battle and fight for survival. Most of his recording discs were destroyed, but he kept three under his tunic and returned them to the British lines so that they could be broadcast on *War Report*. Radio followed the Allied armies across the Rhine, and into the heart of Germany. Radio dramatically conveyed the reality of the Battle of the Pacific. Correspondents waded ashore with the marines at Iwo Jima and cowered in fox-holes during deadly hand-to-hand battles. Radio had come of age but as the NBC correspondent W. W. Chaplin discovered maturity has its price. He wanted to report to the world the image of General de Gaulle making a political speech to one of the liberated villages of Normandy. A mother held the handles of a wheelbarrow containing the body of her child killed in the Allied bombardment.

The censor blocked the report. Chaplin was also prevented from describing the fate of a small town which had been virtually wiped out in the bombing raid. Warning leaflets for the inhabitants had blown away in the wind and they perished in the wreckage of their homes. The Second World War ended with the atom bombs at Nagasaki and Hiroshima. Radio Tokyo tried to describe something they could not understand – an explosion literally searing to death all living things. The ABC network and the BBC later broadcast John Hersey's moving account of what happened to six ordinary people in Hiroshima on 6 August 1945 – the day the atom bomb exploded.

The Second World War generated a huge increase in the number of radio news personnel. The war created huge audiences for news bulletins and news programmes. The war had forced an acceleration in the use of technology and the style of on the spot reporting. The war had challenged the ability of the writer to engage with the imagination of the listener on subjects that had been virtually unimaginable. Radio journalism had come of age.

Part V

International media law for radio journalists

Chapter 19

Defamation

Defamation concerns the restrictions on journalists who attack reputation through publication. In simple terms if the messenger bears news which offends legal protocol the messenger is shot, tortured, hanged, imprisoned or is held upside down to empty his pockets of every pence or cent he has ever owned. Different countries of the world have different ways of dealing with defamation. Roman-Dutch legal inquisitorial systems tend to use criminal procedures with financial and custodial penalties. Adversarial systems based on English and Welsh Common Law tend to use the civil arena where the sanctions are financial and the burden of proof is less rigorous. England and Wales has a system of control which is more weighted against the interests of broadcast journalists.

Defamation has historical roots which you can find in the religious and philosophical foundations of Judeo-Christian civilisation. In the Bible, Exodus XXII 28 states, 'Thou shalt not revile the gods nor curse the rule of thy people'. Leviticus XIX 16 states, 'Thou shalt not go up and down as a talebearer among thy people'. The further back in time you go, the greater the likelihood that the messenger always faced death by hanging, or some other barbaric method of execution. In the Roman civilisation at the time of 450 BC death was the punishment for 'famosus libellus'. In the edicts of Valentinianus I and Valens during the period 364 to 395 AD libel penalties included the disqualification to make a will, imprisonment, exile for life, and forfeiture of property. The Anglo-Saxons were equally bloodthirsty when dealing with malicious gossips and rumour mongers. King Alfred the Great passed 'Lex Talionis' – 'if a person shall be guilty of slander his tongue should be removed or redeemed by the price of his head'. At the time of the English King Henry III (1216–72) there was an offence of 'convicium' which was defined as abusive language addressed to a person, or inciting a crowd to mob or lay siege to a house. Technically 'convicium' still exists in Scottish law. Scotland has retained its own legal system since union in 1707. The law 'carmen famosum' was an offence against attacking the reputation of the ruling elite. Libel or slander can be assessed as a form of political control. It is a system of outlawing criticism and opposition to kings, noblemen and barons. King Richard II passed the Statute of Gloucester imposing gruesome punishments for slanderers against the members of the establishment:

> Every deviser of false news, or horrible and false lyes [sic], of prelates, dukes, earls, barons, and other nobles and great men of the realm . . . shall be punishable by hanging, drawing and quartering the offender, burning him on the forehead, cropping his ears, slitting his nose or by fine, imprisonment and the pillory.
>
> (Richard II's statute of Gloucester. Quoted from Carter-Ruck 1992: 20)

If the purpose of these early sanctions was to preserve the respect for and reputation of the leaders of a society then times have not really changed, only the penalties and sanctions. The invention of the printing press in 1476 created more written publications, and libel – the written form of defamation – became as much of a threat as slander. The notorious English Star Chamber introduced the idea of strict liability. Truth became irrelevant when considering the nature of a libel or slander. Lord Chief Justice Coke in 'de Libellis Famosis' said 'For as the woman said she would never grieve to have been told of her red nose if she had not one indeed'.

Libel is the concern of all radio journalists because English-speaking parliaments have passed laws confirming that radio broadcasting has the same status as a written publication. It was to be several hundred years before England was to experience the development of a popular press. The brakes had been applied by oppressive state censorship on all printed materials and there was also a tendency to impose heavy taxes on paper and pamphlets. The Civil War period leading to Restoration in 17th century England opened up a unique period in journalism history when there was no censorship and the two sides, Royalists and Parliamentarians used 'newsbooks' for propaganda. You can observe all the origins of sensationalism, negative representation, stereotyping of women and libel-free publications in these newsbooks. This extract is contemptuous of reputation and the risk of prejudicing trial by jury. The spelling and grammar is seventeenth-century English:

> Many strange disasters have fallen this week, viz. At Cobham in Kent, a woman jealous of her husband, sent for the suspected female, and having drunk freely with her, she at the last demanded of her, if she would have her nose cut off, or

her bearing part; and immediately she and her maid servants fell to work, and exercised that part of her body which they thought had most offended. Not long after her husband came home, and demanding what there was to eat, she replyed, that she had got the best bit which he loved in the world, and so presented him with that most ungrateful object. Amazed at the horrour of it, he addressed himself to the constable, who carrying both mistress and maid to the next justice, they were both committed to Maidstone Gaol, but the dismembered woman being not dead, they have put in a great bayl to be answerable to justice.

(Raymond 1993: 127)

Most aspects of the human condition are covered in William Shakespeare's plays and libel and defamation is no exception. *Richard II* talks about honour being more important than life:

> The Purest Treasure mortal times afford
> is spotless reputation; that away,
> Men are but gilded loan or painted clay,
> A jewel in a ten-times-barr'd-up chest
> is a bold spirit in a loyal breast
> Mine honour is my life, both grow in one,
> take honour from me and my life is done.
>
> (*Richard II*, I. i., Shakespeare)

Othello also asserts the value of reputation above all the riches of the world:

> Who steals my purse steals trash:
> 'tis something, nothing;
> Twas mine, 'tis his, and has been
> slave to thousands;
> But he that filches from me my
> good name
> Robs me of that which not enriches him,
> and makes me poor indeed.
>
> (*Othello*, III. iii., Shakespeare)

The satirist Jonathan Swift observes wryly: 'Convey a libel in frown, and wink a reputation down'.

So what are the rules? Let us start with England and Wales. In Scotland the principles are broadly the same. In Scotland judges have tended to set the level of damages instead of juries. In addition, exemplary damages are not available in libel, but like the situation south of the border, juries still have a wide discretion to make lottery-style awards against newspapers and broadcasters perceived to be economically and commercially powerful. To fall into the libel trap as a radio journalist in the UK you have to identify the person you have libelled. As radio is a fast-moving medium and radio journalists are generally under sharper deadlines and more intense pressures than their colleagues in the other media, the legal instinct does need to be finely tuned. Radio journalists cannot be specialist libel media lawyers. This section of the book advises on how to create those mental alarm bells which ring loudly when you recognise danger. You should follow two very important principles:

1 When in doubt leave it out.
2 Never assume anything without checking and never take anything for granted.

In the United Kingdom, the penalties for legal transgressions are extremely severe. Libel proceedings can result in awards of damages which are economically crippling. The independent station in Liverpool, Radio City, once suffered the shock of being the defendant when a jury awarded £350,000 in damages to a businessman who had sued them. This was later reduced on appeal. Wherever you are working you need to be aware of the scale of editorial responsibility and leave important decisions on legal judgement to people who are paid to exercise it.

It is important to realise that identification can be implied. The group factor is very important. Generally thirty or more people is regarded as too large a group. In 1971 Old Bailey journalists successfully sued the *Spectator* magazine for the allegation that they were 'beer-sodden hacks'. There were twelve journalists working in the press room at the time and they collected damages. The offending information has to be published to a third party. Apart from a radio or a television programme, publication to a third party can simply be a postcard seen by one other person. Judges in Britain direct juries to consider the ordinary meaning of an offending piece of communication when assessing the existence of innuendo or implied meaning. There are four working definitions of defamation in the UK:

1 Lowering the estimation of right-thinking members of society generally.
2 Exposing a person to hatred, ridicule or contempt.
3 Damaging a person in office, trade, profession, or industry.
4 Causing a person to be shunned or avoided.

I would recommend that you apply these definitions to any piece of radio you are worried about. If you find there are one or more positive answers then you need to consider the main potential defences.

1 Justification is considered by juries on the balance of probabilities, rather than the criminal standard of beyond reasonable doubt. In England and Wales 'reasonable doubt' is not a popular expression used by judges when directing juries. They tend to advise the juries to return a guilty verdict if

the jury is sure of guilt. You need evidence to use this defence. You will need credible and reliable witnesses who will back you up in court.

You need to keep professional notes with information dated and timed and it is very important not to leave malicious comments or flippant remarks anywhere in your notebooks.

2 Fair Comment. If you are considering a fair comment defence then your material will never really be fair. The publication has to be an honestly held opinion made in good faith based on true facts and on a matter of public interest. Good faith means without malice. You have to satisfy all these criteria.

3 Privilege. When it is absolute you will be reporting the Houses of Parliament and the courts. You need to satisfy three important standards; fairness, accuracy and contemporaneous reporting. Fairness means you must never forget to put the other side's story at some stage in your publication. Accuracy speaks for itself. To be contemporaneous you have to make sure your publication is aired on your next bulletin or programme. Accuracy and fairness are more important than being contemporaneous. If you do not satisfy contemporaneous publication your class of privilege simply changes to 'qualified'. Significant inaccuracies and lack of fairness takes away all your privilege. Qualified privilege relates to references to past court cases and parliamentary proceedings. It still requires fairness and accuracy. These publications do not need explanation or contradictions from the other side. There is another qualified privilege which does need explanation or contradiction. You would have this type of qualified privilege if you are reporting meetings of properly constituted associations, local authorities, company meetings, government departments, senior civil servants and a chief officer of the police. The chief officer of the police would normally be the most senior officer available in the press or media department. In Britain legal aid is not available for defamation actions and the damages obtained are tax free. The rich and powerful outside the United Kingdom normally launch libel actions through the English and Welsh system because the dice are generally loaded in favour of plaintiffs. They only have to prove publication within British jurisdiction. There is another remedy available to people in England and Wales in relation to the law of malicious falsehood. This relates to the quality of goods and services. The plaintiff has to show that the publication caused financial loss to the manufacturer and dealers. A valid defence would be that the publication was true, and there is a further defence of showing that the publication was an honest mistake and that a published correction was made at the earliest available opportunity. Plantiffs have also won the right to legal aid from the state for malicious falsehood actions.

In England and Wales, juries are asked to consider the ordinary meaning of alleged libels. This means vocabulary from the 1950s may well have a different meaning in the 1990s. It could be argued that to say somebody was homosexual in 1957 was libellous but it may not be the case in 1997. Liberace successfully sued *Daily Mirror* columnist Cassandra in June 1959 and collected £8,000 in damages. The late entertainment artist had complained that the following passage implied he was homosexual:

> The summit of sex – the pinnacle of masculine, feminine, and neuter. Everything that he, she or it can ever want. . . . I spoke to sad but kindly men on this newspaper who have met every celebrity arriving from the United States for the past thirty years. They all say that this deadly, winking, sniggering, snuggling, chromium-plated, scent-impregnated, luminous, quivering, giggling, fruit-flavoured, mincing, ice-covered heap of mother love has had the biggest reception and impact on London since Charlie Chaplin arrived at the same station, Waterloo, on 12 September 1921.
>
> (Carter-Ruck 1992: 517)

The newspaper tried to argue that the passage did not have the meaning alleged. They did not try to justify the implied meaning. After Liberace died from Aids it emerged that he had been homosexual.

One of the most dramatic libel cases in post-war history was an action by Dr Dering, a Polish doctor who had settled in South London. The best-selling author Leon Uris had written in his book *Exodus*: 'here in block X (at Auschwitz) Dr Wirthe used women as guinea pigs and Dr Schumann sterilised by castration and X-ray and Clanberg removed ovaries and Dr Dering performed seventeen thousand "experiments" in surgery without anaesthetics'. It was a dramatic hearing and the nearest Britain ever came to being the stage of a war crimes trial. Dering won the smallest coin of the realm which at that time was a halfpenny. The gambling nature of the libel system in England and Wales has been compared to a casino. It operates with a cruel twist for plaintiffs who receive damages awards which are less than the amount of money paid into court and offered as a settlement by the defendants. Dr Dering had to pay the legal costs of the losing side.

The biggest risk in radio occurs during live guest or phone-in, talkback-style programmes. In Britain most independent stations have a 'dump' or 'profanity' button which presenters and producers can hit when a libel has been recognised. As there has been a time delay of ten seconds introduced between presentation and transmission the stations can protect themselves from libel actions. BBC local radio services do not use profanity or delay at the time of writing which places an extra stress on live presenters and editorial staff. A new Defamation Act passed in 1996 has raised the possibility of a special defence where a libel has been uttered during a live programme which was unexpected and where the station staff had taken all reasonable steps to avoid it being broadcast. It may also be a legitimate defence for libellous publications on the World Wide Web. However, the theoretical interpretation needs testing in the courts.

Australia has a libel system which closely mirrors the English and Welsh system. Libel definitions such as 'lowering a person's reputation, leading people to ridicule, avoid or despise a person and injuring a person's reputation in business, trade or profession' are almost identical to British libel principles. But there are a number of differences which often stem from the independence of state legal systems. In Australia local councils can sue for libel. In the UK, the Law Lords ruled that local authorities did not have the power to issue libel proceedings. In the states of New South Wales, Queensland and Tasmania the defendant radio station not only has to prove truth on the balance of probabilities, but that the report was also a matter of public interest. This means that radio stations in these states would not be able to safely report accurate stories about the private lives of public figures if the material referred to could not be demonstrated as in the public interest or for the public benefit.

The High Court case of Theophanous v. the Herald & Weekly Times Limited, in October 1994, revolutionised Australian libel law by establishing a constitutional protection for political discussion. It means that Australian radio journalists now have qualified privilege for discussion about the conduct, policies and fitness for office of political parties, public officers and public bodies, and it also includes discussion of political views and the political activities of trade union leaders or other people who are the subject of political debate.

The Americans have the advantage of the First Amendment in their written constitution:

> Congress shall make no law respecting an establishment of religion, or prohibiting the free exercise thereof; or abridging the freedom of speech, or of the press; or the right of the people peaceably to assemble, and to petition the Government for a redress of grievances.

The Americans managed to shake off the shackles of strict liability for libel even before the War of Independence. In a celebrated case in 1735 the British governor of New York sued John Peter Zenger, the editor of the *New York Weekly Journal* which had accused him of corruption and nepotism. At the time the governor William Cosby was hoping to rely on the law of seditious libel where truth was no defence. The jury of colonists returned a not guilty verdict in defiance of the existing law. This case formed the backdrop for the development of the First Amendment.

The Civil Rights movement in the USA during the late 1950s and early 1960s marked the beginning of the liberalising of US libel laws. In the 1964 Sullivan v. *New York Times* case, Civil Rights activists had accused the police commissioner of Montgomery, Alabama of failing to prevent and properly investigate racist attacks and of intimidating Dr Martin Luther King and his family. They published a full page advert in the *New York Times* making these allegations:

> Again, and again, the Southern violators have answered Dr King's peaceful protests with intimidation and violence. They have bombed his home almost killing his wife and child. They have assaulted him seven times – for 'speeding', 'loitering', and similar 'offenses'. And now they have charged him with 'perjury' – a felony under which they could imprison him for 10 years.
>
> (*New York Times*, 1964; Folkerts 1994: 488)

L. B. Sullivan was successful in the Alabama state courts and received an award of $0·5m. Libel suits were being launched in many Southern states in an attempt to censor the news coverage of Civil Rights demonstrations. CBS was defending actions involving damages of $2m. The stakes were high, but the Supreme Court of the USA applied First Amendment protection. The judges established the principle that public officials such as police officers cannot sue for libel. The plaintiff had to prove that the libel was actuated by malice and that the journalists or news organisation knew the libel was false or had a reckless disregard of whether it was false or not. In 1964 Justice Brennan asserted:

> Thus we consider this case against the background of a profound national commitment to the principle that debate on public issues should be uninhibited, robust, and wide-open, and that it may well include vehement, caustic and sometimes unpleasantly sharp attacks on government and public officials. The present advertisement, as an expression of grievance and protest on one of the major public issues of our time, would seem clearly to qualify for the constitutional protection.
>
> (Folkerts 1994: 489–90)

Two further cases in 1967, Curtis Publishing Company v. Butts and General Walker v. Associated Press, extended libel protection to public figures. The Supreme Court declared that libel plaintiffs had to prove a reckless disregard for the truth on the part of journalists. Protection was also defined for news agencies which have to supply news up to the second. The ruling gave radio journalists a useful protection given the demands of the medium. In 1971 another case, Rosenbloom v. Metromedia, extended the protection of journalists from libel actions brought by ordinary people who feature in stories which are matters of public interest. In this case a radio station had investigated a businessman generating huge profits by trading in pornography. The Metromedia group secured an extension of First Amendment protection from the Supreme Court. Since 1971 there have been Supreme Court judgments which have qualified the First Amendment defence. In the 1974 case Gerts v. Welch the judges decided that a lawyer did not deliberately place himself in the public eye or interest so the media was not protected by the First Amendment. In the 1976 case, Mary Alice Firestone v. *Time Magazine*, the judges ruled that an heiress in a notorious divorce case had done nothing to thrust herself into a public controversy. In 1985 the judges ruled in Dun and Bradstree v. Greenmoss Builders that private communications were not protected by the First Amendment. The pendulum swung the other way in the 1988 case of *Hustler Magazine* v. Falwell when the judges ruled that public figures must tolerate ridicule and insult. An obscene and not particularly funny cartoon was covered by the First Amendment.

While the Federal case law invests an obligation on all libel plaintiffs to prove fault, individual states have their own precedents and statutes. Liberal Supreme Court rulings from the 1960s do not mean that US radio journalists should throw caution to the wind. Actions in the state courts can be very expensive particularly if a poor plaintiff has a no-win, no-fee attorney sinking his or her jaws into the financial ankle of a radio station. If the radio news report attacks a public figure or official there will be no First Amendment protection if the station had actual knowledge that the report was untrue, or had a reckless disregard for the truth of the statement. If a news report libels a private person in a public interest story, radio journalists should avoid a charge of negligence in publishing a false statement by seeking the response and explanation from the private person named or identified. Notwithstanding the First Amendment protection, US radio journalists have basic defences which are similar to the position in Britain and Australia. They include truth, fair and accurate reports of court, legislative hearings and public records. Consent is also a defence particularly if the plaintiff realises that he or she is speaking to a reporter and the statements are likely to be broadcast. Opinion based on true facts is another defence.

In Australia, the United Kingdom and USA the dead cannot sue anyone for libel. There was a whoop of delight in many UK newsrooms when the media corporation tycoon Robert Maxwell died in mysterious circumstances while on his yacht near the Canary Islands in 1991. He regularly used the libel laws to intimidate opponents and silence journalists who wished to question his business methods. At the same time there was considerable lament among barristers and solicitors who specialised in libel because Mr Maxwell had generated a considerable 'industry' of litigation. Some countries with libel laws which are not derived from the common law traditions of England and Wales do allow bereaved relatives to take action after insulting and scurrilous attacks on their recently deceased loved ones. Sometimes it does not matter when the libelled subject has died. There was the celebrated Italian case in November 1975 when an author, film producer and film director were prosecuted for alleging that Pope Pius XII knew of the Nazi plans to massacre Italian Jews in the Second World War and chose not to act. The film *Massacre in Rome* starred Richard Burton and was based on the book *Death in Rome* by Robert Katz. The court found that the late Pope was unaware of the Nazi plan. The court imposed suspended prison sentences on the defendants. Katz received fourteen months and film producer Carlo Ponti and director George Pan Cosmatos received six months each. The action had been instituted by the Pope's niece Contessa Elena Rossignani. A BBC television documentary in 1995 repeated the charge that the Pope had failed to use his influence to protect European Jewry. I understand it was not distributed or broadcast in Italy.

Chapter 20

Contempt of court, access to court proceedings and other restrictions

This is another story of contrasts, primarily between Australia, the UK and the USA. In Britain the only constitutional safeguard against government abuse of power is the right of a jury to return a not guilty verdict against an oppressive prosecution or oppressive law which has strict liability. Strict liability means *actus reus* is the crime and the *mens rea*, or mental intent is irrelevant. This means that if you did not intend to commit an offence and you did not have a guilty purpose you should still be found guilty by the court. Governments are rather irritated when juries ignore the strict liability nature of laws and acquit defendants because they do not approve of the law. The government would describe these as 'perverse' verdicts. Others would say that the verdict is an assertion of the principle of liberty. In Britain, there is no right to trial by jury for contempt of court. It used to be tried summarily by the judges themselves. This tended to result in the jettisoning of basic principles of natural justice. Hasty trials, poor representation and apoplectic judges who rule on fact as well as punishment make a powerful cocktail of injustice. Mr Justice Melford Stevenson 'hit the roof' in 1974 when an ex-hippy working as a runner for a firm of solicitors tried to liven up the proceedings of a pornography trial by introducing laughing gas into a neighbouring court. The judge jailed him for six months. After eleven days' incarceration, the Appeal Court set aside the prison sentence so Mr Balogh could continue making daisy chains in the outside world. And that was despite his somewhat provocative remark to the judge who jailed him that, 'You are a humourless automaton. Why don't you self-destruct?' There are many celebrated cases of poor human relations between judges and lawyers, and judges and witnesses, leading to incarceration in the watchtower. It is fortunate that prosecutions of journalists and news organisations for contempt of court have to be instituted in the UK High Court by the Attorney General.

The UK tried to make sense of the various precedents and laws relating to the prejudicing of court proceedings in the 1981 Contempt of Court Act. The British judiciary had been discredited by the prosecution of the *Sunday Times* for contempt over its campaign against the drug company Distillers which had manufactured the drug Thalidomide. Hundreds of children were born with deformities. The paper's editor, Harold Evans, supported coverage of the fight by families for compensation. The High Court proceedings were not being heard before a jury. The newspapers had to appeal to the European Court of Human Rights in Strasbourg for a favourable ruling in 1975. The Contempt of Court Act was the British government's gesture of settlement in that it was now virtually impossible for a news organisation to be in contempt of a High Court hearing being decided by judges alone. Unlike the confused world of libel, the statute clearly defines contempt in the Strict Liability Rule as any publication 'which creates a substantial risk of serious prejudice'. The Act also clarifies the time when the strict liability rule can be applied which is the time of an arrest or the issuing of a warrant for someone's arrest. Mistake or no intention to commit contempt is no defence. In civil cases contempt applies when a case 'is set down for trial'. This means when the court's list office has issued a date for the beginning of the hearing. Generally the risk of contempt in civil cases is somewhat limited because judges tend to decide the facts and awards in civil disputes. However, there is a greater risk when juries decide the factual issues such as in libel cases or actions for damages against the police for wrongful arrest and assault.

The advantage of a clear definition of contempt is that journalists have a better idea of knowing where they stand. The risk has to be substantial. This aspect of the definition concerns the timing of broadcast in relation to the trial and the size of audience. You have to bear in mind the likelihood of a jury remembering the broadcast. In 1994 ITN was acquitted of being in contempt of the trial of an IRA police killer despite broadcasting his Northern Irish terrorist background on the day of his arrest. The judges decided that too much time had elapsed between the prime time television broadcast and the eventual trial.

The prejudice has to be serious and this is a very high standard. The prejudice cannot be remote or slight. The allegations must relate to the issues in the trial such as identification through photographs, accusing a defendant charged with supplying heroin with being a junkie, outlining previous convictions, saying defendants have pleaded guilty or confessed, and publishing anything in a trial heard in the absence of the jury. The first test case of the strict liability arose out of the prosecution of a North London man in 1982 who had climbed into an open window at Buckingham Palace and walked into the Queen's bedroom. Michael Fagan spent some time talking to the Queen who had been waiting for her morning tea. She was still in bed. During the course of their conversation Mr Fagan broke an ashtray but it was clearly an accident. In America or Australia, the full text of their discussion would have become public knowledge, but it was conveniently censored and not read out in open court. Scotland Yard and the country's security establishment were immensely embarrassed by the appalling breach in the Queen's security. The Home Secretary and the Metropolitan Police Commissioner did not feel that they should resign. Instead every mechanism of state prosecution was brought upon the head of Michael Fagan who had been unemployed and somewhat distressed by marital difficulties. He was charged with burglary. It seems that he had helped himself to some wine when exploring a room used to store wedding presents given to the Prince and Princess of Wales. It was a Californian Riesling, but Mr Fagan only felt like drinking half of its contents.

The police also dredged up two offences relating to his domestic difficulties which included assault occasioning actual bodily harm against his stepson and taking and driving away his wife's vehicle without her consent. For this veritable cornucopia of crime Mr Fagan was remanded in custody, and dragged before the famous number one court of the Old Bailey to stand trial before the Recorder of London, Sir James Miskin. The state wanted him locked up in a secure mental hospital without any limit of time on the grounds that he was 'a dangerous schizophrenic' who represented a continuing danger to the public. This was very much a case of the state sledgehammer trying to crack a small nut. The jury was not impressed with the allegation of burglary and acquitted him. The other offences were minor domestic matters. The assault only amounted to slapping during a family row. The judge issued a hospital order but resisted the prosecution's demand for a restriction leaving it to the Home Secretary to decide when Michael Fagan should return to the community. Mr Fagan returned to Islington several months later and recorded a pop song to exploit his notoriety. It was not a hit.

If what I have described smacks of state over-reaction, the newspaper media certainly reflected this in the extent of their prejudicial and imaginative coverage of Fagan's background at the time of his arrest. Several papers homed in on his former heroin addiction. One paper described him as a 'morose, unsociable and unpredictable misfit'. Others conducted alleged interviews with his parents who were quoted as saying that their son was 'good with locks', 'jumped over buildings like Spiderman as though they were not there', 'had been smoking expensive cigars recently which might have been Prince Philip's', 'had stabbed his stepson with a screwdriver', 'had confessed to burglary', and 'was clearly a dangerous junkie'. The *Mail On Sunday* compared Fagan's arrest with the scandalous affair of the Queen's personal bodyguard, Commander Trestrail of the Metropolitan Police who had had an affair with a male prostitute a few months before. The paper also described him as a 'rootless neurotic with no visible means of support'. The Divisional Court eventually found only two newspapers guilty of contempt of court. The *Sunday Times* had falsely alleged that Fagan had stabbed his stepson with a screwdriver and the *Daily Star* had falsely alleged that he had admitted the burglary offence. The others were acquitted. The then Lord Chief Justice Lord Geoffrey Lane had attempted to apply a rather robust analysis of the strict liability rule and it was generally to the media's benefit.

This robust interpretation of the strict liability rule has tended to remain intact despite some celebrated campaigns to have newspapers prosecuted for contempt and mutterings that it was time that a national newspaper editor was jailed for contempt. Two journalists were jailed in 1963 for refusing to reveal their sources during a judicial enquiry into allegations that there was a spy ring assisting a civil servant who had been blackmailed by the KGB. The editor of the *Daily Mirror* was jailed in 1949 for three months for being responsible for a front page splash alleging that an acid bath murderer called Haigh had been responsible for several killings. In 1995 two sisters from South London, Michelle and Lisa Taylor, had tried unsuccessfully to persuade the higher courts to force the Attorney General to prosecute newspapers for sensationalist and allegedly prejudicial coverage of their trial for murder. The sisters had been convicted of murdering Alison Shaughnessy, who had married Michelle Taylor's former lover. Their murder conviction and life sentences were quashed by the Appeal Court which had ruled that the convictions were unsafe and unsatisfactory because the validity of a critical identification witness had been undermined and there had been prejudicial publicity caused by newspapers commenting on, rather than reporting, the trial.

When the sisters' lawyers attempted to compel the Attorney General to prosecute for contempt the High Court judges did not think that the newspapers' coverage had been seriously prejudicial although Mr Justice Butterfield conceded 'some of that coverage crossed the limit of fair and accurate reporting by a substantial margin'. The sisters had objected to the *South London Press* newspaper stating that the best friend of Michelle Taylor 'had torn her alibi to shreds' when giving evidence in the witness box. Lord Justice Stuart-Smith said: 'I think the jury were well able to appreciate that it was their assessment of the witness that mattered'.

A considerable campaign had been mounted on behalf of the Taylor sisters assisted by the civil liberties lobby and the sympathy of left of centre newspapers such as the *Observer* and the *Independent*. The sisters were also ably represented by Geoffrey Robertson QC, the joint author of a leading book on media law and a lawyer who had been associated with cases which supported freedom of expression. The campaign tended to lose some of its momentum when the *Observer* had to apologise to the *Sun* newspaper for wrongly alleging that they had 'doctored', through digital editing, a photograph showing Michelle kissing her former lover at his wedding to the murder victim. The argument advanced in the *Observer* was that the *Sun* had changed the real nature of the still from a video to show that the kiss was more enthusiastic and passionate than an affectionate peck during a wedding ceremony. The *Sun*'s associating headline with the picture was 'Cheat's Kiss'. Lord Justice Stuart-Smith observed: 'It cannot be said to be an inappropriate description. She and Shaughnessy had undoubtedly cheated on Alison as that expression is commonly used in a sexual relationship.' The reactionary climate against the UK media was further stoked up when a judge stopped a trial in 1996 alleging that prejudicial coverage by the newspaper media prevented the former boyfriend of a well-known television actress from receiving a fair trial over an allegation that he had assaulted a taxi driver. Despite the hyperbole of attacks on 'irresponsible news media' the eventual prosecution of newspapers for contempt of court resulted in an acquittal.

Meanwhile many lawyers and anti-media pundits in Britain reacted with horror and moral distaste at the coverage of the 1995 O. J. Simpson murder trial in California. It was regarded as a media circus and British observers failed to understand the balance struck in the USA between the freedom of the media and the right to a fair trial. Britain does not have a complicated process of jury selection which provides safeguards against jurors who might be prejudiced against defendants. There is no written constitution and First Amendment protecting the media from discussing matters of public interest. Judges in the USA do not have the power to make orders infringing freedom of expression rights of citizens outside their courtrooms. The UK 1981 Contempt of Court Act formalised a special power for British judges to postpone reporting of entire trials if they feared a substantial risk of prejudice. In the USA the jurisdiction of the courts in relation to censorship stops at the courtroom walls and doors. The private prosecution of O. J. Simpson for killing his estranged wife and her friend was successful where the standard of proof was on a reduced scale. However, whatever the British criticism of the sensationalist nature of the coverage of the televised murder trial, it could not be argued that O. J. Simpson did not have a fair trial. The Los Angeles Police Department's prosecution probably failed because of the exposure of the investigating detective's racism and the fact that the defendant had a right to silence in the criminal courts which he exercised. In Britain, the racist background of the senior detective in the enquiry would have probably remained secret and concealed from the defence, the jury would have been invited to draw unfavourable inferences from Simpson's exercise of his right to silence and he would probably have been convicted and jailed for life after a two- to three-week trial which would not have been broadcast under any circumstances.

As indicated in an earlier chapter, the development of intense competition between the emerging radio networks in the 1930s may have contributed towards a miscarriage of justice in another 'trial of the century' sixty years before O. J. Simpson's case. The writer Ludovic Kennedy believes that Bruno Hauptmann was framed for the murder of Charles Lindbergh's baby son in 1935. Hauptmann was an ex-soldier in the First World War German army, an illegal immigrant and the American news media had decided upon his guilt before he appeared for trial in the courthouse in Flemington. Radio microphones were allowed in the courtroom for the verdict and the jurors could hear the speculation and comments of radio reporters from a temporary studio on the floor below their hotel accommodation. The case prompted the American Bar Association to ban microphones as well as cameras. Canon 35 of the Code of Judicial Conduct stipulated:

> The broadcasting of court proceedings is calculated to detract from the essential dignity of the proceedings, distract the witness in giving his testimony, degrade the court, and create misconceptions with respect thereto in the mind of the public and should not be permitted.

The ban on microphones and cameras has remained in the federal courts. From 1982 Supreme Court judgements led to a relaxation of the prohibition in state courts. It is unlikely that broadcasting will be permitted in English and Welsh courts despite well researched papers and presentations from the Bar Council. I succeeded in negotiating the exclusive broadcast of the valedictory ceremony for Master of the Rolls, Lord Denning's retirement in 1982. This involved securing permission and approval from the Lord Chancellor, Lord Hailsham, the Lord Chief Justice, Lord Geoffrey Lane, Lord Denning himself, and the Attorney General. It was the first time journalistic recording equipment had been allowed in the Lord Chief Justice's court and the experiment, though hugely successful, has not been repeated. In 1979 Ken Dennis, a freelance reporter for LBC and also the Press Association's Chief Old Bailey correspondent, had succeeded in gaining permission for the recording for broadcast of the retirement ceremony for the outgoing Recorder of London. In Scotland, the senior judges cooperated in an experiment with the BBC which resulted in the television transmission of criminal court proceedings. The whole process was heavily censored and controlled by the judiciary. Every person filmed had to give permission for broadcast. Later a Scottish court gave permission for the filming for broadcast of a sentence hearing without the defendant's consent. If there is to be more progress, it is likely to take the form of either the Lord Chief Justice or Master of the Rolls agreeing to the filming for broadcast of a Divisional Court or Appeal Court judgment.

There is a considerable amount of paranoia and bureaucratic harassment of broadcast media journalists in the crown courts. Despite a custom of interviewing people in the courtroom corridors and on the precincts for thirteen years, in

1996 I was threatened with arrest at the Central Criminal Court if I continued to attempt to record the comments of people being taken down by print journalists outside the courtrooms. Although the Contempt of Court Act only makes it an offence to bring a tape recorder into court for use without the leave of the court, radio reporters are repeatedly harassed and ejected by arrogant and bullying officials throughout England and Wales.

In Australia the courts are more relaxed about allowing radio journalists to use tape recorders to assist with note taking. But there is a strict prohibition on the use of the recordings for broadcast. Radio journalists were allowed to use tape recorders for note-taking purposes by Leeds coroner Philip Gill during the inquest into the death of British nurse Helen Smith in 1982 and part of the first coroner's inquiry into the death of Azaria Chamberlain was televised in Australia in 1981. In 1995 in London the St Pancras coroner permitted sound recording and broadcast of an inquest into an unidentified person. There was also televising in Australia of Sydney's Central Court of Petty Sessions and in 1987 the High Court gave approval for the televising of the swearing in of two High Court judges and the new Chief Justice.

In the USA following a Supreme Court judgment in 1988, all criminal court proceedings are open to the public and radio reporters cannot be denied access. The Supreme Court relied on the common law traditions of England and Wales to justify the absolute nature of the open justice principle. This is rather ironic when the courts in England and Wales have been moving towards a rather arbitrary and questionable pattern of in-camera and in-chambers proceedings with the press and public excluded.

All bail applications at crown court level, however serious the nature of the crimes, are now heard in secret. The same applies to applications by the police for a court order to seize reporters' notebooks, tape and video recordings of events to assist them in the investigation of crime. British judges have 'an inherent jurisdiction' to determine the proceedings before them. This means that UK judges have carte blanche to lock their courtroom doors despite protests by journalists. Under the 1988 Criminal Justice Act judges can investigate applications for in-camera proceedings but journalists who wish to challenge these moves are not permitted to be present at the hearing, nor are their lawyers. The appeals against decisions to approve in-camera proceedings are heard without any advocacy, representation and without the journalists and news organisations being allowed to know the reasons for the secrecy.

In-camera proceedings are normally permitted to ensure a cover-up of controversial deals between police officers and their informers, particularly if the informers have continued to enjoy a thriving and profitable life of crime while being protected and well remunerated by the police. They are also used in Britain to cover up judicial incompetence and interference and attempts to bribe and threaten jurors. The senior judiciary does not appear to be at all concerned about the increasing trend in courtroom secrecy. All hearings relating to the collapse of major financial institutions such as the New Cross Building Society in 1982 and Polly Peck in 1990 have been heard in total secrecy with the result that investors and private citizens were kept in the dark about potential insolvency.

In America judges are required to hold a hearing when deciding to exclude the media or public. In Britain the judges go into secret session first to decide whether to hear the journalists' appeal and the journalists are not allowed to know the reason for the secrecy. In various US states access to civil proceedings and juvenile/youth courts varies, but it is unlikely to be as oppressive as the current position in England and Wales. The Family Division in England and Wales has been operating in near secrecy for decades. If the evidence of desperate telephone callers to one of my overnight phone-in programmes in February 1997 is anything to go by, the secrecy is covering up a serious crisis. If what many of the callers say is true, then the Family Division is using the secrecy of its hearings to hide outrageous abuses of human rights. Callers alleged that week after week, judges with the involvement of social workers permit unsubstantiated allegations of child abuse being made by mothers in adversarial child custody proceedings against fathers, and the partners they are living with. The psychological damage to children interrogated and medically examined, who have never suffered any such abuse or interference, is incalculable. It was also alleged that the judges and masters in the Family Division do nothing to apply any sanction or disincentive to hundreds of people regularly perjuring themselves. No penalties or admonishment are applied when the allegations prove utterly unfounded. Complaints have been made that judges frequently hear cases without properly reading the papers. Cases are frequently handed from one judge to another with no judicial continuity of understanding. Public scrutiny of this legal shambles is covered up with the convenient restrictions and 'in-chambers' status of the proceedings. There is no discipline being applied through the presence of fair and accurate reporting.

The High Court is also giving the judicial go-ahead for doctors to allow people being treated for catastrophic brain injuries to die through the withdrawal of life support. A more extreme use of vocabulary could describe this process as 'judicial culling'. The so-called 'persistent vegetative state' of brain injury victims means that relatives and doctors exhausted by the expense and distress of continued medical treatment regularly go before the High Court seeking legal permission to withdraw feeding and medical support keeping the patients alive. Medical research and treatment in many countries of the world clearly demonstrates that a vegetative state diagnosis is only a matter of medical opinion. Recently, a survivor of the Hillsborough soccer stadium disaster showed signs of recovery and demonstrated that the original diagnosis that he was PVS was wrong. Eventual recovery may be possible. Some social workers and medical professionals have even attempted to widen the judicial permission to allow physically and mentally disabled patients to die. These hearings are either taking place in secret or with restrictions on the identity of the parties. Even the identity of the health trust has been suppressed.

The parties applying for 'permission to die' orders are often anonymous, with the result that severely disabled people are dying in secret. Attempts have been made to continue the secrecy when the public inquest by an independent coroner seeks to investigate the death. In January 1996 the BBC successfully challenged a High Court order preventing journalists from reporting the inquest on a 27-year-old man whose life support system was withdrawn after he had been in a coma for four years. The man's family and the hospital were concerned that they would be harassed by Pro-Life supporters.

Meanwhile in the British criminal courts, social workers and child protection 'professionals' frequently exaggerate the risk of psychological damage of media exposure to young people. Censorship of violent, cruel, and disgusting behaviour by young criminals aged 17 and under is widespread. Killings of elderly people, rape and sexual assaults on women and men, violent robberies and appalling vandalism are censored to the point where no realistic or sensible reporting can be achieved. Judges and lawyers willingly bend to the doe-eyed naivety of social workers so that a 14-year-old psychopath, who will remain a critical danger to any member of the public for the forseeable future, was sent to a secure mental hospital without being identified. He thrust a 10-inch knife into the back of a middle-aged woman walking her dog in Kent without any provocation apart from a diagnosed 'lust to kill'.

A father with a background of inflicting abuse on his children was allowed to live with five of his children in a large council house in Islington, North London, with his wife who had severe learning difficulties. Social workers failed to prevent the parents from killing their 15-month-old son. He died by drowning in his own urine. The council spent public money to maintain reporting restrictions so that the 15-month-old child died with the ignominious public identity of 'child X'. His body lies in an unmarked pauper's grave. The Social Services department exaggerated the impact of the parents' criminal trial on the surviving children so that the parents were convicted of manslaughter and child cruelty without being identified. The father was jailed for seven years without being identified for a horrific and revolting child killing. He will be released back into the community and he could be living next to anyone, fathering more children and society will be none the wiser. The censorship surrounding this case was condoned and extended by lawyers and judges.

In Australia there are similar restrictions which follow the British model quite closely but there are also significant differences. There are strict statutory rules preventing the media from identifying the parties in a family case, such as child custody, but the courts are open to the media for scrutiny. This essential differ-ence may account for the divergence in standards being reported by litigants. In 1991 two newspapers were prosecuted for naming a man who had been protest-ing outside the Sydney Family Court. He was unhappy about the way his child custody dispute had been handled. The media could have properly reported his complaints but by publishing his name they had also identified his wife and chil-dren. The prohibition on identification relates to any picture, voice, names, title, pseudonym, alias, any address where a person lives or works, their job, position or property they own, any description of the way they dress, their relationship with identified relatives or identified business, official or professional acquaintances, recreational interests, political, philosophical or religious beliefs.

The identification of children who appear in children's courts as well as adult courts is also prohibited in Australia. It also applies when children are witnesses, or victims and the age at the time of the offence is taken into account, not at the time of charging or trial. The age is normally 17 and under. In England and Wales the adult courts have to make an order under section 39 of the Children and Young Persons' Act. Just to complicate things, in Scotland youngsters can be identified over the age of 16. In the Australian states of Victoria, Tasmania and Queensland a child has to be under the age of 17 at the time of the offence. In all the other Australian states the threshold is 18 years of age. In Britain journalists have a statutory right to attend youth courts although members of the public are excluded. In Australia journalists have a right of access to children's courts in South Australia, Queensland, the Australian Capital Territory, Northern Terri-tory, Tasmania and Victoria. But in New South Wales, the magistrate has to give permission. In Tasmania publication of the result of a children's court case is forbidden by state law. Reporting of criminal injuries compensation hearings is prohibited in Tasmania. Some Australian states also have specific rules on report-ing suicide cases during inquests to spare the bereaved relatives the added agony of publicity. In New South Wales, Queensland, and the Northern Territory, journal-ists must seek the approval of the coroner to report a finding of suicide. The coroners can even impose reporting restrictions if they suspect that the cause of death may have been suicide.

The other type of restriction common to Australia and the UK is a prohibition on the identification of the victims of sexual offences and any information such as their address, school, place of employment and other details which may lead to identification. In Britain the anonymity is from the moment somebody complains of a sexual offence and it is in perpetuity unless the complainant has provided written consent or a court has been persuaded to lift the restrictions on the grounds that they amount to 'a substantial block to the reporting of the case'.

In federal systems such as Australia and the USA you need to be aware of the particular laws applying in an individual state. For example in Queensland and the

Northern Territory of Australia the accused cannot be identified until committed for trial. In England and Wales there are rather severe restrictions on the reporting of magistrates' courts where accused persons are being processed for trial to the crown court. At the crown court there are also 'preliminary hearings' into complex fraud or sex abuse cases prior to the trial by jury where the defence is trying to have the prosecution annulled. At these hearings it is acceptable to report a successful defence challenge, but it is an offence to report that the prosecution has succeeded and the trial will take place before a jury. It is rather absurd that several weeks later the media are able to report the first trial hearing.

In recent years, Australia and the UK have experienced serious attacks on the open justice principle which has been more successfully preserved in the USA. South Australian courts decided there was no assumed principle of open justice so that judges were therefore able to suppress reporting of public hearings to prevent 'undue hardship' to the accused. This kind of attitude led to appalling censorship and the controversy of a senior drugs squad officer standing trial for more than eighty serious criminal offences and having the privilege of complete anonymity. The constitutional row which followed led to a Federal assertion of the principle of openness and the setting up of an appeal machinery to enable the media to challenge reporting bans.

I had to engage in a major legal and parliamentary campaign in Britain in 1984 when I discovered that there was no common law or statutory provision to appeal against gagging or suppression orders. A case brought before the European Court of Human Rights compelled the UK government to negotiate a settlement by way of new legislation. However, the appeal machinery set out in the 1988 Criminal Justice Act is substantially flawed. The judiciary have placed a ceiling on appeals so that substantial freedom of expression issues cannot be decided before the Law Lords which is the equivalent of the US Supreme Court. Attempts to challenge a wide range of censorship orders have been unsuccessful in the UK courts and at the European Court. The higher courts in Britain are now sanctioning bizarre interferences with the reporting of court cases which have huge public interest value. The Appeal Court maintained a reporting ban on the identification of a father who was fighting to compel his local health service to provide medical treatment for his 11-year-old daughter suffering from leukaemia. The ban remained long after the girl had been fully aware of the court battle and a private benefactor had come forward to fund her treatment after the courts supported the health authority. The first hearings of the attempt by Diane Blood to challenge a decision by the UK Human Fertilisation and Embryology Authority to prevent her using her late husband's sperm for artificial insemination had been subject to a court order preventing her identification. The UK High Court suppressed identification of a 59-year-old British woman who had obtained in vitro fertilisation treatment in Italy and was about to become a mother one year before she was entitled to a state pension. The High Court has imposed blanket censorship on the identity of notorious child killers recently released from imprisonment. Court orders have been used to suppress reporting of the complaints by the former mistress of a leading Conservative politician. She had been seeking to improve the treatment and education of her daughter who had been fathered by the politician. An even more bizarre manifestation of English legal secrecy occurred in March 1997 when the Appeal Court ordered a barrister to pay the legal costs of what the judges regarded as an unjustifiable and unnecessary appeal. The ruling was highly critical of the barrister's conduct. Yet he and all the other people concerned were not named. Several weeks later the *Daily Mail* newspaper interviewed him and he was happy to be named and photographed. Unlike every other profession, barristers in England and Wales have an immunity from actions for negligence.

It does seem that not a year goes by without some additional power of prohibition being granted to UK courts to censor media coverage. The Criminal Procedure and Investigations Act 1996 is an example. Section 58 gives judges the power to make an order censoring reporting of mitigation speeches in criminal trials. The court only has to have 'substantial grounds for believing that an assertion that is false or irrelevant is derogatory to a person's character'. It is yet another shackle on investigative journalism and in my opinion only serves the interests of convicted criminals.

This vista of censorship and interference by judges and lawyers undermines the basic rights of journalists to report matters of considerable public interest. This state of affairs is quite alien to journalists in the USA. The First Amendment and a more liberal culture of 'media rights' means that US radio journalists have more freedom and individual discretion in the gathering and communication of information. There are no statutory controls on the identification of sexual offence complainants, children and other participants in court cases. Many women journalists in the USA have informed me that they would be appalled by the idea of judges banning them from being able to identify witnesses. Whilst they are fully conscious of the agony that sexual offence complainants go through when giving evidence they cite the importance of the way that open reporting underlines the horrific nature of the offence, ensures that witnesses tell the truth, and that other witnesses come forward. Consideration of the position of sexual offence complainants and their desire for anonymity is operated by voluntary codes so that most reporting of US rape trials is not gratuitous and the women are spared the pressure of public attention.

The British criminal courts are now permitting undercover police officers, customs officers and security service agents to give evidence anonymously in court and with their identity withheld from the defence. This fundamental breach of human rights and the basic rules of natural justice is likely to make the British criminal justice system the laughing stock of the world as well as among the most oppressive and unfair. It started with a meltdown in respect for open justice and the tradition of free reporting. The Americans are all too conscious of the dangers of going down that road. As Nina Totenberg, NPR's award-winning legal affairs correspondent told me:

> Is it no wonder that the international reputation of British criminal justice has been destroyed by an unbelievable litany of miscarriages of justice. Guildford Four, Birmingham Six, Tottenham Three, The Maguire Seven, – men and women incarcerated for decades for crimes they had not done. This would not happen in the USA because of our First Amendment and respect for open reporting.

In Australia the sub-judice rules come into play when a warrant for arrest, or summons has been issued and in civil actions when the writ has been issued. Australia also allows for a public interest discussion defence. It is similar to a provision in the UK Contempt of Court Act where there is a defence for a news organization which broadcasts a report or programme which is merely incidental to the court proceedings and which covers a matter of public interest. In Australia the principles of contempt are almost identical to those in Britain. They are based on common sense. As a journalist you should not prejudge a case. You should always avoid publishing the previous criminal convictions of an accused person, and you should be careful to avoid publishing anything which is prejudicial either before or during the trial. Do not publish photographs of defendants where there is likely to be an issue of identification. Do not broadcast evidence prior to it being adduced before the jury and under no circumstances publish information about a confession before it is brought forward as evidence in the trial. When the jury is out do not report the proceedings and do not do anything which might be perceived as applying pressure on a witness or another participant in the case. There is a particular rule in Australia which does not apply in the UK. It is not uncommon for judges and magistrates to stop a lawyer's question being answered by a witness. It is the equivalent of the American facility of 'striking it from the record'. Australian lawyers who have decided not to put a question already started or completed will say 'I'll withdraw that'. In these circumstances the court considers that the question was never asked. Reporting of the question and comment contained within it may be contempt of court and not carry any privilege because the judge would have sustained an objection by the lawyer for the other side.

Juries sit and decide cases in Britain, Australia and America. But they do so in different ways and the media have different rights in relation to investigating the conduct and attitudes of jurors. Generally juries of randomly selected electors are asked to decide the facts of an issue although in some American states juries are invited to give a ruling on whether a convicted murderer should face the death penalty. Scotland has a jury of fifteen with the 'not proven' verdict to enable the criminal courts to make the distinction between a declaration of innocence and the suggestion that the prosecution have not adduced enough evidence. The 1981 Contempt of Court Act in Britain outlawed public discussion by jurors of their deliberations. Journalists soliciting information about deliberations from jurors face an unlimited fine or a maximum of two years of imprisonment. In 1981 I saw the extraordinary arrest and summary imprisonment of a *Guardian* newspaper journalist whose only offence was to chat to a juror about the weather. The newspaper had to send a barrister to secure his release from the cells and placate an Old Bailey judge whose nickname was 'Penal Pete'.

The effect of this oppressive legislation has been to block all research and investigation of the jury process, and suppress the scandal of 'jury nobbling'. Furthermore it has been impossible to assess the real nature of allegedly prejudicial media reporting of criminal trials. The significant issues which weighed in the minds of jurors in celebrated miscarriage of justice cases are never made available to the tribunals sitting to investigate future appeals. The foreman of the jury in the Carl Bridgewater case has said openly for many years that the central plank of the case against the four men originally convicted collapsed when the validity of a confession had crumbled as a result of forensic analysis. The Attorney General has not been invited or taken the initiative to prosecute the foreman or the media organisations who have reported his views. Successive Home Secretaries and an Appeal Court ignored the force of the foreman's comments.

In the USA the regular examination of jurors by prosecution and defence means that arguments about prejudicial publicity and broadcast coverage are rarely issues to concern the courts. The larger size of the country means it is easier to move cases to another part of the state. When judges and the parties to a case are very concerned about the impact of prejudicial coverage during a trial, judges in some states have the power to sequester jurors in secure hotel accommodation with restricted access to the general media. This was the fate of the jurors in Los Angeles during the internationally televised murder trial of O. J. Simpson.

Interviewing jurors in the USA is regarded as a traditional right. Both defence and prosecution are anxious to find out the reasons for the success or failure of their advocacy and evidence. In Australia interviews with jurors are allowed after conviction or acquittal. Throughout Australia radio journalists should not broadcast jurors' views during the trial. Their opinions can be broadcast prior to an appeal but there are some special rules in New South Wales, Victoria and Western Australia. In New South Wales journalists have to wait for jurors to approach them. It is an offence to seek information from jurors or to disclose jurors' identities and addresses. After the verdict identification depends on consent. In Victoria there is a prohibition on identifying a juror or attempting to solicit information about jury deliberations. Publication of jurors' stories volunteered to the media is also an offence if the jurors, or case, are identified. In Western Australia there is a prohibition on publishing jurors' photographs or likenesses.

Many of the contradictions created by illogical reporting restrictions reached an apogee of absurdity in July 1997 when a British mother of three eloped to Florida, with a 14-year-old boy who also happened to be her son's best friend. This was a consensual, though unlawful, sexual relationship. Full coverage of the identities of the two lovers was amplified through lurid and sensational reporting in both tabloid and broadsheet newspapers. There was no evidence of the media seeking to analyse the essential hypocrisy in the approach to the story. This centred around the fact that public opinion appeared to regard an emotional and sexual relationship between a mature woman and an under-age boy to be less morally reprehensible than if it were between an under-age girl and a mature man. There was 'saturation coverage' particularly when the couple were traced to a holiday resort in Florida. Interviews were conducted with the boy's friends and family. The Radio Authority intervened and banned commercial radio stations in the UK from identifying the teenage boy after it realised that their broadcast code, derived from the statutory power of the Broadcasting Act, prohibited naming youths at the centre of sexual allegations. BBC news was not determined by these restrictions, although the published 'Producers' Guidelines' discouraged identification of children in these circumstances. These restrictions did not apply in Florida. Coverage of the story continued with press identification of the boy but with the electronic media suppressing his name. The mother was returned to her native Nottinghamshire and then charged with abducting a child and indecently assaulting a male under the age of 16. The force of the Sexual Offences Amendment Act 1992 meant that now the print media was gagged from identifying the boy. Since identification of the women defendant would inevitably lead to identification of the alleged victim, it could be argued that the woman's name should also be suppressed.

These restrictions were applied in the extraordinary context of the identity of both parties having been exploded in the international public domain. The moral contradictions inherent in this case are not helped by the fact that the people involved in the story are being offered substantial amounts of money for their 'exclusive stories'.

Chapter 21

Sources, election law and other matters

The protection of sources is a fundamental principle in radio journalism. The ethical standards for journalists often conflict with the interests of the state. There is no absolute privilege conferred on journalists to protect their sources in Australia, Britain or the USA. Journalists have been subject to greater harassment in Britain over the last twenty years and the law courts have not been there to provide equitable protection.

The British 1981 Contempt of Court Act actually provides for a statutory protection of journalists' sources but it is taken away with the various qualifications which include national security, the investigation of crime and the interests of the administration of justice. *Guardian* editor Peter Preston was humiliated in 1984 when the Appeal Court forced his newspaper to hand over a leaked document challenging the position of a government minister over the arrival of US cruise missiles in Britain. The *Guardian* thought the new act was a shield. It was not. Peter Preston would have been happy to go to jail to protect the junior civil servant Sarah Tisdall who put the document through the newspaper's letter box in Farringdon Road, London, on her way home from work. But the English courts had developed the crippling penalty of 'sequestration' which means the complete economic annihilation of a business or organization refusing to obey the orders of the court. Sequestration was the weapon effectively employed by the courts to enforce Prime Minister Margaret Thatcher's anti-trade union legislation of the 1980s. Instead Sarah Tisdall was prosecuted under the Official Secrets Act and jailed for six months.

The UK state authorities used a number of other statutory mechanisms to harass journalists and trawl their electronic records for information useful in criminal investigations. The Police and Criminal Evidence Act 1984 gave the police the power to demand notebooks and recordings of any event where they suspected a crime had been committed. In 99 per cent of cases crown court judges have agreed to the police request for material. Although refusal by news organisations forces the police to apply for a court order, the judges normally accede to the police application. The effect of this abrogation of journalistic independence has been to place all journalists under greater risk of attack and reprisal in riots and public disturbances. Since the legislation was passed the number of attacks on journalists and radio reporters in public order incidents has increased. Broadcast reporters have been wounded by shotgun pellets, bludgeoned over the head with iron bars, stabbed, and beaten up. Sometimes the offenders have been police officers. The effect of the new law has been to create the fear and suspicion in alienated and disadvantaged areas of society that the media are agents of authority by proxy. The situation is not helped when some police forces allow their officers to pose as journalists.

Throughout the 1980s repeated attempts have been made in the English and Welsh legal system to suppress publication of embarrassing leaks using the developing law of 'confidentiality' and the threat of contempt of court penalties on journalists who refuse to disclose their sources. The attempt to ban publication of the former MI5 agent, Peter Wright's memoirs *Spycatcher* did little for Britain's freedom of information reputation. Legal moves to ban publication in Australia collapsed after the cynicism of the exercise was exposed by the brilliant advocacy of Malcolm Turnbull. The authorities and courts drew short of jailing journalists to avoid the creation of 'martyrs to the cause'. The BBC, which has an outstanding specialist legal department serving thousands of broadcast journalists in television and radio, has been very adept at consolidating the 'public interest' defence in relation to leaked documents. The BBC lawyers are on call twenty-four hours a day with the result that the expertise and judgement of individual lawyers can often provide advice and support which prevents cases going to court. The BBC legal department is a substantial national asset supported by the licence fee and its contribution to freedom of expression in a country where the interests of journalists are not a priority has not been given enough credit.

One of the more Kafkaesque examples of oppression and intimidation of journalists concerned the unassuming and shy trainee magazine journalist, William Goodwin, who was working for a low circulation engineering publication the *Engineer* in 1990. He had received confidential information about a company and promptly contacted the company to check it out. The full force of the legal system descended on him with a panoply of writs delivered by Uriah Heep-like characters in dark suits. He could have been forgiven for thinking he had become 'Joseph K'. The legal process began in-camera and initially there was some doubt over whether he could consult the National Union of Journalists for legal advice.

The episodes that followed are utterly discreditable for the British legal system which trampled across every basic human right in its unbridled determination to force the young journalist to betray his journalistic integrity. The Court of Appeal created the bizarre scenario that he would only be entitled to an appeal if he was prepared to place the name of his source in a sealed envelope. The document was to be returned to him if he won the appeal, but would be opened and disclosed to the plaintiff if he failed. The British courts failed to recognise his right to protect his source and the Law Lords eventually imposed a modest fine of £5,000. The full European Court of Human Rights in Strasbourg roundly condemned his treatment, and found against the United Kingdom government which has since obdurately continued to block change in the existing law on protection of sources.

In Australia there is no established legal principle enabling journalists or publishers to withhold documents, or to refuse to answer questions on the basis of protection of sources. Journalists have no special legal privilege in this area. The Australian police in most states have the power to seize leaked documents, reporters' notebooks and tapes of actuality and interviews if they have a valid search warrant. Australian courts have the power to punish journalists for contempt of court if they refuse to name the source of information. In libel cases journalists are not forced to reveal their sources before a trial, but refusal to identify a source during the trial would be contempt of court. It is common practice for Australian journalists to provide confidentiality to an important source with the proviso that the source will give evidence in the event of legal proceedings arising out of publication of the story.

The Australian Journalists' Association Code of Ethics asserts the journalistic tradition of protecting sources of information where there has been an undertaking of confidentiality, but the Australian legal system has decided that public interest in all evidence being available outweighs any interest in journalists maintaining confidentiality. Journalists have no lawful excuse when refusing to answer questions. The Australian Law Reform Commission has recommended a more effective way of balancing the need for the courts to receive all available evidence and the need for effective news gathering through the assistance of confidential informants. Sally Walker in *The Law of Journalism in Australia* makes the interesting observation that 'few Australian cases have raised the problem of compulsory disclosure by journalists'. She speculates that this may be the result of governments not being enthusiastic about being seen to attack and intimidate journalists; the special intervention of Australian judges to protect witnesses by asking advocates whether they wish to press questions and the subsequent withdrawal of those questions, and the cultural practice of Australian journalism emphasising attribution in reporting so that public confidence is maintained with the clear definition of sources.

NPR's legal affairs correspondent Nina Totenberg was at the centre of a dramatic protection of sources issue in the USA in 1991. Confidential sources had given her the scoop that Anita Hill was alleging that Judge Clarence Thomas had sexually harassed her while she worked for him at the Equal Employment Opportunity Commission. This story had considerable significance because the revelation was broadcast on the eve of the US Senate's vote confirming Judge Thomas as the first black Supreme Court Justice. Many senators suspected that Anita Hill's allegations had been leaked to scupper Judge Thomas's confirmation. An attorney was appointed to investigate the leaked information with the power to subpoena reporters to force them to identify their sources. Nina Totenberg and a newspaper journalist for *Newsday* attempted to assert First Amendment protection for news gathering. The fact that this information was not central to an investigation of an alleged crime may have been one of the reasons the US Senate did not force the issue.

US journalists are not immune from contempt of court penalties for refusing to disclose confidential sources. The Supreme Court has ruled that the First Amendment does not offer journalists this privilege. In 1972 the court decided that guaranteeing a defendant access to evidence which could be critical in securing an acquittal is a greater priority than journalistic confidentiality. Twenty-eight US states have passed special 'shield laws' to provide journalists with a qualified privilege to protect sources. The privilege will be lost if an applicant can demonstrate that the information cannot be obtained from alternative sources, there is a compelling and overriding interest in the information and it also relates to a likely crime. Judges are likely to pay more respect to the constitutional right to a fair trial compared to any First Amendment right to protect news source confidentiality.

Britain compares badly with the USA and Australia in relation to the broadcasting restrictions that apply in the run up to elections. UK legislation demands that radio broadcasters have to prove that they have maintained fair and balanced election coverage. Radio journalists have to operate different policies at different times. After an election has been announced and before all the candidates have been officially registered, it is unwise to interview or report on their politics and campaigns. After all the nominations have been closed and all the candidates are known, radio journalists have to report the campaign on the basis of balanced and equal time allocation. The UK Radio Authority will advise on the balance of coverage which must be given to each party until the eve of polling day. It is normally based on the proportion of votes cast in the the last election and the number of candidates nominated for the parties. Each station then keeps accurate logs on a day-by-day basis so that each party receives its percentage allocation for the duration of coverage and the placing of the coverage in terms of audience size. The most accurate method of achieving balanced time is to restrict all election coverage to pre-recorded packages. In this way the journalists can control the content for the reports of individual constituencies and ensure that the distribution of coverage exactly matches each party's entitlement. Equal time means what it says. Every time candidates are allowed to make policy statements radio journalists have to make sure that they all have the same amount of time to talk. This is different from balanced time which relates to news coverage of the individual candidates.

UK journalists have to make sure that all candidates in an election take part in the coverage and when they do not, there must be written consent from those not participating. Radio stations can still report candidates in relation to non-political news stories, and candidates who happen to be national figures in a general election campaign can be interviewed in relation to the national campaign provided there are no references to constituency issues. During election campaigns it is essential to scan candidates taking part in phone-in programmes as callers. All callers should be asked as a matter of routine if they are standing as candidates. If producers wish to include candidates in phone-in or talkback programmes then all the candidates must take part and if only one takes part day-by-day, the station has to have written consent from all the other candidates day-by-day. Do not think for one moment that the UK radio journalist's reporting task gets any easier. On the day before voters go to the polls, UK radio journalists cannot run any programmes discussing election issues, but it is still possible to transmit balanced constituency reports and bulletin wraps. On election day itself there is a ban on all campaign reports and interviews with candidates and reporting is reduced to the level of covering a country cricket game. You can report facts about the weather, which the British love to talk about, the likely turnout, the bureaucratic arrangements for counting all the votes, and any predictions you might have about when the returning officer will be able to announce the result. Opinion polls can be published as long as they have not been commissioned by your radio station, and you cannot comment on the implications.

Australia used to have some eccentric restrictions which applied only to broadcasters. Up until March 1983, these included a 48-hour radio and television blackout on any election coverage from midnight on the Wednesday preceding the day of a poll until the close of the poll. There was also a ban on the dramatisation of political events, but these have now been repealed and restrictions now only apply to election advertisements. The 1942 Australian Broadcasting Act places an obligation on radio stations to afford 'reasonable opportunities for the broadcasting of election matter to all political parties contesting the election'. Subsequent interpretations by the Australian Broadcasting Tribunal have demonstrated that the concept of 'reasonable opportunities' only applied to paid political advertising material and does not create an obligation for equal time coverage during an election. The Australian Broadcasting Corporation operates a specific editorial policy during elections for the federal and state parliaments. The ABC estimates the measure of significant public support for any party and grants equal time for election broadcasts to the outgoing government party and official opposition.

In the USA the Federal Communications Commission has enacted rules which aim to prevent broadcasters from favouring one candidate over another and to encourage extensive and fair coverage of political campaigns. Section 315 of the Communications Act places an obligation on stations to allow equal opportunities to candidates for the purposes of making their own election broadcasts. If one candidate pays for an election advertisement and if another candidate requests the same opportunity within seven days they should be granted access. This rule does not apply to news programmes or documentaries. The exemption also applies to reports of news conferences and broadcast election debates, provided these programmes inform the public rather than promote or primarily attack an individual candidate. The equal opportunities rule also applies to the supporters of candidates and supporting groups or organizations set up to campaign for candidates.

Public radio stations in the USA are not allowed to support or oppose political candidates in elections, but they can still transmit editorials on matters of policy. Commercial stations publicly campaigning for a specific party or candidate have to notify the other candidates if they run editorials during an election period, and offer reply time. Any personal attack on an election candidate during editorials or election advertisements must be followed up by informing the person or organization that has been criticised. The criticism must relate to honesty, character, integrity or similar personal qualities. The station must provide a reasonable opportunity for a reply.

The law of copyright is very complicated, but the principles that concern radio journalists are similar in the UK, USA and Australia. The law of copyright in Britain is determined by the Copyright, Designs and Patents Act 1988. This confirmed that copyright exists in original literary, dramatic, musical or artistic works, sound recordings, films, broadcasts or cable programmes and typographical arrangements. It is work and not an idea which can be copyrighted. This means that a radio station is free to steal another radio station's ideas and journalists can do the same. Form is the critical factor and form must demonstrate the use of some independent knowledge, skill, judgement or labour. A table of financial services information or the results of a sporting event may well have copyright ownership if it can be demonstrated that some skill was required in putting it together. The courts look at the substantial content of an original work to identify copyright ownership. The concept 'substantial' can be applied to the creative content or value as much as the length. There is a 'passing off' law which prevents one radio station from broadcasting a service so similar to another that listeners are deceived. Under the 1988 Act employees of a radio station do not have any copyright ownership of the reports and programmes made for the station. The station has ownership. Freelance broadcasters have copyright control if they have not surrendered it by signing a contract. Section 30 of the 1988 Act enables journalists to copy extracts of copyright material for reporting current events and for criticism and review. There are no clear definitions of when fair dealing becomes copyright infringement. This is determined by specialist copyright lawyers but an element of common sense can guide the journalist. The BBC failed in an action against British Satellite Broadcasting in 1991 over the use of short clips from the BBC's coverage of the World Cup in news bulletins. Mr Justice Scott ruled that the fair dealing defence enabled BSB to use short extracts because they were reporting current events.

The 1988 Act introduced two new concepts. The actual speakers in news events now had copyright in their material and could prevent reproduction by journalists and news organisations if they made it clear before beginning a speech that they did not want them broadcast or they were unhappy about one news organisation using the material while all the others were free to quote and use the speech for reporting purposes. This area of the law has not been tested. It could prove problematical if a public figure or somebody involved in a public event wanted to be mischievous. 'Moral Rights' give the author of a copyright work the right to be identified as such, not have the work subjected to derogatory treatment and not to have the work falsely attributed. Copyright should not exist in perpetuity. The 1988 Act ruled that published works remained in copyright fifty years after the calendar year in which the author died. The fifty-year rule also applied to sound recordings and broadcasts. However, a new European Union Directive has extended the duration of copyright ownership to seventy years and this has provided a useful supplement to the estates of authors whose work had been placed in the public domain and was being plundered by broadcasters. In the USA works published before 1978 had been protected for seventy-five years if the author had renewed his copyright interests after twenty-eight years. Australia's copyright laws are very similar to Britain's and are set out in the 1968 Copyright Act. Australia and the USA have a 'fair dealing' defence.

Common to all three countries is the realisation that any radio journalist needs to recognise that using music in a news report or programme has significant copyright implications. Musical composers, performers and the record companies producing music have had historic battles with American and Australian radio networks particularly when music format radio became the viable method of surviving the development of television as the primary medium of mass entertainment in the 1950s. In Britain there are three societies collecting royalties and protecting the copyright interests of musical artists and their record companies. They have their equivalents in the USA and Australia. PRS, PPL, and MCPS police the unauthorised use of music. UK radio stations will establish licence agreements with PRS and PPL on the cost of using music during programming and the amount of music that can be used during programming, otherwise known as 'needle-time' even though music is now transmitted using compact discs. MCPS, or the Mechanical Copyright Protection Society will determine a licence agreement on the dubbing of recorded music or sound entertainment for the purposes of radio production and transmission. Radio journalists using music in reports and programme pieces have to record the exact duration of the music used, the name of the composer or music arranger, the name of the music publisher and the PRS reference number on the cassette, vinyl disc, or compact disc. These records have to be accurately compiled and sent to the royalty collection organisations so that the original owners of copyright interests receive their fees.

Britain, unlike Australia and the USA, does not have a Freedom of Information Act. The American radio journalist has considerably more access to public records at state and federal level. The legislation makes all government records available unless they are covered by the interests of national security, personal privacy and law enforcement. In Australia Freedom of Information Acts have been passed at state and federal level with varying degrees of exception preventing access to government documents. In America government agencies and offices have to specify the reason for denying a journalist access and appeals can be made against the decision to withhold the information. Furthermore, fair and accurate reports of public records can establish immunity from libel proceedings. In Britain journalists have to wait thirty years before they can examine central government documents. Sometimes classification of documents can delay public access for many more decades.

Radio journalists in Britain find themselves subject to further layers of control in relation to taste, decency and ethical behaviour. The UK Radio Authority can impose severe fines and withdraw radio licences for breaches of the broadcasting legislation. Use of obscene or extreme language comes under the Radio Authority remit. I have a copy of a letter from the Radio Authority's precursor, the IBA, which in 1990 threatened LBC with the cancellation of its licence if it permitted the broadcast of the word 'fuck' or 'fucking' during a radio play. The investigation had been prompted by a complaint from one listener after hearing a programme compilation of short plays on Easter Sunday. In addition to the Radio Authority, British commercial broadcasters and their colleagues in the BBC have to experience the attentions of the Broadcasting Standards Council and the Broadcasting Complaints Commission. The former specialised in taste, decency, violence and other matters relating to content, and the latter concentrated on allegations of unfair treatment and invasion of privacy. Both bodies have now combined but their successor still has the power to force publication of its adjudication. The Radio Authority, BSC and BCC were bodies created by legislation and have not been run by publicly elected representatives. The figureheads are political appointments.

The UK Radio Authority believes there is no watershed in radio listening. The US Federal Communications Commission came to a similar conclusion by the late 1980s, but a series of *causes célèbres* had allowed a watershed period between 10 p.m. and 6 a.m. In 1977 the Pacifica Foundation's New York station WBAI had played portions of comedian George Carlin's performance of 'Filthy Word'. It featured the utterance of seven words that Carlin said he could never say on the radio. The very act of stating them explicitly led to the FCC showing how much they agreed with him. The Supreme Court, by a five to four majority confirmed that the FCC had the power to prohibit language regarded as obscene. The lines of censorship became broader in 1988 when the FCC decided to respond to the broadcast by a Californian public radio station of a graphic play on homosexuality, the sexist and 'Playboy' style ramblings of 'Shock Jock' Howard Stern, and the broadcast of a sexually-explicit parody. These programmes did not include the seven deadly words, but the FCC believed the material was indecent. The watershed moved to include the period between midnight and 6 a.m.

This was the start of a long struggle between the FCC, the industry and anti-censorship groups over indecent programming. There have been a number of visits to the Supreme Court. The pendulum swung between support for FCC regulation and striking it down. It would now appear that the Supreme Court in 1995 effectively preserved a watershed for the FCC between 10 p.m. and 6 a.m. thereby preserving a window of opportunity for the broadcasting of more risqué programmes overnight.

At the moment, the US courts have validated the Commission's definition of indecent programming as 'language or material that, in context, depicts or describes, in terms patently offensive as measured by contemporary community standards for the broadcast medium, sexual or excretory activities or organs'. The courts have accepted a compelling governmental interest to support parental supervision of children and protection of the home against intrusion by offensive broadcasts. Judges have tended to rule that broadcasters have fewer First Amendment rights than others because of the unique nature of the broadcast medium.

'Shock Jock' Howard Stern has dabbled on the fault line of indecency regulation through his 6 to 10 a.m. morning sequence on WXRK in New York City, WYSP in Philadelphia and WJFK in Manassas. His programme has propelled his reputation into international celebrity status. He asks guests about their sexual lives, describes his own sexual fantasies, asks women to undress in the studio, comments on the result, and insults phone-in listeners. The FCC imposed fines totalling nearly $1.7 million. Complaints centred on graphic discussions of masturbation, child molestation, and Stern talking about shaving his posterior. It is significant that Infinity Broadcasting Corporation, which owns the three stations, has settled the FCC dispute and no actionable complaints have been filed on Stern's programme since 1994.

In the field of news coverage the FCC handed down a liberating adjudication for National Public Radio's *All Things Considered* programme in January 1991. A news report on organised crime and mafia racketeering in 1989 included audio of an FBI wiretap on mafia boss John Gotti. He used expressions such as 'fucking house . . . this is not a fucking game . . . call your fucking wife . . . my fucking time is valuable . . . you fucking arse . . . I'll fucking kill you'. The news presenter warned listeners that the report contained 'very rough language'. The FCC decided 'we note that the program segment, when considered in context, was an integral part of a bona fide news story concerning organised crime and that the material prompting the complaint was evidence used in a widely reported trial'. I believe this level of tolerance would not be permitted in the UK and other English-speaking countries. Broadcasters would be more likely to 'bleep' the use of the word 'fuck' notwithstanding intervention by regulatory authorities.

In Britain, the BBC has wider discretion and is free from statutory controls. However producer guidelines and editorial policy tend to determine a conservative policy. The use of the word 'shit' or 'arsehole' was regarded as unacceptable in the middle of the afternoon in a play on Radio 4 which I directed in 1995, but highly explicit and indecent language in a play called *Victory* by Howard Barker on the cultural and rather elitist channel Radio 3 in 1995 was acceptable. His play had repeated and liberal use of the words 'fuck' and 'cunt'. Editors and executive producers tend to make an estimation on the likely response of the audience and the risk of young children hearing the programme. Another Howard Barker play, *The Love Of A Good Man*, broadcast on Sunday 9 March 1997, was saturated with extreme language and sexual imagery. It was broadcast without warnings between 7.30 and 9.20 p.m. It would almost certainly have attracted attention from the US Federal Communications Commission.

In Australia the 1942 Broadcasting Act prohibits material which is blasphemous, indecent or obscene. The Australian Broadcasting Tribunal has made it very clear that the words 'fuck' and 'cunt' are not acceptable on radio except in very exceptional circumstances. The Tribunal ensures that no licensed radio station is permitted to broadcast programmes which 'incite, encourage, or present for their own sake, violence, or brutality, simulate news or events in such a way as to mislead or alarm listeners, present as desirable, the misuse of alcoholic liquor, misuse of drugs or narcotics, incite or perpetrate hatred against; or gratuitously vilify any person or group on the basis of ethnicity, nationality, race, gender, sexual preference, religion or physical or mental disability'. In 1989 the Tribunal forced the radio station 2KY to introduce a 10-second delay button for live broadcasting by presenter Ron Casey after he had referred to Chinese and Japanese people as 'those rotten little slant-eye devils to the north of us'. The station also had to introduce training measures to ensure that station staff applied the Tribunal's standards properly.

There is no doubt that radio broadcasters are subjected to more laws and regulations than their print counterparts. Furthermore the very right to broadcast and transmit radio news requires the approval of the state through licence regulation. There would be an outcry that would shake the foundations of public order if any government in Australia, Britain or USA sought to control who had the right to publish a newspaper or magazine. Yet the same standard of liberty is not applied to broadcasting. The broadcast spectrum required mandatory government regulation. The Reverend Robert Schuler failed to challenge the Federal Radio Commission's revoking of the licence for his Los Angeles station KGEF in 1932. He had used his station to vilify the Roman Catholic Church, Jews, local judges and civic leaders and he had also blackmailed prominent figures by warning that he had damaging information which would be announced over the radio unless the people concerned each donated a hundred dollars to his church.

In the famous Red Lion Broadcasting v. FCC Supreme Court Case in 1967 the judges said: 'it is idle to posit an unbridgeable First Amendment right to broadcast comparable to the right of every individual to speak, write or publish'. The idea of a limited spectrum is a controversial one. The BBC exploited ignorance about the limitations of electro-magnetic space for alternative broadcasters for nearly forty years. The monopoly on radio was not broken until 1973. Even now you can twiddle the London FM dial and find large gaps, supposedly reserved for 'emergency frequencies'. Austria was one of the last European countries to deregulate for commercial radio competition against well established state broadcasting services. This had to be fought for at the European Court of Human Rights in Strasbourg. We cannot tell if the explosion in digital broadcasting and World Wide Web publishing will eventually free sound transmission from the control and censorship of state authority. US Federal Communications Commission regulation had been positive for radio journalists when it required all American radio stations to guarantee a minimum of news and public affairs programming, but this has now ended. The old UK Independent Broadcasting Authority guaranteed more fully staffed newsrooms by enforcing promises of news programme performance. But a different kind of deregulation in the 1980s removed these obligations. Employment surveys reveal a substantial reduction in the number of US commercial stations supporting a news service. There is still mobility in the profession, but there has been a trend towards one-person news operations, and smaller salaries. The UK has seen an expansion in commercial services which has compensated for the reduction in the size of newsroom teams and lower salaries. Homage has been paid to the influence of market forces and at the same time regulation has concentrated more on issues of taste and privacy.

The landslide victory by the UK's New Labour party in the May 1997 general election offers the prospect of a more liberal era in journalist and broadcast freedom. The party included a manifesto commitment to a Freedom of Information Act, and the incorporation of the European Convention of Human Rights into British law. However, the weighting against the media in the field of libel, access to courts, and privacy is likely to remain.

The purpose of legal restrictions on freedom of expression in a democratic society is always open to debate. Laws are passed by the State in order to regulate the relations between individual citizens and protect the perceived interests of the State. Media freedom often faces compromise and inhibition when there are clashes with other fundamental civil rights recognised by the State such as privacy, and the right to a fair trial, and pragmatic dilemmas where the State recognises the need for secrecy and confidentiality such as national defence and privileged professional relationships. But existing laws do not control the moral imperatives and determination of radio journalism. These lie with the conscience of the individual journalist and the independent culture of journalistic practice.

Media ethics, ethical standards and moral issues in radio journalism require their own books. Undoubtedly the leading 'bible' exploring these subjects remains *Media Ethics – Cases and Moral Reasoning* by Clifford G. Christians, Kim B. Rotzoll and Mark Fackler (with a third edition published by Longman in 1991). Clifford G. Christians has another influential analysis of this area in *Good News, Social Ethics and The Press* published by Oxford University Press in New York in 1993. The Routledge reader *Ethical Issues in Journalism and the Media*, edited by Andrew Belsey and Ruth Chadwick, enhances the depth and exploration of the moral dilemmas faced by radio journalists. There is a huge spectrum of decision-making for which no radio journalist can relinquish individual responsibility by averring to an existing law.

The use of an interview with an inebriated public figure recorded with content which is largely incoherent is a matter of choice. So is employing lies to obtain information which exposes injustice and wrong-doing. The decision to breach an existing law by asserting the right to know is an ethical decision. Generally journalists will go to jail to protect their sources, but the UK saw no civil disobedience by broadcasters when a Conservative government banned the sound transmission of political parties in Northern Ireland, such as Sinn Fein which had a democratic mandate and subsequently returned two MPs to the Westminster parliament in the general election of May 1997. In Western jurisdictions the law has no easy answer for the radio news editor who has a short-wave recording of hijackers executing a passenger on a jet in the Middle East. The decision to broadcast is made more difficult when the recording discloses the moving and pathetic exhortations for life from the victim. Does the news editor go ahead and broadcast in the full knowledge that the victim's widow and children will hear the actuality? Is there justification in transmitting the actuality in future years as the sound icon of this significant news event?

Part VI

Modern styles of radio reporting and journalism

Chapter 22

The history and development of UK independent radio journalism

This is an uncharted and neglected area of research in radio and the chasm needs to be filled. The political and cultural block on alternative radio news in the UK from 1922 to 1973 was unjustifiable and represents a form of economic and political censorship. Close analysis of Royal Commissions and parliamentary committees of enquiry into broadcasting suggest that competitive motives were responsible for the lack of progress. The newspaper interests in Britain feared a drain on the existing scale of advertising. A public sector broadcasting system funded by tax was a limited threat. The BBC became a very powerful lobby and its parliamentary influence cannot be underestimated. Scientific ignorance also played a part. Politicians were persuaded that the spectrum for radio broadcasting was finite, although now it is difficult to understand how BBC engineers could sustain the argument that BBC transmission waves were so large that there was no room for anyone else. Ignorance and prejudice against foreign commercial radio environments played into the hands of those lobbying against commercial competition. This began to be dispelled when the world became smaller through international communications and jet travel for business and tourism.

The vested interests militating against commercial radio licensing sustained their hegemony from 1955 to 1973 even when ITV and Independent Television News successfully developed an international reputation and challenged BBC TV news in terms of style and audiences. The BBC was fortunate in that the Labour Party during the 1960s and 1970s had a political policy opposed to commercial radio. The BBC was also fortunate that the explosion of pirate radio during the 1960s, stimulated by the huge blossoming of youth culture and popular music had been manipulated by newspapers and political parties into a 'moral panic'. New legislation introduced to the House of Commons in 1967 by Labour Postmaster-General Anthony Wedgwood Benn effectively outlawed pirate broadcasting and the BBC was given the task of responding to the needs of youth culture by transforming its broadcasting networks to meet popular demand. Radio 1 was the result. Most of the new station's disc jockeys had been recruited from the legally harassed and economically disabled pirate services.

Unlike Labour, the Conservative Party was committed to the idea of a competitive market in radio and towards the end of the 1960s, former athlete, Christopher Chattaway MP, was at the centre of a successful campaign to introduce new legislation licensing independent radio. The Local Radio Association and Commercial Broadcasting Associates lobbied strongly for all-party support. A Swiss company was hired to prove that there was enormous capacity in the radio spectrum with varied power medium-wave transmitters. There was a deliberate plan to begin with an all-news radio service modelled on the New York radio station WINS. Local commercial radio was in the Tory Party's election manifesto for the 1970 general election. The Conservative government under Prime Minister Edward Heath between 1970 and 1974 provided the window of political opportunity. Chattaway was appointed minister for Post and Communications. Despite opposition from Labour in the House of Commons the Sound Broadcasting Bill became an Act of Parliament. Opposition spokesman on broadcasting Ivor Richard described the government's proposals as 'nothing more than the establishment of sixty pop stations. It is a piece of Conservative theology which is designed to fulfil an ill-conceived, half-baked pre-election pledge.'

The London Broadcasting Company started its service at 6 a.m. on 8 October 1973 with audio birthday cards from leading politicians including Labour leader Harold Wilson who reaffirmed his party's opposition, but welcomed the radio equivalent of ITN. UK radio had reached the point of no return and BBC radio journalism had to face up to a force of competition which would profoundly change its news-gathering and broadcasting culture over the next twenty years.

LBC and UK independent radio's national and international news service, IRN, have pioneered developments in both the technology as well as the style of radio journalism. Many of these developments have been borrowed from well established traditions in America and Australia. The organisations were sited in the middle of London's Fleet Street newspaper community. Their broadcast journalists were a stone's throw from pubs, restaurants and meeting places frequented by the country's leading national newspaper journalists. This enabled LBC and IRN to have a much more independent journalistic culture and news priority agenda. The sequential nature of commercial broadcasting meant that the station's schedule was much more flexible in accommodating news-gathering and broadcasting responses to dramatic and changing events.

The introduction of talkback phone-in radio brought the journalists in direct

12: Bridget Kendall, BBC foreign correspondent. From 1980 onwards the BBC distinguished itself by employing more women radio journalists on 'the frontline' of reporting. Bridget is a bi-media reporter whose award-winning career has involved being the BBC correspondent in Moscow and Washington.

13: Jenny Abramsky, the most successful woman BBC radio journalist. Her distinguished career has involved editing the *Today* programme, launching Radio Five Live as the programme controller and planning the launch of a twenty-four-hour digital news channel. Her commitment and leadership qualities are legendary. She is responsible for modernising and developing the quality of BBC Radio news journalism.

14: Tim Crook, the author. Britain's first specialist legal affairs radio correspondent covering the Central Criminal Court and Royal Courts of Justice. But he is not allowed to take his tape recorder into the famous Old Bailey building to record interviews and the sound of the proceedings. He was responsible for the first sound broadcast from inside a British courtroom when Master of the Rolls, Lord Denning, retired at the Royal Courts of Justice in the Strand in 1982.

15: Kevin Connolly, experienced BBC radio foreign correspondent. Covered the fall of
the Soviet Union, the storming of the Russian 'White House' Parliament, and the war
in the former Yugoslavia. A courageous and naturally-gifted radio journalist who
was filmed rendering first aid to an elderly Bosnian woman injured by shrapnel when
mortar bombs landed during a funeral in a Sarajevo cemetery.

16: John Schofield, the BBC Radio 4 *World Tonight* reporter shot dead in August 1995
while reporting the war in the former Yugoslavia. He was only 29 years old and one
of more than seventy journalists killed while reporting the conflict.

17: A gallery of distinguished IRN/LBC radio reporters who have become the UK's leading broadcast journalists at Independent Television News.

(*i*) Jon Snow, the former social worker who decided to get involved in the early days of LBC news. He is remembered for travelling around London on a racing bike to beat the traffic and his competitors to deadlines. The first reporter to use a radio telephone for a live report at the end of the Balcombe Street siege in London, the recipient of many awards and now presenter of Channel Four's television news.

(*ii*) Paul Davies. He spent most of his IRN reporting career travelling to the world's most dramatic news stories with a battered Marantz superscope tape recorder. He won awards for his brilliant television reporting of the fall of Ceauşescu's regime in Bucharest, and the siege of Dubrovnik. One of his most memorable radio reports was the ad-lib from the Toxteth Liverpool riots of 1980.

(*iii*) Carol Barnes. Along with the late Joan Thirkettle and Tricia Ingrams, one of the first women radio reporters at LBC and now a popular main presenter of ITN news. Her friendly and supportive personality is loved by viewers as well as her colleagues. She is a sensitive and thoughtful journalist who dispelled the myth that you have to be aggressive and ruthless to get on in journalism.

(*iv*) Andrew Simmons. When sent by IRN to cover the Israeli invasion of Beirut in 1982 the first hotel he was booked into was razed to the ground during his first night in the city. Fortunately, he was being given hospitality at another hotel by colleagues. A conscientious and dogged broadcast journalist who was arrested by Saddam Hussein's Republican Guard while trying to report the crushing of the post Gulf War revolt by Arabs in the Basra region.

(*v*) Lindsay Taylor. Conscientious and thoughtful IRN reporter who was travelling home one night with a reporter's kit over his shoulder when he noticed that his underground train did not stop at King's Cross station, London, because of smoke. He got off at the next stop and ran to the scene of a horrific fire. He ad-libbed as paramedics tried to resuscitate a dying firefighter. His reporting that night won him the award UK Sony Reporter of the Year in 1987 and a job as a reporter on ITN's Channel Four News. His first radio reporting job was with the tiny Moray Firth community station in Inverness, Scotland.

(*vi*) Jo Andrews. LBC's local government correspondent when London still had a metropolitan Greater London Council, which was abolished in 1986 by Prime Minister Margaret Thatcher. Mrs Thatcher was not prepared to tolerate the ruling Labour group baiting the Conservative government with a banner proclaiming the latest unemployment figures. The banner was draped on County Hall opposite the Houses of Parliament. Jo worked in broadcast news in Australia before returning to Britain as a staff ITN news reporter when she was appointed ITN's US correspondent.

IRN Stations

Classic FM • Capital • Essex Radio • Invicta • Kiss 100 FM • The Beach • Ocean Sound • Central • 100.7 Heart FM • Great Yorkshire Gold • Choice FM London • Downtown • Great North • Gold Radio • GWR West • 2-10 FM • Leicester Sound • Trent FM • Chiltern • Severn Sound • SGR FM • Island FM • Kix 96 • Orchard FM • Q102 • Sabras Sound • Radio Forth • Spectrum • Stray FM • Townland Radio • Radio Wyvern • Talk Radio UK • The Bay • Asian Sound • Power FM • Century • Galaxy • Cheltenham Radio • Eleven Seventy • Piccadilly • Hallam FM • Fox FM • Jazz FM 100.4 • Brunel Classic Gold • Beacon • Mercia FM • New Hereward • Horizon • Broadland • Q96 • KCBC • Moray Firth • Pirate Radio • Radio 1521 • Radio Wave • Scot FM • NorthSound • Spire FM • Sunrise Radio • Wessex • Atlantic 252 • City Beat 96.7 FM • BRMB • Southern FM • CFM • Channel 103 • Country 1035 • Aire FM • Red Dragon • Metro FM • Gemini • Jazz FM 102.2 • Isle of Wight • WABC • Classic Gold • KL FM • Northants • Amber • Fortune • KFM • NECR • Plymouth Sound • Radio Maldwyn • Radio XL • Radio Borders • Radio Tay • Spirit FM • Sunshine 855 • West Sound Radio • A1 FM • The Bear • South Coast Radio • Heart 106.2 • Choice FM B'Ham • Country Sound • City FM • Red Rose • TFM • Viking • GWR East • 2CR • Gem • Ram FM • Q103 • 96.6 FM • SGR Colchester • Mercury • Kiss 102 • Nevis Radio • Premier • The Pulse • RTM • Radio Clyde • London Greek Radio • London Turkish Radio • Signal • Star FM • Swansea Sound • News Direct 97.3 • • • • •

INDEPENDENT
RADIO NEWS
200 GRAY'S INN ROAD
LONDON WC1X 8XZ
TEL 0171 430 4090
FAX 0171 430 4092

18: The board listing IRN subscribers in 1997.

19: Derval Fitzsimons. IRN's first woman editor at a time when IRN is probably the most successful news provider of its kind in the world. Derval Fitzsimons had worked previously in the trusted and highly popular newsroom of Downtown Radio in Northern Ireland, before moving to ITN's radio service. IRN now has a near monopoly of UK commercial radio news by virtue of its successful commercial marketing. The selling of advertising within its breakfast bulletins returns a profit to carrier stations.

20: The newsrooms of LBC and News Direct 97.3FM at 5.40 a.m. LBC and News Direct 97.3FM are adjacent to each other in the basement of the ITN building. The LBC 'talkback' station is calmly operating with a producer and presenter and the interaction of callers on the telephone. News Direct – the rolling news format station – has a buzzing newsroom. The sequence editor *until lunchtime* is writing up the 'running order', reporters are researching the background to developing stories, and producers are using computers to compile news packages.

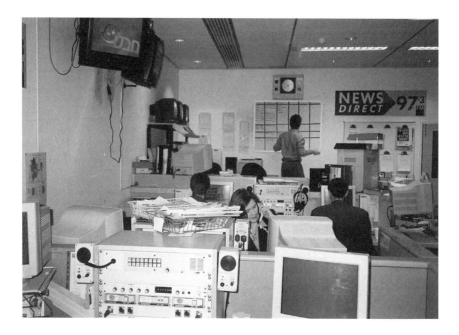

communication with listeners who were allowed to articulate opinions and views and provide direct information. In the beginning IRN only had one member of staff, Fred Hunter, who had been recruited from the government's information service, the COI. IRN's development depended on the further licensing of local commercial stations who had to pay a subscription fee based on audience size, turnover and profits. In 1975 IRN received £20 for every thousand listeners. The first major story was the Yom Kippur war between Israel and its neighbouring Arab countries. IRN's first news bulletin was presented by Australian radio journalist Ken Guy. The first words of the bulletin were in a popular direct style: 'The Middle East War'. The writing was short, simple and concrete. The first report, on 8 October 1973, was an ad-libbed actuality based 'voicer' from UPI radio correspondent, Richard C. Groce, in Northern Israel. You could hear the rumble of tanks driving towards the Golan Heights as he talked into his microphone:

> Here comes another one I think. And this one has its gun facing forwards. Two men staring out the top turret. This main street actually in more normal times is like a main street anywhere. Traffic here is tanks, armoured half tracks, command vehicles and jeeps, the stuff of any army on the move. That's because this town is hard by the frontier with the occupied Golan Heights. Here comes another tank . . . tank commander gave a wave. The troops and vehicles have been moving through this town on the way to the front since Israel first started mobilizing its troops on the first day of the war. If I turn around I can see pops of white smoke on the hills on this side of the heights that face Israel proper. And from there are dulled explosions that one can hear from time to time. The soldiers here have been mobilized hastily and some of them are still wearing dungarees, civilian shirts, or teeshirts and they're either going to change into uniform away to the front or else go fight in their dungarees. Traffic here is heavy, the heaviest it has been since the last war in 1967. One soldier told me 'This time it is going to be the last one'. This is Richard C. Groce at a small town in Northern Israel near the occupied Golan Heights of Syria.
>
> (Crook and Rose 1993)

LBC and IRN relearned the basics of radio journalism by changing the outmoded and bureaucratic practices of reporters who had been recruited from the BBC and importing the skills of mainly Australian and New Zealand itinerant radio journalists who were on their 'world trips'. An influential figure was John Herbert who had been in the thick of ABC's battles with Gough Whitlam's Australian Labour government in 1972, had worked at editorial level at the BBC World Service and later wrote the first book on radio journalism which averred to practice outside the BBC. There is an apocryphal story that LBC were at one point so desperate for experienced freelances that an editor was despatched to the Aldwych, which was a traditional gathering point for international travellers from 'down under'. Here, travellers sold their camper vans on to compatriots wishing to take on the world tour via Katmandu. The story goes that the editor had to move from camper van to camper van saying, 'Anyone here a radio journalist from Australia or New Zealand?'

In the next twenty years IRN/LBC became a substantial training ground for broadcast journalists who now figure prominently as international bimedia correspondents and programming executives. Generations of reporters learned their trade in reporting London news events and many journalists in their early twenties found themselves flying around the world with a battered Marantz cassette recorder, 'Comrex' telephone transmission enhancement unit and a personal credit card which would eventually be reimbursed by the station's expenses accountant, Tony Darkins. Years later he would be recruited by News Direct 97.3FM as a producer for rolling news format programmes.

The lively, ambitious and enthusiastic community of journalists walking in and out of the basement headquarters in Gough Square changed the face of UK radio journalism. The most influential editors and managing directors included former ITN reporter George Ffitch, former *Daily Sketch* and *Daily Telegraph* journalist Peter Thornton, Keith Belcher, Ron Onions, Linda Gage, Dave Wilsworth, Robin Malcolm, Charlie Cox, and John Perkins. There were many others in the chain of editorial command who determined the style and content of the news coverage including bulletin editors, intake editors and network editors such as John Greenwood, Jim Keltz, Derek Grant, Rick Thomas, Rory McLeod, Nigel Charters, Colin Parkes, Steve Butterick, Julian Rush, Stephen Kyte, Tim O'Mara, Charles Morrissey, Vince McGarry, Chris Shaw, Charlie Rose, Vivienne Fowles, Kevin Murphy, Stephen Gardner, John Sutton, and Marie Adams. I can only apologise for omitting the names of many other journalists who made a significant contribution during this period.

Up until 1987, IRN's resources had expanded with the subscription fees provided by the burgeoning ILR network of stations and this had been combined with a subsidy from the sister company LBC. The operation was labour intensive, but despite fluctuations in funding and the threat of redundancies in four- to five-year cycles, LBC was a remarkable success. The station was protected by a limited radio market. For many years there were only two commercial stations in London and the competition was music format in the form of Capital Radio. UK spending on radio advertising remained stubbornly restricted to 2 per cent. The introduction of *Newslink* in 1988 with a spectacular presentation on the Orient Express radically changed IRN's funding base. *Newslink* was the UK's first national radio network advertising opportunity. The IRN morning bulletins would include commercials and the revenue earned from this selling point meant that IRN carriers would no longer have to pay subscription fees. Soon IRN's commercial prowess would result in carrier stations receiving a *Newslink* dividend. Previous

IRN subscribers became significant shareholders and IRN was no longer a financial subsidiary of LBC. A former IRN/LBC industrial correspondent and negotiator for the National Union of Journalists, John Perkins, successfully steered IRN to commercial success and domination of the news provider market through the late 1980s and 1990s.

Many attempts were made to challenge the IRN hegemony. They included expensive loss-leader news services from Network News, ITN and Reuters, but these were unsuccessful. IRN contracted out the service provision to ITN in 1991 after a major decline in LBC's fortunes. In 1989 LBC's new owners Crown Communications made a series of poor management decisions which included leaving Gough Square, changing the identity of the station by launching two new services on the AM and FM frequencies and failing to match expenditure with income. By the time the Radio Authority withdrew the licence in 1993, IRN had found a new home in the highly resourced multimedia ITN building in Grays Inn Road. LBC returned to the London radio scene with another change of ownership in 1996 and the sensible decision to return to the original branding. It is ironic that the LBC of the present day is again operating on the same floor as IRN and its sister FM station News Direct 97.3FM.

Although it is an analysis born of nostalgia, it is quite clear that maintaining the pre-1987 economies of scale at Gough Square and a continuity of radio journalism culture would have preserved LBC's unique position of qualitative news and current affairs-based broadcasting which had been the envy of the BBC. From 1987 successive managements failed to appreciate the value of audience loyalty and brand identity of a 20-year track record in broadcasting, over-estimated the threat of an expanding radio market and under-estimated the expansion in adver-tising expenditure. Another catastrophic mistake included relocating to an inaccessible suburb of London in an expensive leasehold office block which became a white elephant when property prices in the City collapsed shortly after the move. LBC/IRN could have remained in Gough Square with a peppercorn rent and would have been adjacent to powerful decision-making centres of finance, politics and law. The history serves to show how a vibrant and creative centre of journalism culture can be undermined by a series of organisational failures in a liberal democracy and capitalist economy that allows business takeovers and the buying and selling of media assets. The 'regulation' by the old IBA and succeeding Radio Authority is open to question. Should the IBA have permitted the Australian media entrepreneur David Haynes to buy LBC/IRN from the Canadian con-glomerate Selkirk Communications in 1987? Should the unelected Radio Author-ity have been allowed to withdraw LBC's licence in 1993 when the station had successfully recovered from its earlier losses and had re-established its share in a more competitive London radio market? Politics may have been influential in a highly unpopular decision. The station's owners Chelverton Investments were inextricably linked to former Westminster Council leader Dame Shirley Porter who was being accused by the District Auditor of selling council homes to buy Conservative votes.

The Radio Authority awarded the franchise to the group led by LBC's former Managing Director Peter Thornton. But Peter Thornton's group did not have the necessary financial base to launch the new services and had to sell out to Reuters which had been a rival franchise bidder. These events undermined the credibility of regulation and leave uncomfortable question marks over whether the politics of broadcasting were more important than the merit of broadcasting operations. Many of these questions are difficult to answer because the Radio Authority conducted its decision making in secret and was not obliged to provide any reasons for its decisions.

IRN/LBC reporters demonstrated a faster response to news events from 1973 onwards. Sometimes reporters as a result of receiving tip-offs from freelances monitoring emergency service frequencies, or telephone calls from listeners, would be on the scene of major crimes before the police. There was one celebrated occasion when an LBC reporter conducted an interview with the victims of an armed robbery. They had been locked inside their warehouse. As questions were asked and answered through the letterbox police sirens could be heard getting closer and closer. Another reporter conducted a bizarre interview with an anti-immigration National Front supporter while he was fighting with an Anti-Nazi League protester. Interviews with Captain Mark Phillips and Princess Anne prior to their wedding in 1973 betray sexist cultural values of the period. Princess Anne is asked if she would make a good housewife, and would she cook her husband's breakfast before he goes off to work? She was also asked if she could sew on a button. She replied with considerable equanimity that she had been quite well educated.

The IRA's mainland terrorist campaign from 1973 onwards produced dynamic and disturbing actuality reports from reporters Ed Boyle and Jon Snow. News packages are produced with ad-libbed links mixed with the actuality sound of interviews and location recordings. Ed Boyle arrived on the scene of the pub bombing in Guildford shortly after the fatal explosion. His language is imagistic and direct:

> The quaint shopping streets littered with broken glass, footprints in blood outside a clothing store, people crying, policemen everywhere, Guildford has never seen and never wants to see again anything like it.
>
> (Ed Boyle, IRN/LBC 1974; Crook and Rose 1993)

Ed Boyle became IRN/LBC's political editor by 1975 and on Monday 9 June of that year commentated on the first broadcast from the House of Commons. In that year Jon Snow became the first radio reporter to use a radio car phone to broadcast the end of a dramatic siege of an IRA active service unit that had been cornered in a flat in London's Balcombe Street. The four men who gave themselves up adamantly indicated that they had been responsible for the pub bombings at Woolwich and Guildford, but the British judicial system continued to detain eleven people who became known as the Guildford Four and Maguire Seven for crimes they had plainly not been responsible for. LBC interrupted its regular schedule to take this live report from Jon Snow who was well known for travelling to the scene of London news stories on a racing bicycle:

> The four gunmen have come out. The siege here has just ended one minute ago. There is still a great deal of activity here, but a blue flashing lighted van has just swept off into the distance with its siren wailing. Briefly, a figure came out onto the balcony, looked over, went back in again. Another came out, looked over, went back in again, and then suddenly we saw the four being led across the street into the police van and away they've been swept. There is still a very heavily armed presence all round. I am just getting further information. Just one moment.
>
> [*Another journalist says 'that's a gunman with a white handkerchief'.*]
>
> 'A gunman with a white handkerchief has literally just come out. Really, it is so dark up that end now. We are obviously going to have to wait for the firm confirmation of the police but the evidence so far is that we are right at the very end of this siege'.
>
> (Jon Snow, IRN/LBC 1974; Crook and Rose 1993)

IRN's parliamentary unit covered the major political events of these two decades and in particular the rise to power and triumphant general elections of Mrs Margaret Thatcher. Ed Boyle was succeeded as political editor by Peter Allen who successfully drew out of this politician views and opinions about sound domestic housekeeping which were to become the cornerstones of 'economic Thatcherism'. Peter Allen left IRN to pursue a successful career as a television political specialist and is now co-presenting the successful breakfast programme on BBC Radio Five Live which is drawing listeners away from the Radio 4 flagship *Today*. He was succeeded as IRN's political editor by Peter Murphy who is admired for his wit and ability to focus on the real news value of political developments.

In 1975 LBC reporter Julian Manyon travelled to Saigon to witness the fall of the South Vietnamese regime to the Vietcong and North Vietnamese army. He stayed behind after the frantic evacuation of the American embassy by Chinook helicopters. He produced a remarkable 5-minute-long ad-libbed telephone account of Vietnam's fusion into one country. It combined dramatic, concrete description with assured analysis of the significance of what he had seen. Here is an example:

> Whatever one's political views about the rights and wrongs of the war what is undisputed is that the North Vietnamese and Vietcong soldiers were far better disciplined, far better controlled and just basically obeyed orders.
>
> (Julian Manyon, IRN/LBC 1975; Crook and Rose 1993)

In 1980 IRN/LBC journalists were broadcasting live on the dramatic end to the Iranian embassy siege. It was a sunny Sunday afternoon when the British Home Secretary gave his permission for the SAS to attack the building. By this time Iranian separatists had begun to shoot hostages and dump their bodies on the steps outside. The first to die was the Iranian press attaché. BBC personnel had been inside the building when the siege began. Producer Chris Cramer had been allowed to leave after being taken seriously ill. A duty BBC television reporter, Kate Adie, was also present with the IRN reporting team of Malcolm Brabant and Peter Deeley. The journalists there were clearly shaken and shocked by the blasts of percussion grenades, the outbreak of firing and an enveloping fire. Kate Adie has been criticised for screaming when the firing began, but she has rather pointedly observed that her friends and colleagues were inside the building as hostages and she feared that they were being murdered. Her accomplished live reporting of the event for BBC television brought her to the notice of editors and in the following years she became the BBC's Chief News Correspondent and Britain's most popular broadcast journalist. It is a salutary tribute to radio journalism that she learned her trade as a radio reporter for seven years in local BBC stations. The young Malcolm Brabant was challenged by the struggle of having to provide accurate and live eye witness description to LBC listeners while being completely unaware that SAS soldiers were entering the building in a ruthless military operation which would result in the deaths of all but one of the gunmen. His ability to keep his head under fire stayed with him through the rest of his career which has included award-winning reporting of the war in the former Yugoslavia.

Like America in the 1960s, Britain in the 1980s was to witness severe outbreaks of public disorder caused by decades of economic deprivation, racial prejudice and aggressive police tactics in Asian and Afro-Caribbean communities. Youths attacked police officers with petrol bombs, and business premises were looted. IRN/LBC like every other area of the media was poorly represented by non-white journalists. IRN reporter Paul Davies witnessed the first petrol bombs being thrown at poorly protected police officers at Toxteth in his native Merseyside:

[*Shouting and beating of batons on shields.*]
And the noise that you can hear now is the police beating on their riot shields as they move into a barrier in the centre of the road. They are coming under fire now. Missiles. There's a large crowd of youngsters at the other end of the street. They seem to have got hold of a civilian car. They've turned the person out of it and they're pushing it towards the direction of the police barricade.

The police are moving up the street and they're coming under heavy fire. They're now forming what looks rather like the old Roman system of using their riot shields to protect not only their sides, but also their heads. And bottles are coming in. One just landed very near to me and a stone just there. The police are having to duck for cover beneath their riot shields. The stones really are flying in. Some of the youths, their faces hidden by scarves and masks. That car that was just taken has been crashed into some railings and the police are now moving in again, beating their riot shields and trying to break up a crowd of youths who are now sprinting back up the street, still throwing bottles, and bricks at the police . . .

[*Shouting, cries and smashing glass.*]

And there goes the first petrol bomb that I have seen. It came flying over the ranks of the policemen. Burst into fire. Nobody seems hurt at this moment. Policeman putting it out with a fire extinguisher. But there comes another one. A bottle straight into the ranks of the policemen. The crowd screaming as that Molotov cocktail burst into flames.

(Paul Davies IRN/LBC 1980; Crook and Rose 1993)

By the early 1980s IRN/LBC had developed a comprehensive team of staff reporters, correspondents and specialist freelances who could make a decent living on retainers and piece work deals with editors. This meant the services could benefit from the first broadcast legal affairs team covering the Royal Courts of Justice and Central Criminal Court day by day. After 1983 I was concentrating on Old Bailey trials and cases heard outside London. My colleague Tim Knight covered civil hearings and appeal court cases at the RCJ. The BBC duplicated specialist resources in legal affairs several years later.

LBC's local government correspondent Jo Andrews provided live links from County Hall opposite the House of Commons on the controversial reign of left-wing GLC Labour Leader Ken Livingstone. Notable freelance specialists included diplomatic correspondent David Spanier and defence correspondent Paul Maurice. Andrew Manderstam covered the USA in Washington DC. IRN staff reporters covering world events during the 1980s included Barbara Groom, Andrew Simmons, Margaret Gilmore, Chris Mann, Mark Mardell, Sue Jameson, Mark Easton, Lindsay Taylor, Martin O'Neill, David Loyn, Antonia Higgs, John Draper, and a young journalist recruited from the Birmingham ILR station, BRMB – Kim Sabido who found himself despatched on a naval task force to cover the Falklands War in 1982.

The Falklands War demonstrated that LBC/IRN could cover a national emergency as well as any other news organisation. The BBC, in particular, became disturbed that in the Greater London area, listeners tuned to LBC because it maintained sequential news and current affairs programming twenty-four hours a day and would interrupt light programme, entertainment slots for important developments. BBC Radio 4 found that the structured tradition of block programming prevented news flashes being broadcast in the middle of pre-recorded one and a half hour plays. During the Gulf War, the BBC responded by turning its national FM frequency over to a concentrated news and current affairs service concentrating on that war's coverage.

The Ministry of Defence excluded all foreign journalists from accompanying the naval Task Force sailing to the Falklands. The four broadcast specialists, Robert Fox for BBC radio, Brian Hanrahan for BBC television, Kim Sabido for IRN, and Michael Nicholson for ITN worked on a pool basis. During the events all the reporting was radio. Television pictures were not allowed out until after the islands had been recaptured. The only woman broadcast journalist covering the war was IRN's Antonia Higgs who reported the Argentine side in Buenos Aires. This tough, resourceful general reporter was also the first British broadcast journalist to land on the Caribbean island of Grenada after the US invasion by marines.

Kim Sabido's journalism during the Falklands War was in the best tradition of war reporting – honest, vivid, sensitive, and informative. He decided to join the troops 'yomping' through the marshy peat bogs to do battle in the mountains behind Port Stanley:

> [*Gunfire.*]
> You can hear now the bullets whizzing around us. Ricocheting off the rocks. A heavy salvo of small arms fire, machine-gun fire coming both down the hill and then up the hill in reply from the British troops ahead of me.
> [*Gunfire and explosions*]
> More incoming gunfire. From Argentine batteries around Stanley. Keeping everybody's heads down.
> [*Cries and shouting.*]
> Somebody's been hit up front.
> [*Loud explosion and crack of shrapnel against rock.*]
> Good Heavens! Everything now landing far too close for comfort. I just heard somebody up front about twenty or thirty feet has received a bullet in the leg or something.
>
> (Kim Sabido, IRN/LBC 1982; Crook and Rose 1993)

In one of the despatches he sent, Kim Sabido made the poignant observation:

> I can honestly say that my thirst for action, if that is what it was, has been fully satisfied. I pray earnestly I shall never have to face another night like that again. And I can assure you that there are many more young men here who share that sentiment.
>
> (*ibid.*)

In an interview with media sociologists afterwards, he also made the professional observation that military censorship severely hampered the quality of journalism during the war and that the presence of American reporters would have increased standards.

IRN's Andrew Simmons was recovering from a back operation during the Falklands War. Although frustrated by missing the opportunity of reporting such an important news event, he was to have no shortage of drama as IRN's reporter in Beirut during the Israeli invasion of Lebanon. After checking in at his hotel, he went out with colleagues and returned later to find it had been reduced to a pile of rubble. The Israeli bombardment created human suffering on a vast scale. At one point he simply decided to describe events into the microphone as a mother wailed with uncontrollable grief:

> You can hear the screaming of a mother who believes her child is underneath the huge piece of concrete. I can't really describe in any acceptable tone what I can see now.
>
> [*The sound of digging with spades and the engine of earth moving machinery.*]
>
> There is the body of a man underneath the massive slab of concrete – only a leg showing. There can be no hope for rescuing this man. But the mother insists she heard the screams of her child underneath all of this and so the bulldozer moves forward and relief workers crowd around what really can't be anything else but a massive hideous concrete graveyard.
>
> [*Screaming voice of bereaved mother. Siren of ambulance blocked by the bulldozer driving backwards and forwards.*]
>
> (Andrew Simmons, IRN/LBC 1980, Crook and Rose 1993)

As world news events broke throughout the 1980s and 1990s, IRN reporters were present to provide a fresh, popular approach to radio journalism. Dave Loyn's reporting of Indira Ghandi's assassination won him the Sony Reporter of the Year in 1985. Lindsay Taylor's reporting of the King's Cross fire also earned him the same accolade in 1988. IRN reporter John Alcock won the award in 1989 for his reporting of the PanAm disaster at Lockerbie and the assassination of the President of Pakistan. In one year the Sony judges refused to make an award because there had been no IRN/LBC entries and they were not satisfied with the standard offered by BBC radio reporters.

However, this golden period of independent radio reporting seems to have passed. The journalistic infrastructure that served both IRN and LBC was broken up through aggressive management policies in the early 1990s. Key journalists took voluntary redundancy or found alternative employment in other broadcast services. The transfer of IRN personnel to ITN's managed service saw further reductions in staffing levels and experience. Network stations no longer demanded 30 to 40-second voice reports and wraps which used the medium skilfully. The demand in the late 1990s has been characterised by short cuts of actuality, and 2-minute bulletins written in a predominantly tabloid newspaper style. The editing of the service by its first woman editor Derval Fitzsimons required a more complex balance of resources to provide different outlets to a larger and more demanding market. Access to ITN's reporters and international news bureau created a bimedia service which meant that expensive international connections could be achieved by interviewing and asking for reports from television reporters many of whom used to be IRN reporters. Derval has shown that she is more than up to the task. IRN recently won the contract to provide news to British Forces Broadcasting from the BBC.

There is every sign that IRN continues to be in the front line of award-winning coverage. In 1996 Andrew Bomford's documentary on the trial of serial killer Rosemary West won a gold medal at the International Radio Festival of New York and twenty-one years after his report on the fall of Saigon, Julian Manyon's radio reporting of the Chechen war with Russia was also recognised at the 1996 Festival. In recent years independent radio has vied with the BBC in the battle to command the majority share of radio listening in the UK. IRN continues to be a powerful competitor, but the BBC has responded with substantial investment in news and current affairs since 1987. BBC radio reporters have more outlets and greater capacity for varied coverage of news events. The all news and sport network Radio Five Live, staffed by many former LBC/IRN journalists, continues to enjoy substantial increases in listening figures. The depth of IRN radio news coverage may be limited by the fact that News Direct 97.3 FM is only a London service and Classic FM's six o'clock *Classic Report* is the only opportunity for a national platform for independent radio reporting.

Chapter 23

Contrasting styles of contemporary radio journalism

It did not take me long to realise that by writing this book I could never do justice to the rich and varied practice of radio journalism in the modern world. As I became overwhelmed by the thousands of cassettes of news bulletins, documentaries and showcase reels featuring the work of broadcast journalists from all around the world and the never-ending trail of recommendations and stories offered by enthusiastic colleagues, I came to the conclusion that radio journalists deserve their own library. It could justifiably be packed with millions of books, scripts and recordings. It is my hope that some day there will be an international centre of research and cultural celebration of this priceless craft and art form. The development of the International Radio Festival of New York archive at Goldsmiths College, University of London, is a start.

In January 1997 a 26-year-old Venezuelan radio journalist William Ojeda was behind bars and his book *How Much Is A Judge Worth?* was removed from circulation. He had been imprisoned by the very people he had exposed. As I have mentioned in an earlier chapter, legal systems based on Roman Law provide the power to impose prison sentences for libel and Mr Ojeda was jailed for one year for defaming two judges in a book which reveals a legal system riddled with corruption. Mr Ojeda refused to reveal his sources. There were 1,950 outstanding complaints of corruption against Venezuelan judicial officials. One judge was caught with a £535 bribe concealed in her underwear. At the centre of this scandal is a legal system based largely on secret written processes. Now Venezuelan politicians are considering a more open system with oral hearings open to the public. William Ojeda is a young radio journalist who has highlighted the consequences of secret justice in his own country. The trend towards secret hearings in Britain has been indicated elsewhere in this book. He has had the courage of his convictions. He has asserted the independent cultural imperatives of radio journalism.

In any year radio journalists are jailed, beaten up, tortured and assassinated for maintaining freedom of expression through their work. Two attempted military coups in Venezuela in 1992 created a climate of oppression. The Interior Minister at the time, Luis Pinerua Ordaz ordered the police to vandalise the premises of Radio Rumbos because he wanted to restore order by banning news broadcasting. Government planes also shelled the station's transmitting aerials. However, one microphone 'got away'. It had been concealed in the pocket of one of the station's journalists. Radio journalists face harassment in rather unlikely situations. The Pope's visit to a Latin American country would not appear to create dangerous conditions for the radio reporter. But Columbian radio reporter Antonio Caballero was beaten up by the Pope's security guards after attempting to ask him if he had a message for the people of Columbia. Although the Pope made a gesture of disapproval as his security service personnel proceeded to throw Mr Caballero to the ground and kick him, the Pontiff was heard to remark 'these journalists, they never learn'. Radio journalists investigating organised crime frequently find themselves the target of intimidation and assassination. Philippines journalist Gloria Martin who worked for Zamboanga Radio was shot in the back by two men on a motorcycle in December 1992. She died instantly. She had been receiving death threats following her broadcast reports criticising the authorities' failure to properly investigate and prosecute kidnappings by criminals and Moslem separatists.

The Palestinian Al-Qods radio station owned by Ahmad Jibril's People's Front for the Liberation of Palestine found that its broadcasts to the occupied territories were frequently jammed by the Israeli authorities. The conflict in Haiti led to exiled radio journalists such as Jean-Claude Olivier and Fritz Dor being assassinated in Miami in 1991. The owners and editors of private radio stations which sought to question the military dictatorship were frequently assassinated until democracy was eventually restored. Mexican university lecturer and radio broadcaster Ramon Garcia de la Mora Bueno was probably killed by government troops while attending a conference on radio journalism in Guatemala in February 1992. It had been organised by the Latin American Centre for Journalism Studies. His family say his body bore the signs of torture. The Mexican government demanded an enquiry and it is suspected that he was killed because he sought to challenge human rights violations by the Guatemalan government which claimed he was 'a mercenary and had been working for a pirate radio station linked to an anti-government guerilla group'.

The war in the former Yugoslavia claimed the lives of many radio journalists. They had sought to continue balanced and fair broadcasting to communities which succumbed to a nasty ethnic conflict that placed a higher premium on bigotry and racism. Those who have survived the war have had to confront the forces of censorship even in peace time. The independent station Radio 101 in Zagreb has been fighting for its survival. It was a station for former young communists and became the only journalistic outlet for political groups opposed to President Franjo Tudjman's government. Those of us living in stable liberal democracies find it difficult to understand why Drazen Vrdoljak, a producer of music programmes on the state-run Radio Zagreb, was forced to resign on 14 February 1992 after being accused of treason over his decision to broadcast two rock songs composed and performed by Serbians.

The bloody war that followed claimed the lives of many foreign journalists who struggled to find a way of measuring the risks of reporting a conflict where bullets and shrapnel came in all directions. One of the many tragedies was the death of BBC Radio 4 *World Tonight* reporter John Schofield in August 1995. By the time of his death broadcast organisations had invested in armoured vehicles, body armour for staff and strict safety codes. Despite these precautions, John was shot through the neck after sending a series of sensitive and evocative reports which concentrated on the impact of the war on ordinary people and explored the ramifications of ethnic conflict:

> Croatian marching songs played on a radio in the main street in Petrinja this afternoon. The front of the radio had been blown off, adding to the broken glass that was everywhere. The signs of the Serb inhabitants' hasty departure this weekend could be seen all around. Clothes still hanging on washing lines; bread in plastic bags dropped on the pavement, ice cream in a cafe melting and turning brown in its tubs.

The *World Tonight* programme which was broadcast on the day of his death is a monument to the dignity and professionalism of this programme as well as a fitting tribute to a young reporter who gave his life so that others would know the truth of human suffering on Europe's doorstep. It is astonishing and appalling that the UK's so called professional trade magazine for television and radio, *Broadcast*, seemed unable to provide any coverage of his death. It is also a shame that the industry's radio institutions such as the Sony Awards and Radio Academy could not find any way of posthumously recognising his contribution and the qualities of the programme he served.

Radio journalists in liberal democracies have had to fight to preserve their freedom. It was the small and eccentric Pacifica network station in New York, WBAI, which in 1962 resisted anonymous bomb threats and warnings from the Justice Department to broadcast criticisms of J. Edgar Hoover's dictatorial command of the FBI. Only WBAI had the guts to put former special agent Jack Levine's story to air. The mainstream broadcasting and newspaper organisations would not investigate Mr Levine's complaints of quasi-legal FBI procedures, anti-liberal, anti-black and anti-Semitic attitudes inherent in the FBI hierarchy. WBAI became the first authoritative media outlet for these complaints. The station's reporters and producers covered the Civil Rights movement without the stringent time limits of the network reports. The station's programme director Chris Koch produced an award-winning series of reports and interviews of the Freedom Summer of 1964 which were unrivalled by the highly resourced and well funded networks.

WBAI also pioneered a more critical and extensive coverage of America's involvement in Vietnam. But the boldness of the station's journalistic coverage was nearly responsible for its destruction. The enterprising Chris Koch told his station in 1965 that he was going to spend his vacation in Paris. Instead he travelled to North Vietnam and returned with hours of material providing the first opportunity to tell the story of 'the enemy' to US radio listeners. The documentary material was powerful and controversial. It challenged government propaganda. Koch found that he was being censured for deceiving his employer about his trip to North Vietnam and he was also horrified to find that his hour-long programmes were being censored because the station's Board of Directors feared they were too sympathetic to the voice of the Hanoi government. Koch walked out and so did about half of his colleagues. Listener subscriptions plummeted.

Somehow WBAI survived and developed a 'free form' style of cultural and musical programming which suited the hippy counter-culture period of the 1960s. Overnight presenter Bob Fass opened his *Radio Unnameable* programme to an astonishing series of live reports from hippies who had become the focus of police violence after a gathering of thousands of young people at Grand Central Station in March 1968. The Grand Central 'Yip-In' was not covered by television news services. It is believed the violent police response was provoked by some over-exuberant hippies removing the hands from the Grand Central Station clock, letting off a couple of 'cherry bombs' that must have reverberated in the large scale ambient acoustics of the station and the chanting of some rather impolite anti-police slogans. The violent clashes were therefore described clearly and dramatically on live radio through the night. WBAI's staff reporter Dan Drison recorded the events on a portable tape machine and brought it into the studio by 2.15 a.m. Listeners could hear the actuality of happy chanting turning into screams and frightened descriptions of police brutality. WBAI closely followed the subsequent demonstration outside the Democratic convention in Chicago and the violent and brutal police response. The station campaigned for the defendants in the 'Chicago Conspiracy' trial which followed. The Pacifica stations still maintain 'a counter-culture' spirit. In the 1970s and 1980s WBAI and KPFA in Berkeley, California have sought to address the representation of non-white Americans in cultural and news and current affairs programming.

An analysis of radio journalism entries to the International Radio Festival of New York in the years 1994, 1995, and 1996 is testimony to the quality of radio reporting throughout the world. BBC Radio's Kevin Connolly submits a portfolio of brilliant radio reports of the battle for the Russian White Parliament in Moscow in 1993. Alan Little's evocative report on the corruption of United Nation's troops in the dying city of Sarajevo uses evocative writing and subtle actuality to convey an atmosphere and truth about human nature. The literary and reflective qualities of BBC radio correspondents are perhaps best illustrated by Fergal Keane whose moving letter to his new-born son first broadcast on the BBC's *From Our Own Correspondent* has resulted in the book publication of his journalistic writing.

The news station KFWB in Los Angeles provides breathtaking energy in its response to developing news stories with reporters hovering in news helicopters and climbing devastated terrain in four-wheel drive news-gathering vehicles to get to the very heart of stories. The station's coverage of recent earthquakes, bushfires, and the arrest and trials of O. J. Simpson has been outstanding. The ABC station 2BL 702 in Sydney, Australia offered a similar standard of professionalism when seeking to report the bushfires of January 1994 which came to within a few kilometres of the centre of Sydney. The use of mobile phones enabled the station's coverage to be on a suburb-by-suburb basis. The risk of panic-stricken, or sensationalist coverage was minimised by the good judgement of experienced journalists. 2BL sports reporter Tracey Holmes found herself in the middle of an inferno when she had simply travelled to a seaside resort to look for a place to rent. As the fires enveloped multi-million pound homes like 'howling wolves coming across the bay' she had to seek refuge on a boat which did not offer much protection while she was broadcasting her reports. Dramatic and skilful reports were also provided by 2BL's commercial competitor in Sydney, 2UE.

The courage and resourcefulness of the individual radio journalist is well illustrated by Radio New Zealand Don Rood's coverage of the French nuclear testing at Mururoa Atoll in 1995. He flew to Tahiti to board the Greenpeace flagship *Rainbow Warrior Two* and report on the anti-nuclear protest off Mururoa. The French authorities seized his equipment as soon as he arrived in French Polynesia. He fell ill out at sea and when French commandoes boarded the Greenpeace vessel he was captured, detained and interrogated by soldiers, held on Mururoa and later in Papeete. In the riots that erupted after the first nuclear test he was tear-gassed, stoned, threatened, and shot at. Over three weeks he provided on-the-spot coverage. Sometimes he resorted to secret recording to avoid the seizure of his interviews and actuality recordings by the French military.

But radio also continues to support investigative journalism at a very high level. BBC Radio maintains a *File on Four* investigative team at its Manchester centre which on a weekly basis thoroughly explores and investigates stories of national and international significance. Commercial news stations in America still support investigative reporting despite the drive for profits and cost cutting in newsroom operations. WJR AM 760 in Detroit submitted an outstanding file to the 1996 International Radio Festival of New York on the work of veteran radio reporter Rod Hansen. WJR has resisted the trend of many radio news operations to 'rip-and-read' or follow up the stories that other journalists have originated in the other media. The station supported him in his quest to reinvestigate the murder conviction of Ricky Allen Amolsch. Rod Hansen uncovered inconsistencies in the prosecution case. His investigative work was crucial in securing Amolsch's release and revealing new evidence pointing to a new suspect for the murder of Janie Fray. Hansen had worked for WJR for 28 years. His news director Richard Haefner observed:

> In a season when terror in Oklahoma City, the O.J. Simpson case and the agonies of British royalty dominated the news, Rod Hansen did his work on a different plane. It did not grab international headlines, but it had the only impact that really counted: justice for the wrongly accused and for the family of the murder victim.

WJR AM 760 is a radio station which has a commitment to its journalists and a pride in a qualitative culture of news reporting and journalistic broadcasting. As we hurtle into a new century they are values that are worth cherishing. They also underline the value of the radio journalist's independent function in broadcasting and the contribution that radio journalism can make to human civilisation.

The future for radio journalism looks hectic and highly technological. Multi-skilling and the versatile applications of digital technology are likely to place more pressure on radio journalists as well as increase the speed of productivity and response times to breaking news stories. At the same time the disruptive hands of censorship, regulation, and cost-cutting management are likely to generate the occupational hazards facing radio journalists throughout the world. But I believe the indomitable spirit of the unknown radio reporter will continue the honourable tradition of bringing the world's most important stories to the ear first and with accuracy, authority, sensitivity and decent social purpose.

Bibliography

Published Texts

Alexander, J. (1981) 'The mass news media in systemic, historical and comparative perspective', in E. Katz and T. Szescko (eds) *Mass Media and Social Change*, London: Sage, pp. 17–51.

Angina, Maschio (1996) *The Quest for Radio Quality: The Documentary*, Rome: Radio Televisione Italiana, Prix Italia.

Australian Broadcasting Corporation Legal Department (1992) *The ABC Guide to Media Law*, Sydney, Australian Broadcasting Corporation.

Australian Broadcasting Corporation (June 1993) *ABC Editorial Policies*, Sydney: Australian Broadcasting Corporation.

Baird, L. (1992) *Guide to Radio Production, Australian Film, Television and Radio School*, Australia and New Zealand: Allen & Unwin.

Baker, P. (1995) *Making It As A Radio Or TV Presenter*, London: Piatkus Books.

Barbrook, R. (1995) *Media Freedom*, London: Pluto Press.

Barendt, E. (1992) *Freedom of Speech*, Oxford: Clarendon Press.

Barendt, E. (1995) *Broadcasting Law, A Comparative Study*, Oxford: Clarendon Press.

Barendt, E., Lustgarten, L., Norrie, K. and Stephenson, H. (1997) *Libel and the Media – The Chilling Effect*, Oxford: Clarendon Press.

Barnett, S. and Curry A. (1994) *The Battle For The BBC – A British Broadcasting Conspiracy*, London: Aurum Press.

Barnouw, E. (1966) *A Tower in Babel*, New York: Oxford University Press.

Barnouw, E. (1968) *The Golden Web*, New York: Oxford University Press.

Barnouw, E. (1970) *The Image Empire*, New York: Oxford University Press.

Baron, M. (1975) *Radio Onederland – the Story of Independent Radio in the UK*, London: Dalton.

Belsey, A. and Chadwick, R. (1992) *Ethical Issues in Journalism and the Media*, London: Routledge.

Bernstein, C. and Woodward, B. (1974) *All The President's Men*, London: Quartet Books.

Benthall, J. (1993) *Disasters, Relief and the Media*, London: I. B. Tauris & Co.

Berry, C. (1990) *Your Voice and How To Use It Successfully*, London: Virgin Books.

Berry, C. (1992) *The Actor And His Text*, London: Virgin Books.

Bliss, E. Jr (1991) *Now The News, the Story of Broadcast Journalism*, New York: Columbia University Press.

Borrie, G. and Lowe, N. (1983) *Borrie and Lowe's Law of Contempt*, London: Butterworth.

Boyd, A. (1993 2nd edn) *Broadcast Journalism – Techniques of Radio and TV News*, London: Focal Press.

Braithwaite, N. (ed.) (1995) *The International Libel Handbook*, London: Butterworth, Heinemann.

Briggs, A. (1995) *The History of Broadcasting in the United Kingdom in five volumes: The Birth of Broadcasting (1896–1927), The Golden Age of Wireless (1927–1939), The War of Words (1939–1945), Sound of Vision (1945–1955)* and *Competition (1955–1974)*, Oxford: Oxford University Press.

Briggs, S. (1985) *Those Radio Times*, London: Weidenfeld & Nicolson.

British Broadcasting Corporation (1993) *Producers' Guidelines*, London: BBC.

Brown, G. (1995) *Exposed!*, London: Virgin.

Brown, M. and Newmark, T. (1978/1988) *Bush House Newsroom Guide and Style Book*, London: BBC.

Bryson, B. (1994) *Dictionary for Writers and Editors*, London: Penguin.

Cain, J. (1992) *The BBC – 70 Years of Broadcasting*, London: BBC.

Callender Smith, R. (1978) *Press Law*, London: Sweet & Maxwell.

Cantril, H. (1966) *The Invasion from Mars – A Study in the Psychology of Panic*, Princetown, NJ: Princeton University Press.

Carter-Ruck, P. F., Walker, R., Starte, H. N. A. (1992 4th edn) *Carter-Ruck On Libel and Slander*, London: Butterworth.

Carey, J. (1987) *The Faber Book of Reportage*, London: Faber & Faber.

Chantler, P. and Harris, S. (1992) *Local Radio Journalism*, London: Focal Press.

Chippendale, P. and Horrie, C. (1993) *Stick It Up Your Punter! The Rise and Fall of the Sun*, London: Mandarin Books.

Clayton, J. (1994) *Interviewing For Journalists*, London: Piatkus Books.

Cole, J. (1996) *As It Seemed To Me – Political Memoirs*, London: Phoenix.

Cooke, A. (1981) *Letters From America – A Selection From His World Famous Radio Programme*, London: Penguin.

Cox, B. (1975) *Civil Liberties in Britain*, London: Penguin.

Crisell, A. (1994 2nd edn) *Understanding Radio*, London: Routledge.

Crisell, A. (1997) *An Introductory History of British Broadcasting*, London: Routledge.

Crone, T. (1995 3rd edn) *Law And The Media*, London: Focal Press.

Curran, J. and Seaton, J. (1991 4th edn) *Power Without Responsibility – The Press and Broadcasting in Britain*, London: Routledge.

Curtis, L. and Jempson, M. (1993) *Interference on the Airwaves – Ireland, the Media and the Broadcasting Ban*, London: Campaign for Press and Broadcasting Freedom.

Day, R. (1989) *Grand Inquisitor*, London: Weidenfeld & Nicolson.

Dahlgren, P. and Sparks, C. (1993) *Communication and Citizenship – Journalism and the Public Sphere*, London: Routledge.

Denis, E. E. and Pease, E. C. (1993) *Media Studies Journal – Radio The Forgotten Medium*, New York: Columbia University Press.

Dimbleby, J. (1975) *Richard Dimbleby – A Biography*, London: Hodder & Stoughton.

Donovan, P. (1992) *The Radio Companion, The A–Z Guide to Radio From Its Inception To The Present Day*, London: Grafton.

Dougary, G. (1994) *The Executive Tart and Other Myths*, London: Virago.

Douglas, G. H. (1934 *The Early Days of Radio Broadcasting*, Jefferson, NC and London: McFarland & Company, Inc.

Folkerts, J. and Teter, D. L. Jr (1994) *Voices of a Nation – A History of Mass Media in the United States*, New York: Macmillan College Publishing Company.

Franklin, M. A. and Anderson, D. A. (1990 4th edn) *Cases and Materials on Mass Media Law*, Westbury, New York: The Foundation Press, Inc.

Franklin, B. (1994) *Packaging Politics*, London: Edward Arnold.

Gage, L. (1990) *Guide To Independent Radio Journalism*, London: Duckworth.

Gall, S. (1982) *Don't Worry About The Money Now*, London: Hamish Hamilton.

Gellhorn, M. (1993) *The Face of War*, London: Granta Books and Penguin.

Gondin, W. R. and Mammen, E. R. (1970) *The Art of Speaking*, London: W. H. Allen.

Grace, A. (1993) *Battledress Broadcasters*, London: SSVC, Chalfont.

Grant, T. (1994) *The Best of From Our Own Correspondent Volume 5*, London: I.B Tauris.

Harding, R. (1979) *Outside Interference – The Politics of Australian Broadcasting*, Melbourne: Sun Books.

Hargreaves, I. (1992) *Sharper Vision – The BBC and the Communications Revolution*. London: Demos.

Hartley J. (1993) *Understanding News*, London: Routledge.

Harris, G. and Spark, D. (1993) *Practical Newspaper Reporting*, London: Focal Press.

Harris, R. (1994) *The Media Trilogy – Gotcha! Selling Hitler, Good and Faithful Servant*, London: Faber & Faber.

Hawkins, D. (1994) *War Report D-Day to VE-Day – Radio Reports from the Western Front 1944–5*, London: BBC.

Head, S. W. and Sterling, C. H. (1991) *Broadcasting In America*, Boston, MA: Houghton Mifflin Company.

Hetherington, J. (1988) *Australians – Nine Profiles*, Melbourne: F. W. Cheshire.

Hickman, T. (1995) *What Did You Do In the War Auntie? – The BBC At War 1939–45*, London: BBC.

Hicks, W. (1993) *English For Journalists*, London: Routledge.

Hoffman, A. (1992 4th edn) *Research For Writers*, London: A & C Black.

Holland, P. (1997) *The Television Handbook*, London: Routledge.

Horrie, C. and Clarke, S. (1994) *Fuzzy Monsters – Fear And Loathing At The BBC*, London: Mandarin.

Horstmann, R. (1991 2nd edn) *Writing for Radio*, London: A & C Black.

Howes, K. (1993) *Broadcasting It!*, London: Mansell.

Hudson, R. (1993) *Inside Outside Broadcasts*, Newmarket: R & W Publications.

Hunter, Fred, *Hilda Matheson and the BBC 1926–1940*. Published chapter and paper supplied to author.

Inglis, F. (1994) *Media Theory – An Introduction*, Oxford: Blackwell.

Jankowski, N. *et al.* (1992) *The People's Voice*, London: John Libbey & Co.

Karpf, A. (1988) *Doctoring The Media – The Reporting of Health and Medicine*, London: Routledge.

Karpf, A. (1996) *The War After: Living With The Holocaust*, London: Heinemann.

Kay, M. and Popplewell, A. (1992) *Making Radio – A Guide To Basic Radio Techniques*, London: Broadside Books Ltd.

Keeble, R. (1994) *The Newspapers Handbook*, London: Routledge.

Kent, R. (1994) *Measuring Media Audiences*, London: Routledge.

Knightly, P. (1989) *The First Casualty*, London: Pan Books.

Korthals Altes, W. F., Dommering, E. J., Hugenholtz, P. B. and Kabel, J. J. C. (1992) *Information Law Towards The Twenty-First Century*, Boston, MA: Kluwer Law and Taxation Publishers.

Lazar, R. (1980) *From Our Own Correspondent – Twenty-Five Years of Foreign Reports*, London: BBC.

Lawrence, A. (1972) *Foreign Correspondent*, London: George Allen & Unwin Ltd.

Levin, B. (1988) *All Things Considered*, London: Jonathan Cape.

Levin, N. (1975) *The Holocaust- The Destruction of European Jewry 1933–1945*, New York: Schocken Books.

Lewis, C. (1993) *All My Yesterdays*, London: Element Books.

Lewis, P. M. and Booth, J. (1989) *The Invisible Medium, Public, Commercial and Community Radio*, London: Macmillan.

Maidment, R. and Dawson, M. (1994) *The United States in the Twentieth Century: Key Documents*, London: Hodder & Stoughton.

MacArthur, J. R. (1992) *Second Front – Censorship and Propaganda in the Gulf War*, New York: Hill and Wang.

MacDonald, B. (1994) *Broadcasting in the UK*, London: Mansell.

MacDowall, I. (1992) *Reuters Handbook For Journalists*, London: Butterworth, Heinemann.

McChesney, R. W. (1994) *Telecommunications, Mass Media & Democracy – The Battle For The Control of US Broadcasting, 1928–1935*, New York: Oxford University Press.

McDonald, T. (1993) *Fortunate Circumstances*, London: Weidenfeld & Nicolson.

McDougall, I. (1980) *Foreign Correspondent*, London: Frederick Muller Ltd.

McIntyre, I. (1993) *The Expense of Glory*, London: HarperCollins.

McKain, B., Bonnington, A. J. and Watt, G. A. (1995) *Scots Law For Journalists*, Edinburgh: W. Green/Sweet & Maxwell.

McLeish, R. (1994 3rd edn) *Radio Production*, London: Focal Press.

McNair, B. (1994) *News And Journalism In The UK*, London: Routledge.

Mayer, M. (1993) *Making News*, Boston, MA: Harvard Business School Press.

Miall, L. (1994) *Inside The BBC, British Broadcasting Characters*, London: Weidenfeld & Nicolson.

Michael, K. C. and Krause, J. M. (1989 2nd edn) *The Radio Station*, London: Focal Press.

Miller, D. (1994) *Don't Mention The War – Northern Ireland, Propaganda and the Media*, London: Pluto Press.

Milner, R. (1983) *Reith – The BBC Years*, London: Mainstream Publishing.

Milne, S. (1994) *The Enemy Within – MI5, Maxwell and the Scargill Affair*, London: Verso.

Moran, A. (1992) *Stay Tuned – An Australian Broadcasting Reader*, Sydney: Allen & Unwin.

Morrison, D. E. and Tumber, H. (1988) *Journalists At War – The Dynamics of News Reporting During The Falklands Conflict*, London: Sage Publications.

National Public Radio (1996) *NPR Production Guidelines*.

Negrine, R (1994) *Politics and the Mass Media in Britain*, London: Routledge.

O'Kane, B. (1993) *Essential Finance For Journalists*, London: Oak Tree Press.

O'Malley, T. (1994) *Closedown? – The BBC and Government Broadcasting Policy 1979–92*, London: Pluto Press.

Orlik, P. B. (1992) *The Electronic Media*, Boston: Allyn and Bacon.

Paxman, J. (1991) *Friends In High Places – Who Runs Britain?* London: Penguin.

Peak, S. (1992) *The Media Guide 1993*, London: Fourth Estate.

Peak, S. (1994) *The Media Guide 1995*, London: Fourth Estate.

Peak, S. and Fisher, P (1995) *The Media Guide 1996*, London: Fourth Estate.

Petersen, N. (1993) *News Not Views – The ABC, The Press, and Politics 1932 – 1947*, Sydney: Hale & Iremonger Pty Ltd.

Pile, S. (1979) *The Book of Heroic Failures*, London: Futura Publications.

Pimlott, J. Dr (ed.) (1988–1994) *Images of War*, London: Marshall Cavendish and Imperial War Museum.

Popham, M. and Spink, G. (1991) *The Best of From Our Own Correspondent Volume 2*, London: Broadside Books.

Popham, M. and Spink, G. (1992) *The Best of From Our Own Correspondent Volume 3*, London: Broadside Books.

Potts, J. (1989) *Radio In Australia*, Sydney: New South Wales University Press.

Price, B. and Dyer, Jonathan (1993) *Freelance Reporting For Newshour: A Beginner's Guide*, London: BBC.

Price, S. (1993) *Media Studies*, London: Pitman.

Raboy, M. and Dagenais, B. (1992) *Media, Crisis and Democracy*, London: Sage Publications.

Raphael, A. (1993) *Grotesque Libels*, London: Corgi Books.

Raymond, J. (1993) *Making The News, An Anthology of the Newsbooks of Revolutionary England 1641–1660*, Gloucestershire: The Windrush Press.

Read, D. (1992) *The Power of News – The History of Reuters 1849–1989*, Oxford: Oxford University Press.

Reporters Sans Frontières (1993) *Freedom of the Press Throughout the World 1992 Report*, London: John Libbey.

Reporters Sans Frontières (1994) *Freedom of the Press Throughout The World 1993 Report*, London: John Libbey.

Robertson Q. C. G. (1992 3rd edn) *Media Law*, London: Penguin.

Robertson Q. C. G. (1991 6th edn) *Freedom, The Individual and the Law*, London: Penguin.

Rosenblum, M. (1993) *Who Stole the News?* New York: John Wiley.

Sampson, A. (1993) T*he Essential Anatomy of Britain, Democracy in Crisis*, London: Coronet Books.

Sanderson, T. (1995) *Mediawatch – The Treatment of Male and Female Homosexuality in the British Media*, London: Cassell.

Sayer-Jones, L. (1992) *Law Brief – The Australian Film and Television Industry in The Nineties*, New South Wales, Australia: Trade News Corporation.

Schlesinger, P. (1978) *Putting 'Reality' Together – BBC News*, London: Constable.

Scannel, P. and Cardiff, D. (1991) *A Social History of British Broadcasting, Vol. I, 'Serving The Nation, 1922–1939'*, Oxford: Basil Blackwell.

Sebba, A. (1994) *Battling For News – The Rise of the Reporter*, London: Hodder & Stoughton

Shirer, W. (1987) *Berlin Diary – The Journal of a Foreign Correspondent 1934–1941*, New York: The American Past Book of the Month.

Sidey, P. (1993) *Hello Mrs Butterfield*, London: Kestrel Press.

Siegel, B. H. (1992) *Creative Radio Production*, Boston, MA: Focal Press.

Sinclair, J. (1993) *BBC English Dictionary*, London: HarperCollins.

Snoddy, R. (1993) *The Good, the Bad and the Unacceptable*, London: Faber & Faber.

Southill, K. and Walby, S. (1991) *Sex Crime In The News*, London: Routledge.

Spink, G. (1993) *The Best of From Our Own Correspondent, Volume 3*, London: I.B. Tauris.

Spink, G. (1994) *The Best of From Our Own Correspondent*, Volume 4, London: I.B. Tauris.

Taylor, G. (1993) *Changing Faces — A History of the Guardian 1956–88*, London: Fourth Estate

Thompson, R. (1993) *A Style Guide for Writing News Scripts For Regional Television or Local Radio*, London: BBC.

Tomaselli, R., Tomaselli, K. and Muller, J. (1987) *Broadcasting In South Africa*, South Africa: The Natal Witness Printing and Publishing Company.

Tusa, J. (1992) *A World In Your Ear — Reflections On Changes*, London: Broadside Books.

Van Dijk, T. A. (1991) *Racism and the Press — Critical Studies in Racism and Migration*, London: Routledge.

Voss, F. S. (1994) *Reporting the War — The Journalistic Coverage of World War II*, Washington DC: Smithsonian Institution Press for the National Portrait Gallery.

Wagman, R. J. (1991) *The First Amendment Book, Celebrating 200 Years of Freedom Of The Press and Freedom of Speech*, New York: Pharos Books.

Walis, R. and Baran, S. (1990) *The Known World of Broadcast News*, London: Routledge.

Walker, A. (1992) *A Skyful of Freedom — 60 Years of the BBC World Service*, London: Broadside Books.

Walker, S. (1989) *The Law of Journalism In Australia*, Sydney: The Law Book Company.

Watkinson, J. (1994) *The Art of Digital Audio*, London: Routledge.

Welsh, T. and Greenwood, W. (1995) *McNae's Essential Law for Journalists*, London: Butterworth.

Wilby, P. and Conroy, A. (1994) *The Radio Handbook*, London: Routledge.

Williams, G. (1994) *Britain's Media: How They Are Related*, London: Campaign for Press and Broadcasting Freedom.

Windschuttle, K. (1988) *The Media, A New Analysis of the Press, Television, Radio and Advertising in Australia*, Victoria: Penguin.

Woolf, M. and Holly, S. (1996) *Broadcast Journalists 1995/96*, London: Skillset.

Yorke, I. (1990) *Basic TV Reporting*, London: Focal Press.

Young, J. (1971) 'The Role of the Police as Amplifiers of Deviance', in S. Cohen (ed.) *Images of Deviance*, Harmondsworth: Penguin, pp. 22–61.

Internet Publications

The Journalism of the Holocaust, Marvin Kalb, (27 February 1997) Lecture delivered at the US Holocaust Memorial Museum: www.ushmm.org/misc-bin/add_goback/lectures/kalb.htm

The Media Coverage of Waco – Summary of A Special Task Force Report by The Society of Professional Journalists, (26 November 1993) Listerv@ulkyvm.louisville.edu

Yippie by Andrew Salciu (21 January 1996) WBAI World Wide Web home page. (Pacifica Network)

Newspaper Articles

Bardgett, S. (18 April 1993) *A Tragedy The World Ignored*, London: the *Observer*.

Bates, S. (9 November 1996) *Small, Quiet Voice From The Front*, London: the *Guardian*.

Bell, A. (29 November 1993) *Turn On, Stay Tuned*, London: the *Guardian*.

Churchill, R. (24 April 1945) *Education For Murder*, London: the *Daily Mail*.

Cox, G. (30 December 1993) *William Shirer Obituary*, London: the *Independent*.

Forbes, P. (30 July 1944) *We Must Not Betray Them*, London: the *Sunday People*.

Gordon, H. (20 March 1997) *The Authentic Voice of Joe Sixpack*, London: the *Daily Telegraph*.

Hilton, I., Rado, G. and Gowing, N. (11 August 1995) *Obituary on John Schofield*, London: the *Guardian*.

Karpf, A. (25 June 1996) *Children of the Holocaust*, London: the *Guardian*.

Knight, J. (25 January 1997) *Corruption Expose Lands Author In Jail*, London: the *Guardian*.

Milne, M. (9 May 1995) *The Holocaust: Why Auntie Stayed Mum*, London: the *Independent*.

O'Brien, R. B. (9 September 1994) *Blackout That Shrouded the V-2 Menace*, London: the *Daily Telegraph*.

The *Sunday Pictorial* (6 September 1942) Pictures from the Dieppe Raid.

Ungoed-Thomas, J. and Harvey, M. (14 February 1997) *Murderers, The Mail Accuses These Men of Killing. If We Are Wrong, Let Them Sue Us*, London: the *Daily Mail*.

Training Videos and Publications

Australian Film Television and Radio School, PO Box 126, North Ryde, NSW 2113.

Radio Production

The Radio Studio, Announcing and Presentation, Radio Writing, Radio News

Editing

Cut and Dub, The Radio Interview, Radio Talkback, Copyright, Writing for Radio.

British Broadcasting Corporation. BBC Training. Videos on broadcast journalism, interviewing, news reporting and the law. Produced at Borehamwood. Marketed through BBC Worldwide, Woodlands, 80 Wood Lane, London W12 OTT

Published Audio-cassettes and Compact Discs

Academy Lecture, Mark Tully and John Birt (July 1993) Published by the UK Radio Academy, London.

America Before TV, (1987) Greatapes, USA 1523 Nicollet, Minneapolis, MN 55403.

Aviators, Voices of the Great Pioneers, Eye Witness Accounts, (1991) Pearl, Pavilion Records Ltd, Sparrows Green, Wadhurst, East Sussex, England.

Bi Media Journalism, What's In It For Radio? (July 1991) The Radio Academy, published by Audio Assignments, Cleckheaton, BD19 3RR.

Blaze of Day, The Suffragette Movement, A Documentary Survey, (1992) Pearl, Pavilion Records Ltd, Sparrows Green, Wadhurst, East Sussex, England.

Concentration Camp Horrors, Broadcasts Heard in 1945, (1990) Radiola Records, Box C, Sandy Hook, Conn. 06482.

Crisis Coverage, The Gulf War, (July 1991) The Radio Academy, published by Audio Assignments, Cleckheaton BD19 3RR.

Crook, T. and Rose, C. (1993) *LBC News 1973 to 1993 – 20 Years of the Best News Reports From The London Broadcasting Company*, London: IRDP – The Drama Collection. PO Box 518, Manningtree, Essex CO11 1XD.

The D-Day Invasion. From the First Beach-Head, Live on Radio, 40 Consecutive Hours of WEAF – NBC station in New York, (1990) 38 cassette collection. Radio Yesteryear, Box C, Sandy Hook, Conn. 06482.

D-Day Despatches, Original Recordings From The BBC Sound Archives June 1944 and Spring 1945, (1989) BBC Radio Collection.

Don't You Know There Is A War On? The Story of The Home Front in WWII, (1995) BBC Radio Collection.

The Falklands War, March–June 1982, Original Recordings From The BBC Sound Archives, (1992) BBC Radio Collection.

Great Speeches of the Twentieth Century, (1991) USA, Rhino Records Inc, 2225 Colorado Avenue, Santa Monica, CA 90404–3555.

The Great War, An Evocation in Music and Drama Through Recordings Made At The Time, (1989) Pearl, Pavilion Records Ltd, Sparrows Green, Wadhurst, East Sussex, England.

Iwo Jima — Combat Actualities, February 1945, (1990) USA, Radiola Records, Box C, Sandy Hook, Conn. 06482

Matthews to Moore 1948–1966 Commentary and Interviews From The BBC Sound Archives, (1992) BBC Radio Collection.

National Public Radio, The Best of NPR, Twenty Years, (1990) Dove Audio, 301 North Canon Dr, Beverly Hills, CA 90210.

National Public Radio, Retrospective On The Gulf, The Questions of War, (1991) Dove Audio, 301 North Canon Dr, Beverly Hills, CA 90210.

Outlook, BBC World Service (1992) PO Box 76, Bush House, Strand, London WC2B 4PH.

Quality Radio — How Do You Define It?, (July 1991) The Radio Academy, Published by Audio Assignments, Cleckheaton, BD19 3RR.

This Was A War, (1994) WJR Am Radio 760, Detroit, Michigan, USA — produced and narrated by Michael Whorf in 13 episodes.

This Was Radio, FDR, Churchill, The Hindenberg: Radio's Most Famous Moments, (1990) Great American Audio Corporation, 33 Portman Road, New Rochelle, NY 10801.

The Rise of Fascism, Documentary Recordings of the Time From Germany, Italy and Britain, (1992) Pearl, Pavilion Records Ltd, Sparrows Green, Wadhurst, East Sussex, England.

Second World War, Original Recordings From The BBC Sound Archives, (1989) BBC Radio Collection.

Sounds of the Third Reich, Hitler's Inferno (1990) Radiola Records, Box C, Sandy Hook, Conn. 8482.

Victory Broadcasts of WWII on American Radio 1938–45, (1991) Greatapes, 1523 Nicollet, Minneapolis, MN 55403.

The Voice of Richard Dimbleby, (1966) Music for Pleasure (EMI) Introduced by Wynford Vaughan-Thomas.

Broadcast Radio and Television Programmes

Arena Night, BBC Radio Four (18 December 1993) *Back To Square One.* Producer: Dilly Barlow.

Richard Dimbleby Remembers Belsen, Introduced by Jonathan Dimbleby (January 1995) BBC2.

Document, *The Unspeakable Atrocity,* BBC Radio Coverage of the Holocaust. BBC Radio 4 (26 August 1993). Producer: Nigel Acheson.

How Radio Won The War (June, July, August 1995) BBC Radio Five Live. Produced by Concept Creative Production.

Forty Years of From Our Own Correspondent, (28 September 1995) BBC Radio 4. Producer: Tony Grant.

The Friend In the Corner, 1936, (25 November 1992). Producer: Alastair Wilson.

Front Lines, (29 April 1995). Presented by Mark Laity on BBC Radio 4. Producer: Kate Whitehead.

Pope Pius XII, (January 1995) *Timewatch*, BBC2.

In Time of War, (1992) TVS. Presenter/subject: Robert Fox. Director/producer: Graham Hurley.

Radio Lives, Edward R Murrow: A Nation's Conscience? (1993) BBC Radio 4. Producer: Fiona McLean.

Reith – Face To Face. BBC Television.

Shoa, Parts 1 and 2, (7–8 January 1995) BBC2.

The Wilderness Years, (18 December 1995) Episode Three, Channel Four Television.

Radio and Radio-related Web Sites

ABC Radio USA. Radio news, weather, sports and commentary from one of the major networks. http://www.abcnews.com/

Addicted to Noise. A service for modern music news. http//www.addict.com/

ATN/Air Force Radio News. News produced by the US Air Force. http://www.brooks.af.mil/realaudio/newsbyte.html

Australian Broadcasting Corporation. http://www.abc.net.au

AMI News Recreative Network. http://www.aminews.com/

Boston Radio Archives http://radio.lcs.mit.edu/radio/whatfiles.html

British Broadcasting Corporation. www.bbc.co.uk/ – several radio news sites. Real Audio is delivered during special events such as the general election. The BBC is continually updating its internet and web services.

The Broadcasting Archive, Barry Mishland. http://www.oldradio.com

Broadcast Education Association. http://www.usa.edu/~bea/noframe.html

Canadian Radio Stations on the Internet. http://www.breaktech.com/ca_radio.htm

CBC Radio Home Page. http://www.radio.cbc.ca/

CBS Radio Networks. http://www.cbsradio.com/

Chicago Radio Resources Page. http://miso.wwa.com/~janik/radio.html

Corporation For Public Broadcasting (USA). http://www.cpb.org/

Cylink Information Services Ltd. Media, Press and News Agencies on the Web. http://www.cylink.net/weblib/businf/mediapress.html

Deutsche Welle. http://www-dw-gmd.de/english/index.html

Dutch Public Service Broadcasters. http://www.omroep.nl/

England: Newspaper Services on the Internet. http://www.mediainfo.com – this site lists national, regional and local newspapers that are published on line. There are also links to web lists of newspapers in Africa, Asia, Oceania, Canada, Europe, Latin America, Middle East, and United States.

Federal Communications Commission. http://www.fcc.gov/

Greek News and Music. 101.6 Kyriakatiko FM in Thessaloniki, Greece. http://www.diavlos.gr/kyriakatikosFM/radio.htm

History of Broadcasting in San Franciso by John Schneider. http://www.aa.net/~rfs/

Internet Sources For Journalists and Broadcasters at CBC. http://www.synapse.net/~radio/welcome.html

Media History Project at the University of Memphis. http://www.mediahistory.com/radio.html

Martin Bensman at the Department of Journalism, University of Memphis. http://www.people.memphis.edu/~mbensman/

Memphis University of, Department of Journalism. http://www.people.memphis.edu/~jourlib/

Mike's page on radio stations which broadcast on the Web. http://www.Geocities.com/hollywood/hills/4229

Minnesota Public Radio. http://www.mpr.org/

The MIT List of Radio Stations on the Internet. This is a very extensive resource for radio stations throughout the world. The list is divided into countries and areas of the world with indications of those services which have sound transmission. http://wmbr.mit.edu/stations/list.html

National Association of Black Journalists. http://www.nabj.org/

National Association of Broadcasters. http://www.nab.org/

National Public Radio (USA). http://www.npr.org/

NBC. http://www.nbc.com/

New Zealand Radio. http://www.rnz.co.nz

NHK – Japanese Broadcasting Corporation. http://www.nhk.or.jp/

NRK Norsk Rikskringkasting. http://nrk.hiof.no/

The Newsroom Index. http://www.auburn.edu/~vestmon/news.html

Ocean RealAudio Server. A site containing archived presidential speeches and other sounds. http://www.ocean.ic.net/

Old Time Radio History. http://www.old-time.com/toc.html

Pacifica Network News. http://www.webactive.com/webactive/pacifica/pnn.html

Positive News. A Positive Place on the Internet. http://www.positive-place.com

Radio Days A Soundbite History. http://www.otr.com/main.html

Radio services at ABC, Australia. www.abc.net.au/surf/radio.htm

Radio Television Hong Kong. http://www.rthk.org.hk/

The Radio and Television News Directors Association. http://www.rtnda.org/ rtnda/

The Radio and Television News Directors Association. Journalism and Media Resources. http://www.rtnda.org/rtnda/media.html

Radio News at Mid Century. http://www.missouri.edu/~jourvs/apr52.html

Real Audio Radio Stations. Stations and services that provide sound. http:// www.timecast.com

South African Broadcasting Corporation. http://www.sabc.co.za

The Virtual Media Library, Steve Opfer at University of Memphis. http:// www.infi.net/~opfer/library.htm

Vancouver talk station and British Columbia's most listened to station. http://www.cknw.com

Women in US Radio News. Produced by Vernon Stone at the Missouri School of Journalism. http://www.missouri.edu/~jourvs/radiowom.html

World of Radio by Glenn Hauser. Real Audio links to stations throughout the world. http://www.wrn.org/gh.html

New York Radio Festival

International Radio Festival of New York, 186 Fifth Avenue, 7th Floor, New York, NY 10010. Tel: 914 238 4481, Fax: 914 238 5040. Website: http:// www.nyfests.com.

Archivist to Radio Festival: Tim Crook, Head of Radio, Goldsmiths College, University of London, Lewisham Way, SE14 6NW. 0171 919 7611. Fax: 0171 919 7611.

Festival Entries for 1994, 1995, 1996, and 1997 are now archived and available for examination by scholars.

Entries referred to:

ABC Radio, 2BL 702, *The Sydney Bushfires* (1995).

Black Radio, *Telling It Like It Was.* (1995) Radio Smithsonian, American History Building, MRC 645, 12th and Constitution NW, Washington, DC 20560.

New Zealand Public Radio, *A Week In French Polynesia.* (1995) Reports by Don Rood.

WJR AM Radio 760, Detroit, Michigan, *Rod Hansen, Investigative Reporter.* (1995).

Index